GRAND RAPIDS FURNITURE

The Story of America's Furniture City

by Christian G. Carron

with contributions by
Kenneth L. Ames
Jeffrey D. Kleiman
Joel Lefever

Public Museum of Grand Rapids

The Public Museum of Grand Rapids

THE PUBLIC MUSEUM OF GRAND RAPIDS, established in 1854, is the oldest and largest institution of its type in the state of Michigan. Its holdings include one of the nation's most important collections of nineteenth- and twentieth-century furniture. In addition to furniture, the Museum holds collections of wood-working machinery, design drawings, manufacturing photographs, and thousands of trade catalogs, making it an important center for the study of American design and industrial history. Two of the Museum's facilities, the Van Andel Museum Center and Voigt House Victorian Museum, offer innovative exhibitions, tours, and programs that interpret the region's rich furniture making heritage.

Public Museum of Grand Rapids

Copyright 1998 The Public Museum of Grand Rapids
272 Pearl St. N.W.
Grand Rapids, Michigan. 49504-5371

ISBN: 0-9666524-0-1
Library of Congress Catalog Card Number: 98-96573
First Printing

Editor: Karen McCarthy
Art Director: Thomas Kachadurian

Photography:
Corporate Color
John Corriveau
Steve Milanowski
Craig Vander Lende

Printed in Traverse City, Michigan by Village Press, Inc.

Foreword

In 1979, as the Public Museum of Grand Rapids celebrated its 125th year of "preserving and presenting the times," it embarked on a project to collect and study the history of the furniture industry, which defined the city's growth and dispersed the name "Grand Rapids" worldwide as a trusted household phrase and a hallmark of quality. The Museum's long-term goal was to organize and present a major permanent exhibition on the subject, drawing upon the institution's comprehensive collection of some 2,600 examples of Grand Rapids-made furniture.

"The Furniture City" exhibition opened in November, 1994 on the Museum's 140th anniversary, in a new home—Van Andel Museum Center. In the mammoth process of its organization, curators came to realize that "writing the history" of the industry was a necessary first step in organizing the volumes of artifacts and historical data that had been collected. Surprisingly little had been published about the Grand Rapids furniture industry, except a few company sketches and several graduate student theses and dissertations focused on narrow subject areas.

The exhibition has garnered public and academic acclaim since its opening. Now, four years later, The Public Museum is pleased to present this major publication, which expands on the content of the exhibition and seeks to disseminate the scholarship that is its foundation.

For most of its history, the identity of Grand Rapids has been linked to the making of a single product—furniture. Those tables, desks, sofas, chairs, and bedsteads; the people who make them today; and the ways they used to make them and sell them have defined this community. As the furniture industry grew and changed, it affected Grand Rapids and the lives of its residents. *Grand Rapids Furniture* is therefore more than just a book on the decorative arts. It is the story of the people of Grand Rapids: the lives they led, the chances they took, the town they built, and the products they created. It is to them that this book is dedicated.

Timothy J. Chester

Timothy J. Chester, Director
The Public Museum of Grand Rapids

The Johnson-Handley-Johnson Co. produced many pieces decorated with marquetry designs. This elaborate Jacobean-style, gate-leg desk was made ca. 1925. Its English oak and oak burl surfaces are ornamented with delicate floral inlays of wood, ivory, and mother-of-pearl.

Table of Contents

Although most Grand Rapids furniture was made using machinery, detailed hand craftsmanship often provided it with distinctive beauty. OPPOSITE: The considerable amount and variety of carving on this regal-looking armchair from around 1920, attributed to the Berkey & Gay Furniture Co., made it a fitting seat for the Chairman of the Board of the Mutual Home Federal Savings & Loan in Grand Rapids. ABOVE: The simple shape of this ca. 1930 chest of drawers afforded the hand decorators at the Century Furniture Co. the perfect surfaces to paint with chinoiserie motifs in bronze powders over raised lacquer work.

The Grand Rapids Furniture Record

Kenneth L. Ames, Chair for Academic Programs at the Bard Graduate Center for Studies in the Decorative Arts in New York, discusses the social forces that helped make Grand Rapids "The Furniture City."

Good Timing and a Flair for Leadership

by Kenneth L. Ames

Grand Rapids. To millions of Americans today the name is still synonymous with furniture. Grand Rapids is the Furniture City, America's Furniture Capital. Why did this small city in western Michigan attain such prominence within the furniture trade? In this essay I approach this intriguing question by examining the fuller context in which the people and products of Grand Rapids functioned. Understanding context is important, because success depends on many factors. One of the most important—and often most unacknowledged—is the existence of enabling conditions. In the middle of the last century, conditions were highly conducive to the growth and prosperity of the furniture trade. For that matter, it was a propitious time to enter many lines of business, as the market for countless categories of both traditional and novel goods was expanding dramatically.

Some of this market expansion was linked to the extraordinary growth of the population in the United States. The official government census figures for 1850, when Grand Rapids itself was still a very small settlement, list United States population at something above twenty-three million people. By 1860 the number had risen to over thirty-one million and by 1870 to more than thirty-eight million. Each successive decade up to 1900 showed a gain of at least ten million. After that date, growth was at a rate closer to fifteen million per decade. We can assume that, as is usually the case when a census is taken, quite a few people avoided being counted, and that the population was actually somewhat greater than official figures indicate.

Another demographic pattern promised benefits to manufacturers located away from the East Coast. As the years passed, the center of the United States population moved gradually westward and, throughout the nineteenth century at least, closer to Grand Rapids. In the eighteenth century, most Americans of European or African descent lived in a narrow band along the Atlantic seaboard. At the time of the first national census in 1790, the population center was somewhere east of Baltimore. Westward migration carried the popu-

OPPOSITE: Beautifully illustrated covers of *The Grand Rapids Furniture Record,* like this one from September, 1911, reflected the Victorian culture of domesticity that encouraged the consumption of home furnishings. BELOW: Immigrants like those in this ca. 1904 photo represented both a work force and a growing market for Grand Rapids' furniture industry. Courtesy, Collection of the Maryland Historical Society.

lation center through Parkersburg, West Virginia to Chillicothe, Ohio, then to Cincinnati by 1880. From that date until 1940 the center of population crept slowly westward across the state of Indiana, never more than a few hundred miles from Grand Rapids.

Population growth meant more potential buyers, while the westward drift meant that a significant proportion of those buyers were close to Grand Rapids. This would not have mattered much to the furniture industry, however, if the average American family had been content to buy a chair or two and then quit. But the American public was in a mood to buy more furniture than ever. In 1850, the golden age of furniture consumption had begun.

This golden age owed something to population growth, but more to a complex web of ideologies and values that were gaining ascendancy in the mid-nineteenth century, and that encouraged Americans to place a premium on furniture as a conveyor of important social and cultural meanings. The furniture industry flourished because people deeply believed in furniture. They believed that it expressed important truths about them as individuals, about their personality and character, about the quality of their lives, and about the level and nature of their civilization. To most people who shared the values of mainstream Victorian culture, living the good life meant living with good furniture.

By the first decades of the twentieth century, however, this cluster of values had begun to fall apart. It has sometimes been tempting to blame the decline of Grand Rapids' prominence in the household furniture business on the general disruption caused by the Great Depression. It would be more accurate to say that the Depression only accelerated a process that was caused by the decline of Victorian cultural values. In other words, the rise and fall of the Grand Rapids household furniture business correlates with the rise and fall of Victorian culture in America.

Victorian Culture Values Furniture

Two strands of Victorian culture stand out as particularly critical for the high valuation of furniture: the rise of gentility and the ideology of domesticity. The rise of gentility means the process by which more and more Americans lived in a style and with possessions formerly associated with the aristocracy, with the gentry. The ideology of domesticity refers to a belief system that confined women to homes while simultaneously assigning to domestic environments paramount importance in the shaping of character and behavior. Both factors encouraged increased sales of household furniture.

In the case of the rise of gentility, or what historian Richard Bushman calls "the refinement of America," levels of furnishing once limited to the upper classes increasingly became the norm for people further down the economic scale. This process of gradual refinement was enabled by patterns of emulation, by a belief in upward mobility, and—a very important point —by actual and relative declines in the prices of goods brought about by the systematic industrialization of virtually every object made for household use.

Evidence of the rise of gentility is widespread. We can see it in the imposingly scaled and lavishly furnished houses erected in the last century. Set beside houses of the eighteenth century built for people of comparable wealth and status, Victorian-era houses impress us by their greater size, more extensive ornament, and denser patterns of furnishings. They also possess a degree of specialization previously unknown in American homes. This specialization, a key component of the process of refinement, had a remarkable impact on the furniture trade.

One of the most distinctive features of the typical Victorian house is its organization as a series of specialized experiences, a series of functionally discrete spaces—hall, dining room, parlor, bedrooms, kitchen. Victorians knew which space was which partially by its location but even more by the furniture in it. They recognized halls because they were furnished with hall-stands and hall chairs. Dining rooms were defined by dining tables, dining chairs, and sideboards. Parlors were furnished with parlor chairs and sofas, parlor tables, whatnots or etageres, parlor cabinets, and perhaps pianos or parlor organs. When they encountered bedrooms they found bedsteads, chests of drawers with mirrors, dressing cases, and washstands.

This all seems obvious and unremarkable today, but for people in Victorian America it was both new and positive. When Victorians compared their standard of living to that of the past, most of them saw dramatic signs of progress. Having a house with entire rooms assigned to various individual functions was clearly a mark of elevated status. In the seventeenth century and well into the eighteenth, even people of significant means had lived in only a few multi-function rooms. Beds, for example, appeared in parlors well into the eighteenth century in this country. For many immigrants who arrived in the nineteenth century, this was true of the rural houses and crowded city dwellings they left behind and of the congested tenements or slave cabins they encountered here. The better lives they hoped for meant larger homes with specialized rooms.

Victorian Americans patterned their rationally organized and commodious dwellings on palaces, castles, villas, and country houses built for the European wealthy. They also patterned the furniture for their newly specialized rooms on genteel European prototypes from the past. Evidence of upper-class historical antecedents can be seen with particular clarity in the Victorian enthusiasm for suites of furniture. A suite is a matching set or group of furniture in which each part typically constitutes one element of an ensemble that furnishes or nearly furnishes a room. Most popular in Victorian America were parlor suites and chamber or bedroom suites.

Parlor suites, produced extensively in Grand Rapids by the 1870s, typically included a man's chair, a woman's chair, four smaller chairs, and a sofa. Although the individual pieces varied in size and proportion, all were typically ornamented and upholstered in the same manner, which unified them visually and identified them as a suite. For thousands of middle-class and upper-middle-class families, these sets of furniture brought into their homes courtly echoes and a connection to the grand suites of rooms created for the royalty and wealthy in the eighteenth century. To ordinary Americans newly able to afford a parlor full of seating furniture, these specialized suites provided compelling evidence of their rising status and increasing levels of refinement. We get some sense of the pride people took in these new possessions from the wonderful images recorded by Wisconsin photographer Andrew Dahl. Hundreds of surviving photographs from the 1870s show us

ABOVE: Victorian consumers created a demand for specialized forms like this hall-stand in the 1895 Voigt House Victorian Museum, Grand Rapids. BELOW: Manufacturers offered suites of matching parlor furniture, allowing customers to outfit entire rooms. *Michigan Artisan*, Sept. 10, 1888.

ABOVE: Nineteenth-century photo by Andrew Dahl shows a family proudly posing with their newly acquired parlor furniture. Courtesy, State Historical Society of Wisconsin. BELOW: The Phoenix Furniture Co. was founded in 1870 to meet consumer demand for suites of parlor furniture, which included pieces like this ca. 1880 rocking chair.

families proudly posing in the recently purchased seating furniture they carried out into their front yards especially for the occasion of the photograph.

Even with these images it is difficult for us today to fully empathize with the sense of positive excitement and achievement these suites brought to thousands of people when they were new. While furniture is just as important for self-definition today, we no longer look to it for evidence of the progress of our civilization. Yet in the nineteenth century, dramatic technological advances and Darwinism combined to fuel a vision of ever-improving conditions. Parlor suites, at least for a while, seemed to confirm that vision, for back in the eighteenth century only the wealthy owned upholstered furniture. Textiles were usually numbered among a household's most precious and costly furnishings. Textile production, however, was one of the first trades to industrialize. Mechanized production on increasingly grand scales lowered the cost of textiles, including upholstery fabrics, and put them within the reach of the expanding middle classes. The declining cost of textiles and the long-standing cachet of upholstered furniture combined to propel exceptional sales of fabric-covered furniture.

Artifactual evidence indicates that during the 1850s many people purchased the first sofa anyone in their family had ever owned and consequently enjoyed an elevated standard of living. Yet the next generation of that same family moved up to an entire suite of upholstered furniture. From cane-seated chairs and plank-bottom settees to an upholstered sofa and then to a parlor suite in less than half a century was a dramatic trajectory. At each stage, what had previously been a luxury was transformed into a necessity.

Parlor suites were potent commodities because suites were associated with courtly grandeur and exploited the positive connotations of textiles. Historian Katherine Grier has shown that the rise of culture and comfort went together in the last century. As life became refined it literally became softer, more enveloped in textiles. Richly upholstered parlor suites were evidence of rising levels of culture and comfort.

The emerging taste for parlor suites depended on the furniture trade, and at the same time provided it with great opportunities. The individual forms that made up parlor suites were not new, for upholstered seating had been manufactured in this country since the eighteenth century, albeit for a limited market. The real change was the creation of new markets. A Grand Rapids giant, Phoenix Furniture Company, was founded in the 1870s with the specific objective of producing parlor seating furniture for the middle and upper-middle market, an idea that would have been nearly inconceivable even two decades earlier.

Nelson, Matter & Company had already established a specialty of chamber suites in the 1860s. Here again, industry expansion had less to do with new goods than with new markets. Chamber suites provided bedrooms with coherent sets of furnishings, replacing the motley assortments of unco-ordinated goods found in middle-class sleeping areas before the mid-nineteenth century. Repeated design elements, materials, and finish helped people see at once that these objects were designed to be installed and used together. Part of the appeal of suites was their ability to convey the appearance of significant wealth, for they suggested that their owners had the financial resources to buy an extensive set of furniture in one purchase.

Because the sale of a suite always meant the sale of more than one piece, suites were obviously good for the furniture business and a number of Grand Rapids firms specialized in them.

The most basic chamber suites consisted of a bedstead, a chest of drawers with mirror, and a washstand. Large and expensive suites also contained a dressing case with mirror, a bedside stand, a tea table, four tea chairs, a nurse or sewing rocker, and a towel bar. As with parlor suites, each individual furniture form had precedents, sometimes quite ancient. Bedsteads, for example, were known in classical antiquity. Washstands, in one form or another, also can be traced to the ancient Greek and Roman past. Chests of drawers were of more recent origin.

Yet none of the objects in typical Grand Rapids chamber suites of the 1870s looks exactly like these antecedents, in part because they had not normally been conceived as components of suites. Typically, case pieces and bedsteads were the products of different design traditions and technologies. Case pieces were made by joiners or cabinetmakers, bedsteads often by turners. In Victorian America, both forms were produced within the same factory according to the same principles of industrialized cabinetmaking. This centralized the design process and allowed for greater integration of the forms. Bedsteads were given expansive headboards that rose high on the wall and dominated the room. Chests of drawers typically had attached looking glasses with elaborate wooden frames that duplicated the major design features of the headboards. The washstand, a less assertive piece, usually repeated principal design elements of the other two objects. As a result of this emphasis on design coordination, furniture for bedrooms acquired a degree of impact and impressiveness that it never had before. This design presence, in turn, made people more attentive to furnishing bedrooms, and that meant more furniture sales.

Furniture As Evidence of Gentility

Another facet of refinement that was helpful for selling furniture was the gradual replacement of shared objects with objects for individual use. Benches gave way to individual chairs, eating from a communal bowl to eating from individual plates with one's own spoon and then fork, and so on. A similar pattern affected the use and occupation of bedrooms. In the eighteenth and early nineteenth centuries many country people lived in cramped quarters, often with several sleeping in the same room. But for the middle class, having one's own bedroom with one's own bedroom furniture became tangible evidence of gentility. Married couples typically shared a room, but if they were affluent enough, their children could expect separate rooms and furniture. This too spurred furniture sales.

Parlor and bedroom suites had historical antecedents, but sometimes the past failed to provide models of furniture appropriate to the Victorians' notions of genteel living. In such cases, the Victorians invented them. The hallstand is one of the best examples of this creativity. We might say that hallstands were invented to help the Victorians live out the cultural drama they had written for themselves. Hallstands were unknown until the early years of the nineteenth century. They combined in one form a looking glass, hooks or pegs for men's hats or outer garments, holders for umbrellas,

The New England Furniture Co. specialized in the production of "Painted chamber suits," aimed at Victorian Americans hoping to create room settings to reflect their status. *Michigan Artisan*, **April 1, 1886.**

and sometimes a small table or stand. These mundane elements were synthesized within an elaborated architectural framework that drew attention to, dignified, and ceremonialized their function.

Hallstands survive as eloquent witnesses to the Victorian emphasis on ritual, on daily life as a series of performances, for they made people self-conscious about the otherwise unremarkable acts of entering or leaving a house. They testify to the Victorian obsession with appearance, since their mirrors helped people adjust clothing or hair, and the umbrellas they held were tools for maintaining a genteel exterior in spite of the elements. No one manufactured hallstands in the eighteenth century, but Grand Rapids furniture houses were turning them out in large numbers in the last third of the nineteenth century. Beliefs that objects such as hallstands were essential for living a refined life shaped the contents of thousands of American homes, and brought prosperity to Grand Rapids.

Hallstands were specialized forms, designed for specialized spaces within homes. As the century wore on, other such forms emerged, including tea carts, smoking stands, stackable bookcases, and telephone tables. The appeal of specialization was in part due to its associations with affluence. But in Victorian culture, specialization was also valued because it served as evidence of the application of reason. It meant that a function, a problem, a phenomenon had been identified, analyzed, and in some way conquered or at least ordered by the human mind, subordinated to the human will. Extensive specialization was then equated with a high level of cultural development and of civilization.

When the exploration and empire-building of the nineteenth century brought Europeans and Americans in close contact with people around the world, these people were ranked on a scale that ranged from savagery to civilization. Material culture typically played a major role in determining that ranking. People who had little or relatively unspecialized material culture were defined as near savagery and those with extensive and specialized material culture as civilized. Using this scale, the materialistic Western world defined itself as the most highly civilized.

When people entered Victorian homes, they saw the marks of civilization as the western world understood it. They also saw in material form the same values that created industrialization: the processes of living had been subjected to the same rational analysis that characterized factory production, the same segmentation into discrete parts and units. Yet they could also see that this specialization was sanctioned by reference to courtly precedents. The rich had long known that living well meant living with refined, specialized goods. The great accomplishment of the nineteenth century was to make such goods available to a mass audience.

Specialization was a product of the modern mind, but the notion of gentility was constructed from the culture of the courtly past. Courtly material culture was characterized by richness and intricacy of design, materials, and

ABOVE: **This parlor in the Grand Rapids residence of William F. Hake, ca. 1885, illustrates the soft gentility and elaborate ornamentation favored by Victorian consumers. One of the pieces from the suite in this photo is pictured on page 36.** BELOW: **This settee is part of a parlor suite received in 1884 by the Manwaring family of Grandville, Michigan from Berkey & Gay Furniture Co., in lieu of a shareholder's dividend payment.**

fabrication. From 1850 to 1890, a similar emphasis prevailed within furniture design, producing the elaborately ornamented forms we usually think of as Victorian. Examples of this self-conscious evocation of courtly splendor are abundant, but few may be better known than the wonderful bedroom suite exhibited by Berkey & Gay Furniture Company at the Centennial Exposition in Philadelphia in 1876, long in the collection of the Public Museum of Grand Rapids and pictured on this book's cover.

Massive and lofty, richly adorned with burl walnut panels and gilded incised decoration, the design of the bed is a marvel of purposeful elaboration, illustrating the energized and willfully complex quality of Victorian design. Planes moving back and forth in space, a variety of shapes that defy easy identification, a stunning, arresting pediment, and multi-directional finials are all orchestrated into a coherent form, a visual parallel to a Victorian symphony.

The Aesthetic of Denseness

The elaboration seen in this bedroom suite and in other individual goods typified entire domestic interiors. Here too we can see the imprint of the rise of gentility. The wealthy of the past not only had objects of fine design and impressive execution, but they often had a great many of them. Believing that more was better, wealthy Victorians or those who wanted to appear wealthy gave their rooms a density we find almost inconceivable today. For we sit on the other side of a great aesthetic divide that occurred around 1900. Up until that time, household interiors had become increasingly dense. Wall and ceiling papers were of different patterns; rugs were piled on top of rugs; framed pictures, small brackets, and shelves holding endlessly varied bric-a-brac adorned and nearly obscured walls; mantelpieces and tabletops were packed with elaborate goods in many materials; and, above all, numerous pieces of carved, inlaid, or turned furniture were packed into rooms, transforming interiors into intricate and thickly textured landscapes that testified to western claims to domination of the natural and cultural worlds past and present.

All of this can be seen in splendid detail in surviving photographs of the period. The high point of this density seems to have been reached during the 1880s. By 1900 a new aesthetic of relative spareness had already begun to spread rapidly. Interiors of this later period seem to have been swept by a wind that had blown away fully half of the furniture and bric-a-brac. Interiors have never been as dense as they were in the 1880s.

The aesthetic of denseness meant unprecedented levels of furniture sales. Furniture manufacturers and dealers came to believe that the hyperconsumption that led to this denseness during the 1870s and '80s was the norm. When furniture sales began to drop off around 1900, furniture manufacturers identified the problem as underconsumption. In a sense they were right, for by the standards of the 1880s, people were underconsuming. But that same pattern of relative underconsumption has continued with only minor changes up to the present.

Rising levels of gentility would have meant little for the household furniture trade if they had not been paired with the ideology of domesticity. The home was celebrated as a repository for important social values. Homes were understood to provide a moral counterpoint to the unbridled individualism and cut-throat economic competition that characterized the newly industrialized society. Women became guardian angels of the home, saintly consumers responsible for providing a sheltering haven and retreat from the heartless outside world for their husbands. In these homes they created nurturing and supportive environments intended to shape the morals and character of their children in positive ways.

Women were encouraged to use material culture prominently in their attempts to construct these domestic retreats, for Victorians believed that the objects in homes simultaneously reflected and shaped character and behavior. Victorians accepted and endorsed the old proposition that there was a direct correlation between doing good and doing well. Well-furnished homes could be evidence of lives lived morally. They could also be important tools in forming the outlook and values of people, particularly children, who lived in them. As *The Grand Rapids Furniture Record* put it, "Home building means character building." In Victorian America, many people believed that good homes made good people.

Good Furniture Means Good Morals

This idea made sense to people who subscribed to a form of environmental determinism. Victorian Americans shaped their domestic environments in order to shape the people within them. Today we recognize that character, values, and behavior are affected by many factors, including environment. Comfortable and stimulating surroundings not only enhance the quality of life but promote mental health and a positive outlook. Conversely, dull or dingy surroundings depress and can contribute to lack of ambition, low self-esteem, and a negative outlook on life. The Victorians knew all this and therefore accepted it as a moral imperative to furnish and embellish a home with well-made furniture of good design.

Photos such as this were published in *American Home Culture* to teach women how to turn their homes into domestic retreats.

Such furniture had its own moral components. Buying poorly constructed furniture was wasteful at best and deceitful as well if that furniture was also ostentatious. Poor design revealed incompetence or ignorance, neither of which was admirable. Well-made furniture of good design showed that its owners were moral people, responsible and informed. The linking of morality and design took even more explicit form during the later years of the nineteenth century and the early years of the twentieth. Both the Aesthetic Movement of the 1870s and '80s and the Arts and Crafts Movement of the early 1900s exploited moralistic interpretations of household furnishings. Styles, woods, and methods of construction and ornament were all assigned either positive or negative moral value. Today the arguments that raged over furniture surprise us, but a century or so ago, people wrote and argued passionately about furniture. And that passion helped Grand Rapids prosper.

Furniture inside homes created a sense of refuge and retreat. It documented the owners' civilization and their knowledge of design history. It provided a nonverbal projection of their personality and taste. In homes people used furniture, in combination with countless other goods, to construct artifactual portraits of themselves. These portraits shared certain general traits, but each home had its own personality. The projection of individuality within each home was facilitated by an exceptional differentiation of products within the furniture trade. Objects were differentiated not only by style, association, and cost, but by a host of more mundane factors including woods, finishes, fabric grades, and colors. More similar to clothing than to vehicles, furniture was produced to offer customers an extensive range of fairly minute variations. The purpose and result were congruent: just as no two families were quite the same, no two homes should look the same. Victorian concepts of domesticity meant that certain general traits characterized all socially acceptable homes but also that each home needed some elements that would personalize it and set it off from all the rest. Thus, even if people purchased the same model parlor suite, they could vary the color and pattern of the upholstery fabric. Furniture allowed for fairly subtle self-definition. Every home could be specially crafted to reflect the values and tastes of the people who lived within it and to exert a distinctive influence on them.

This emphasis on providing consumers with a wide range of options has at least something to do with the decentralization of the household furniture trade during the nineteenth century and with the large number of firms coexisting within the field. By the end of the nineteenth century, the furniture market had developed many niches. The development of those niches was related to the expansion of stylistic options as the century progressed. In 1850, middle-class people had relatively few stylistic options from which to choose.

By about 1900, however, the furniture trade and its customers had learned a good deal about the history of furniture. Designs from the past became options for buyers. Century Furniture Company, for example, produced an extensive line of reproductions of historic forms. This meant that customers could select from a broader, more subtly nuanced range of choices, and furniture could reveal their learning. To people who knew furniture history, the objects they encountered in the homes of others could be as telling as the books they saw on the shelves.

The manufacture of historic reproductions meant that conditions were changing. Grand Rapids firms began to sell reproductions in response to the growing interest in antiques. Yet people who bought authentic antiques were not likely to buy much new furniture. Some people were content to mix old and new, but the rediscovery of old furniture ultimately meant less business for furniture manufacturers. Here, then, was yet another factor beyond its control that ultimately had a profound impact on the furniture trade in Grand Rapids.

Factors beyond our control often shape our destiny. I have tried to suggest some of the many conditions beyond the control of Grand Rapids manufacturers that encouraged sales of household furniture in the second half of the nineteenth century. The rise of gentility, a pervasive sense of progress, aspirations to upward mobility, and the desire to make homes centers for moral and cultural development all played a part, as did that competitive activity called fashion. Fashion is a mechanism to promote constant jockeying for position among those who fancy themselves as cultural leaders. In a society where emulation played a prominent role, many frequently adjusted to conform to the dominant fashion. This too fostered furniture sales.

ABOVE: This page from a 1920s Century Furniture Co. catalog reveals how variations in fabrics and frame shapes offered consumers a range of historic forms. BELOW: When this Century chair was covered with fabric resembling a medieval tapestry, its simple shape became appropriate for a period room setting. A change of fabric made it equally at home with Art Deco furnishings.

Grand Rapids Stands Out

But I have said little about factors that helped Grand Rapids stand out from its competitors. Four seem particularly significant. The first I see largely as an accident of timing. The furniture trade flourished in Grand Rapids because it profited from the painful transition from craft to industry that had taken place at considerable human cost in other, generally eastern, parts of the country. A major transformative chapter in American furniture history took place before Grand Rapids became a significant center of the trade. During the first half of the nineteenth century, small, artisan-owned shops gradually and reluctantly gave way to larger factories owned by capitalists. These factories were increasingly organized according to rationalized industrial processes. The results, which came about only slowly, were the relative de-skilling of furniture artisans and real declines in their autonomy, status, and earning power.

Much of this transition was worked out in New York, Boston, Philadelphia, Cincinnati, and elsewhere. In the early 1870s Grand Rapids owners were able to erect what were at the time some of the nation's largest and most aggressively rationalized factories. Established after most of this transition had taken place, Grand Rapids was at a relative advantage. It learned from and built upon transformations initiated elsewhere but was relatively free from the disruption, contention, and ill will generated in older furniture centers. As so often happens in the world of competitive business, the new was able to build at the cost of the old.

Three other advantages resulted from deliberate acts of good judgment. The first was the establishment of the Grand Rapids Furniture Market, which capitalized on the large concentration of furniture manufacturers in the Grand Rapids area. But the furniture market would never have worked, would never have drawn large numbers of buyers and outside exhibitors, if Grand Rapids manufacturers had not established themselves as leaders in the middle and upper-middle markets, exactly where the bulk of furniture sales were concentrated. Grand Rapids attracted outside interest because it had forged a firm reputation as a manufacturer of solid quality goods at the upper end of the domestic line.

The second inspired idea was the establishment of *The Grand Rapids Furniture Record*, first published in 1900. Journals devoted to the interests and needs of the furniture trade had been published in this country since 1870 but the *Record* stands out as one of the finest and most enduring. Like Grand Rapids furniture, the *Record* was a quality product. Large format, glossy paper, handsome design and layout, copious well-printed photographs, and color covers and frontispieces when color was still rare in periodicals made the *Record* superior to most competing journals.

Browsing through old issues of *The Grand Rapids Furniture Record* is enjoyable and informative. Some of the enjoyment comes from the high quality of the art work within the journal and on its covers. Produced by many talented hands and remarkably varied, these wonderful covers provide an engaging visual commentary on changing concerns and emphases within the furniture trade. Each issue has a freshly designed cover highlighting some topic related to furniture: domestic interiors, individual

Phoenix Furniture Co. finishing room, ca. 1895. For their day, Grand Rapids factories were models of rational thought and large-scale production.

pieces of furniture, people using furniture, store windows, delivery trucks, Art Nouveau or poster-style semi-abstractions, the principal buildings of the Grand Rapids Furniture Market, and other furniture-related images. The covers of the *Record* constitute a striking exhibition of purposeful art.

But the contents of the periodical provide hard data about the interests and concerns of the furniture trade over the years. Virtually all aspects of the furniture business in Grand Rapids and across the nation are regularly discussed in the *Record*. Articles and brief notices provide current information about particularly strong and weak areas of sales, emerging or fading styles, new upholstery fabrics, hints to salesmen, styles of furnishings, outdoor furniture, modern business methods and managerial structures, practical lessons in salesmanship, cash versus credit sales, combatting mail order houses, modern merchandising methods, designing new store fronts, arranging furniture on the sales floor, woods, seasonal sales suggestions, and so on. One regular feature printed inquiries from and responses to retailers seeking manufacturers of specific kinds and grades of goods. The *Record* also provided hints on publicity or laying out show windows, news from various conventions and about furniture people, listings of new trade catalogs available, obituaries, and many other relevant matters. A 1914 issue, for example, included a discussion of delivery trucks and commentary from a dealer who found trucks more reliable than horses. Most issues were also embellished with full-page photographs or drawings of new or current goods from factories in Grand Rapids and elsewhere.

The *Record* also carried notices and reviews of books. The titles reviewed in the February, 1914 issue provide a nice cross-section of interests, showing a balance of scholarship and business concerns. Books reviewed included Luke Vincent Lockwood's *American Colonial Furniture*, George Leland Hunter's *Home Furnishings*, and Frank Farrington's *Selling Suggestions*.

Attention to scholarly study of furniture was a component in Grand Rapids' strategy to establish itself as "a leading educational center for all matters pertaining to good furniture." The *Record* played a prominent part in that strategy but a more important ingredient, and the third deliberate factor in Grand Rapids' high visibility, was the furniture library established at the Grand Rapids Public Library. In 1903 the Public Library decided to create a major reference library for students of all aspects of furniture. The first substantial acquisition brought to Grand Rapids all titles on furniture shown by the French book trade at the 1904 St. Louis fair. Over the next two decades or so, new acquisitions swiftly diversified the collection.

In December of 1927, to commemorate the one hundredth semi-annual Grand Rapids Furniture Market, the Public Library published a list of furniture library holdings. Although comparative data is hard to come by, in 1927 this may well have been the country's leading collection of furniture books. And what a wonderful collection it was. Trade designers had collaborated with library staff to identify important titles, and a remarkable number had been collected in a relatively short time. Books on French furniture were abundant. The list includes seemingly endless French titles from the nineteenth and early twentieth centuries, including Pierre de la Mesangere's important *Meubles et objets de goût* (Paris, 1796 - 1830) and Henry Havard's massive multi-volume *Dictionnaire de l'ameublement* (Paris,

Articles like this one, from the August, 1911 *Grand Rapids Furniture Record*, informed retailers about every aspect of the furniture business.

4181 Special Furniture Reference Library Containing
Rare Furniture Books and Plates for Designers' Use.

This stereocard, produced in 1928, shows the furniture study area of the Grand Rapids Public Library.

1887 - 90), still an essential reference work for the study of French furniture.

The library had acquired a number of furniture history classics from other areas of the world, including Frederick Litchfield, *Illustrated History of Furniture* (London, 1892), Wilhelm Bode, *Die italienische Hausmobel des Renaissance* (Leipzig, 1902), Herbert Cescinsky, *Chinese Furniture* (London, 1922), and Gisela Richter, *Ancient Furniture* (Oxford, 1926), as well as many more specialized studies, particularly of European furniture.

English furniture was extensively documented in studies by the pioneering figures of English furniture history, such as Percy Macquoid, *A History of English Furniture* (London, 1904-08). Even richer were the library holdings of the works of major English designers, including a 1754 edition of Thomas Chippendale's famous *Gentleman and Cabinet-maker's Director* (London) and Robert Adam's *Works in Architecture* (London, 1773 - 1822).

British neo-classicism was well represented in Grand Rapids by Thomas Sheraton, *The Cabinet-maker and Upholsterer's Drawing Book* (London, 1802) and Thomas Hope, *Household Furniture and Interior Decoration* (London, 1807). The emergence and flowering of the Romantic styles were documented in Augustus Charles Pugin, *Gothic Furniture* (London, 1827).

The evolution of more modern styles was recorded in Bruce James Talbert, *Gothic Forms Applied to Furniture* (Birmingham, 1867) and *Examples of Ancient and Modern Furniture* (Birmingham, 1876).

Perhaps because the library was formed when interest in the American colonial past was just emerging, holdings on that subject were extraordinary, starting with Irving Whitall Lyon, *The Colonial Furniture of New England* (Boston, 1892). The furniture library also owned Luke Vincent Lockwood, *Colonial Furniture in America* (New York, 1901), Wallace Nutting, *Furniture of the Pilgrim Century* (Boston, c. 1921), and R. T. H. Halsey, *A Handbook of the American Wing* (New York, 1926), which documented the museumization of American colonial furniture in New York's Metropolitan Museum of Art.

Equally well represented in the furniture library were books on interior design, starting with the first American title of any consequence, Andrew

Jackson Downing, *The Architecture of Country Houses* (New York, 1851), and continuing with most major American and English texts, including Charles Locke Eastlake, *Hints on Household Taste* (Boston, 1872), Clarence Cook, *The House Beautiful* (New York, 1877), Edith Wharton and Ogden Codman, *The Decoration of Houses* (New York, 1897), and many others.

Added to all of these titles were long or short runs of over a dozen furniture trade periodicals and numerous trade catalogs from firms in Grand Rapids and elsewhere. The furniture library had become an impressive collection that reflected and facilitated a scholarly understanding of furniture.

Leadership Out of Self-Reliance

These three factors—the market, the *Record*, and the library—might not have emerged if Grand Rapids had been a bigger city or had been within the sphere of some larger center. For the truth remains that New York, Chicago, Philadelphia, and other cities produced more furniture than Grand Rapids. Yet within these big cities, furniture manufacture was just one industry among many others. The high proportion of furniture manufacturing compared to other industries helped Grand Rapids stand out as "The Furniture City."

Gardner, Massachusetts was also a furniture city—the eastern center of the chair business. Yet it never developed a major market, produced a leading trade publication, or established a nationally significant library. Only fifty miles from Boston and less than twenty from Worcester, Gardner had little need to fall back on its own resources. Grand Rapids, on the other hand, was over a hundred miles from Detroit by land and from Chicago by water. Grand Rapids had to become a center itself if it wished to become a leader within the trade.

Why Grand Rapids? The answer turns out to be complex. Enabling cultural conditions, fortuitous timing, focus on a critical part of the market, attention to quality in design and construction, personal and civic ambition, and location are all part of the explanation. Whatever the exact causes, however, Grand Rapids' accomplishment remains an established fact and appropriate cause for congratulation and celebration.

The official civic flag of Grand Rapids, adopted in 1896, celebrated Grand Rapids' identity as a one-industry town.

In just a few short decades, furniture making in Grand Rapids moved from the small shops of local craftsmen to large factories employing hundreds of workers.

Arrivals & Beginnings

In the previous chapter, Ken Ames explained why Grand Rapids became America's "Furniture City." But how did a furniture industry begin in Grand Rapids in the first place? What combination of people, resources, technology, capital, and know-how came together to make this city devote its energies to one enterprise?

Commerce Defines a City's Character

There are many similarities among the stories that describe the growth of various urban areas on the American frontier. Richard C. Wade points out in his book, *The Urban Frontier: Pioneer Life in Early Pittsburgh, Cincinnati, Lexington, Louisville, and St. Louis,* that most "Western" frontier cities were established for the purpose of commerce. Grand Rapids was founded in 1831, at the site of Louis Campau's fur trading post, which he built at the intersection of several Indian trails and the rapids of the Grand River in 1826. Here, whites and Native Americans could exchange furs for manufactured goods and supplies.

Around this same time, farmers began moving west in search of tillable land. Anything they could not grow on the farm they had to purchase in a commercial center. So farmers brought their crops to merchant establishments in Grand Rapids, to exchange for goods made in factories in the East.

Transporting these goods over the mountains and through the great forests of the West was slow and difficult. Since few roads had been constructed, and those became impassable whenever it rained or snowed, lakes and rivers were the most practical highways between cities in the nation's interior. The Grand River, which runs through the middle of Grand Rapids and empties into Lake Michigan at Grand Haven, became the principal artery for people and goods flowing into Grand Rapids.

Most people venturing west converted their possessions into cash, because a purse of money was easier to transport than a bulky household. A

Michigan's timber resources seemed endless to the nineteenth-century settlers who came to exploit them.

few who had room on their wagon, or could afford to pay the freight expenses, brought prized pieces of furniture with them. A number of such pieces survive in Michigan. A small, ornately carved Elizabethan and Rococo Revival-styled side chair, attributed to cabinetmaker Elijah Galusha of Troy, New York, was brought to Grand Rapids circa 1855 by a family from Vermont. A canopied cradle of late eighteenth-century vintage was brought by the Smith family from Bell's Falls, Massachusetts to Battle Creek, Michigan in the mid-nineteenth century. One can imagine the reasons, both sentimental and utilitarian, that the family might have had for bringing that particular piece of furniture.

Merchants and Cabinetmakers Supply Local Needs

Once settlers arrived in the West, they converted their cash back into tools and furnishings. Initially, local merchants supplied these goods by transporting them west from Eastern factories. But high transport expenses provided an incentive for the merchants to begin manufacturing some items locally, especially things that were heavy and difficult to transport, including furniture.

The firm of Eagles and Pullman (1850 - 1854) sold furniture, both manufactured in New York City and locally custom-made. The company disbanded circa 1854, when two of the partners, George and A. B. Pullman, moved to Chicago, where they soon began to manufacture George's signature invention, the Pullman Palace railroad cars. The partnership of Boynton & Creque (circa 1866 - 1872), later just J. P. Creque (circa 1872 - 1883), retailed lounges, mattresses, upholstered furniture, looking glasses, picture frames, and parlor pieces. These were likely manufactured elsewhere. They also sold what advertisements in city directories described as "common furniture" for the bedroom and dining room, which was probably produced in their own factory.

The first people who earned their living making furniture in the new village of Grand Rapids were cabinetmakers and chair makers. As the community grew, it attracted a variety of businessmen and artisans in search of greater opportunity, including those trained to make furniture in a system that had changed little for centuries. Typically, a worker was apprenticed to a master cabinetmaker or turner while still in his teens; he moved up over time to become a journeyman, and eventually became a master craftsman and opened his own small shop.

By most accounts, William "Deacon" Haldane was the first person trained in this tradition to open a cabinetmaking shop in Grand Rapids. Born in Delhi, New York in 1807, Haldane was the son of poor Scottish immigrants. His first important woodworking job was reported to have been carpentry for the construction of a church in Ohio in 1831, where he met and married the niece of the minister. In 1836 they traveled by horse and wagon to Grand Rapids and built a small frame residence at the corner of Pearl and Ottawa Streets, with a room in the back for his first cabinet shop.

Haldane made a wide range of products: case pieces, beds, chairs, tables, and, as was common for many traditional cabinetmakers, coffins. In his first year, he made several sleighs or cutters to earn extra money. In 1855 he won two prizes at the Kent County Agricultural Society's annual fair, for a bedstead and a bureau. A hoop-back Windsor armchair in the collection of The Public Museum of Grand Rapids, which was originally finished with a dark red-brown wash, has long been attributed to Haldane. It was made from a combination of Michigan woods including oak, hickory, maple, and poplar. Surprisingly, even though Haldane had a lathe in his shop, the spindles that form the chair's backrest were not turned but crudely fashioned with a spoke shave.

An advertisement that Haldane ran in the *Grand Rapids Weekly Enquirer* for July 11, 1845 listed several specific forms that he made: Jackson Chairs, Clay Settees, and Birney Sociables. These forms take their names from American politicians, who presumably owned similar pieces. The "Jackson Chair" was probably named for Andrew Jackson, who was President of the United States from 1828 - 1836, around the time when Haldane first arrived in Grand Rapids. The "Birney Sociable" took its name from James Birney, an editor, abolitionist, and presidential candidate for the Liberty Party in 1840 and 1844. The "Clay Settee" was likely derived from a piece owned by Senator and presidential candidate Henry Clay. It seems appropriate for the name of this strong promoter of westward expansion to be associated with early furniture made in Grand Rapids.

Haldane's shop saw limited success, growing to employ seven men, but the 1845 advertisement indicated that Haldane would still take barter in the form of produce, lumber, or shingles in exchange for his furniture (hardly the practice of a capitalized manufacturer). He reportedly led his workers in prayer and Bible reading every morning before they began their work, one of the activities that earned him the nickname "Deacon." As early as 1845 he had installed several pieces of water-powered machinery in his shop, which by that time had been moved out of his house to a location on Canal Street. In 1854 Haldane took Enoch W. Winchester as a partner, but this partnership was dissolved after one year. In 1859 he closed his shop.

Though he was later chosen by promoters of the Grand Rapids Furniture Market to be venerated as the "Father of the Furniture Industry," he seems to have played at best a minor role in the industry's founding. To make such a claim is comparable to saying that the first seamstress to land in Manhattan was responsible for New York's fashion industry, or that the first kindly soul to house an overnight guest in Honolulu should somehow be credited with Hawaiian tourism. The fact that Haldane may have been the first person to put together a chair in Grand Rapids should not be confused with the important factors that actually established furniture making as the city's identity and principal industry. In fact, at the time when Grand Rapids' furniture industry was beginning to compete on a national scale, Haldane switched careers to sell real estate!

Yankees Open Mechanized Factories

Before the 1820s, nearly all furniture in this country came from cabinetmakers in small shops. Customers purchased furniture directly from the man who made it. The craftsman generally made the entire piece himself, from rough cut wood to finished product, although larger shops employed additional workers to perform some steps under the direction of the master.

Reliance on this system began to change when, in 1818, Lambert

The oldest piece of signed Grand Rapids furniture was made by German immigrant Bernard Orth, who had come to Grand Rapids by 1857. It is a circular sewing or work table with painted oak graining, supported on a turned pedestal with three scrolled legs. Its lines are suggestive of the Biedermeier style, hinting at the German origins of its maker. Inside the table, on unfinished portions of the frame, Orth wrote not only his signature for posterity, but also this cryptic message in a pidgin of German and English:

"Bernard Orth from Badendorf on the Rhein [sic] Germane [sic] via Prussia between Coblenz and Cologne fixed this table 25 Jan. 1859 for present of my wife and she is a good wife. It is a difficult time, because there is work again after a period of 2 years.

"Grannet [sic] Rapids, 25 January [18]59 Honored Reader. Be happy with your life and use your gifts because when you grow old, it is too late to be joyful.

"All is vanity. Farewell, World. I must depart. Goodbye."

Although Orth sounds in this writing as though he is near death, he is listed as a cabinetmaker in Grand Rapids city directories as late as 1866.

Jonathan Green, who worked as a cabinet-maker, upholsterer, and wagon maker, left a message with letter punches on the back of the crest rail of a chair that he made ca. 1866. It indicates that Green, who served in the First Regiment, Michigan Engineers and Mechanics during the Civil War, was commissioned by his company to make the chair for presentation to its Captain, J. C. Herkner, as a token of respect. The form, a military campaign chair with folding curule legs, shows that its maker had some knowledge of classical styles. However, its decoration, which includes a double American eagle on the crest rail and a crouching bull dog on each armrest, is somewhat crude, betraying the limitations of his skills.

Hitchcock founded the Hitchcock Chair Company in Hitchcocksville, Connecticut. This company adapted for furniture the assembly-line production of standardized parts, and the division-of-labor principles already used by other New England factories that made guns and clocks. In Hitchcock's factory, workers were soon cutting, assembling, and decorating fifteen thousand chairs per year. Most were small and light, making them easy to transport to distant markets. Their forms were simplified from eighteenth-century Sheraton designs, and most decoration was painted or stenciled, which kept production costs down. Ruth Berenson pointed out in her article "Hitchcock Furniture," from *Nineteenth Century Furniture: Innovation, Revival and Reform*:

> . . . Lambert Hitchcock, merits an honored place in American industrial history, not just because of his chair's distinctive appearance but because, as the first person to apply mass-production methods and labor-saving devices to cabinetmaking, he was the progenitor of Grand Rapids.

By the time Yankee settlers began leaving New England in search of opportunity in Michigan during the 1830s and '40s, the success of Hitchcock's methods were quite well-known. Some chose to apply these same techniques in new locations further west. For entrepreneurs willing to invest the capital and accept the risks, success stories similar to Hitchcock's soon began to emerge from Grand Rapids.

Ebenezer M. Ball, born in New Hampshire, moved to Grand Rapids because his uncle, John Ball, was one of the city's founders. In 1849, Ebenezer invested some of his father's money in a partnership with William T. Powers, a distant relative. They shipped lumber and chairs west across Lake Michigan and east down the Erie Canal, into upstate New York. Theirs was likely the first Grand Rapids company to use power machinery to make furniture to sell in markets beyond the city's limits.

Letters that Ball wrote to his father in New Hampshire between 1845 and 1853, now in the collections of The Public Museum of Grand Rapids, describe how he overcame inexperience with determination and persistence:

> After I had been with him [William T. Powers] about a week he went over the lake with his lumber leaving me drove to death with business, half a dozen men to look after and no experience in the business which has made it very hard but I got along much better than I anticipated.
>
> **Ebenezer M. Ball**
> **Letter to his parents, Nov. 29, 1849**

After a year they already found it necessary to improve their business by securing the use of water power to run their machinery:

> We shall try to get a shop up this fall. It is running in debt more than we wished but we could rent no good shop and were compelled [to] secure a water power or do business to a great disadvantage. We have pretty strong competition and shall have to make strong exertions and manage economically to carry through what we have undertaken but I think it can be done if we have no very bad luck.
>
> **Ebenezer M. Ball**
> **Letter to his parents, June 25, 1850**

Once their new shop was up and running, they were able to double the number of men in their employ, and the shop quickly began to pay for itself:

> *William has been engaged in our new shop all winter fitting up machinery and I have had to attend to the finishing and sale of furniture and have not been away scarcly [sic] an hour during the whole time. We comenced [sic] work in our new shop about the first of Jany. and when we get all the machinery put up that we intend to shall be able to supply not only this market but furnish conciderable [sic] for the markets over the lake. We have just completed our machinery for making Winsor [sic] chairs which works finely so that we can almost as it were throw in whole trees into the hopper and grind out chairs ready for use. We have contracted to furnish one firm in Chicago with 10,000 the coming season.*

Ebenezer M. Ball
Letter to his parents, March 8, 1851

Sometimes men trained in the traditional methods of cabinetmaking successfully integrated machinery with their craft, and used their skill in making and designing furniture to greatest advantage. One such family of cabinetmakers was that of George Widdicomb and his sons. Trained in Devonshire, England, George Widdicomb immigrated to New Hampshire in 1843, where he trained his four sons, John, Harry, William, and George, Jr. In 1857 William moved to Grand Rapids, and was soon joined by his father and brothers. In that same year they opened a small shop. William made a trip to Milwaukee in 1858 to find retailers for their furniture, and later claimed to have been the first traveling furniture salesman from Grand Rapids. Just as the business was beginning to take off, it closed, because all four brothers enlisted in the Union Army, to fight in the Civil War.

George, Jr. died during the war, and the three surviving brothers returned to Grand Rapids to form a new partnership with Theodore F. Richards on Canal Street. There they began to produce low-end bedsteads with lathe-turned spindles and simple, milled boards. These were easy to mass-produce by machine, lightweight to ship unassembled, and inexpensive because they left the factory mostly "in the white," or unfinished. By the time of the company's incorporation as the Widdicomb Furniture Company in 1873, the plant had been moved to Fifth Street on the city's west side, where its successor, the John Widdicomb Company, still operates today. By 1887 promotional literature claimed that Widdicomb was the largest manufacturer of bedroom furniture in the world.

Grand Rapids furniture manufacturers made use of so much mechanized technology in their factories that a whole secondary industry of woodworking machinery manufacturers became established in the town. Another Yankee, Charles Buss of Marlborough, New Hampshire, began learning about machinery in 1834 at the age of fourteen, when he was apprenticed for five years to J. A. Fay & Company, a manufacturer of woodworking machinery in Keene, New Hampshire. J. A. Fay & Company introduced the first power mortising, tenoning, and moulding machines ever manufactured. When his apprenticeship ended, Buss opened his own machine shop, patented a hand vise, and won prizes for his Buss panel planer. After the railroad reached Grand Rapids in 1858, Buss sold his belt-driven planers and band saws there.

In 1878 he moved his entire manufactory to Grand Rapids, along with all four of his grown sons, and eighty-four tons of patterns, models, tools, and machinery! According to an advertisement he placed in the Grand Rapids city directory, he made the move so that he could better serve his customers there, and because he recognized the city as a principal and

ABOVE: Widdicomb Brothers & Richards used uncomplicated milling and turning machinery to make this bedstead from locally available hard maple, ca. 1870. BELOW: John, Harry, and William Widdicomb pose with employees in front of their factory, ca. 1871. Note the number of children, who made up nearly one-third of the company's work force.

growing market for his machines. Once re-established, Buss expanded the variety of machines he offered, until the company could contract to supply the entire machinery needs of factories, which it did into the 1950s. On the whole, Buss's machines were not all that different from those offered by competitors. The company's success came from its ability to create custom devices and provide a full line of woodworking machines, and from simply being nearer to its customers.

Another woodworking machinery manufacturer, the King Carving Machine Company, founded in 1889, had a profound impact on the entire furniture industry. Its King Four Spindle Carver allowed manufacturers to create multiple carved pieces simultaneously, with only one machine operator tracing a hand-carved piece with a stylus.

Industry Exploits Forests and the River

But all the Yankee ingenuity and machinery would have done little good without access to wood, and lots of it. Michigan's landscape appeared to be one endless forest to the Easterners who moved there in the 1830s and '40s. In New England, a large percentage of the hardwood forests had already been harvested and used for cabinetmaking and homebuilding. But ninety-five percent of Michigan, totaling thirty-five million acres, was still covered with virgin forests, which land speculators believed were so great that they could never be exhausted. Grand Rapids was situated at an ideal location to exploit the forests. North of town were large stands of white pine, a softwood used for building houses, telegraph poles, railroad ties, and sometimes the backs or hidden insides of furniture. To the south grew walnut, oak, maple, ash, cherry, and other hardwoods, which were favored by furniture makers.

The first farmers in Michigan worked hard to clear the land of timber and bring order to the wilderness. Some wood was used to build cabins and for firewood; the rest was simply piled up and burned as rubbish. As the flood of settlers increased, small sawmills were built along the Grand River and its tributaries, which provided water power to run the mills. A canal was completed on the east side of the Grand River in 1842, to capture river water at a higher elevation above the rapids, then pass it through turbines in the mills to the lower water level downriver. A second canal was built by William T. Powers in 1867 on the river's west side.

The Grand River also provided an easy means of transportation from the forest to the mills. Millions of board feet of logs were cut upriver from Grand Rapids, marked with a brand designating their owners, then floated downriver and collected at the mill, where they were sawed into lumber for use in frame houses, plank roads, barrels, wagons, and furniture. Those finished products that were not used locally were loaded onto river boats and sent around the rapids on the canals, and downriver to the port city of Grand Haven, where they were loaded onto steamships, which took them through the Great Lakes to their final destination.

This situation was key to the development of furniture making as an industry in Grand Rapids. Great quantities of the right kinds of wood and relatively easy transportation made the cost of materials low. The seemingly endless supply of wood created a feeling of optimism: investors saw the cutting and processing of timber as a tremendous opportunity.

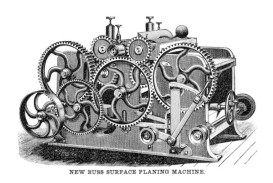

NEW BUSS SURFACE PLANING MACHINE.

ABOVE: Buss produced a succession of new machines for its customers, like this one from an advertisement in the *Michigan Artisan* Dec. 1, 1884. BELOW: Slocum's Grove, seen here ca. 1900, was only one of many sawmills established along the Grand River and its tributaries to harvest hardwood timber for the furniture industry.

ABOVE: The Grand River made transporting the region's timber resources possible, placing Grand Rapids in the center of traffic. Here, logs float under the Pearl St. Bridge in the middle of the city, ca. 1875. BELOW: Walnut "Berkey Table" with white marble top, ca. 1870. Berkey Tables were so successful that the Berkey Brothers Co. changed its entire production from architectural products to furniture.

The story of Charles Carter Comstock embodies many of the forces responsible for Grand Rapids' early success, including building of infrastructure, investment risk, and the exploitation of natural and human resources. Comstock left New Hampshire for Michigan to supervise the construction of a plank road between Kalamazoo and Grand Rapids, using locally milled timber. Through this job he was presented with an opportunity to purchase timber land from the government at a low price, and later resell it for a large profit, some of which he used to open a sawmill and a barrel factory. Many of his employees were African-Americans who moved from the South after the Civil War. He constructed company housing for his workers, known as "Comstock's Row," which became one of Grand Rapids' first African-American neighborhoods. He also invested some money in the Winchester Brothers Furniture Company; when they defaulted on the loan he wound up owning the company, as he described in his *Early Experiences and Personal Recollections of Charles Carter Comstock*:

> In the Fall of 1857 Enoch and Samuel [Winchester] became embarrassed [had financial problems]. I had endorsed some of their paper which they were unable to pay. . . . On Sept. 15 . . . [I] bought out their property and business. . . . Fifteen days after this purchase came the noted crash of 1857. . . . [These] dark days . . . were beyond any description . . . Though severely embarrassed, I nearly doubled my factory and machinery. . . . I must have both in order to make any money in the furniture trade, and . . . I must sell more than I could sell in Grand Rapids.

Comstock soon was selling his furniture through retailers in Chicago, Milwaukee, St. Louis, and Peoria. His furniture is thought to have been the first shipped from Grand Rapids by rail. He eventually sold his interest in the company, which became Nelson, Matter & Company, one of Grand Rapids' largest manufacturers in the nineteenth century.

Many of the city's first bona fide furniture factories actually began as lumber or "sash and blind" mills, which processed cut logs into architectural elements. Because some forms of furniture could be made with the same machinery used to fashion doors, cornice brackets, and newel posts, and because there was a demand, many mills started making a few chairs or cabinets with scraps of wood, and gradually increased their production until they made furniture exclusively.

Mill owner William A. Berkey moved to Grand Rapids from Ohio in 1855 to open a new mill for the manufacture of window sashes and other wood products for home building. His brother Julius came to work there as a planer. According to an article in the *Grand Rapids Press* from January 27, 1923, Julius and partner Alphonso Hamm started making a few small tables with scalloped edges in a corner of the mill in 1861, to help fill local demand:

> In those days furniture had to be brought from the east, horse hauled from Detroit or around the lakes by boat. . . . In response to

pressing local demand Julius Berkey, a skilled woodworker, added
furniture to his production.

The simple design of "Berkey Tables," as they were called, was limited to
the production capabilities of the machinery in the sash and blind mill. The
tables soon became so popular that the mill dropped all sash and blind production in favor of furniture. Later the company became the Berkey & Gay
Furniture Company, and by the 1920s was one of the largest furniture manufacturers in the nation.

Manifest Destiny

These seeds of a furniture industry—technology, natural resources, capital
investors, etc.—were planted in Grand Rapids at the right time. The pervasive national mood was optimistic, inspiring the city's founders to take risks.
The successful businessmen who uprooted their families and moved to the
edge of the frontier believed not only that was it possible to civilize the
wilderness, but that it was their God-given destiny. They felt that the
forests and rivers were created for them to exploit and subdue, and they
built roads, canals, railroads, and factories at an unprecedented pace. When
the currency necessary to build all of this infrastructure was scarce because
of their remote locations, they simply founded banks that issued their own
scrip. Bank notes carried images of ships, trains, canals, and bellowing
smokestacks, all under the approving eye of Columbia, the symbol of
America's bounty. Investors were mostly local, creating a close relationship between those who spent the money and those who benefited by
lending it. Businessmen combined their knowledge and family fortunes to create enough capital for companies to expand.

William Widdicomb, in his *The Early History of the Furniture
Industry in Grand Rapids*, reflected the bold optimism and determination of many of his contemporaries when he stated: "It is one of my theories
that it is not so much location or natural advantage that secures business
success, but rather, the personality of the men who happen to originate and
develop it."

In 1858 a public improvement arrived in Grand Rapids that forever
changed the city's commercial access to the rest of the nation. On July 10,
the first passenger train of the Detroit, Grand Haven, and Milwaukee
Railroad rolled into Grand Rapids, reducing travel time to New York from
two or three weeks to two or three days. The *Grand Rapids Daily Eagle* for
July 12 recognized the significance of the occasion:

> *With this day commences a new era in the city of Grand Rapids.
> We are now connected by railway with all the great cities of the east
> and west, and bound by railroad ties to nearly all the Atlantic States.
> This morning, for the first time, have the people of the Valley City
> [Grand Rapids] had the privilege of leaving their home by another
> public conveyance than that of our river steamers and the old-fash-
> ioned stage coaches. We are now but a few hours' distance from
> everywhere. Let us shout over the triumph.*

Grand Rapids was now truly positioned to expand from supplying the local
region to supplying the nation with furniture.

The growth of this industry coincided with the greatest period of migra-

ABOVE: C.C. Comstock's employees pose with
the products of their sash and blind mill, ca.
1875. As in other Grand Rapids sawmills,
their tools and skills provided a transition to
furniture manufacturing. Courtesy, Grand
Rapids Public Library. BELOW: Five-dollar note
issued in 1858 by the Exchange Bank of
Daniel Ball & Co., to fund construction of the
Michigan City and South Bend Plank Road.
When money was scarce, many Michigan
banks issued private scrip to fund
infrastructure projects.

The invention of devices like the multiple carving machine created demand for a new breed of skilled laborers, like this one in an unidentified factory, ca. 1890.

tion ever seen. Millions of white Americans moved west, and millions of white Europeans made the difficult ocean journey to settle in America. After the Civil War, immigration from Europe continued to rise: the largest numbers to come to Grand Rapids were from the Netherlands, Poland, and Germany. African-Americans freed from slavery also moved to the area in search of jobs.

Most of these immigrants had been peasants or farmers in their old homes. When they arrived in Grand Rapids without the cash necessary to purchase farmland, many took jobs in the factories. Mechanization created a need for these unskilled applicants, who could be easily trained to perform many of the repetitive tasks required. A greater percentage of Canadian, English, German, and Scandinavian workers had received formal training in woodworking in their former homes, and so secured more of the higher-paying jobs. Children were also an important source of inexpensive, unskilled labor: boys between the ages of twelve and sixteen sometimes made up as much as one-third of a factory's labor force. Though there were exceptions, job opportunities for African-Americans and Native Americans were limited to back-breaking, day labor activities.

The constant arrival of immigrants created an important advantage for furniture makers who employed a high percentage of unskilled or semi-skilled laborers. These people were willing to work long hours for low wages, and if they complained or attempted to organize, there were always more coming behind them who would take their jobs without complaint. During the 1910s and '20s, Berkey & Gay's in-house newsletter, *The Shopmark*, frequently featured the "coming over" stories of European immigrants who had found work in its factories. The March, 1924 *Shopmark* talks about Martin Slabbekoorn, who arrived in Grand Rapids in 1890. He worked for a clock and mantel company for twenty-one years before entering the finishing room of Grand Rapids Upholstering Company, a subsidiary of Berkey & Gay.

> Martin was born in the province of Zealand, The Netherlands, a little more than 60 years ago. Here he was a plowman, tilling the soil on the low lands of Holland, but at the age of 28, he saw visions of better things in America and with his wife and two children sailed to this country. Straight to Grand Rapids he came and at once commenced work with the Clock and Mantel Company. . . .

Jake Tanis, another Hollander, ran the factory elevator at Berkey & Gay for more than thirty years. His trip to America is recounted in *The Shopmark* from February, 1917:

> In April, 1880, Jake and his family [including his wife and twelve children] arrived in America on the Zaandam. Jake said that they were only 21 days on the boat, but the voyage lasted him for weeks after that. The ocean gave a little celebration for Jake the last few days of the trip and when it was over, Jake says that all the lifeboats were smashed and the wooden shoes were floating around the ship like decoy ducks.

Often one family member would arrive in this country, then work until he had saved enough money to send for a parent or a cousin. When the family member arrived, he would board with the relative and go to work for the same factory. Some factories had three generations of the same family in their employ.

There was another advantage created by this great migration of people: they served not only as Grand Rapids' labor force for the making of furniture, but also as the principal market for buying it. As the population of Midwestern cities multiplied, there were, very simply, more people within close range to buy Grand Rapids' products. Since many immigrants arrived at their new homes with few possessions, they often needed inexpensive "starter home" furniture. Grand Rapids recognized this tremendous need, and stepped up to fill it, unself-consciously supplying "cheap goods" to the masses. Its furniture may have been a little old-fashioned, made from domestic woods, derivative of higher-quality makers, or a bit lacking in carved decoration, but it was affordable and accessible. Families struggling to establish a homestead on the prairie, or paying rent in a Chicago tenement, cared little about such details; they just needed chairs to sit on and a bed to rest in at the end of a long, hard day. The fineries of life could come later, and when they did, Grand Rapids would be there to supply those, too.

Thousands of immigrant peasants like Martin Slabbekoorn, shown here in *The Shopmark* from March, 1924, became the inexpensive labor pool for Grand Rapids' factories.

Holland Historical Trust Curator Joel Lefever examines three Grand Rapids firms that changed public attitudes toward the production of fine furniture with machinery in the late nineteenth century.

They Make Furniture with Machinery

by Joel Lefever

What set Grand Rapids apart in the furniture industry was the impact that its companies had on the way furniture was perceived by both the trade and the public. Traditionally, high-quality, stylish, expensive furniture had been handmade. During the period from 1870 to 1885, the leading Grand Rapids companies, in particular Berkey & Gay Furniture Company; Nelson, Matter & Company; and Phoenix Furniture Company, helped machine-assisted production of fine furniture to gain acceptance.

These three companies, which are considered the most significant early Grand Rapids firms, exhibited large bedroom suites at the Centennial Exposition in Philadelphia in 1876, and all three won awards, signaling that machine-assisted production had matured.

Longer-established cabinetmakers and factories did not readily accept that the same machinery used to make inexpensive "cottage furniture" could also be applied to high-end furniture. Customers, who were not concerned with construction methods, were easier to convince: they simply wanted substantial furniture that looked good for a reasonable price.

The trade did not object to the use of machinery for production of "low" to "medium" furniture. Machines were used as early as the 1850s for preparing, shaping, and turning wood. However, when Grand Rapids applied the same technology to upper-end furniture in the 1870s, the furniture trade took notice, and some began to complain bitterly. The industry was divided between those who embraced technological advances and those who did not. Ultimately, only those who accepted new woodworking technology could survive.

These three major Grand Rapids companies contributed to the city's emergence as a furniture manufacturing center. They combined keen businessmen, raw materials, available work force, technological advances, professional furniture designers, and aggressive marketing to create a significant impact on the industry.

Before the 1870s, most fine furniture was manufactured in the East, while Midwestern manufacturers mostly produced inexpensive furniture for the country's still-developing regions. In the 1840s, Cincinnati, Ohio became the largest furniture manufacturing center in the area, as successful

ABOVE: Walnut, grained, ebonized, and gilt table with marquetry and incising, attributed to Berkey & Gay Furniture Co., ca. 1875. Despite its complex appearance, most of the ornamentation was produced with machinery and applied in layers.

Dovetails Aid Identification

Early patented drawer joining machines offered a way to cut labor costs. Workers could produce ten times as many drawer joints per day using machinery, which helped to lower the final cost of production and the price charged to the consumer. Most consumers were probably not concerned with the intricacies of drawer construction, since the joints are hidden when the drawers are closed.

As early as the 1860s Berkey Bros. & Co. used machine-cut dowel joints; by the 1870s dowel joints had replaced dovetails on the drawer fronts and backs of mid-grade and expensive furniture. Some expensive furniture attributed to Berkey & Gay from the 1870s has pointed, hand-cut dovetails with scribed guide lines parallel to the dovetail ends on the drawers.

During the early 1870s, Nelson, Matter & Co. used hand-cut, blunt-ended (unpointed) dovetails on their higher-quality furniture. On their cheaper furniture they used rough hand-cut, blunt-ended dovetails and rabbited joints.

By 1873 Nelson, Matter had started to use a Knapp dovetailing machine, patented in

1872, which produced a scallop and dowel joint at the front of the drawer. The back of the drawer had a dowel joint.

Documented Phoenix furniture (1876 at the earliest) has joints made by a gang dovetailer on both the drawer fronts and backs. These joints were used from at least 1876 through the end of the century and were possibly made by "Boult's Patent Reverse Motion

Continued on page 35

firms like Mitchell & Rammelsberg located there. Although that company manufactured all grades of furniture, the majority was inexpensive, fashioned by workers using steam-powered machinery.

The industry in Chicago was also developing during this period. Initially, cabinetmakers and chair makers moved to that area to produce much-needed furniture for a dramatically increasing population. From 1850 to 1860, the number of furniture factories in Chicago increased from thirteen to twenty-six; after 1852 many of them were powered by steam. The majority of their products were, as the *Democratic Press* newspaper described them in 1854, "rather more in the common and useful line, than the luxurious and expensive." Luxurious furnishings had to be ordered from Boston or New York.

The furniture industry in Grand Rapids followed this same pattern. In the 1850s, Nelson, Matter and Berkey & Gay were established from modest beginnings manufacturing inexpensive furniture. Phoenix was founded in 1870 by a group of investors specifically to produce quality furniture for the middle-class market. By the early 1870s the economy in Grand Rapids had developed to the extent that the local furniture industry was an attractive place to invest capital. Grand Rapids companies were also ready to manufacture higher-quality furniture and market it nationally.

These three companies all built impressive factories, powered by water and/or steam, and used the latest machinery and technology to manufacture furniture. They all owned large tracts of timber land in Michigan, which supplied wood for manufacturing. They built their own sawmills and dry kilns, installed elevators and fireproofing in the factories, and laid tracks through the buildings to move furniture. They established markets, employed hundreds of workers, and helped provide an economic climate that encouraged the establishment of other manufacturers and suppliers in Grand Rapids.

As early as 1875 a Grand Rapids promoter proclaimed: "Grand Rapids will, at no distant day, be as famous for its manufactures of wood as Pittsburgh is for its iron." This prophecy came true: after the rapid growth between 1870 and 1885, Grand Rapids furniture manufacturers could claim "a reputation the world over." The American furniture industry of the 1870s and '80s looked to Grand Rapids with envy and fear: few other manufacturing centers or individual companies produced stylish furniture at lower prices.

Today, late nineteenth-century, cheap, mass-produced American furniture is often called "Grand Rapids furniture" or "Grand Rapids style" because of the huge quantities of furniture manufactured there, and the machine production methods used.

Edward Odlin, a reporter for the *American Cabinet Maker*, astutely observed in 1883:

> One thing in which the Grand Rapids manufacturers are probably in advance of any others in the country is in the adoption of new machinery. It has always been their policy to adopt the latest improvements, believing that the saving in the cost of manufacture more than offsets the price of the machinery.

Among those who objected to the use of machines for making fine furniture was a Cincinnati manufacturer who in 1887 contemplated the state of the American furniture industry. He evidently felt that handcrafted furniture was inherently superior, and could not understand "why the trade buys so largely in Grand Rapids. The manufacturers there are not cabinet makers; they make furniture with machinery." In reply, the editor of the *Michigan Artisan*, a promoter of Grand Rapids furniture products, asked, "if machines can be made to do more and better work than men can perform, what is the objection to their use?"

Three Tiers

This complaint reveals the distinctions made in the nineteenth century among grades of furniture, and how manufacturing technique defined quality. Historian and Curator Catherine Hoover Voorsanger points out that there were three levels of furniture makers. The finest held the title "cabinetmaker," and relied on traditional hand construction methods. Among the best-known of these were Herter Brothers, Julius Dessoir, John Henry Belter, Alexander Roux, Leon Marcotte, and Pottier & Stymus of New York City; Thomas Brooks of Brooklyn, New York; Elijah Galusha of Troy, New York; John Jelliff of Newark, New Jersey; Davenport & Co. of Boston; and George Henkels and Daniel Pabst of Philadelphia.

In the second tier were the manufacturers who used the terms "furniture" or "furnishings" to distinguish their products from fine cabinetmaking. It was to this class of manufacturers that most Grand Rapids companies initially aspired. Every advertisement placed in city directories and trade journals by Berkey & Gay; Nelson, Matter; and Phoenix, from their inception until 1885, used the word "furniture" to describe the companies' products, indicating to consumers that their products did not pretend to be traditional handmade cabinetry.

The trade in the 1870s knew that, although Grand Rapids makers were not cabinetmakers, they did produce high-quality furniture. William LeRow, of the *American Cabinet Maker*, indicated the level of furniture quality when he wrote:

> Manufacturers [outside of Grand Rapids], in offering their goods not infrequently say, "this is as good as the Grand Rapids work" while others less honest and more mum, appropriate the designs, and palm them off as their own creations. It is the high quality of the work produced here, rather than the great amount of it, that has caused this place to take the dominating position in the American furniture trade. The bulk of the work produced by the leading firms here, is of the grades ranging from medium to fine, adapted to the wants of the middling classes of society. The marked success of the manufacturers here is attributable to their comprehension of the needs of the times, in design, construction and finish, which, it is needless to say, means that they have succeeded for many years in producing highly desirable work at modest prices, and holding and increasing their annual business, in the teeth of the fiercest competition from other sections.

Grand Rapids companies were keenly aware of the "needs of the times," and provided appropriate furniture for the exploding middle-class market. But Berkey & Gay; Nelson, Matter; and Phoenix sought to raise the standards of design, ornament, and finish for factory-made middle-class furni-

Paneling, Variety Moulding & Dovetailing Machine" manufactured in Battle Creek, Michigan by the Battle Creek Machinery Company. A labeled ca. 1878 Phoenix secretary bookcase also has rabbited drawer joints on small letter drawers. A photograph of a high-end sideboard with open drawers in a ca. 1876 Phoenix album indicates that hand-cut dovetails were also occasionally used on expensive furniture.

After about 1880, furniture had machine-cut dovetails at the front of the drawers and dowel joints at the back. Hand-cut dovetails are never found after this time, since the three companies adopted the latest drawer-joint machinery. Until dovetail machinery became more standardized in the 1880s, companies tended to alternate between hand- and machine-cut dovetails, depending on the customers' wishes and the circumstances of manufacture.

A labeled 1880s mahogany dresser and washstand have very regular machine-cut dovetails at the front of the drawers, made by a gang dovetailing machine, and dowel joints at the drawer backs. Gang dovetailers cut joints using the rotary action of cutter heads. The cuts made by the heads left semicircular voids that appear on the inside of a drawer after it is assembled. Smaller drawers in the dresser have rabbited joints. Berkey & Gay also used gang dovetails and dowel joints in the 1880s.

As woodworking machinery developed and became more standardized, Berkey & Gay and Nelson, Matter used the same type of machinery to produce wedge-shaped dovetails on drawer fronts. Nelson, Matter stopped using the Knapp dovetailing machine by 1885, possibly because its cutters were difficult to keep sharpened. From the 1870s on, Phoenix continued to use rotary dovetailing machines that produced traditional-looking dovetails on both the fronts and backs of drawer sides.

The frame for this armchair was made in Chicago on contract for Berkey & Gay, and may have been part of that company's display in the Michigan Building at the 1876 Philadelphia Centennial Exposition.

ture and as a result received the praise of journalists like LeRow . . . and a sizeable share of the furniture market.

Furniture makers in the third level were known by the terms "slaughter" shops, "butcher" shops, and "auction" shops. Many of these low-quality furniture producers were located in large cities and sold furniture assembled in lots at auction. Owners of these shops hired poorly trained workers for low pay and kept their operations small. The Midwestern manufacturers, including those in Grand Rapids, put many of these makers out of business in the 1870s and '80s by offering higher-quality yet inexpensive products.

Eventually Berkey & Gay and Nelson, Matter eliminated the most common furniture from their lines, while Phoenix continued to manufacture some "cheap" furniture. In the late 1870s, most of the least expensive beds, tables, dressers, and washstands disappeared from the photographed furniture albums and from descriptions of the latest furniture lines in trade journals. Yet other companies in Grand Rapids specialized in inexpensive products, and occasionally companies re-directed manufacturing efforts to supply a demand as when, in 1884, Phoenix developed a "Special Order" department for contracted work while they continued to produce their regular line.

By the 1870s, Grand Rapids (especially its three leading companies) was known for producing bedroom furniture or "chamber suits." The large exhibition bedroom suites manufactured for the Centennial Exposition helped to foster this reputation. Period trade journals often described Grand Rapids bedroom suites and frequently reported on the companies' receiving contracts for furnishing American hotels.

Other furniture manufacturing cities also became known for specific products. Chicago, for example, excelled in producing "parlor frames," the wooden frames for upholstered parlor sofas and chairs.

This specialization may be attributed to the availability of differing raw materials. Grand Rapids had an abundance of wood available; case furniture and beds required more wood than parlor chairs. Chicago, on the other hand, had the transportation network required for importing upholstery fabrics and padding. Chicago also had stockyards, which provided leather for chair coverings and curled hair for cushion stuffing.

Various furniture forms were not consistently manufactured by all the companies between 1870 and 1885. For example, in the 1870s Berkey & Gay and Nelson, Matter did not manufacture parlor frames, although they did upholster chair frames manufactured in Chicago. Phoenix originally manufactured upholstered parlor furniture because company president William A. Berkey saw a potential market for it. In 1882, however, Phoenix discontinued this line.

Men and Machines

The Grand Rapids factories were busy worlds of workers and machinery; mechanical advances in the nineteenth century had not eliminated the need for human labor. Machinery required skilled operators, and furniture assembly and ornamenting still required craftsmanship. There were four categories of tasks in a factory: machine operation; assembly, ornamentation, and finishing; factory production assistance; and marketing and management.

Although most of the machinery in the Grand Rapids factories between 1870 and 1885 was used to prepare wood for final hand assembly, the machines were different enough to necessitate strict division of labor for skilled operators. There were circular saws, band saws, jigsaws, scroll saws, jointers, planers, sanders, shapers, moulders, lathes, stampers, and carving machines.

After machine operators shaped the pieces of wood, there was much work to be done by hand. Cabinetmakers assembled the prepared wood into case furniture, a task known as "benchwork." Other hand work was done by bedstead makers (probably assemblers), caners, wood fillers, finishers, gluers, lock fitters, marquetry cutters, decorators, upholsterers, veneerers, and wood carvers.

Factory production assistants included the engineers, firemen, machinists, pipe-fitters, blacksmiths, and carpenters who kept boilers and machinery functioning; pilers, laborers, and elevatormen who moved fuel, raw materials, and finished products from place to place; and the lumber inspectors, stockroom keepers, clerks, bookkeepers, cashiers, and shipping clerks who guaranteed that appropriate materials were available, that workers received pay, and that furniture made it to market. These workers created the support network required for an efficient factory.

Management and marketing, although not directly involved with production, were essential for continued operations. It was the management of the Grand Rapids factories, including the owners, presidents, secretaries, and treasurers, who made a commitment to quality products and who made innovative production methods possible. Furniture photographers, showroom salesmen, and traveling salesmen (called "drummers") kept the whole factory system operating, by moving products to consumers.

Organizing such an intricate network of tasks and workers required specialized, rationally organized factory buildings. Berkey & Gay's manufacturing complex, a good representation of the Grand Rapids factories, was described in 1882. Its yard held two million feet of lumber and a dry kiln. Nearby stood the four-story, 70-by-120-foot machinery building, which included a sawmill and woodworking machinery. The adjacent Grand River powered two water wheels, and a steam engine provided emergency power. Beside the machinery building was a similarly proportioned benchwork building, where furniture was assembled and ornamented. Across Canal Street stood a six-story building containing the finishing areas, warehouse, and salesrooms. At the time, Berkey & Gay employed 500 people.

Inside the buildings, workers were organized into departments overseen by foremen. Specific departments included sawmilling, cabinetmaking, carving, veneering, finishing, upholstering, packing, and stocking. Members of the same family (at least with the same surname) frequently worked together in a department. Three members of the Biggs family (Isaac, Josiah J., and Thomas) worked in the upholstery department of Berkey & Gay between 1873 and 1884. Josiah became the upholstery foreman at least by 1881 and possibly helped Isaac and Thomas find work.

Although they were located in close proximity, Berkey & Gay; Nelson, Matter; and Phoenix tended to use different machines or methods to construct furniture in the 1870s. Examining the dovetails and joints used to

Grand Rapids salesmen quickly learned that it was easier to carry photo catalogs than train loads of furniture.

The furniture pictured in the 1873 and 1876 Nelson, Matter catalogs illustrates the differences of quality and expense that the furniture trade termed "common, medium, & fine." The least expensive had no carving and very little moulding or shaping of surfaces, and were the only pieces available in "white-wood" (tulip poplar).

Medium-quality furniture, which constituted the broadest range, generally had more complex design and ornamentation, including moulded surfaces and applied mouldings, although the forms were similar to "common" furniture. Medium furniture was available in ash and black walnut, walnut being the highest quality available in that line.

Fine furniture generally had quite complex designs, heavier and more expensive applied ornaments, better hardware, and a multiple-layer hand-rubbed varnish finish. Parlor tables, sideboards, and bedroom dressers and washstands (also called commodes) often had marble tops. Courtesy, Grand Rapids Public Library.

construct drawers reveals distinct differences and similarities among the three, helping to differentiate their products, and indicating the rate at which they adopted new machinery.

All three companies used hand-cut dovetails on expensive furniture in the early to mid-1870s, but changed to machine-cut dovetails even on the best furniture grades. Although the industry seemed to expect handcrafted dovetails on expensive furniture, by about 1876 the companies rarely produced drawer joints by hand.

Ornamentation Indicates Luxury

In addition to changing the way drawer joints were produced, manufacturers looked for innovative and cost-effective ways to ornament their furniture. Ornamenting could be as simple as varnishing wood black to make it look like ebony, or purchasing ornaments made elsewhere and gluing them into place. By the late 1870s, enough skilled carvers and wood inlay workers were located in Grand Rapids to produce furniture that could compete with the high-end products of other, longer-established companies.

Varnish was the most popular protective finish used in Grand Rapids. It was applied in several coats, with a worker (called a rubber) buffing after each application. Most manufacturers did not want to risk having finishes damaged during shipping, so they sold furniture to retailers unfinished (in the white). Retailers often had their own finishing rooms and varnished the furniture themselves. Furniture sold directly from factories to local consumers was probably sold finished.

Other finishes were used to make furniture look more luxurious without increasing the cost. "Graining" achieved the look of ornamental, expensive burled walnut veneer: the wood was painted to resemble burl. By the 1870s, both Berkey & Gay and Nelson, Matter employed grainers.

Expensive furniture was ornamented with marquetry. Exotic wood veneers were cut and pieced in layers to make flower and foliage designs, musical and gaming "trophies," or scenes. Although Phoenix occasionally used marquetry on parlor chairs between 1870 and 1885, it was Berkey & Gay and Nelson, Matter that excelled in this art. A ledger attributed to Berkey & Gay at the Public Museum contains many drawings of marquetry designs.

Metal marquetry ornaments, probably inlaid brass cut-outs, were used by Nelson, Matter, with simpler, more abstract designs. They also used patented artificial wood drawer pulls and ornaments on their furniture in the 1870s, supplied by O. A. Nathusius & Company of New York City. The ornaments were made out of a pressed sawdust and binder composition. An unfinished Nelson, Matter walnut secretary bookcase with a Grecian female head wholesaled at $45 in 1876, making the ten-cent cost of the ornament a small part of the overall expense of manufacture.

In the late 1870s, however, Nelson, Matter stopped using Nathusius ornaments on expensive furniture, preferring hand-carved ornaments made in their Grand Rapids factory. This shift was probably due to the changing furniture market and increase in Eastern sales. The new styles popular in the East by the mid-1870s, namely Modern (Reform) Gothic and "Eastlake," eschewed artificial ornaments on expensive furniture.

Carved elements are often found on furniture from the three companies.

Some close-grained wood was "ebonized," or finished to look like ebony. Nelson, Matter & Co. used real ebony wood in the carved columns on its exhibition suite at the Philadelphia Centennial. Nelson, Matter and Berkey & Gay also used ebony veneer for marquetry work. But ebony was more difficult to obtain than cherry or maple, and these local woods ebonized successfully, so imitation ebony was common. Berkey & Gay tended to combine lighter woods like walnut with ebonized wood on parlor tables in the mid- to late 1870s.

Phoenix probably produced substantial amounts of ebonized furniture by 1881: during that year, company records listed four workers as ebonizers. Phoenix advertisements in the city directories of 1880 to 1882 illustrate a writing desk with mirror. This ebonized version of the desk with different hardware is in the collection of the Public Museum of Grand Rapids. The underside of one drawer bears a rare employee's signature of John W. Hagelgans, a cabinetmaker and trimmer for Phoenix.

Carving became more profuse as the 1870s progressed; for a few years in the early 1880s, elaborate hand carving was a characteristic of expensive Grand Rapids furniture. At this time, enough wood carvers worked in the area to establish the Grand Rapids Furniture Carvers' Guild.

A high-quality bedroom suite by Berkey & Gay, now in the collection of the Public Museum of Grand Rapids, exemplifies the carved Eastlake style of the 1880s. A pot of daisies forms the crest of each piece and lotus blossoms decorate the frieze (both decorative elements from the Aesthetic Movement). The mouldings are heavy and carved, and panels are incised. A similar Queen Anne bedroom suite by Phoenix described in an 1882 trade journal had "rope pillars and a profusion of carving."

Mid-grade furniture often had less hand carving, or had machine carving that was concentrated on panels or mouldings. Machine carving was used increasingly in the 1870s and '80s as machinery improved. According to historian Michael Ettema, a carving machine was developed in 1876 for Berkey & Gay by a man named Clarke. Although city directories list no Clarke working for Berkey & Gay (possibly due to spotty record-keeping in the 1870s), G. H. Clark, a founder of the Valley City Table Company in 1888, is given credit for introducing machine carving to Grand Rapids.

Machine carving either removed excess wood before hand carving or traced design templates, carving duplicates simultaneously. Lower-end furniture had either very simple machine carving or none at all. During this period, cost is generally related to the extent of handwork, and even machine carving required a competent operator, adding expense.

Berkey & Gay; Nelson, Matter; and Phoenix probably reacted to the criticism of their making "furniture with machinery" by adorning expensive furniture with handmade ornamentation. When they started using exclusively machined joinery, they simultaneously added exceptional carving and marquetry that could not be produced by machinery. Handmade ornament compensated for the coldness of largely machine-produced furniture by giving it warmth and individuality.

Styles and Designers

This nimble ability to adapt furniture production to the demands of the market contributed to the Grand Rapids companies' success. They were also quick to adopt new fashions, following the lead of the rapidly changing styles on the East Coast. Furniture illustrated in Nelson, Matter's 1873 catalog reflects mostly the Renaissance Revival style, with hints of earlier Rococo and later Neo-Grec in furniture crests. Library tables have Elizabethan turnings. On the East Coast, most of these styles had peaked by 1870.

In the 1876 Nelson, Matter catalog, Neo-Grec design is shown on expensive furniture, and there are elements of Rococo, Elizabethan, and Renaissance Revival in the less expensive furniture. The catalog's frontispiece has a photograph of a sideboard in the more fashionable Reform/Eastlake style. Berkey & Gay and Phoenix produced tables and parlor suites, respectively, in the Louis XVI style in the late 1870s, but examples of this style are rare, partly because it relied on expensive marquetry and gilt bronze or porcelain plaques for ornament.

Eastlake became the most popular style in Grand Rapids by 1880.

ABOVE: The musical and floral marquetry on this ca. 1875 tabletop is typical of the designs drawn by John Keck for Berkey & Gay.
BELOW: This ca. 1880 Reform or Aesthetic-style washstand is part of a bedroom suite by Berkey & Gay which traveled more than 3,000 miles to reach its purchaser. After moving by rail to the wareroom in New York City, it was placed on a ship which took it to the port of Indianola, Texas. It then traveled overland to its final destination, the small farming community of Llano, Texas.

ABOVE: Designer John Keck of Ann Arbor, Michigan, probably sketched this bed for Berkey & Gay sometime in the 1870s.
BELOW: In Kendall's own hand, the words above this ink and wash drawing read, "The first piece I drew at the Phoenix. DWK" ca. 1882.

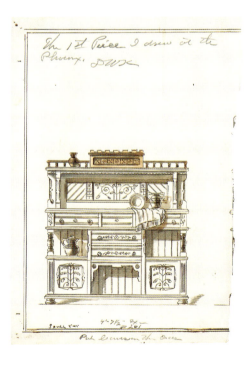

Although Grand Rapids Eastlake was usually put together with "dishonest" dowels and often had "false" veneer panels and occasionally high relief carving, it followed the general rectilinear forms promoted in British tastemaker Charles Eastlake's *Hints on Household Taste*. Examples of Modern Gothic, Anglo-Japanese, and Turkish/Moorish are all represented in furniture lines by 1885.

In order to maintain their share of a constantly changing market, the companies contracted with designers, who created furniture in different styles, which helped the companies to keep up with the demands of fashion.

John Keck of Ann Arbor, Michigan was probably an early contracted designer for Berkey & Gay. Furniture sketches signed by Keck are in the same ledger as the attributed Berkey & Gay marquetry designs. The Keck drawings include designs for Renaissance Revival/Neo-Grec-style as well as Reform/Eastlake-style furniture.

Keck was born in Wurtemberg, Germany in 1839; at age fifteen he immigrated with his family to Washtenaw County, Michigan. In 1867 he started designing and manufacturing furniture in Ann Arbor. One sketch of a bed by Keck is nearly identical to a bed from a labeled Berkey & Gay suite at the Cappon House Museum in Holland, Michigan. The original design was altered to accommodate machine production and standardized parts, permitting a less expensive bed with no carving.

A designer named Charles Radcliffe, originally from Wiscasset, Maine, worked for Nelson, Matter from 1877 until the firm closed in 1917. He designed the company's regular line and special orders for hotels and public institutions, and worked until his death in 1919. In 1881, President Chester Arthur purchased a Radcliffe-designed bedroom suite from Nelson, Matter for his personal use in the White House. An art critic of the time called the suite a "poem in wood."

Asa Lyon and David Wolcott Kendall were two Phoenix designers commended in trade journals in the 1880s. Lyon was described in the July, 1884 *Michigan Artisan* as the "new designer" for Phoenix who had "produced many new and novel features in furniture." Kendall was born in Rochester, New York in 1851, learned cabinetmaking there from his father, then moved to Grand Rapids, joining Phoenix as a draftsman in 1879. By 1882 he was designing "plain" (Reform/Eastlake) bedroom suites.

Marketing Techniques Develop

In marketing, the Grand Rapids companies cooperated. Separately, they used marketing methods like advertising, traveling salesmen, catalogs, and showrooms. But they also found that joint exhibitions, markets, and manufacturing associations helped spread the name Grand Rapids more effectively than individuals promoting the products of an isolated lumber town. A reporter for the *American Cabinet Maker* observed the spirit of cooperative marketing when he wrote in 1882:

> In some cities a visiting dealer will be terribly bored by the manufacturers [trying] to induce him to buy the goods of his manufacture, and to keep him from visiting rival factories. None of this spirit will be found in Grand Rapids. It is . . . as if all the furniture was made by one factory consisting of the whole of them.

This sense of cooperation was surprising to the rest of the furniture industry but gave Grand Rapids a marketing advantage. If one factory did not offer a specific product, another would. Grand Rapids had become a one-stop furniture showroom by 1885.

Initially the three leading companies advertised in Grand Rapids newspapers and city directories to sell furniture to local residents at retail prices. Before 1885 national advertising in print was probably not very important, since it was mostly intended for the furniture trade, not for consumers.

Among the earliest marketing accounts are the reminiscences of Charles Jones, a shipping clerk for Berkey Brothers & Company who sold furniture locally. Following the Great Fire of 1871, Jones traveled to Chicago, and later made other sales trips along the Lake Michigan shore. He left the company in 1874 but not before traveling east, where he found dealers incredulous that Grand Rapids produced furniture, since they thought "there was nothing but woods and Indians out (there) . . . they couldn't make furniture . . . and if they did the Indians would likely go on the warpath and kill everybody before it could be shipped out of the woods."

One of the first sales trips to the East occurred in the late 1860s when George Washington Gay, a partner in Berkey Brothers & Gay, took two train cars of furniture to New York and Philadelphia and sold the stock. Trips east, west, and south developed into annual or biannual events.

The companies soon discovered that catalogs, with either photographs or wood engravings, were more convenient and less expensive for the companies to send on selling trips than actual furniture. The earliest existing catalog and price list (although not the first) are dated 1873 from Nelson, Matter. The catalog contains numbered photographs while the price list describes the furniture and gives ordering information. Catalogs were either carried by traveling salesmen or sent to furniture dealers who placed orders from the numbered items. Photographs permitted retailers to see the variety and styles of the Grand Rapids industry. By the mid-1870s all three companies had photographers and skylit studios in their factory buildings.

Showrooms could reach both retailers and the public with the newest furniture products. The three companies originally sold from the factories

FURNITURE PAVILION AT NEW ORLEANS,
ERECTED AND OCCUPIED BY THE
Furniture Manufacturers' Association of Grand Rapids, Mich.

Public exhibits offered the opportunity to reach a broad public. At the 1871 Northern Michigan Agricultural and Mechanical Fair, Nelson, Matter exhibited chamber and parlor furniture and was awarded "the first premium." But it was the Philadelphia Centennial Exposition that permitted a large United States audience to compare Grand Rapids products with those of other states and countries. Phoenix displayed two bedroom suites, one made specifically for the exhibition and one from the regular line, and a hallstand, sideboard, and table. Nelson, Matter showed an exhibition bedroom suite valued at $10,000 that was said to be the most elaborate at the Centennial. It featured a bed and matching dresser that stood eighteen feet high, with niches for carved statues of patriots from the American Revolution, and topped with life-sized eagle finials. Berkey & Gay exhibited a bedroom suite of Michigan black walnut with French burl panels and lounges. All three companies won awards and were commended in categories including workmanship, finish, and selection of materials. Courtesy, Grand Rapids Public Library.

The public saw Grand Rapids furniture not only in the Main Exhibition building but also in the Michigan Building where Berkey & Gay furnished a parlor organ, a bedroom suite, a parlor suite, and draperies.

The 1884-85 World's Industrial and Cotton Centennial Exposition in New Orleans offered another opportunity to call attention "to the extent and character" of the Grand Rapids furniture lines. An association of one Chicago and twenty Grand Rapids companies built the Grand Rapids Pavilion, LEFT. From the *Michigan Artisan,* Nov. 1, 1884.

but soon developed salesrooms. By 1872 Berkey & Gay and Nelson, Matter had separate buildings for showing and selling furniture.

Berkey & Gay opened a New York City showroom, managed by John E. Foster, in 1875; it was first listed in an 1876 New York business directory at 17 Elizabeth Street, in the Little Germany section of Lower East Side Manhattan, an area known in the 1860s and '70s for producing inexpensive but "respectable" furniture. The New York showroom gave Berkey & Gay direct access to the Eastern furniture market, allowing buyers to purchase Grand Rapids furniture without traveling to Michigan. By 1876 the company was selling to every state, as well as to Great Britain and Australia; foreign sales helped sustain companies during market downturns.

Phoenix and Nelson, Matter also went to New York City, where they opened "warerooms." The Phoenix showroom was established in 1876 or 1877 under the direction of C. W. Baldwin at 177 Canal Street. Nelson, Matter opened a wareroom under James W. Wheelock in 1878 at 202 & 204 Canal Street. Both of these showrooms were literally around the corner from Berkey & Gay.

Identification and Attribution

Although the Grand Rapids companies were perhaps best known for their bedroom suites, they produced a variety of furniture, and much of it was unlabeled in the nineteenth century. With such a broad spectrum of furniture forms varying widely in construction and style, it is difficult to look at a piece and say that it is from Grand Rapids, let alone from a particular company. Style and decorative motif are not often helpful in identifying furniture, because there was a considerable exchange of designers, workmen, and component suppliers among the companies.

There are clues that help attribute certain pieces to certain manufacturers. Drawer construction (joints and dovetails), identification marks, and workers' signatures all provide evidence. A single identifying characteristic does not prove a manufacturer, but combinations of these features can lead to strong attributions of unlabeled furniture.

Early turned whatnots and simple tables have few significant manufacturing characteristics that distinguish one factory's products from another's. They are currently identifiable only through illustrations in scarce catalogs or advertisements. Upholstered furniture is difficult to attribute, partly because the upholstery hides construction details and labels. Also, of the three leading Grand Rapids companies, only Phoenix manufactured upholstered parlor furniture frames before the 1880s. Berkey & Gay and Nelson, Matter upholstered chair frames manufactured elsewhere and sold them in the local retail market.

Factory labeling is the most effective way to identify furniture, but most Grand Rapids firms labeled furniture only sporadically in the 1870s and '80s. Very few labels remain on early furniture, and many pieces give no indication of ever having had them.

When they did label, Berkey & Gay; Nelson, Matter; and Phoenix used white cards with text printed in black ink. Examples of card labels tacked to the backs of furniture survive for all three companies, although infrequently on earlier pieces, since they tended to tear or fall off as the paper deteriorated.

ABOVE: The Phoenix Furniture Co. was a model of efficient and fire-proof factory design when constructed between 1873 and 1880. Though razed in 1988, a portion was salvaged and recreated in the Public Museum of Grand Rapids' exhibition. "The Furniture City." BELOW: This turned crib was attributed to Nelson, Matter & Co. because it appears in the company's 1876 catalog.

To identify component parts or pieces of furniture, factories used penciled, chalked, painted, stenciled, stamped, or scribed markings. All the factories seemed to mark pieces such as drawer components with penciled numbers.

Berkey & Gay often used scribed, or scratched, Roman numerals along with the painted numbers to identify furniture. The scribed Roman numerals were two to three inches high and were placed on component furniture parts such as a mirror and dresser base that went together. Occasionally, chalk was used to mark Roman numerals on furniture. Stenciled numbers were also used on case pieces from the 1880s.

Nelson, Matter seldom marked furniture. When they did, they used thick black paint on unfinished backs. They also used black paint to write the destination of furniture being shipped. This practice has caused some Nelson, Matter furniture to be misattributed, because the destination was often a finishing factory or retailer.

Nelson, Matter used Roman numerals along with painted black numbers. On some early attributed furniture, Roman and Arabic numerals less than an inch high were scribed on unfinished backs. Later they used white chalk. Small, punched, Arabic numerals marking hinge and latch placement have been found on an 1873 Nelson, Matter desk.

Phoenix used die-stamped, or punched, numbers on a dresser from the 1870s. The numbers, approximately half an inch high, are "1" over "384." Occasionally numbers were marked in black paint, and white chalk marks such as "2/2" and "2/17" have been found on furniture backs. Drawers and their corresponding placement in the furniture case were marked in blue or black wax pencil. No Roman numerals were found on Phoenix furniture.

In the 1870s, suppliers of marble sometimes marked the marble slab's unpolished underside to distinguish orders intended for different companies. White marble is more often marked than colored marble.

Factory workers in Grand Rapids occasionally signed the furniture that they produced, which helps in attribution. City directories list the occupation and place of employment for many Grand Rapids residents. An 1880s ebonized desk attributed to Phoenix was signed "John W. Hagelgans, Grand Rapids, Mich." under a drawer. Hagelgans was a cabinetmaker and trimmer for Phoenix.

Berkey & Gay furniture is the most easily identifiable because of the unusual dowel joints they made during the 1860s and '70s, and because the distinctive two- to three-inch-tall scribed Roman numerals were not observed on furniture by any other company. Phoenix is probably the most difficult to identify because the machinery they used to produce rotary (gang) drawer joints was also used by other companies around the country by the mid-1880s. Eventually, as more pieces are attributed, studies of the style and motif of specific companies will be possible for the unidentified late nineteenth-century furniture known as "Grand Rapids."

Recently, interest in the furniture of late American-Victorian Grand Rapids has increased, in dramatic contrast to previous attitudes. Interior decoration advisor Elsie de Wolfe revealed an intense and representative dislike when she wrote in 1911:
"I fancy the furniture of the mid-Victorian era will never be coveted by collectors, unless someone should build a museum for freakish objects of house furnishings. America could contribute much to such a collection for surely the black walnut era of the Nineteenth Century will never be surpassed in ugliness and bad taste, unless—rare fortune—there should be a sudden epidemic of appreciation among cabinetmakers which would result in their taking the beautiful wood in the black walnut beds and wardrobes . . . and make it over into worthwhile things."

Raymond F. and Marguerite Yates, authors of the 1949 *A Guide to Victorian Antiques*, who held views similar to De Wolfe's, illustrated their guide with examples of top-of-the-line Berkey & Gay bedroom furniture. They felt that the furniture, made for "Mr. Moneybags of the 1870's," was "badly proportioned, gawky, knobby, and with crotch walnut veneer" and "hideous in the extreme, yet already a candidate for antiquity."

FRANK J. DÁVIDHÁZY.
1934

Dr. Jeffrey D. Kleiman, Associate Professor of History at University of Wisconsin-Marshfield, explores the relationships between workers and owners that led to "The Great Strike."

Making Connections
by Jeffrey D. Kleiman

The people in the furniture trade in Grand Rapids at the turn of the twentieth century lived, for the most part, in two distinct, separate worlds. The owners of the manufacturing firms formed a tightly knit circle of canny businessmen who lived closely and worked cooperatively, in both the furniture industry and banking, to ensure their continued power and position in the city. The work in their factories was largely done by immigrants from the Netherlands, Poland, Germany, and other European countries, who had varying skills and interests, attended diverse churches, and lived in small, heavily mortgaged houses in scattered ethnic neighborhoods.

Although these two worlds seldom intersected, the lives of the two sets of people were actually connected, because of the furniture industry, the economy, and the careful planning and control exerted by the manufacturers and their managers. This socioeconomic structure became more and more tense, and eventually led to one of the most explosive episodes in Grand Rapids history.

The Rule from Above: Owners' Organization

The rise of the furniture industry in Grand Rapids was the result of conscious planning by business leaders. Within a few years after the Civil War, the city lost its initial advantage as a natural site for furniture manufacturing. Compared to Chicago or Detroit, Grand Rapids lacked easy access to raw materials, transportation, labor, and capital. Growing competition caused businessmen to face an important choice: whether to permit a variety of manufacturing in town, or to focus on one industry in all its phases. By 1906, they had chosen the furniture trade, bringing that industry to a national prominence out of all proportion with the size of the city. Through tightly managed sharing of information in banks, employment bureaus, and executive boards, furniture men worked together to make the most of local resources. Business interests were reinforced by social contacts, as many members of this inner circle relaxed at the same city club, played golf at the same country club, and worshiped at the same church.

OPPOSITE: This portrait of Phoenix spindle carver and turner Jack Weaver was painted by Frank J. Davidhazy in 1934. The image, which was reproduced in publications and hung in the company's offices, portrays Weaver as a benign and skilled craftsman busily working at his bench. Weaver worked an incredible 66 $\frac{1}{2}$ years for the same employer.

ABOVE: Company officers formed both formal and informal alliances with other influential men for mutual advantage. This golf foursome included James Muir, the owner of a furniture catalog printer; James Bayne, the owner of a furniture photography studio; William Cox, a lumber supplier; and Dr. Alfred Wishart, the politically active minister of a prominent Protestant church.

Members of the Furniture Manufacturers Association, 1908.

An inner circle of powerful men shared interlocking directorships in both furniture manufacturing and banking. These entrepreneurs exercised tremendous influence on the economy of Grand Rapids by controlling its major industry and by holding the mortgages of many of their employees.

William Hovey Gay, president of Berkey & Gay Furniture Co., also served as president of the People's Savings Bank and director for the Fourth National Bank and the Michigan Trust Company. These positions put him in proximity to the more powerful Kent State Bank. Combined, the Fourth and Kent Banks wielded assets approaching a million dollars. Gay and his partner, John Covode, used their common knowledge of these banks to influence the West Side Savings and Loan, the third largest such institution in the city and a vital center for mortgage money for homeowners.

The Kent State Bank was directly interlocked with the Old National and City National Banks, whose combined assets approached two million dollars. On Kent State Bank's board of directors were Robert Irwin and Alexander Hompe, president and vice-president of the Royal Furniture Co., and Elijah Foote, who founded the Imperial Furniture Co. and served as an officer of Grand Rapids Chair Co. These banks were also influenced, along with other commercial banks and mortgage-granting institutions, by William Widdicomb. In manufacturing,

Nineteen firms formed the heart of the city's furniture industry, wielding enormous influence on unemployment, wage levels, and production. These companies were the largest in the Furniture Manufacturers Association (FMA). They accounted for a quarter of the city's entire labor force and more than eighty-five percent of the furniture workers. Eight of these firms formed a special inner circle of power: Berkey & Gay Furniture Company, Grand Rapids Chair Company, Imperial Furniture Company, The Macey Company, Oriel Cabinet Company, Phoenix Furniture Company, Royal Furniture Company, and Widdicomb Furniture Company. Each employed more than four hundred men, and each turned out a variety of items directed at furnishing the expansive urban market.

Berkey & Gay, Oriel, Grand Rapids Chair, Royal, and Phoenix were at the center of a network of interlocking directorates in both the furniture industry and the banking community. Berkey & Gay and Oriel shared executives William Hovey Gay and John A. Covode, Jr., and Phoenix and Royal were part of a consortium headed by Robert W. Irwin and Alexander Hompe. William Hovey Gay was born in Grand Rapids in 1863, the son of a prosperous furniture manufacturer and the grandson of William Hovey, a pioneer settler and entrepreneur. The FMA was established in 1881 as a result of Gay's efforts. His business partner, John A. Covode, Jr., came to Grand Rapids at age twenty-three and applied his college education to making money. Both men were Baptists and supported the Fountain Street Church.

Alexander Hompe was born in upstate New York, attended Cornell University, and moved to Grand Rapids at age twenty-six in 1891, where he moved up to the rank of vice-president in the Royal Furniture Company. He maintained an intimate business relationship with Robert Irwin, owner of both the Royal and Phoenix Companies. Through interlocking executive positions, the two exercised control over more than fourteen hundred workers.

Elijah Foote, who founded Imperial and served as an officer of Grand Rapids Chair, had come to Grand Rapids, from upstate New York, as a child with his family before the Civil War. William Widdicomb influenced several banks and directed a number of furniture firms as well, including Grand Rapids Chair, Royal, Phoenix, Macey, and of course, the William Widdicomb Company.

These men shared the neighborhood on the bluff overlooking the downtown and factory districts (now referred to as Heritage Hill), looking across the river to the working-class neighborhoods on the West Side. They got involved in banking partly because competing successfully in the national furniture markets required access to funds for expansion. It was estimated at one time that these interlocking firms held in excess of thirty percent of the national market for their respective goods. Yet rather than turn to major financial centers in Chicago or New York, they sought control of the four principal commercial banks in Grand Rapids. They also created new banks and mortgage companies, all headed by furniture executives.

This deliberate concentration of power eventually regulated wages and working conditions. Furniture manufacturers created their own privately funded Employers Association in 1905; a public group, the State Free Employment Bureau, was established the same year. The Employers

Association kept a card on every worker who had been employed in the city's furniture factories. With these cards, the manufacturers monitored wages, productivity, and union sympathies among workingmen.

The Association determined which employees were "competent or worthy" of employment; it provided encouragement "to all such persons in their efforts to resist compulsory methods sometimes employed by organized labor" to unionize a shop. Members were promised protection ". . . against Legislative, Municipal, and other political encroachments" on their professional autonomy. The Association enforced uniform wage levels, discouraging competition for skilled workers. One example concerned a disgruntled worker who left one company to seek a job with another firm in town. He had received $2.00 per day on his former job, and asked the other company for $2.25 per day without mentioning his old wage. Returning the following day to see about the job, he was told that since he had received $2.00 earlier that was all he could expect in the future. Presumably any complaint would have rendered him no longer "competent or worthy" to continue working in Grand Rapids.

Such a possibility would have had dire consequences given the very high chances that he would have been a homeowner. Grand Rapids reflected national trends with increases in the housing supply and its financing. From 1890 to 1910, outstanding mortgage debt for private homes nearly doubled. On a household basis, this translated into an increase in family debt from $289 to $316, quite a burden when many wage earners relied on the contribution of the entire family to bring in an annual income of $700.

On the eve of World War I, nearly half the homes in Grand Rapids were owner-occupied, and the majority of those were mortgaged to local banks and savings and loan associations. Although the lending institutions were small neighborhood firms, they were tied to the established network of money and capital markets, and the city's chief savings and loan companies shared officers with the major banks and with furniture factories.

As the number of homes in Grand Rapids rose, the influence of the banks and furniture manufacturers increased accordingly. Any pretense that the city's five separate savings and loan associations competed with one another or stood apart from the major banks ended in 1911, when it was announced that these five mortgage companies would pool their resources into a single fund. For those who had committed themselves to long-term debt in the form of a home mortgage, this made their dependence on their jobs even greater.

Indeed, the city's workingmen became part of this network if they chose to pursue home ownership and savings accounts. Their wages, if placed into banks, fell back into the control of their employers. In this way, one-third of the city's wage earners trusted the security of their employment to a single industry, while even more fed their savings into the pool of capital that was dominated by industrialists who could tap those very savings for expansion or other commercial investment. By 1911, the Grand Rapids furniture workers had become involuntary partners in financing the companies they worked for, yet would be denied any voice in determining their wages or hours.

Widdicomb was the hub to several major interlocked furniture companies.

In addition to controlling the principal commercial banks in Grand Rapids, these industrialists helped to create new financial institutions through which to conduct their business. In the years after 1905, three new banks, headed by furniture executives, opened in the city. The manufacturers sitting on the boards of directors and in executive offices of these new banks were men from the largest, interlocked furniture concerns in the city. The City Trust and Savings, the Kent State Bank, and the Grand Rapids National City Bank all brought in individuals whose

ENTRANCE OF
The Grand Rapids National City Bank
CORNER MONROE AND OTTAWA STREETS
Capital Surplus and Profits $1,350,000.00

companies employed more than two hundred workers each.

Earlier banks and savings concerns were led by a wide variety of locally prominent businessmen, in sharp contrast to the homogeneous leadership of the newer ones. In fact, the federal government recognized the extent to which the Grand Rapids banks exercised a virtual monopoly in their region. After the Clayton Anti-Trust Act was passed in 1914, all banks and their directors had to apply for exemption from that portion of the Clayton Act barring interlocking directorates. Many directors were denied exemptions; five percent of the national total of denials involved Grand Rapids, including the Kent State and Grand Rapids Savings Banks.

Dutch language newspaper of the Holland Furniture Workers Union No. 45 of Grand Rapids, Sept. 15, 1892. Workers who shared a common language, beliefs, and ancestry often banded together inside and outside the factory. While this created a close safety net for those within the circle, it also created a gulf between workers and owners, and fragmented workers along ethnic lines.

Workers' Lives

Wage earners in the Furniture City were as disjointed as the owners were collaborative. While their work provided a common thread to their collective lives, it was a slender thread at best: only one-third of the total labor force worked for the furniture factories. The lives of most working-class people in Grand Rapids centered on their ethnicity and religion, expressed in closely knit neighborhoods of small homes scattered around the city. The backbone of the furniture work force in Grand Rapids was formed by immigrants from Poland and Holland.

Dutch immigrants brought with them to Grand Rapids the antagonistic relationships that existed among the provinces of their homeland; they settled around the city in various pockets according to these provincial differences. Rather than speaking of one "Little Holland," it would be more accurate to speak of "Little Zeeland," "Little Friesland," and "Little Overijssel." Distinct neighborhoods developed on both sides of the river, united only by a commitment to the Reformed Faith and the Dutch language. By 1900, Netherlanders accounted for more than one quarter of the city's population. This was due to larger-than-average family size, and to the fact that the Dutch immigrated earlier than other Europeans.

Religious motives figured prominently in the drive for migration to the New World. Certain that the Netherlands state church was doomed to corruption, many families sought an environment in which to practice a "purer" religion. From the very earliest settlement, the Dutch pursued policies of cultural and ecclesiastical isolation. The Dutch language served as the vehicle of instruction; not until 1902 was any concession made to church services in English, and not until 1910 was a Holland paper published in English. One prominent Dutch spokesman noted, "In our isolation is our strength."

An incident in which religious belief set the Dutch community against the larger culture took place in 1888. The Grand Rapids Street Railway Company ran steam-powered engines on a regular Sunday excursion to Reeds Lake, a popular resort. Because of the clatter of the engines, disruption of services, fear of danger posed to children, and the "common rowdyism and drunkenness prevalent among the merry-makers," the local church requested suspension of that line on the Sabbath. When the company refused, men and women of the congregation tore up the track and began a battle that lasted more than a month. Peace was restored when the Kent County Circuit Court enjoined the company from operating that line on Sunday.

Such deeply felt religious sentiment did not prevent disruption within the ecclesiastical community. By the late nineteenth century, the Christian Reformed Church and the Reformed Church in America had split over concerns about "worldly" matters. It was felt that the Reformed Church had dallied too readily in matters of this world by its sanction of secular fraternities and open discussion on the property of labor unions. This, coupled with theological differences regarding hymns, revivals, and prayer meetings, forced a series of eruptions as congregations split along doctrinal lines. "We are convinced that ecclesiastical alliances of any kind between orthodox and liberal are contrary to the word of God," pronounced the regional synod in 1924.

An episode in June, 1905 brought one of the few censures from the community to the Dutch immigrants. When a smallpox epidemic swept through the city, killing thirty-four people, the Dutch represented a high proportion of those infected. The city physician and health officers noted that the greatest opposition to vaccination came from the Netherlander neighborhoods. The City Council passed an ordinance closing public meeting places and limiting the operational hours of private meeting places in an attempt to curtail the dangers to public health. The Christian Reformed Churches protested the mandated closures, but the conflict slowly abated.

While not all Dutch immigrants became furniture workers, about half of the seven thousand furniture workers were Dutch. Slightly more than forty percent of the remaining workers were Polish. Even though they accounted for only a tenth of the city's population in 1910, Poles remained highly visible, because they constituted a disproportionate element in the furniture industry, they remained mostly on the city's West Side, and their Catholic faith made them stand out in a predominantly Protestant city.

Just as Old World divisions had animated the Dutch in their provincial and religious suspicions among themselves, traditional hatreds followed the Polish immigrants. The Germans had come to Grand Rapids earlier and taken hold of the skilled jobs in the furniture factories. German artisans became the foremen and shop directors, supervising both Dutch and Polish immigrant wage earners. Yet the Germans also dominated the Catholic ecclesiastical structure and never really let the Poles forget that just as their native country had been absorbed into the German Empire, so too were they still dependent upon the Germans in spiritual matters.

The Catholic diocese of Grand Rapids was created in 1882 with German-born Henry Joseph Richter as its Bishop. Poles sought to build a church modeled on the Basilica at Trezenieszno in their homeland. Construction began before Bishop Richter's appointment, but when the church was dedicated, he named it for Saint Adalbert, a German monk who had brought Christianity to the Poles in the ninth century (in the wake of an invading army). Adalbert's shrine stood in eastern Poland, from which many of the West Side immigrants had come. Later, when the city's East Side Polish parish chose Saint Stanislaus for their church, Richter overrode them and dedicated it to the German Saint Isidore.

The Bishop acted again in 1904 to maintain a distinctly German bearing to his diocese when he transferred Father Simon Pognis out of Grand Rapids to the more distant reaches of Gaylord, Michigan (then referred to jokingly as "Siberia"). Pognis, the first Polish priest ordained for the Grand Rapids parish, arrived five years after Richter. He served St. Adalbert's well, but infused his services with a call for Polish nationalism. Such actions not only set him into personal conflict with the German Bishop, but served as a

The Eastern Avenue Church and parsonage served as a center of activity for one of the city's many Dutch neighborhoods. Courtesy, Calvin College and Seminary Archives.

St. Adalberts Church, Grand Rapids, Mich.

The towers of St. Adalbert's Roman Catholic Church dominated the West Side Polish neighborhood of the Widdicomb Furniture, John Widdicomb, and American Seating Companies.

direct challenge to the established church structure. Pognis also urged Poles to act in an organized way to assert their political influence in Grand Rapids. He founded the Polish Political Club in 1899, which worked to mobilize immigrant votes on behalf of their countrymen.

The principal basis for the differences between Dutch and Polish workers in the furniture factories was the fact that the Dutch arrived in Grand Rapids on average five years earlier. This translated into economic advantage: Dutch immigrants tended to earn more and have larger, older families by 1910. First-generation Dutch earned a yearly average of $559, compared with the annual Polish income of $511. Second-generation Dutch workers rarely remained in the furniture factories, but those who did had a significantly higher wage, bringing home about $646 a year. Given these factors, the Dutch wage earners had a different experience than the Poles, helping to create rifts that could only be closed in some extraordinary circumstances. On the other hand, second-generation Germans and Swedes tended to continue to work in the industrial shops, rising to the position of foremen and management. They thus commanded even higher wages than second-generation Dutch, earning more than $700 annually.

The wage differences carried over into the household economy and the way in which the Dutch and Polish families of furniture workers supplemented their main income. The Dutch family cycle began earlier, so that by 1910, Dutch families had five children, while the Poles averaged two. Dutch children were older and more likely to work outside the home, contributing forty percent of the supplemental income to Dutch households. Among Polish families, children working outside the home brought in barely one quarter of extra incomes. Polish families tended to make additional money by letting out sleeping space to boarders and lodgers, usually other Poles or the growing numbers of Lithuanians. Approximately one-third of Polish families in Grand Rapids derived more than half their household income from boarders, while another third used boarder income to supplement furniture factory wages.

Many immigrants felt an overwhelming need for supplemental income because they owned their own homes: tax payments, mortgage payments, and improvements all loomed on a regular basis. More than half the Polish and nearly three-quarters of the Dutch workers were homeowners. Home ownership did not mean opulence, nor ownership free and clear. Rather, the majority of homes in Grand Rapids were small, inexpensive, and heavily mortgaged. Rates of encumbrance were high, as were mortgage rates and interest, and the cost of a city lot.

Twenty-nine percent of all the mortgaged homes in Grand Rapids were valued at less than $2,500. These small, wooden houses carried an average debt of $872—over fifty percent more than the average Dutch furniture worker earned annually, and about seventy percent more than the yearly income of a Polish wage earner. The next largest group of mortgaged home owners comprised half of all the encumbered property owners. Their homes were worth about $3,325 and carried a typical debt of $1,439. These debts depict Grand Rapids as a city of property owners who carried a heavy burden for small, encumbered houses.

Thus the control Grand Rapids' manufacturers retained over the flow of capital in their city through interlocking directorates was complemented by the increased dependence of workers on that capital. In the larger economic and social environment of Grand Rapids, property represented a sheet anchor of conservatism: the pervasive commitment the workers held to property, family, church, and neighborhood inhibited a truly broad-based action. But when these debt-ridden homeowners eventually decided to challenge the furniture trade, they were overwhelmingly supported by fellow property owners.

The Great Strike

Inflation caused the workers' initial concerns. A rapid expansion of the national marketplace in all walks of life drove up the cost of living all through 1909. In Grand Rapids, grocery prices climbed so quickly that one alderman circulated a petition demanding that the stores take action. In the face of such circumstances, forty-five workers from the Oriel Cabinet Company plant asked to speak with management about bringing wages into line with the cost of living. These men were among the most highly paid, skilled cabinetmakers. Oriel management wanted to postpone discussions until after the busy season. The workers honored this request, and returned two months later to find themselves fired as "agitators."

Management's refusal to grant any concession aroused anger. The *Evening Press* complained that wage rates in Grand Rapids were so notoriously low that newly arrived immigrants earned more money doing street work in Detroit. The newspaper noted that "the South is the only part of the country where wages are as low as they are in Grand Rapids." The FMA met with a representative of the United Brotherhood of Carpenters and Joiners (UBCJ), and then agreed to continue discussions after the critical Market in June, 1910. Workers acceded, waited, and returned in August only to be told that no collective bargaining would take place under any circumstances. Only individual laborers in each factory might bargain with their respective employers over the issues of hours and wages.

An entire year had been spent since January, 1910 in good faith efforts by workers to improve their wages. Responding to efforts by the UBCJ to promote negotiation, the FMA distributed a letter to all employees in their factories, declaring that there was no place for organized labor in their industry. No organization had any right to "confer with us about the management of our business," said the letter, which asserted that individual employees had always been treated fairly on the basis of ability. The letter further claimed that each company had "always recognized the liberty of every man to sell his labor freely, independently, and at the best price obtainable," without mentioning the Employers Association's power to monitor wages.

For the manufacturers, the vital issues were not wage rates and the right of collective bargaining, but managerial autonomy and complete control of the workplace. According to them, the fault lay not with the industry, but with outside agitators who had come to this content town to stir up trouble.

ABOVE: The factory of the Oriel Furniture Co. dwarfs the surrounding working-class houses in its neighborhood. Trouble between the company's labor and management began when workers were fired for attempted collective bargaining, leading to the Great Strike of 1911. BELOW: Parade banner of the cabinetmakers' local union of the United Brotherhood of Carpenters and Joiners of America, ca. 1910.

Workers show support for their unions at a Grand Rapids Labor Day Parade, ca. 1900. Courtesy, Grand Rapids Public Library.

Alarmed at the increasing bitterness between workers and owners, city newspapers voiced fears of how disruptive any confrontation might be. Social order and economic stability must come before any private gain, urged the *Grand Rapids Press* as it asked workers and manufacturers to compromise. The *Evening News* noted that "the interests of the people . . . are interdependent." Although privately owned, the furniture factories were a public concern, declaimed the *Evening Press*: "The conclusion has been reached that anything which affects our safety, our happiness and our pocketbooks, like a strike, is very much the public business." In counterpoint, the *Evening News* concluded that it was "the meanest employer in any line of business that fixes the standard of wages in that particular industry."

Workers had shown restraint through the spring of 1911, postponing strike votes in hopes that some conciliation might appear. A special mayoral commission failed to produce concrete results. Optimism collapsed, and the next two days brought a flurry of activity. The UBCJ sent labor organizers and money to workers in Grand Rapids.

On April 19, more than three thousand workers walked off the job. By April 21 virtually every major furniture plant in Grand Rapids stopped producing as a thousand more workers joined the ranks of strikers. Despite this show of strength, the manufacturers closed ranks and pooled their economic resources. There were enough experienced workers and other shop floor managers to keep up the appearance of output. At the Michigan Chair Company, twenty men out of four hundred struggled to maintain production. Torn by ethnic and religious differences and suffering under severely reduced incomes, laborers tried to close down any continuing work by keeping nonstriking workers from going back to the factories.

Union pickets posted at the factory gates made no attempt other than talking to workers to keep them from going in. The Union was concerned that the strike be conducted in a respectable way and that Union men be above reproach. However, some wage earners returned to the plants, and some strikers felt that Union victory and economic survival outweighed restraint and respectability. Confrontations increased in the month after the walkout, suggesting a growing dissatisfaction among strikers as their fellow workers drifted back. Victor Marek, a striker at the Luce Furniture Company factory, yelled to a strikebreaker, "If you don't quit I'll kill you!" Maybe the death threat was an exaggeration, but strikers did begin to arm themselves with stones, boards, and other makeshift weapons to deter nonstrikers.

Manufacturers and managers were not exempt from the tension. Police grabbed a club from Luce manager John Hoult, who was swinging it from his car as he drove through a crowd gathered at the firm's gates. An employee of the American Seating Company stood by the door of one workshop waving a large target pistol while shouting for the crowd to disperse. "The attitude of the man and his orders to the crowd angered peaceable men," reported the *Evening News*, and soon hundreds of angry men, women, and children chased him down the street.

As the Union tactics brought only stalemate, larger numbers of people milled around the factory gates, especially on the city's West Side, where homes and factories sat cheek-to-cheek. Strikers were joined by their families, who appreciated both the risk and the importance of the struggle undertaken. Entire neighborhoods organized to ambush strikebreakers on their way home from the Harry Widdicomb factory near Fifth and Davis Streets. The attack worked: where once 150 men had returned to work, only twenty-five showed up the following day. Nonstrikers persisted, and the next day, fifty men ran the gauntlet of sticks, stones, and verbal abuse.

A Surprise Announcement

In the midst of this tense environment, the FMA announced to its members and the public at large that the strike had been broken! Work would resume May 15, and all workers not at their usual positions would be out of luck. This was news to both the Union strikers and the city government. A widely circulated remark by Grand Rapids Showcase Company Treasurer Samuel Young added to the tension. He reported that his firm had placed a very large order to outside companies and would not need any more local help: it appeared to him that the workers wanted a "little vacation, and I guess we will let them have one."

The announcement of a deadline, combined with Young's taunts and the inability of the Union to bring any concrete results, produced an explosive mixture. The crowded West Side erupted into a full-scale attack on factories in the Davis Street area. But this riot was unlike the sporadic harassment that involved a few hundred people: more than two thousand men, women, and children poured into the streets to demonstrate the solidarity and effective action that was needed to move the strike to some conclusion.

Gathering in the factory district around Fifth and Davis Streets on the evening of May 15, striking workers, their wives, and even some small children showered nonstriking workers with stones as policemen and fire companies tried to disperse the crowd. The greatest violence took place around the Widdicomb factories. Both Harry and William Widdicomb had been especially provocative in the weeks before this evening. J. P. Steen, the captain of the pickets, blamed William Widdicomb as the first man to display firearms during the week of May 7, walking around his factory, waving a revolver in the air. "No one else had shown any weapons or acted [as] if he wanted trouble," stated the police. From the strike's beginning, Harry Widdicomb had driven strikebreaking employees to and from work in his own large automobile, exchanging hostile words and gestures with strikers at his factory entrance. This evening began no differently, except that the verbal exchanges were meaner and the numbers of people were greater.

One of these routine shouting matches set off violence that night. Several hundred people attacked Widdicomb's car as he tried to drive out of the factory gates. Women formed the front ranks of the rioters, some with children in their arms, creating a wall behind which strikers tossed stones and other debris. Several women offered their shoes when bricks ran out, and no one backed off when pistol shots from an unidentified source rang out. Harry retreated back behind the factory gates. When police finally showed up, one angry mother dropped her child, picked

ABOVE: The Widdicomb Furniture factory was the site of the greatest riots of the 1911 Strike. BELOW: Some furniture buyers stayed away from Grand Rapids companies during the furniture strike, fearing that it would affect the delivery of their orders. This advertisement from the September, 1911 *Grand Rapids Furniture Record* was part of a campaign launched after the strike to reassure customers that factories were at full capacity.

In 1911, Grand Rapids' fortunes were so economically tied to the furniture industry that it seemed that every resident's life was affected in some way by the strike. Factory owner William Widdicomb reacted to his

striking employees as a loving father who had been wounded by his children. He continued the paternalistic practice of purchasing a christening gown for every child born to an employee during the strike, yet threatened picketers at his factory with a gun.

Outspoken activist Viva Flaherty sympathized with the laborers and their families, whom she had come to know through her work at the Bissell Social Settlement House in Grand Rapids. During the strike she condemned the treatment of factory workers with editorial letters to the newspapers, and authored a tract entitled *History of the Grand Rapids Furniture Strike with Facts Hitherto Unpublished.* She also resigned her position as the secretary for social programs at Fountain Street Baptist Church, to which many of the factory owners belonged.

up a club, and came out swinging at an officer.

The violence began around 5:30 p.m.; within an hour fire engines appeared and turned a stream of water on the crowd in an attempt to break up the gathering. Unsuccessful, the engines returned to their various station houses. After a brief appearance by the mayor urging an end to the violence, Harry tried to escape once again, this time protected by policemen who stood on the car's running boards. The crowd spotted him and rushed after him, heaving a volley of stones, pulling back only after the policemen raised their guns. Fire engines reappeared and turned their hoses on the crowd again. "Hundreds were drenched, but they retreated reluctantly and their mood was ugly," reported the *Evening Press*.

During the lull, Harry Widdicomb finally rode out of the factory, accompanied by armed policemen, and took half a dozen workers home. Despite the arrival of more police, the fighting continued until "the street was filled with madly running and cursing men and women." In a final display of fury, the largest body of rioters lined Davis Street and began a barrage of rocks, bricks, and boards against Harry Widdicomb's factory, shattering every window in the building. With his flight and that of the nonstriking workers, there seemed little reason to stay; strikers and their families headed home around 11:00 p.m. Never had such widespread or intense violence been seen in Grand Rapids; never had it lasted so long.

Tensions rose dramatically as gun sales increased across the city. Mayor Ellis hoped to curb the growing alarm by appointing a special police force to patrol the city. One hundred auxiliary policemen appeared by the end of the week armed with night sticks, their ranks filled with striking workers. Theodore Roosevelt praised this "workingman's militia," but the furniture manufacturers only complained loudly about the city government's catering to the voters. The factory owners looked for help outside the city and found it in the person of Kent County Sheriff Hurley, who showed his sympathies for the industrialists by deputizing dozens of nonstriking workers to defend the furniture plants. The city was transformed into an armed camp.

As production losses mounted, the factory owners moved to import strikebreakers in greater haste than before. At the end of May, Grand Rapids Showcase set up dormitories for 150 laid-off workers from Pullman, Illinois. In a desperate attempt to increase the number of strikebreaking workers, owners began to recruit unskilled labor from the surrounding area. This stopped suddenly when the city physician announced that one group bound for Grand Rapids from Ionia County was infected with smallpox and that some had already made it into the city.

Yet despite these apparent reversals, the factory owners outlasted the strikers. By the end of August, the majority of workers had returned to their places on the line without any formal concessions by the employers. What happened? Why did the strike fail to produce any long-lasting results, let alone a short-term victory? There are three basic answers to those questions.

First, larger economic forces outside the city made it easier for manufacturers to withstand a drop in production, reducing the pressure to settle with workers, and increasing their ability to resist unionization efforts. A sudden and deep recession began early in 1911 and spread across the country. The economy weakened, reaching its lowest point during the summer of the strike. This permitted manufacturers to use older styles and materials already in stock during the July Buyers Show. Demand was down, and therefore the work withheld by strikers was not felt as keenly as it might have been in times of a rapidly expanding economy.

Second, the workers' strike wages were insufficient to support them, especially since most workers lived in a single-wage household structure. Money from community groups came slowly and sporadically, frequently from ethnic and religious organizations. This meant that resources were not shared equally among the striking workers. Union assistance went largely to the more skilled Germans, but even there it fell to less than half regular wages by July. Polish workers who relied on boarders to supplement their incomes found themselves especially hard hit. If renters were also furniture workers, then a double hardship ensued: both landlord and renter were forfeiting the income they needed to maintain their households.

Finally, important religious differences influenced the strike's outcome. The Catholic Church supported the strike; Bishop Richter had been temporarily side-stepped by Auxiliary Bishop Schrembs, an active proponent of the Church's more progressive responses to industrialization. Schrembs had maintained a high profile, always speaking at any public forum on behalf of the strikers' cause and the legitimacy of trade unions like the UBCJ. The Christian Reformed Church, however, found the Union incompatible with the church's doctrines, given that the trade union was "for material purposes only." For nearly a thousand of the remaining strikers, perhaps a third of the total still not working, this was a serious loss of moral support.

Divided City, Common Ground

Life in the Furniture City for its workers and owners rarely centered on any commonality. In the factory, owners maintained a clear role of authority, collaborating among themselves to ensure a united front against all challenges. The FMA served as the focal point for major political, as well as economic, activity in Grand Rapids through the better part of the twentieth century. Manufacturers, bankers, and other industrialists lived together in the hilltop district overlooking the city, exchanging ideas informally through social and religious networks. They stayed together in order to survive and flourish, since competition on the national level was fierce, and Grand Rapids was a city with limited resources.

Workers faced fifty-five-hour weeks with wages sufficient to sustain limited home ownership and purchasing power. Although there was some improvement in hourly and piece rates after the strike, inflation over the next four years eroded whatever gains they had made. Ironically, the prosperity of the Roaring Twenties helped Detroit more than Grand Rapids, as Americans began to put more money in automobiles than new furniture. Still, the furniture industry was one of the few full-time, year-round jobs that required skilled labor and offered some hope for advancement. Laborers spent their time with family, church groups, and fraternal organizations. Work was a means to have all this, and not an end in itself.

RIGHT: Roman Catholic Auxiliary Bishop Schrembs supported the many striking Polish and Lithuanian Catholic workers from his pulpit, but was suddenly transferred to another diocese soon after the factory owners broke the strike. Courtesy, Catholic Diocese of Grand Rapids.

BELOW: Despite his church's objection to organized labor, furniture worker Garrit Verburg was both a member of the Burton Heights Christian Reformed Church and an officer of his union. Here, Verburg and his family enjoy the annual Grand Rapids Labor Day festivities. As a union officer during the Strike, Verburg believed his name was placed on a "blacklist" by the manufacturers. After the strike ended, he was never able to find employment in a furniture factory again.

Innovative manufacturing techniques and unified marketing made Grand Rapids Arts and Crafts and Revival furniture much sought-after commodities in America, and secured the reputation of "Grand Rapids Made" as a hallmark of quality.

Grand Rapids Made

The Grand Rapids furniture industry matured as it moved into the twentieth century. Manufacturers cooperated in promoting and protecting the reputation of Grand Rapids as "The Furniture City." Their self-consciousness about the increasingly negative image of factory-made furniture prompted manufacturers to hire trained designers and skilled artisans. Some expanded their offerings for not only dining rooms and bedrooms, but also living rooms, dens, libraries, sewing rooms, and even kitchens, sunrooms, and front porches. Others specialized in new areas, producing refrigerators, retail showcases, outdoor furnishings, lodge seating, church pews, school desks, clocks, or office furniture. A few Grand Rapids firms became leaders in the industry, introducing new forms and styles, which manufacturers in other cities began to copy. They also tapped new market segments with sophisticated advertising and consumer education. The phrase "Grand Rapids Made" became a recognizable trademark across the nation.

Yet, even as Grand Rapids succeeded in adjusting the industry for the new century, its own rapid consumption of Michigan hardwoods forced further change. What had seemed an inexhaustible supply of lumber was largely gone in the southern half of Michigan's lower peninsula before the turn of the century. The last log runs on the Grand River in the early 1890s signaled that one of Grand Rapids' principal geographical and economic advantages was disappearing. Since the ability to extract large supplies of walnut, maple, and cherry from nearby forests was no longer reliable, the industry would now have to depend on ingenuity.

Phoenix Furniture Company designer David Wolcott Kendall found a way to use a plentiful but not particularly popular hardwood, oak, by developing new finishes that were pleasing to the eye. One folklorish tale suggests that he developed his "antique oak" stain after noticing how furniture workers' tobacco spit brought out the wood grain and a pleasing golden brown tone in the factory floor, when it missed the spittoons. Kendall eventually set up an entire chemistry laboratory in the basement of the Phoenix factory, to replicate this effect and experiment with other methods, including chemical reactions between the natural acids in the wood and different chemical fumes. Kendall has been credited with pop-

Since the favored hardwoods had become scarce and expensive, why not apply technology to cheaper softwoods to give the appearance of hardwood? This was the goal of Grand Rapids inventor A. Harry Sherwood, (OPPOSITE), who in 1885 established the Grand Rapids Panel Co. and devised a system by which inexpensive and available pine could be stained, then mechanically grained to look like almost any wood. Flat surfaces could be transformed with a graining machine, with large drums similar to a printing press. Small or curved components were grained by hand using carefully carved ink rollers, which transferred the printer's ink from a gelatin plate onto the wood surface in a grain pattern. Furniture manufacturers like the Arcadia Furniture Co. of Arcadia, Michigan, which produced this ca. 1910 dresser, (ABOVE), found that the process provided pieces that looked right to the consumer, but cost less than nearly identical pieces made with the actual wood.

 ABOVE: Nineteenth-century loggers clear-cut Michigan's forests, wiping out most stands of virgin timber in a single generation. BELOW: Oak bookcase attributed to David Kendall for Phoenix Furniture Co., ca. 1895. The lively play of light and dark on the cabinet's surface is created by Kendall's distinctive Cremona finish.

ularizing oak as a cabinetmaking wood in late nineteenth-century America. His finishes transformed oak and ash into hues of green (Malachite), grey-black (Flemish), tan (Cremona), and even a Canary Yellow.

As sophisticated techniques for finishing furniture developed, it became more important for pieces to leave the factory finished. Fewer pieces were sold unfinished or "in the white." The use of golden oak finish became so widespread that the term "Golden Oak" was used to categorize all furniture finished in that manner, even pieces made of maple, ash, or gumwood. Golden Oak furniture came in a wide variety of revival styles, ranging from Italian Renaissance and Louis XVI to Queen Anne and Empire. Some was massive and highly carved with mascarons, mythological griffins, and Chimerae, but much was inexpensively made for middle-income consumers.

Sears & Roebuck and Montgomery Ward mail-order catalogs from the 1890s through the 1910s were filled with machine-made oak furniture, generically captioned "shipped direct from the factory in Western Michigan." Any consumer with access to a train station and a catalog could now order Grand Rapids oak furniture directly, and have it delivered. The Macey Company innovated its own mail-order catalog, which offered a variety of oak and mahogany office furnishings and supplies.

Some Grand Rapids entrepreneurs set out to find new sources of hardwood. By the 1880s and '90s, water and rail transportation had developed sufficiently for manufacturers to base their production at least partly on imported woods. If manufacturers no longer had the advantage of close proximity to timberlands, they could gain a different advantage by controlling the entire vertical system of harvesting and distributing the wood they used. One manufacturer who attempted this was Charles R. Sligh, who started his own lumber import business in 1883 when his furniture manufacturing firm was a mere three years old. His Honduras Mahogany

Company purchased mahogany timber from the tropical rain forests of Central America, shipped it to New Orleans where it was cut into lumber, then transported it to Grand Rapids to be made into bedroom furniture.

As Grand Rapids' furniture industry earned more respect, many of its factories consciously moved their production away from cheap goods. The Furniture Market changed the image of Grand Rapids from a frontier town striving to compete with larger urban centers into the place where thousands of store owners, designers, and reporters from across the continent flocked each season to see the latest styles. Grand Rapids boosters bragged about the fine work of the city's high-end factories and berated the work of out-of-town competitors. At the same time, they drew less attention to the city's considerable low-end production. For example, the John Widdicomb Company gained much publicity over the first prize awarded to its Empire Revival mahogany bedroom suite at the Paris Exposition of 1900. But less was said about the more than 200,000 sewing machine cabinets the company contracted to produce for Singer in 1901.

While older Grand Rapids firms were working hard to upgrade the image and quality of their products, new companies were being established as high-end from their inception. The Century Furniture Company, started in 1900, favored imported fabrics, exotic woods, and heavy carving in designs based mostly on revivals of highly decorative styles from England, France, Italy, Spain, and the Netherlands. Rather than relying on high-volume sales of inexpensive pieces, Century maintained an extensive catalog of designs which were produced in small batches as orders came in. This allowed for greater customization of such cosmetic details as finishes and upholstery materials. Each piece required considerable production hours, because of the amount of hand carving, finishing, or painted decoration. But whatever the company gave up in high-volume profits, they made up in the high cost per piece.

The Arts and Crafts Movement was largely responsible for the change in manufacturers' attitude toward the quality of their furniture. The Arts and Crafts style in America traces its roots to a social movement in England. By the middle of the nineteenth century, many of that country's small, local craft shops had already yielded to the establishment of large-scale, nationwide manufacturers. Anti-industrial reformers like William Morris and John Ruskin criticized the mass-produced furniture of these mechanized factories as shoddy and inferior, while romanticizing the skills and dedication of artisans before the industrial revolution. They sought to save and restore the role of the artist/craftsman in society, and to improve the quality of furnishings available to consumers.

Oak combination furniture by the Welch Folding Bed Co. was ideal for use in small apartments and summer cottages, because each piece performed several functions. The front featured a combination, such as a writing desk, chest of drawers, vitrine, and chifforobe. It rotated on its castors, and a Murphy bed folded out of the back, instantly turning a tenement parlor into a bedroom.

The Grand Rapids furniture industry developed in much the same way, with large factories replacing the cabinetmakers' shops. By the time the Reform Movement began its spread to America in the 1880s and '90s, Grand Rapids was already becoming self-conscious about its reputation as a place where mass-produced, inexpensive furniture was made.

Most Grand Rapids firms adopted the style, if not the substance, of the Arts and Crafts Movement. Pieces were made from solid cuts of wood instead of veneers. Forms lost the heavy Victorian carving and decoration, which at its worst became busy and complicated, in favor of simple, solid

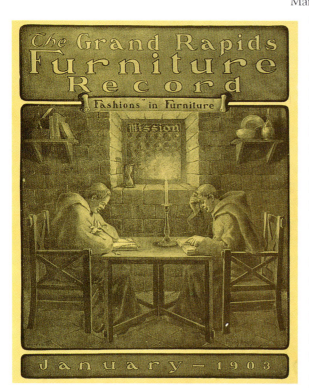

By January of 1903, Grand Rapids had so embraced the marketability of the Arts and Crafts style known as "Mission" that the cover of *The Grand Rapids Furniture Record* was illustrated with a pair of Spanish monks in their Southwestern adobe outpost, sitting on Grand Rapids Arts and Crafts chairs under the heading "Fashions in Furniture." Inside was a feature article entitled "Mission and Kindred Styles" which made the following prediction: "If, as is claimed, the popularity of the simple modes of furniture and decoration are a reaction from the surfeit of elaborateness that has preceded them, it must be admitted that we have gone nearly to the extreme. It is undeniable, that the people of today desire their furniture plain, the popularity of the Colonial and the so-called Mission effects furnishing abundant evidence of this taste. The severely simple yet graceful and utilitarian appearing Mission may be a fad, as some critics affect to believe, yet it is certain to leave impress on the furniture styles of the future."

forms almost devoid of ornamentation. Elements of construction such as keyed mortise and tenons, butterfly wing joints, wooden pegs instead of nails, and an occasional geometrical cut-out often provided the only breaks in a piece's rectangular form.

Manufacturers and designers traveled from Grand Rapids to centers of the Arts and Crafts Movement, where they found new sources of inspiration and kept abreast of changes. Albert Stickley established a second Stickley Brothers factory in London in 1897, allowing for a direct flow of ideas between his facilities in England and Grand Rapids. Charles Limbert made trips to the Netherlands to study Dutch furniture, which inspired the Dutch Arts and Crafts line that he introduced in 1902. He also traveled to Vienna, Austria, as did Sligh Furniture Company designer John Brower, to study the modernist work of the Jugendstil and Secessionist artisans there. David Kendall traveled not only to England, Scotland, and continental Europe to see new forms and decorative motifs, but also to more exotic locales like Japan and Central America.

The increasing influence of the Movement prompted Grand Rapids firms to hire designers and craftsmen from these Arts and Crafts centers. They brought their own ideas on design and craftsmanship with them, transforming Grand Rapids into one of the leading centers for the production and promotion of Arts and Crafts goods in America. The Michigan Chair Company began to produce furniture showing influences of American Mission, Prairie, Glasgow Art Nouveau, and Vienna modernist styles after Boston architect Edgar Somes became its chief of design in 1901. Stickley Brothers' "Quaint Arts and Crafts" line flowered after the company brought Scottish designer David Robertson Smith to Grand Rapids in 1902. Timothy Conti, who came to town in 1895, won a series of awards from international expositions in Malta, Florence, and London for his marquetry work. Conti and his son worked as independent producers of marquetry for the industry until they entered the employ of Stickley Brothers from 1900 to 1905. After that time they again produced independently for Stickley Brothers and other manufacturers, from inside the Stickley Brothers factory.

New York metalworker Forrest Emerson Mann arrived in 1903, to teach classes in pottery and metalworking. He founded the Grand Rapids Arts and Crafts Society and published *Le Dernier Cri*, an Arts and Crafts journal along the lines of Gustav Stickley's *The Craftsman*. He operated his own shop for the production and sale of jewelry, ceramics, and metalwork under the name Forest Craft Guild, which he eventually moved to the former New York business address of Louis Comfort Tiffany in 1917. It is likely that at least some of the hand-cut and hammered metal hardware and accessories seen in the catalogs of Charles Limbert and Stickley Brothers were actually designed and produced by Forest Mann. Mann may have also trained the Turkish, Armenian, and Russian metalworkers whom Stickley Brothers began to recruit in 1904. These artisans produced hand-hammered copper hinges and drawer pulls for the company's furniture, as well as copper lighting, jardinieres, vases, and desktop accessories.

Most Grand Rapids manufacturers departed from the Movement's purists by using machinery and large-scale production. They adopted the style because it sold well, but found no conflict in the use of the latest technology to produce it. Many details that gave pieces their Arts and Crafts character were actually mass-produced to appear handcrafted.

Ironically, it was in places like Grand Rapids that one of the tenets of the Movement was best achieved: to make better-quality design and construction available to every household. Small craft shops in England and America produced limited quantities, making their pieces too scarce and expensive for most buyers. But in Grand Rapids, virtually the same styles and forms were made in large factories that employed power machinery and hundreds of workers. Their Arts and Crafts designs demonstrated the same simplicity of form and structural strength, but were readily available, distributed nationally, and affordable to all categories of buyers.

Charles Limbert went to greater lengths than his fellow manufacturers not only to produce furniture that looked the part, but also to effect real change in the lives of his workers. He believed that Grand Rapids, as an urban industrial center, was full of the sorts of social maladies that came between workers and their work. So in 1905 he moved his factory to the nearby small town of Holland, while keeping his showrooms in Grand Rapids. He explained the reasons for this move in a catalog from the period:

> As the work extended and became greater in importance, the influence of a busy manufacturing city became more and more uncongenial for these artistic craftsmen who were inspired to put their best efforts into every piece which was to bear the Limbert Trade Mark, so an environment more conducive to artistic effort and a higher quality of craftsmanship was sought and eventually discovered in the little town of Holland, Michigan.

Some pieces by Grand Rapids Arts and Crafts manufacturers demonstrate an awareness of the work of Rene Mackintosh, Josef Hoffmann, C. F. A. Voysey, Charles Rohlfs, and Frank Lloyd Wright, but were toned down for less adventuresome, middle-class consumers. Designs that were too severe often failed to attract buyers. Many of Grand Rapids Bookcase and Chair Company's "Lifetime Cloister" pieces, for example, resemble those designed by Harvey Ellis for Gustav Stickley's New York-based Craftsman Workshops, but lack the gentle curves and more delicate proportions that relieve his designs from becoming too heavy or rectilinear.

The Arts and Crafts Movement had several lasting effects on the furniture industry in Grand Rapids. One was the beginnings of a tension in design between modernism and historicism which continues to shape the city today. From the time of the Arts and Crafts Movement onward, the prevailing styles have swung back and forth between the principles of modernism: honesty of materials, simplicity of form, and functionality; and the principles of historicism: romance, beauty derived from decoration, and faithfulness to style. Frequently, both sets of principles have enjoyed popularity at the same times, even within a single company. This has had less to do with ideology than with keeping customers happy by offering all the choices they might want.

Another lasting change that came as a result of the Arts and Crafts Movement was the increased importance of the designer in the process of

ABOVE: This side chair by the Michigan Chair Co. resembles a design that Frank Lloyd Wright created in 1902 for his Prairie-style Ward Willis House, with the same quarter-sawn oak, square spindles and legs, and upright back. However, the Michigan Chair piece is shorter, its spindles end at the seat rail instead of below it, and the backrest lacks the subtle taper seen in Wright's design. These changes probably made it less extreme-looking to uninformed buyers, while still following the style of the day.

David Kendall's McKinley Chair, designed for the Phoenix Furniture Co., is a good example of Grand Rapids' role as a trend setter. Designed in 1894, its straight, square oak spindles and broad, flat armrests make it one of the earliest examples of the Arts and Crafts style which a decade later would become the rage in America. It quickly became a top seller for Phoenix, and was even further popularized because U. S. President William McKinley owned one. According to Don Marek's *Arts and Crafts Furniture Design: The Grand Rapids Contribution*, Kendall's McKinley Chair was soon copied by companies in cities that previously wouldn't have given Grand Rapids a second thought, including Joseph McHugh Company of New York, Paine Furniture Company of Boston, and Ford and Johnson of Chicago. Such open plagiarism of his design caused Kendall to patent the McKinley Chair in 1897. It remained in production, with several variations, until at least 1912.

making and marketing furniture. Grand Rapids designs from the 1830s through the 1860s had mostly followed traditional forms that cabinet-makers learned as young apprentices, or designs published in style books that were already out-of-date by the time manufacturers copied them. But by the late nineteenth century, most of the larger Grand Rapids companies had hired staff designers with academic training in art history or architecture. Both large and small manufacturers also employed free-lance designers, who set up their own shops in Grand Rapids. These men were keenly aware of what was happening in the world's great centers of art and culture, and often contributed to the popularization of new styles. This concentration of designers, constantly looking to innovate the next new fad in American home furnishings, changed Grand Rapids' image from trend follower to trend setter.

By 1917 there were enough designers in Grand Rapids to form the Grand Rapids Furniture Designers Association. Still active today, it is the oldest group for designers in the nation. Over the years, many of Grand Rapids' most prominent designers have served as leaders of the Association. In 1931, the Grand Rapids Furniture Market hosted the first meeting of the American Institute of Decorators, which became and remains the national trade association for interior designers.

In order to make the best furniture, Grand Rapids firms hired their design talent from the world's most prestigious companies. Many of them trained at certain interior design houses. English-born Tom Handley apprenticed in the London shops of Waring & Gillow, then worked for the exclusive firm of W. & J. Sloane in New York City before coming to Grand Rapids as a designer for Luce Furniture Company. Not long afterwards, he formed the Johnson-Handley-Johnson Company with the Swedish-born Johnson brothers in 1906. Handley focused the company on historical British and French styles.

Other designers followed Handley's path to Grand Rapids. Stanley Green, also English, apprenticed at Waring & Gillow before designing English pieces for the John Widdicomb Company. William Millington received his training from the Royal College of Arts in London, worked for both Waring & Gillow and Sloane, then came to work for the Phoenix Furniture Company in 1917. William Hoffmann trained to be an architect at the Cooper Union school in New York, and worked for several years at Sloane before being recruited by the Robert W. Irwin Company in 1921. American Frank C. Lee began at Sloane, then headed Waring & Gillow's branch office in Madrid, Spain, where he designed interiors for the Spanish royal palace. In 1921 he returned to the United States, where he was eagerly hired as a staff designer at Berkey & Gay Furniture Company.

The deliberate move toward the high end also prompted Grand Rapids manufacturers to recruit highly skilled craftsmen. The furniture created by the new class of designers called for intricate and sophisticated marquetry: inlaid, carved, and painted decorations. Mechanization was still used for much of the work, but the decoration and finishing now required many hours of hand labor, increasing the quality and appeal to the consumer, and also the price per piece.

Realizing that trained craftsmen might not easily make their own way to

Grand Rapids, company owners went to great lengths to locate and collect the talent they needed. Frank J. Davidhazy was born into a family of Hungarian cabinetmakers. He received formal training as a painter in New York, then went to work as a decorative painter at W. & J. Sloane. The young decorator's abilities became known to Robert Irwin in 1920, perhaps through the designers he had recently hired from Sloane. Irwin asked Davidhazy what it would take to convince him to move to Grand Rapids to head his company's decorative finish department. Davidhazy had no real interest in leaving his family, friends, and job in New York, so he replied with a salary amount so high he guessed it would bring an end to the conversation. But to his surprise, Irwin readily agreed, and Davidhazy boarded a train bound for Michigan.

As the revival of foreign furniture styles from earlier periods gained popularity, some manufacturers drafted artisans from abroad. Leopold Baillot was one of thirteen master carvers who were located in Florence, Italy for Berkey & Gay and convinced to immigrate to Grand Rapids by the U.S. consulate in Italy. They created many of the highly carved Italian grottoesque pieces that Berkey & Gay produced beginning in the 1890s. James M. Seino received training as a painter from the Imperial Academy in Tokyo, and studied art in Paris and New York, before becoming the first Japanese resident of Grand Rapids. He headed Stickley Brothers' decorative painting department from 1914 until 1938, during which time the company promoted Japanese raised lacquer work as one of its specialties. Fuji Nakamiso was also recruited to leave his native Japan and work as a decorative painter for Berkey & Gay.

The Arts and Crafts Movement left Grand Rapids furniture makers with a greater appreciation for furniture styles of the past. Arts and Crafts proponents' often-romanticized interest in pre-industrial furniture survived even after the demise of the Mission style. Designers searched for Medieval and peasant forms to re-interpret, and discovered the same ideals of good design and craftsmanship in other styles. As consumers tired of the hard, unadorned lines of some Arts and Crafts furniture, designers turned to reproducing these other styles, in order to stimulate buying. Collections of antique furniture in art museums, colonial homes, and European castles provided endless inspiration for their drawing boards.

A revival of interest in the decorative arts of an earlier time was hardly a new concept, nor was it a Grand Rapids invention. Most eighteenth- and nineteenth-century styles were loosely based on elements from the past, but were not accurate reproductions. During the years surrounding the American Centennial in 1876, nationalism caused a swelling of interest in creating a uniquely American folklore to rival the older heritage of European nations. Families brought old, forgotten pieces of eighteenth-century furniture down from their attics and into their parlors. A growing number of furniture makers began to create Colonial Revival furnishings, which were still mostly amalgams of elements from the William and Mary, Queen Anne, Chippendale, Federal, and sometimes American Empire

ABOVE: Believing that his creations would become heirlooms, Tom Handley's Johnson-Handley-Johnson Co. was one of the first to place a decal of the designer's signature onto each piece it manufactured. BELOW: "Dutch" and "Ash" chairs from the Dutch Arts and Crafts line of the Charles P. Limbert Co., ca. 1905. Note that the pegged mortises and cordate cut-outs are the chairs' only surface ornamentation.

styles. As America's economic stature in the world grew, so did interest in Colonial furniture.

The revival of historical styles of furniture also followed a renewed interest in historical architecture. The 1893 World's Columbian Exposition in Chicago and the increasing influence of the Ecole de Beaux Arts in Paris ushered in an era of classical architecture inspired by Mediterranean villas, French chateaux, and English country houses, as well as New England salt-boxes and Tidewater plantations. To furnish these new mansions, furniture manufacturers began to produce Venetian grottoesque stands, Louis XV mirrors, Georgian beds, Gothic dining suites, and Chippendale wing chairs with greater attention to accuracy.

For many Grand Rapids manufacturers, production of Colonial and European Revival styles continued throughout the Arts and Crafts period. For others, there was a definable point of transition. Stickley Brothers produced a substantial number of Colonial Windsor chairs before turning all its energies toward the Mission style around 1903. Then again, after 1909, soft sales in their "Quaint Mission" and "Quaint Arts and Crafts" lines prompted the company to reintroduce ornamentation and historical reference with the "Quaint Tudor" line. Still based in the same passion for British antiques, Quaint Tudor took advantage of the factory's ability to interchange parts in the assembly process by substituting heavy ball-turned legs on its Mission oak tables, thus instantly creating new period revival pieces with components from the old Mission line.

This success prompted Stickley Brothers to continue introducing other period-inspired variations, labeled "Quaint Jacobean" and "Quaint Peasant." Their last foray into Arts and Crafts came around 1914 with "Quaint Manor," which used caned panels and sleek, Austrian-inspired lines to create a simple, geometrical beauty. But in that same year the company also began its Japanese lacquer line, and by the end of World War I, all Stickley Brothers furniture was richly carved, painted, and ornamented.

Grand Rapids Bookcase & Chair Company followed a similar path beginning in 1913, when it added spiral turnings to "Lifetime Cloister" designs, thus creating "Lifetime Jacobean." Slender, gently arching redesigns of the old Cloister Mission pieces were attempted in 1917. This remake line was named "Lifetime Puritan" to tap into the interest in Colonial Revival, despite the fact that it bore little resemblance to anything ever used by the colonists who lent it their name.

To appreciate the authenticity and artistry of Grand Rapids furniture, consumers had to know something about design. Manufacturers' abilities to design and market furniture appropriate for dozens of different architectural styles meant little, unless buyers felt that finding the correct style was important, and knew which style they needed. Educating the consumer became one of the primary ways to sell period revival furniture. A large advertising, photography, and publishing industry thus developed in Grand Rapids, producing interior magazines, style guides, and color brochures to teach the general public how to decorate tastefully. The more homeowners learned about the history of furniture styles and Grand Rapids quality, the more they wanted to own it.

Good Furniture, "The Magazine of Good Taste," was published monthly by the Dean-Hicks Company of Grand Rapids beginning in 1914. It featured articles with titles like "Furniture: An Expression of Art," "On The Relation of Furniture to its Architectural Setting," "A Story of Antiques," and "Chairs of the Golden Age." Illustrations included photos of pieces from the collections of the Metropolitan Museum of Art, room installations from European palaces, and plates from Thomas Chippendale's *Cabinetmaker's Director*. Advertisements in the front and back of the magazine showed furniture by Grand Rapids companies that imitated the styles discussed in the articles.

Style guides were generally written and produced by people or companies connected with the industry, but their detailed illustrations and rich binding gave them an air of legitimacy. *How to Know Period Styles in Furniture* by W. L. Kimerly went through several editions by a number of Grand Rapids publishers, beginning in 1912. It featured sketches and descriptions of styles beginning with ancient Egypt and Assyria, and moved through seventeenth- and eighteenth-century English styles, American Colonial, and Mission. *Furniture As Interpreted by the Century Furniture Company*, a leather-bound, gilt pocket volume first published in 1926, followed a similar progression, including Roman, Gothic, Italian, Spanish, Flemish, Dutch Renaissance, and all the French and English style designations, ending with American Colonial. It even dictated which styles were appropriate for certain uses in the home:

> Modern usage has disregarded completely the excessively rococo style of Louis XV furniture, but on the whole it has been adapted to many modern types of furniture. Where a rich and sumptuous effect is desired, furniture of this period will provide it.

But rather than showing illustrations of actual pieces from the periods described, the book cleverly substituted photos of Century's interpretations of each style, leading the reader to believe that their products were the pinnacle they should attempt to reach.

Berkey & Gay was perhaps most adept in using history to sell furniture. The company reprinted Eugene Field's poem "In Amsterdam," from his 1892 *Second Book of Verse*, in advertisements and catalogs because of the romantic picture Field painted about Berkey & Gay's revival furniture.

For some Berkey & Gay advertisements from the 1920s, copywriters wrote their own fairy tales about the period and country from which each style originated. These helped buyers to imagine themselves as Henry VIII sitting down to feast at his new banquet table, or "King Fritz der Foorst" slumbering in his royal bed.

Another series of Berkey & Gay ads from 1926, which ran in leading periodicals like *The Saturday Evening Post*, took a different tack. No longer simple photos of furniture with descriptions of finishes or charming stories, these ads used subtle phrases and imagery to appeal directly to consumers' secret desires, and call attention to their worst fears. For the status-conscious, rising middle class, one ad asked:

> What do the chauffeurs hear? When the final bridge score has been settled, and your guests are motoring home - what is the verdict?
> What impression of you and your home are they carrying away?

For isolationist Americans, who worried that free immigration might

The Victorian sentiments in Berkey & Gay advertisements such as this one, produced for the November 13, 1926 edition of *The Saturday Evening Post*, offered conservative, historical furniture as domestic protection from the outside world.

In 1929 Berkey & Gay took the concept of selling history quite literally with its limited edition of one hundred "Old Ironsides Tables." During the late 1920s, restoration had begun in Boston Harbor on the *U.S.S. Constitution*, the ship nicknamed "Old Ironsides" during the War of 1812. Some of the original materials removed from the orlop deck of the ship were sold to help fund the project. Berkey & Gay purchased these pine timbers and carved them into eagle decorations, which were placed on the front aprons of Colonial Revival tables based on a design from a Wallace Nutting book. A plaque was attached inside the drawer of each table as a certification of authenticity, and each purchaser was given a small fragment of the wood.

bring ruin to the country, another ad likened the comparison between native-born Americans and immigrants to the comparison between thoroughbreds and mongrels under the header "A trait that reflects good breeding." For immigrants struggling to prove that they were true Americans, buying the right furniture was a symbol to others that they had arrived. An ad proclaiming that Berkey & Gay had been "Patronized by three generations of gentlefolk" dropped the hint that if they wanted to fit in, they should buy from Berkey & Gay. Still another ad, entitled "Bulwarks against the Age of Jazz," played on white Americans' latent racist views toward African-Americans:

> Inside the home—a little group of growing, gracious lives. Outside, like a circling threat, the lure of shoddy, vulgarizing things. . . . Tawdry jazz-music with the jungle-rhythm . . . stained cheap drama . . . "snappy" literature . . . dance hall nights. How shall we protect our children from all this cheapness? By surrounding them with forms of beauty! Good books, good music, good furniture. . . .

What relief they must have felt, to learn that Berkey & Gay furniture could actually save their children from the evils of life on the street!

As reproductions of antiques became popular, Grand Rapids manufacturers developed techniques to give their new furniture the appearance of age. Beautifully crafted pieces of factory-new furniture were stained, bleached, worn, and beaten to simulate the patina that real antiques develop from centuries of use. Many consumers preferred these "new antiques" because they had the charm of the real thing, but were easy to purchase and adapted for modern convenience. They made sense in the context of their new English Tudor cottages, French chateaux, and Southern plantation homes, which were constructed throughout suburban America in the 1920s and '30s. But most of all, they gave the false impression that they had been passed down through many generations of careful acquisition.

As consumers were taught more about the correct proportions and decorations of various styles, they became more willing to pay for reproductions that were accurate. Some designers and manufacturers traveled abroad, not just to study furniture styles, but to acquire pieces and bring them home, where they could serve as models for reproduction. Hollis M. Baker, owner of Baker Furniture, Inc., amassed a collection of furniture through his travels and from antique dealers and auction houses, eventually numbering more than four thousand pieces. Examples were collected from Europe, Egypt, the Far East, and America, and dated as far back as 2000 B.C. In 1941 the company opened The Baker Museum for Furniture Research, which it dedicated to "the Study and Convenience of Students of Furniture Design and for the Furtherance of Public Interest in the Furniture Arts and Crafts." A portion of the Baker Collection is now owned by the Grand Rapids Art Museum.

Smaller firms without the means to acquire so large a collection found other ways to obtain and even borrow antiques for reproduction. As late as the 1950s and '60s, Donald Thompson made annual trips to New England to locate antiques. He would stay in Colonial-era homes converted into bed and breakfast inns, and scout nearby villages or even the inn where he stayed for pieces to borrow. After he had convinced its owner that his request was legitimate, he would load the piece into his car and drive back to Grand Rapids. Thompson would return the piece the following year, when he went back in search of more inspiration.

Some Grand Rapids firms developed relationships with museums that allowed them to measure, study, and reproduce pieces from their collections. This provided new sources of inspiration for designers, and the name of the institution that owned the original was mentioned in ads and catalogs, adding prestige to the reproduction. In the 1920s, the Johnson Furniture Company manufactured a line of reproductions based on pieces at the Metropolitan Museum of Art, and dropped that name in all their catalogs.

The Century Furniture Company, which often cited European museums and palaces as the sources for its reproductions, didn't copy only the original construction materials and details. Century also reproduced the signs of age and wear on its furniture, as in a ratchet-arm sofa copied from Knole in England. Its stretchers were carefully planed to simulate wear from centuries of rubbing boots; dark stain in the corners approximated the build-up caused by dirt and cleaning over time; and its velvet upholstery was dyed with a pattern of faded areas, and randomly woven with lighter-colored threads, to make it appear sun-faded and worn.

Grand Rapids furniture manufacturers received new respect for their early American reproductions in 1931, when they were selected by a distant relative of George Washington to furnish a replica of his Mount Vernon home for the International Colonial and Overseas Exposition in Paris. After the Exposition, the pieces were given a special label and sold through exclusive American retailers. For those Americans who couldn't afford the rising costs of genuine antiques, Grand Rapids offered the chance to purchase exact copies of the reproductions used in the replica of the home where George Washington slept! Such patriotic furnishings undoubtedly made some buyers confident that their national loyalties would be above reproach.

As part of their efforts to reach new markets nationwide, Grand Rapids furniture companies improved consumers' recognition of their products. This deliberate effort coincided with a national trend away from unlabeled, locally produced goods, toward nationally distributed products with name-brand recognition. According to Susan Strasser's *Satisfaction Guaranteed: The Making of the American Mass Market*, branding and trademarking allowed manufacturers to regain control of the relationship they had lost with consumers. Cabinetmakers from a generation earlier knew the people who bought their products, and sold to them directly. But late nineteenth-century consumers knew only what their local retailer told them about the Grand Rapids company that manufactured the furniture. When manufacturers advertised, they provided product education that enabled buyers to

The desire to make the home's interior reflect the opulence of an earlier age sometimes overshadowed the novelty of modern conveniences. When new forms had to be introduced into a space that was decorated in the style of a particular period, they were sometimes disguised as antique forms. For instance, throughout the 1920s the H.E. Shaw Furniture Co. disguised its desks, intended for use in living rooms, as spinet pianos. Around 1925, the Shear-Maddox Furniture Co. manufactured this Spanish Renaissance-style chest-on-stand with wrought iron stretchers and hand-decorated leather by Wilson & Beckwith Studios. The small crank handle extending from one end is the only outward evidence that a phonograph is hidden inside.

associate their company's name with certain favorable traits. Consistent labeling of products with memorable brand names and recognizable trademarks made consumers remember what they read, and demand specific company products by name.

Trademarks were developed to help consumers differentiate between similar products by competing manufacturers. Even if a consumer couldn't remember a company's name, a cleverly designed trademark might be distinctive enough to be recognized. A trademark also told consumers that the manufacturer was willing to stake its reputation on the quality of its products. Beginning in 1870, a number of ineffective attempts were made at legislating protection for corporate trademarks. Finally, in 1905, two bills were approved that allowed one company or organization to sue another for infringement upon its trademark or brand name. In order for a trademark to provide evidence of ownership for a particular product, it had to be attached in some visible way (such as a tag, label, or decal), and incorporate original and consistent lettering and designs to make it unique.

The Century Furniture Co. reproduced the signs of age and wear on this ca. 1925 copy of a seventeenth-century ratchet-arm sofa from Knole House in England.

The adoption of trademarks and brand names by some Grand Rapids furniture makers placed them at the forefront of this revolution in American business. Before the 1890s, few Grand Rapids companies consistently placed trademarks on their furniture. Some pieces had company names stenciled or burn-marked in generic lettering. Other pieces were labeled, but only for shipping purposes. In the late 1890s and early 1900s, companies like Stickley Brothers, Charles P. Limbert, Macey, Michigan Chair, Berkey & Gay, and Grand Rapids Bookcase & Chair began to register and use trademarks consistently in advertising and labeling.

Since all of these companies were at that time producing Arts and Crafts furniture, they often blended the modern notion of trademarks with the centuries-old European craft tradition of placing hallmarks, denoting standards of purity or royal license, on pieces of silver or ceramics. The Arts and Crafts furniture makers' trademarks mimicked the bold, simple designs of these hallmarks.

Several Grand Rapids companies created their own successful brand names. Stickley Brothers used the brand name "Quaint," the British style term for Arts and Crafts furniture. Ramsey-Alton's "Oak Craft" brand name represented strength and craftsmanship. Grand Rapids Bookcase & Chair's "Lifetime" brand name suggested permanence of construction and design. Even today the Lifetime brand name is more generally recognized by Arts and Crafts collectors than the name of the company that invented it. The "Steelcase" brand name adopted by the Metal Office Furniture Company in 1920 became so commonly known that the company eventually changed its name to Steelcase, Inc.

But more significant than all of these individual company trademarks was the one adopted by the collective membership of the city's Furniture Manufacturers Association. Commonly known as the "Grand Rapids

Made" logo, this red triangular trademark was applied to every piece of furniture made by every FMA member company between 1899 and about 1913. Its appearance on a piece of furniture was meant as an assurance of quality, and an authentication that the piece originated from Grand Rapids, Michigan. A campaign was launched in 1900 by the FMA, which placed advertisements like this in leading magazines of the day:

> *This step is made necessary for the protection of the buying public, so much inferior furniture being foisted on the market yearly under the Grand Rapids name and reputation. This trade mark is a guarantee of honest material and superior workmanship. Furniture bearing this label is guaranteed to be exactly as represented.*

A number of Grand Rapids firms also incorporated the "Grand Rapids Made" triangle into their corporate trademarks. The triangular shape became so recognizable that it was widely copied by suppliers to the furniture industry in Grand Rapids, and by furniture manufacturers in other cities, who hoped to confuse consumers into thinking that their product bore the Grand Rapids seal of approval.

The FMA not only promoted the "Grand Rapids Made" trademark, it vigilantly protected the exclusive use and good reputation of the name "Grand Rapids." In 1913, a feature article in *The Grand Rapids Furniture Record*, entitled "Misrepresenting Grand Rapids," exposed the fraudulent use of the term "Grand Rapids furniture" by the Grand Rapids Cash Furniture Company of Spokane, Washington in describing its products. The Ahdawagam Furniture Company took advantage of consumers' confusion by advertising its location in Grand Rapids, Wisconsin. But in 1919 the FMA successfully sued several stores in the Cleveland, Ohio area for using the name "Grand Rapids" even though they didn't sell Grand Rapids furniture.

Such cooperative solidarity among so many potential competitors seems extraordinary, but it served Grand Rapids manufacturers well. None of the companies individually held enough market share to reach the complete name recognition achieved in other industries, but as a group they did. It was too much to expect the average consumer to keep straight the reputations of dozens of different companies, but they could remember that "Grand Rapids Made" was their assurance of quality.

Misrepresenting Grand Rapids.

THE Grand Rapids Advertisers' Club, at a recent meeting adopted resolutions unqualifiedly condemning the practice which is indulged in by many dealers all over the country in offering furniture which is represented as Grand Rapids furniture, but which is as unlike Grand Rapids furniture as it is possible to imagine. These resolutions were published in the March number of THE FURNITURE RECORD. Other resolutions of the same general character have been adopted at different times, but nothing has been done to check this fraudulent trading on the good name of Grand Rapids for good furniture. There are numerous retail establishments throughout the United States which are, presumably for the distinction which the name may possibly imply, known as the "Grand Rapids Furniture Store," or the "Grand Rapids Furniture Co." Some of these stores are stores of quality, but others are stores in which a piece of Grand Rapids furniture is rarely to be found. There ought to be some way to put a stop to these practices for the use of the name of Grand Rapids in connection with some of the stores which are to be found throughout the country, and the use of the name Grand Rapids in connection with much of the furniture which is offered as Grand Rapids furniture is damaging to the reputation of the manufacturers of furniture in this city. There are one or two firms in Chicago which are constantly advertising Grand Rapids samples and Grand Rapids furniture, the representatives of which rarely, if ever, buy anything in this market. These stores handle only cheap furniture, such as is not made in this city, and very little of which is ever shown in this city during the market season.

Attention has been called to a very flagrant misuse of the reputation of Grand Rapids in the advertisements taken from a Spokane, Wash., paper. There is no reader of THE FURNITURE RECORD familiar with what the Grand Rapids manufacturers make who will be deceived by the illustrations shown in the ads. No such furniture is made in this city. Seven-dollar dressers do not grow in this vicinity—even at wholesale—to say nothing of dressers that can be sold at retail at that price. Our information states that instead of being dressers from the Berkey & Gay Furniture Co., and the Nelson Matter Co., as sometimes represented, the goods sold are cheap, coast-made goods. Our correspondent asks if there is not some way to stop misrepresentation of this kind.

Yes. In some of the states, thanks chiefly to the work which is being done by the local adver-

tising clubs of the country and the associated advertising clubs, legislation is being secured against fraudulent advertising of this sort. Such a law has recently been enacted in Ohio. Here is the way it has been put in the Ohio law:

"Any person, firm, corporation or association who, with intent to sell, or in any wise dispose of merchandise, securities, service, or anything offered by such person, firm or corporation or association, directly or indirectly, to the public for sale or distribution, or with intent to increase the consumption thereof, or to induce the public in any manner to enter into any obligation relating thereto, or to acquire title thereto, or an interest therein, 'knowingly' make, publishes, disseminates, circulates, or places before the public or causes directly or indirectly to be made, published, disseminated, circulated or placed before the public in this state in a newspaper or other publication, or in the form of a book, notice, handbill,

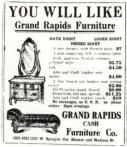

poster, bill circular, pamphlet, or letter, or in any other way an advertisement of any sort regarding merchandise, securities, service or anything offered to the public, representation or statement of fact which is untrue, deceptive or misleading, shall be guilty of a misdemeanor and on conviction thereof shall be punished by a fine of not less than ten dollars or more than fifty dollars or by imprisonment in the county jail not exceeding twenty days, or both said fine and imprisonment."

The bill before the Indiana legislature, and which at last accounts had passed one branch of that body, is slightly different and reads:

"That any person, firm, corporation or association, or any agent, attorney or employe of such person, firm, corporation or association, who shall hereafter, knowingly, publish, circulate, distribute or in any manner place before the public in any newspaper, circular, book, booklet, poster or sign, make any fraudulent or false statement concerning any article of merchandise, goods, wares, work

This article, from The Grand Rapids Furniture Record for April, 1913, describes the prompt action taken by the FMA when a Spokane, Washington dealer tried to profit from Grand Rapids' good reputation. The "Grand Rapids Made" logo was used by the member companies of the Grand Rapids Furniture Manufacturers Association to collectively market the reputation of their goods.

OPPORTTAS

1919

OPPORTUNITY

The Furniture Market brought thousands of buyers to Grand Rapids to order the latest styles and to celebrate the city's livelihood.

Selling Style

For eighty-seven years Grand Rapids played host to one of the largest events where furniture was sold. Officially known as the Grand Rapids Furniture Exposition and commonly referred to as "The Market," this semi-annual trade show attracted buyers from across America and around the world. The Market transformed the shape of downtown Grand Rapids, and brought a steady stream of clients to the front doors of the city's factories. Satisfied visitors helped spread the reputation of Grand Rapids as "The Furniture City." Part convention and part carnival, the Grand Rapids Furniture Market became a festival of the furniture industry, just as county fairs celebrate farming. Civic leaders recognized furniture as the source of the city's wealth, and so each return of the industry's leaders to Grand Rapids provided a cause for celebration. Market was vital to the success of many local businesses. The months when Market was held, January and June, were busy times, as Grand Rapids pulled out all the stops to show visitors a good time. When buyers came to town they bought not only furniture, but also the idea that Grand Rapids knew all about style and comfort.

Origins of Market

A number of origin myths developed, attempting to explain the founding of the Grand Rapids Furniture Market. Historian Frank Ransom, in his book *The City Built on Wood*, contends that the earliest evidence of a cooperative furniture sale by local manufacturers can be found in an article from the November 15, 1873 issue of the *Grand Rapids Daily Eagle*:

> The next ten days will be a lively period in the furniture business. The Berkey and [sic] Gay Furniture Company have extensively advertised in this and other states their trade sale which begins next Wednesday, and it is expected that dealers in furniture will be here to attend the sale and buy what they need. Other furniture manufacturers, Nelson Matter [sic] and Company, and the Phoenix Furniture Company also propose to sell at a reduction in price to suit the times.
>
> Why would it not be a good idea for our furniture manufacturers to combine for an annual trade sale? Such a course would bring a great many dealers here, and once here to see facilities that our man-

ufacturers have for making and shipping furniture, and the elegant goods that are produced, they would be sure to come again. . . .

Other accounts of the first Market disagree on the date as well as on other details. On the occasion of the hundredth Market in January of 1928, a reporter for the *Grand Rapids Herald* interviewed "old-timers," asking about the actual beginnings of the event. The answers varied widely. Charlie Jones, described as "Dean of the Furniture Salesmen," recalled:

> . . . *William A. Berkey, one of the Berkey brothers, decided to retire from the Berkey Bros. & Co. . . . They had quite a lot of furniture to divide and dispose of . . . letters were sent out to dealers announcing an auction sale of the furniture. . . . That was in 1872 and something like a dozen or fifteen dealers came to Grand Rapids to buy at that auction sale. . . . That was the first furniture market ever held here.*

Furniture man Frank M. Sparks remembered its beginnings differently:

> *In those days it was an altogether normal thing for the dealers to come (to order furniture) in January and in June or July, and the result was that year after year found a growing group of dealers in Grand Rapids. . . . Then came the discovery of the Grand Rapids Market in 1877. . . . It so happened that a salesman for a manufacturer not located in Grand Rapids happened to be in Grand Rapids about his business. He was surprised to find here a large number of retail dealers. . . . He trotted out his pictures and around the hotel lobby showed them to the dealers assembled there and took some orders . . . the result was that in January, 1878, when the dealers arrived they found in Grand Rapids at least one other line.*

Ed Morley, who represented a number of furniture firms, fondly remembered the days of the early Markets:

> *The Market in those days was a gay time. Business was only sort of incidental to the joy of the occasion. . . . Today they give the furniture a chance in a proper setting. In those days the furniture had to tell the whole story against the most impossible odds.*

Frank Ransom also looked to the hotels in his attempt to document the first Market. He found that at least eleven furniture buyers from Chicago, Philadelphia, Boston, Milwaukee, and Toledo were registered at Grand Rapids hotels on December 22, 1878. The Grand Rapids Furniture Market Association also adopted December of 1878 as the official date of the first Market. They attributed the interest that out-of-town dealers showed in Grand Rapids to the attention the city's factories had received at the 1876 Philadelphia Centennial Exposition. As these buyers began to make the journey to Grand Rapids to place their orders, local companies set up showrooms inside their factories. Companies located elsewhere soon realized that buyers were passing them by, on their way to one-stop shopping in Grand Rapids, so they sent their own salesmen, armed with catalogs.

The showroom of Berkey & Gay Furniture Co., shown in this stereocard ca. 1878, typifies the method of display for the period. One sample of each piece made by the company, plus complementary products by other manufacturers like Hunzinger, were simply lined up in rows, on an open floor of the wareroom building.

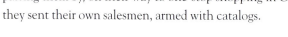

The Grand Rapids Furniture Market quickly became a regular, organized event. Sections of local factories were permanently designated as showroom spaces. Out-of-town manufacturers, who previously used vacant storefronts, contracted with local sales representatives who rented space in downtown buildings to display six or eight lines of furniture.

According to an article in the November, 1915 issue of *The Furniture Manufacturer and Artisan*, the Grand Rapids Market Association was newly formed to coordinate the various activities that took place during Market-time, and to advertise the Market to retail customers and potential new exhibitors. The Market Association replaced the Grand Rapids Association of Furniture Exhibitors, and was itself replaced by the Grand Rapids Furniture Exposition Association in 1931. The Association solicited funds and represented the interests of local manufacturers, exhibition buildings, civic groups, and out-of-town companies. Beginning in the early 1920s, the Association sponsored the National Retail Furniture Institute during the closing week of Market. It provided educational courses on furniture design, manufacturing techniques, and retailing for Market attenders. The Association also published *Buyer's Order Books*, which listed all of the exhibitors for each season, and *The Marketeer*, which was distributed throughout the furniture industry prior to each Market.

The Furniture Market was responsible for much of the growth of Grand Rapids. As attendance reached into the hundreds and then thousands, the event outgrew its available space. Hotels, theatres, bars, and restaurants were built to serve visitors, and enormous showroom buildings, some a block long, were constructed to showcase furniture. By the early twentieth century visitors required guidebooks to find their way around. These included maps from the hotels to the showroom buildings and listed the companies displayed in each. Many support businesses like restaurants and night clubs advertised special offers for Market goers, including limousine services that picked up and delivered dealers to their doorsteps.

The Market Transforms the City's Image

The growth of the Furniture Market changed the way the city looked. As the Market became national and international in scope during the 1910s and '20s, civic leaders envisioned their town becoming one of the country's great cities. To position Grand Rapids to compete with larger cities (particularly Chicago, which also hosted a furniture market), they worked to beautify downtown, so that Grand Rapids could be dressed appropriately to teach about design and style trends. Important-looking monuments and classical-style buildings began to replace the more modest structures in the city's center. The influence of the Ecole de Beaux Arts, the great school of fine arts in Paris, became evident in the architecture of the city. New exhibition halls, hotels, theatres, and office towers were grandly constructed and lavishly decorated. Resembling Grecian temples and Renaissance palaces with rows of columns, arcades, swags, and laurel wreaths, these buildings made Grand Rapids seem more sophisticated.

City planners were particularly concerned about the appearance of the factories that dominated the Grand Rapids riverfront. Schemes to beautify the business district and riverfront areas were drafted by professional vision-

Steve ran onto a bunch of salesmen who used to call on him.

Illustration from *The Awakening of Steve Randall: The Story of a Rejuvenated Furniture Store*. This novella was published in 1913 by the Grand Rapids Association of Furniture Exhibitors and sent to retailers across the nation to excite them about Grand Rapids. It described a man who turned his business and life around by taking a journey to the Furniture Market. A secular version of the parable of the prodigal son, it was written with all the zeal of a religious mission tract.

The 100th Market

Grand Rapids' advertising machine went into overdrive in January of 1928. The Furniture City hosted the twice-yearly Furniture Market for the hundredth time, and the industry rose to the occasion with gusto.

The special "100th Market Edition" of *The Grand Rapids Herald* spared no words in proclaiming the day: "Ninety-nine Milestones has Grand Rapids set across the Flowerland of Civilization. Ninety-nine times have her Gates flung wide to Welcome those who make the Hearthside dear. Ninety-nine times have Portals opened to present to Man the rarest children of the Brain, the most beautiful Craftsmanship of high skilled Hands that may be found in all the World. . . . Now Grand Rapids is set for another Milestone, a Bigger and more Beautiful and more Imposing Shaft, the stone which bears the simple legend: One Hundred."

The circumstances of the celebration were almost as grand as the pomp. A delegation representing the Market Association set out in 1927 to visit the White House and invite President Calvin Coolidge to attend. Although they presented to him this elaborate marquetry invitation, he declined to come.

Presidential invitation, courtesy, John and Carol Sindelar.

Undaunted, organizers devised a new plan, enabling the president to press a button in the White House, which lit up two miles of street decorations and window displays along Grand

aries in 1908 and 1924. The 1924 Bartholomew Plan recommended that factories be covered with coordinated classical facades. The evidence of industry was to be disguised by cornices, balconies, and colonnades. The plan also called for wide boulevards terminating at heroic sculptures, and park spaces along the Grand River. Neither of the facelifts was ever implemented, but the idea of beautification took root. Most of the factories are now gone from the riverfront, replaced with civic buildings, museums, open plazas, walking paths, and public parks.

Grandiose images of the city were used by promoters to attract furniture dealers to Market. Popular decorating magazines kept the event in a national spotlight with reviews of each season's new introductions. Advertisements by the Market Association in Grand Rapids-published trade journals spared no modesty trying to convince retailers that attending Market was crucial to their success. They depicted the city with gleaming domes and triumphal arches reaching to the clouds. Some spun elaborate tales likening a trip to Market to a religious pilgrimage by crusading knights. A June, 1914 advertisement in *The Grand Rapids Furniture Record*, with the heading "The Road to Success Leads Thru the World's Market at Grand Rapids," showed furniture dealers hurrying toward the shining city of Grand Rapids. An inset just above their heads depicted a familiar biblical story, comparing these smart retailers to the wise men who followed the Star of Bethlehem.

An advertisement in the January, 1914 *Grand Rapids Furniture Record* gave the Market a personality: "the Spirit of the Grand Rapids Market" personally invited buyers to come to "his" city. Many ads and illustrations portrayed the Market and the furniture industry as a benevolent goddess who protected the city just as Columbia protected the country. Other ads showed her guiding a designer's hands, or showering blessings on all who visited the city.

Dealers Flock to Market

Many Market visitors traveled to Grand Rapids by train, and were greeted by the tall tower of the Grand Trunk Terminal or the imposing columns of Union Station. Others came by private automobile or a combination of lake steamer and interurban line. The nation's first regular passenger airline service began in 1926 between Grand Rapids and Detroit, and companies like Furniture Capital Airlines soon offered air travel to Market.

However they arrived, visitors were soon whisked to their hotels in chauffeured limousines. The Morton House, managed by J. Boyd Pantlind, was the original inn of choice for Market goers. In 1900 Pantlind became part owner of the Hotel Ottawa on Lake Michigan. He convinced many dealers to enjoy the lakeside amenities of the Ottawa in the evenings, then travel each morning into town on the interurban train. In 1902 he reopened the former Sweets Hotel as The Pantlind Hotel, gaining control of more than half of the area's available hotel rooms. The new Pantlind became the center of activity for the Market, with its large, grand lobby (furnished by Grand Rapids manufacturers) and an elegant ballroom for formal banquets and social events.

Several smaller hotels, including the Cody, Herkimer, and Livingston, were located farther from the exhibition buildings, but offered more affordable rooms. Hotels hosted everything from dignified receptions to smoky all-night card games. Service businesses like restaurants, hotels, newsstands, and cigar shops hired extra help during Market, relying on African-Americans and recently immigrated Eastern European women to work long hours as cooks, waiters, bellhops, doormen, maids, and janitors.

After settling into their hotels, dealers set out to see and order furniture in the exhibition buildings, most of which were near the major hotels, within walking distance of one another. Advertisements for the Market from the 1910s and '20s referred to that portion of downtown as the "Furniture Exhibition District," in an effort to convey the size and convenience of the Market's infrastructure.

In 1887 only seven out-of-town companies rented space to show their furniture at the Grand Rapids Market. Two years later, D. A. Blodgett, a local lumber baron and financier, opened the Blodgett Building at Ottawa and Louis Streets as a multi-use office building. Two enterprising sales agents, Philip J. Klingman and Charles P. Limbert, who represented a number of furniture manufacturers, rented two floors and eventually the entire Blodgett Building for furniture displays. By 1900 the number of outside manufacturers showing in Grand Rapids had increased to 225! All the vacant lodge halls, stores, and office buildings in town could no longer provide enough space for the furniture displays.

In 1899 Klingman partnered with Dudley E. Waters, a prominent local banker, to construct a building entirely devoted to wholesalers' displays of furniture. They soon added a sixth floor. The demand for space continued to increase, so in 1904 they put up another building. Following this success, between 1907 and 1914 several more large, significant buildings were constructed in the same area. Then, in the early 1920s, several existing buildings were renovated to house furniture showrooms.

Klingman innovated another successful concept when he opened an outlet store. Klingman's Sample Furniture Company sold display samples after Market ended, saving manufacturers the cost of shipping pieces back to their factories. This grew into the Klingmans Furniture store, which still specializes in the sale of Grand Rapids-made furniture and is one of the largest furniture retailers in the nation. Several other sample furniture stores soon opened downtown.

Only people who worked in the furniture trade could tour the showroom displays, so the sample stores offered a glimpse of the coming season's newest introductions to the general public. One regular customer of the sample stores was the family of prominent retailer and flour miller Carl G. A. Voigt. Despite their newly acquired wealth, the Voigts often preferred furnishing their rooms one bargain at a time, rather than purchasing a suite ensemble at full price. The Voigt House is now operated as a house museum by The Public Museum of Grand Rapids.

Inside the early showrooms, displays consisted of unsophisticated, tightly packed rows of furniture. But by the 1910s manufacturers began displaying their products attractively in room settings, a technique they learned from their clients, the retail stores. With pieces arranged in groupings, buyers could visualize how they might look in their stores, and determine if they fit the level of sophistication and purses of their customers. Reporters for

Rapids' Monroe Avenue and its cross streets. Factory whistles screeched out their greetings across the city. The party went on without the president, and no one seemed to mind his absence.

Many manufacturers released special lines of furniture to commemorate the anniversary, like the sideboard from the "Phoenix Suite" (ABOVE), produced by the Robert W. Irwin Furniture Co. for the 100th Market.

Any lines that were even shown at the 100th Market were required to display special Grand Rapids Furniture Market tags in retail stores across the country. The Market Association sponsored a contest among retailers for the best 100th Market window displays in their hometowns. The campaign ensured that Grand Rapids furniture was featured in all participating stores, and made the name "Grand Rapids" visible to consumers nationwide.

ABOVE: Hundredth Market display window, Ryder Furniture and Carpet Store, Beaumont, Texas.

ABOVE: The Pantlind Hotel, headquarters for many visitors to Market. BELOW: The Furniture Exhibition Building, later known as the Waters Building, was the largest trade show building in the country until Chicago's Merchandise Mart was completed decades later.

national magazines were welcomed into the showrooms, with the hope that they would identify a manufacturer's new line as a wave of the future.

Designing showrooms became a separate, specialized job. Temporary walls created more intimate spaces inside the cavernous showrooms. Reproduction coats of arms, Chinese vases, and sculptures were used as props. They enhanced the rich appearance of the furniture, made the interpretations of historical styles seem more authentic, and evoked romantic images of elegance and antiquity. Items representing beauty, adventure, chivalry, morality, or excess could be placed in the setting. Their meaning became as important a selling point as the actual quality of the furniture.

By the middle of the 1920s Grand Rapids boasted ten furniture exhibition buildings which provided nearly one and a half million square feet of showroom space to 561 manufacturers. These figures did not even include the dozens of local companies that maintained showrooms at their factories. But just when the Grand Rapids Market seemed to reach its zenith, its promoters began to see signs of its vulnerability.

In 1925 the American Furniture Mart opened for the competing Chicago Furniture Market. This huge structure eclipsed Grand Rapids' exhibition buildings in both size and elegance. Its opening was advertised in *The Grand Rapids Furniture Record* magazine, invading the home turf of the Grand Rapids Market.

In less than a year G. A. Hendricks, the developer and owner of the newly opened Fine Arts Exhibition Building, responded to this threat from the west with his proposal for the Furniture Capitol Building. Design drawings showed a tower taller than that of the American Furniture Mart, connected to the Fine Arts Building on the site where the Amway Grand Plaza Hotel tower now stands. Its thirty-five stories would have dwarfed all other buildings in Grand Rapids, with one million square feet of showrooms, restaurants, and club rooms, an interurban train station, and even a furniture museum. The plan was shelved for good after the 1929 stock market crash.

Companies with showrooms inside their factories rolled out the red carpet for guests. Dealers were lavished with attention, food, cocktails, and factory tours. Small dining rooms were constructed adjacent to some showrooms expressly for entertaining during Market. Many hired part-time cooks to prepare special meals for the lucky, invited few. One can only imagine the smells of food being prepared as they mixed with the smell of fresh sawdust! The luncheons held around the Imperial Furniture Company's "Round Table" gained such renown that one was featured on the cover of *The Grand Rapids Furniture Record* in August, 1918.

But these luncheons had a hidden agenda. Eating and touring occupied a considerable amount of the buyers' time, which might otherwise have been spent touring the showrooms of out-of-town competitors. When the visitors were finally allowed to escape from their hosts, it was in limousines that drove them to the next local company's showroom down the road.

Salesmen Entertain Around the Clock

After a long day touring the showrooms, visitors were ready to relax and have a good time. The city lit up for them at night, and the streets of downtown bustled with activity. Many salesmen for Grand Rapids manufacturers treated their best clients to dinners in their own homes, fostering long-term, personal friendships, which ensured steady orders for years to come.

Some clients were treated to an evening of theatre. Grand Rapids opera and vaudeville, and later motion picture theatres, planned their seasons to peak during January and June, when they were assured full houses. An enormous theatre olio, or backdrop, was created by scenic painter Basil Bradley for the Savoy Theater, which stood on Market Street near Monroe Avenue. Used as a background for short acts during vaudeville performances, the backdrop depicted a Grand Rapids that only existed in the dreams of promoters. Many actual buildings were represented, but their size and grandeur were exaggerated. Local advertisers paid to have their names cleverly depicted as billboards, which could be rear-illuminated. When the stage lights were adjusted, the scene could change from the bustle of mid-morning to the magical sparkle of evening. All of the storefronts at street level were painted as filled with furniture displays, as they actually were during the 1928 Centennial Market, when every downtown storefront became a furniture showcase. The scene memorialized the first companies that rented vacant stores for their displays in 1878. Market goers who attended the theatre must surely have recognized and enjoyed this salute.

Special entertainment events were often staged just for Market goers. At the January, 1927 Market, cowboy humorist Will Rogers entertained an audience of more than thirteen hundred buyers and salesmen. To show their appreciation, the furniture men presented Rogers with a chair by the Century Furniture Company. The January 14, 1927 *Grand Rapids Herald* reported: "The crowd cheered itself hoarse when the chair was presented and never was satisfied until [it] was finally placed on stage and Will had climbed up to sit on it." In response, Rogers joked about the chair:

> It's a fine chair. . . . It's beautifully upholstered with enough in it to feed a horse. That's a lovely covering, too. It would make a splendid vest pattern. I am not sure just what period it belongs to. I can't tell whether those legs are Queen Anne or Aimee McPherson, but they're alright [sic] anyway. . . . I probably could tell more about it if it had a price tag on it. . . . It was the Egyptians who first invented furniture. But they didn't fight with the federal trade commission over designations of wood. They just went out to a stone quarry and cut their furniture out. . . . William and Mary formed the first furniture firm, but the only contribution of America to furniture design has been cigaret burns and price tags.

Those who preferred to be entertained outdoors also found much to their liking. Streetcars took visitors to enjoy the carnival rides at Ramona Park on Reeds Lake in East Grand Rapids, and the adjacent Ramona Theater. The interurban train carried furniture men to picnics and day outings at Lake Michigan beaches. Golf tournaments and "Furniture Field Days" were held at area country clubs. Robert W. Irwin, owner of the Robert W. Irwin Furniture Company, hosted large hunting and fishing trips to his cabin on the Pere Marquette River. Alexander "Skipper" Hompe, owner of the Royal Furniture Company, entertained clients while sailing on Lake Macatawa.

In 1917 the manufacturers' sales representatives organized a salesmen's club. In 1933 they reorganized as an adjunct to the Exposition Association,

A Grand Rapids showroom interior, ca. 1925.

Frank J. Davidhazy, head of the hand-decorative painting department for the Robert W. Irwin Furniture Co., reproduced paintings for the showrooms as part of his job. After designers told him the historical periods of the new lines to be introduced, he worked from plates in books to hand-paint facsimiles of classic works of art from those periods. These were then used as room decor in the showroom. During one Market, he received a phone call at home in the evening. It was a salesman, telling him that his painting had helped to sell a big order. In fact, the buyer thought that it set the mood so well, he convinced the salesman to give it to him off the wall, to take home and hang in his own store! Left with a blank spot in the display, the salesman called Davidhazy and asked him to produce another before the showroom opened the following day. When morning came the new painting was on the wall, still a bit wet to the touch.

calling themselves The Furniture Salesmen's Club of the Grand Rapids Furniture Exposition. The Club's by-laws described its purpose as combatting unethical sales practices and elevating selling to a higher standard of performance. However, most of the Club's funds and energies were poured into planning and executing entertainment for the visiting furniture men during Market. Its funding came from individual and company membership dues, and the profits of its annual Furniture Frolic Ball. Formal events like banquets and the Ball were attended by the dealers, salesmen, and company owners who brought their wives and daughters for an evening of polite socializing. Those who attended remember the Furniture Frolic Balls as highlights of the Grand Rapids social calendar.

The goal to keep buyers coming back was an important one during the Great Depression. As Market attendance decreased in the 1930s, the Exposition Association began looking for ways to continue enthusiasm for furniture buying. In 1936 they sponsored a large celebration called the "Centennial of Furniture." It marked the hundredth anniversary of the arrival in Grand Rapids of "Deacon" Haldane, the small-scale cabinetmaker whom they proclaimed the "father of the furniture industry." Depression-weary Grand Rapidians celebrated a century of furniture making with more than thirty floats, sponsored by furniture companies and civic groups, parading through the streets of downtown.

A companion event, billed as a mammoth spectacle, "The Romance of Furniture" was a dramatic tableau performed at Houseman Field on the city's Northeast side. Hundreds of costumed furniture workers portrayed great events in furniture history, beginning with the discovery of the chair by a caveman. The great saga continued with throngs of worshipping Babylonians and Queen Elizabeth on her throne. Many of the re-created events were meant to be silly and entertaining, but the timeline progressed ever upward, until it ended with furniture making in Grand Rapids at the highest point of achievement.

In 1936 the city of Grand Rapids and the Exposition Association together opened the Grand Rapids Furniture Museum, in a large Tudor Revival house overlooking downtown. Reproduction pieces representing various stylistic periods were lent by local manufacturers, and mixed with genuine historical pieces in room settings. The purpose of the Museum was twofold: to educate Market attenders and the general public about furniture styles and the history of furniture making, and to validate Grand Rapids as part of that history. It lasted until 1960, when the Market was in its final years. At that time, the loans were returned, and almost five hundred historical pieces of furniture were transferred to the Grand Rapids Public Museum. The building still stands, as part of the Davenport College campus.

Souvenirs Proclaim City's Identity

When Market was over and the dealers left Grand Rapids, they carried with them the identity of Grand Rapids as "The Furniture City." This nickname came into common use during the 1890s, when furniture first became the city's leading industry. Grand Rapids adopted the Furniture City flag, with its bellowing smokestacks symbolizing prosperity, as the official civic flag in 1896. Many businessmen followed suit and adopted "Furniture City" for their companies' names, even if they had no direct connection to the making of furniture. Visitors could sip a brew from the Furniture City Brewing Company, attend a meeting of The Furniture City Elks Lodge No. 48, have their suits pressed by the Furniture City Cleaners and Dyers, or enjoy the sounds of the Furniture City Band. They brought their families souvenirs ranging from playing cards and post cards to silver spoons and commemorative plates, decorated with cornucopias overflowing with chairs and puffing smokestacks, all bearing the nickname "The Furniture City."

A second nickname for Grand Rapids, "The Furniture Capital of America," was used by groups like the Chamber of Commerce and the Market Association beginning in the late 1920s. Its appeal to civic leaders was that it described Grand Rapids not simply as a place that made furniture, but as the center of the industry in America. However, it never caught on with the local or visiting public.

The Market Declines

According to Howard Silbar's *Notes on the Furniture Industry of Grand Rapids: 1836 - 1964*, the number of buyers attending Market rose fairly steadily throughout the 1910s and '20s, from 2,500 in 1914 to 4,800 in 1925, and more than 6,000 for the Centennial Market in 1928. Spring and fall exhibits were added in 1926, increasing Grand Rapids' schedule from two to four Markets a year. In 1943, government restrictions on materials and consumption due to the war effort reduced the need back to two annual Markets. After World War II there was some resurgence in the Grand Rapids Market, following the favorable economy of the 1950s and the demand for home furnishings during the baby boom. In 1953 the city celebrated the "Diamond Jubilee," or seventy-fifth year of the Grand Rapids Market.

Yet the Market steadily lost influence. One reason for this decline was the decrease in the number of residential companies based in Grand Rapids. As a greater percentage of America's furniture, particularly in the lower and middle market ranges, began to be produced in Virginia and the Carolinas, the attention of many dealers was drawn to this new center of the industry. By the time of the Diamond Jubilee only two structures remained as exhibition buildings in downtown Grand Rapids. Many companies moved their showrooms from Grand Rapids to the Southern Market in High Point, North Carolina. Most of the companies that continued to maintain showrooms at the Grand Rapids Market focused on the higher end of the consumer range. Eventually even the Grand Rapids manufacturers opened secondary showrooms at High Point, or closed their Grand Rapids showrooms altogether. Others chose to operate a number of regional showrooms year-round, in cities like New York, Chicago, Los Angeles, Atlanta, and Dallas.

Market Guides from the final Grand Rapids Furniture Markets of the early 1960s show no more than two dozen high-end companies still exhibiting in Grand Rapids. In 1965, with ever-declining numbers of exhibitors and buyers, the Grand Rapids Furniture Market Association decided to discontinue the exhibition in Grand Rapids. The remaining companies scrambled to find space in the exhibition buildings of High Point. After eighty-seven years of selling style, the Grand Rapids Furniture Market came to an end.

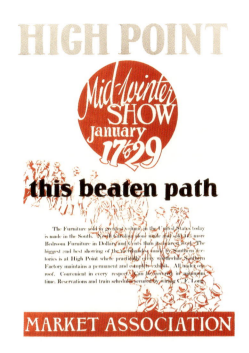

Many aspects of today's Furniture Market in High Point, North Carolina bear a striking resemblance to the one previously held for so many years in Grand Rapids.

The FURNITURE MANUFACTURER and ARTISAN

38TH YEAR
VOL. 76 No. 5

NEW SERIES
VOL. 15 No. 5

WOMEN as FACTORY WORKERS

MAY 1918

SUBSCRIPTION
$ 2.00 PER YEAR

SINGLE COPIES
20 CENTS

In the 1920s, changing economic conditions and growing competition began to threaten Grand Rapids' place of prominence in the furniture industry. Manufacturers tried new designs and sales techniques in an effort to maintain their position and their share of the market.

Transitions: Grand Rapids Furniture Matures

Grand Rapids' original advantages had been its supplies of lumber, cheap labor, and investments in technology. But beginning in the 1920s, other parts of the country, especially North Carolina, enjoyed some of the same advantages. Michigan's old-growth forests had largely been cut, forcing Grand Rapids manufacturers to import lumber. Southern forests had only begun to be harvested, and were fast becoming a leading source of the nation's lumber, reducing Southern furniture manufacturers' costs for raw materials.

Furniture workers' wages in Michigan had increased considerably, partly due to the rise in auto workers' pay. Furniture companies were forced to increase their wages or lose their best workers. The automotive industry ushered in a new wave of unionization, which also increased wages. New manufacturers in the South found labor costs to be lower, since there were relatively few unions or competing companies.

Grand Rapids manufacturers had chosen to focus on producing higher-quality, more expensive furniture, which took considerable skilled handwork. Wages for skilled workers were higher than for unskilled machinists, so the cost of doing business went up. North Carolina furniture was mostly inexpensive and machine-made, just like Grand Rapids furniture had been a generation earlier. This, too, made Southern labor costs lower.

By the 1920s, many of Grand Rapids' factories were growing old. Some of the largest plants, approaching half a century of use, were oversized and inefficient. Most were built on multiple levels, which were less practical for assembly-line production than one single level. Much of their machinery was just as old, making it slower than newer models, and costlier to repair.

Even some of the management of Grand Rapids companies was showing signs of old age. Since many of the companies were family-owned, they depended on having another generation of male children to take over. By the 1910s and '20s many of the aggressive, risk-taking founders of Grand Rapids' leading companies were reaching retirement age. Some families groomed the next generation by sending their sons for schooling in business at the University of Michigan or the Ivy League, then having them take their expected positions within the company. But some had only daughters, who were expected to marry money rather than generate it themselves.

OPPOSITE: The first and second World Wars impacted Grand Rapids' furniture industry in many ways, one being a greater acceptance of women as factory workers. While many of the men left to fight for their country, women stepped into their jobs in the furniture plants, continuing production for civilian use, and manufacturing goods for the war effort. When the men returned, some of the women kept their jobs, leading the industry to a more diversified work force. Cover, *The Furniture Manufacturer and Artisan*, May, 1918.

ABOVE: As the twentieth century progressed, competition from Southern states for home furnishings market share increased. North Carolina and its neighbors built their own industry on many of the same advantages that allowed Grand Rapids to succeed: available lumber, cheap labor, and investment in new technology. Advertisement from *The Furniture Manufacturer and Artisan*, April, 1924.

CHICAGO
The Furniture Market of Greatest Convenience to the Greatest Number

CHICAGO is the greatest furniture market in the country, because it is the market place of greatest convenience to the greatest number—the only centrally located, mutually accessible market place where *the merchant* may find the widest opportunities for selection and purchase, coupled with ample provision for his personal comfort—where he may find the most highly perfected machinery for doing business and the most inviting diversions for his leisure hours—where he may, in fact, find all the material requisites of a great national wholesale market amid surroundings that best contribute to his wellbeing, both as a merchant and as a man.

Midsummer Exhibition Opens July First

CHICAGO anticipates with pleasure the great gathering of Furniture Merchants within her gates *during the month of July* and assures them of a most cordial welcome and every convenience for their profit, comfort and entertainment.

Ample Hotel Accommodations in Chicago

The Grand Rapids Furniture Market faced stiff competition. Chicago also held a national, semi-annual furniture market, which had begun in 1891. Chicago was easier for buyers to reach than Grand Rapids, and had more and better hotels and exhibition buildings. Despite Grand Rapids' concerted efforts at advertising its market, some of its firms moved their primary showrooms to Chicago. The Chicago Market eventually out-drew all other furniture markets in the country.

But by the time Grand Rapids held its last Market in 1964, it was clear that the residential furniture market in High Point, North Carolina would ascend to the throne. High Point had held a small regional market for years, and it grew with the Southern industry. By the mid-1950s, the Grand Rapids Market had shrunk so much that its promoters could no longer pretend it was the primary national market, and by the early 1960s virtually no manufacturers outside of Grand Rapids maintained showrooms there any longer. Even most of the remaining local companies had secondary showrooms at High Point or Chicago. The cancellation of the 1965 Grand Rapids Market created little disruption for the city's manufacturers. It did however, strike a blow to the city's claim to the title of "The Furniture Capital of America." Advertisement for the Chicago Market in *The Grand Rapids Furniture Record*, June, 1912.

Others had sons who showed no interest in the family business, and abdicated their birthrights. Some willing sons accepted directorship of their companies, but were not suitable leaders. Still other owners produced no heirs at all, and were forced to sell upon their retirement. Mrs. Clarence (Foote) Dexter, daughter of the owner of the Imperial Furniture Company, reflected on this predicament in a 1971 oral history interview now in the collections of the Grand Rapids Public Library:

> . . . in many cases there were no sons to carry on the business. Now while my father . . . built the Imperial, he had no sons that were interested in carrying that on so we sold it and that was the case in many of the factories. After the original leaders died the factories were liquidated and sold [to] outside corporations. Now Mr. Robert Irwin of the [Robert W.] Irwin Furniture Company had no sons to carry on. It was very pathetic, because if they had had sons that were more interested and were capable of carrying on the business I think the industry would have stayed intact longer. . . .

North Carolina steadily grew to become the leading producer of furniture for the middle- and lower-end markets, which Grand Rapids had given up in its effort to improve quality. By 1945 more than half the country's residential furniture came from factories in the South. Even though few Grand Rapids companies actually moved or built Southern plants, the percentage of Grand Rapidians employed in making furniture decreased because of the competition.

The Great Depression struck another crushing blow to Grand Rapids' furniture industry. Even when disposable incomes were on the rise during the 1920s, the furniture industry had begun to slide. An article entitled "Furniture Pieces Increase, Prices Drop," from the January, 1927 *Furniture Manufacturer and Artisan*, sounded the alarm that all was not well. It indicated that the increase in production had out-paced the nation's needs for new furniture. As a result, more furniture was being produced than ever before, but wholesale prices and manufacturers' profits were also lower than ever before. The article quoted the Bureau of Labor Statistics for 1925, which calculated that "prices received for furniture made in 1925 [were] only 44 percent more than in 1913, although labor, materials and overhead [were] approximately 108 percent more."

After the stock market crashed in 1929, and millions of Americans were thrown out of work, disposable income was greatly reduced. Families had to spend their precious dollars on food and other essentials, so the decision to postpone redecorating the dining room was an easy one. Grand Rapids' chief products became unattainable luxuries. According to historian Frank Ransom's *The City Built on Wood*, national furniture production between 1926 and 1929 had already declined to 86% of the 1923 - 1925 average, and by 1932, production had plunged to a mere 25.6%. Suddenly finding themselves deeply in debt from expansion in the early 1920s, many Grand Rapids furniture companies failed.

Berkey & Gay, the largest furniture manufacturer in the city, had been around since the early days of the Grand Rapids furniture industry. When it closed its doors in 1931 the city's people were stunned. The company had expanded aggressively throughout the 1920s, until it encompassed five plants covering one and a half million square feet. When the market crashed in 1929, Berkey & Gay was unable to make payments on the debt from these expansions. A majority of shares in Berkey & Gay stock were sold to the Simmons Company, a rival from Chicago. After two years of continuously falling sales, the new owner declared the company bankrupt and closed its doors. The remaining local stockholders sued Simmons over the closing. In 1934 they received two million dollars, at that time the largest civil suit award in American history. Berkey & Gay re-opened under the management of these shareholders in 1935, but never regained its former position as an industry leader. In 1948 Berkey & Gay's local owners closed the factory for the final time.

Census of Manufactures figures for 1929 and 1940 show that Berkey & Gay's failure was far from an isolated occurrence in Grand Rapids. Of seventy-two furniture companies operating before the market crash, only forty-seven, or two-thirds, remained after a decade of economic malaise. In the remaining factories, the number of employees fell from more than twelve thousand in 1929 to under three thousand in 1940. In *The Reorientation of the Grand Rapids Furniture Industry in the Twentieth Century*, Kirk Vredevelt determined that Grand Rapids' average furniture wage plummeted from sixty-three cents per hour in 1929 to just thirty-three cents in 1933.

Partly because of the reduction in wages, hours, and jobs, and partly because of the rising dominance of the automobile industry in Michigan, labor unrest and strikes increased during the 1930s. A strike was launched in May of 1937 against three companies associated with the Irwin family: Irwin Seating Company, Robert W. Irwin Company, and the Macey Company. Robert Irwin had become a spokesperson for the furniture industry on a national level, and his opposition to New Deal initiatives had made him a highly visible target for union efforts. When the work stoppage began, management immediately retaliated with a court injunction banning picketing.

One month into the strike, the workers abided by the court order in exchange for management's agreement to negotiate. The resulting agreement allowed the companies to resume production in exchange for granting workers the right to organize, a modest wage increase contingent on sales, overtime pay, and job protection for unionized workers. Emboldened by their partial success, employees of other Grand Rapids factories attempted similar strikes. But the Depression had left workers without cash reserves, and most returned to work without concessions after only a few weeks.

Faced with such challenges, the city's manufacturers again turned toward collaboration, with efforts like the Grand Rapids Furniture Makers Guild, as a means to gain advantage over their competitors. The formation of the Guild in 1931 accomplished several goals: it provided a new avenue for marketing Grand Rapids furniture during the Depression; it ensured that a large number of retail dealers would consistently carry Grand Rapids goods; it educated the general public about style and craftsmanship in furniture; and it advanced the reputation of Grand Rapids as the place where high-quality furnishings were made.

Initially composed of nine Grand Rapids companies, the Guild cooperatively marketed products from each of its members through exclusive Guild

One effort to encourage sales reminded everyone associated with Grand Rapids of the enormous hardship its residents endured. In the early 1930s, a parade wound through the streets of the city with floats urging onlookers to "Buy to Increase Employment." The furniture manufacturers were represented by a series of flat-bed trucks carrying suites of furniture. A truck carrying a dining table and chairs informed viewers that "The purchase of this dining room outfit furnishes work for 29 men for one day," while another topped by a bed and dresser stated that thirty-two men would be supplied with work if someone purchased that suite.

Grand Rapids Goes Hollywood

During the Depression and World War II era, Americans found an escape at the movies. Spectacular sets and exotic locations captured movie-goers' imaginations, allowing them to forget their own hardships. Ordinary people became obsessed with Hollywood stars, and dreamed that they could live such glamorous lives. Grand Rapids played a role in the Hollywood fantasy. From the early 1930s through the mid-1940s, *The Stylist* magazine maintained an arrangement with Metro-Goldwyn-Mayer to publish photos of the studio's contracted stars. Often they were shown in their homes, or in room settings furnished by the Grand Rapids Furniture Makers Guild. Lucille Ball, Spencer Tracy, Clark Gable, Jeanette MacDonald, Lana Turner, Hedy Lamarr, Van Johnson, Don Ameche, Tyrone Power, and other legends of the silver screen were elegantly photographed, relaxing on their sofas or entertaining in their dining rooms. Readers were left with the impression that these actors cared deeply about their homes, and that they filled them with Grand Rapids furniture.

Lucille Ball in an MGM film set. *The Stylist*, **Fall, 1944.**

Some Grand Rapids designers left Michigan to work for motion picture studios in California. Movie set designers from the major studios routinely attended the Grand Rapids Furniture Market to purchase props for their latest productions. Frank Vander Ley was part owner of a small family-run company that made upholstered Victorian Revival furniture. In an interview for the May 5, 1974 issue of the *Grand Rapids Press*, he recalled an encounter with a studio designer during Market: "One afternoon a man walked into the showroom, and before I could get my pad

dealers across the nation. According to Ransom, the number of Guild retailers grew quickly, reaching 222 by 1937. Every piece of furniture sold by a Guild dealer was registered by number, and marked with a special tag identifying it as "Guild certified." When the piece was purchased, the consumer received a certificate proving its authenticity and listing its pedigree.

The Guild offered its dealers a number of services. Manufacturers of home decorating products such as wallpaper, paint, carpeting, lighting, and household accessories were licensed to produce official Guild lines to be sold in association with Guild furniture. Advertising art and copy were distributed to dealers for their local newspaper ads. Retailers were allowed to distribute complimentary copies of *The Stylist: A Magazine for the Homemaker* to their customers. Published by the Guild from 1932 until 1967, *The Stylist* offered tips on home decorating in both modern and traditional styles.

Furniture made by Guild factories was prominently marketed through the magazine's articles. Makers were referred to only as "Grand Rapids Furniture Makers Guild member companies."

Guild companies also attempted to boost sales by providing furnishings for Hollywood, since many people sought an escape at the movies during these difficult times. Stars of the silver screen were elegantly photographed in room settings filled with Grand Rapids furniture, and movie set designers often furnished their sets with pieces purchased at the Grand Rapids Furniture Market.

The founding of Kendall College of Art and Design by the widow of David Wolcott Kendall in 1928 made Grand Rapids a leading producer of furniture designers. As furniture factories reduced their work forces, some Grand Rapids designers left to work for motion picture studios in California.

A New Look for a New Tomorrow

Another attempt to stimulate sales of new furniture was the radical shift on the part of some manufacturers from European revival styles to the new, sleek-looking Art Moderne, or Art Deco. As over-production caused a sales slump in the mid-1920s, manufacturers hoped that the style's rich materials would appeal to the increasingly affluent middle classes. Grand Rapids furniture publications had followed with interest the development of the style since it was thrust upon the world stage at the Exposition Internationale des Arts Décoratifs et Industriels Modernes in Paris in 1925. Many industrial designers in this country admired the clean, sensual lines, cubist geometry, and combination of exotic natural and new synthetic materials. But revivalism had become so deeply entrenched in American minds that Art Deco was slow in gaining acceptance.

One of the first American manufacturers to introduce a line of Art Deco furniture was Baker Furniture, Inc. of Grand Rapids. Baker's 1925 Grand Rapids Furniture Market showrooms included the "Twentieth Century Shop," which pre-dated New York's introduction of the style by several years. The showroom was outfitted with room settings of furniture in rosewood and olive burl. Josef Urban designed a rectilinear bedroom group of bubinga wood (a dark rosewood) with silver-plated hardware for Baker. Urban had received his training from the Wiener Werkstatte in Austria before immigrating to America, where he became chief designer for the Metropolitan Opera in New York.

In the early 1930s Baker also produced Art Deco furniture designed by American Donald Deskey, who in 1932 created the spectacular interiors of New York City's Radio City Music Hall. The front page of the *Grand Rapids Press* for January 9, 1930, proclaimed the introduction of several lines of tubular steel and rattan furniture designed by Deskey for the Ypsilanti Reed Furniture Company of nearby Ionia, Michigan. The writer, Sidney B. Coates, tried to convince the reader of the furniture's merit, and to reassure that its startling appearance was within the bounds of good taste:

> At first glance this new furniture, which the word "contemporary" best describes, finds no kindred note in furniture conception. It resembles the moderne French, but the atmosphere is distinctly different. It is strictly American. . . .
>
> This contemporary furniture and its contemporary surroundings are the conceptions of the modern designer, Donald Deskey of New York City, who made them for Ypsilanti.
>
> In them he has done with metal, rayon, wood, windows, lamps and reed what Gershwin has done in music with chords and sequences that mirror the life of a great city.

The *1933 Bulletin of Progress*, produced for the summer Grand Rapids Furniture Exposition, described two new bedroom suites designed by Deskey for the Widdicomb Furniture Company. Deskey also designed for the Luce Furniture Company of Grand Rapids and the Estey Manufacturing Company of Owosso, Michigan, during this same period.

In 1928, Grand Rapids' Johnson Furniture Company commissioned David Robertson Smith, who twenty years previously had created Arts and Crafts designs for Stickley Brothers, to design its first Art Moderne line, which it called "Dynamique Creations." The company described Dynamique as the first complete line of Moderne offered in this country. Smith was influenced by leading French designers like Emile-Jacques Ruhlmann, Pierre Chareau, and Nics Frères, though many of his creations are nearly contemporary with theirs.

Dynamique catalogs in the collections of The Public Museum of Grand Rapids reveal a wide range of forms, including tall vertical bookcases and stair-stepped secretaries reminiscent of Paul Frankl's famous "skyscraper" furniture. A series of occasional tables supported by bold U-shaped or cyma-curved bases rest on architectural plinths, like those Deskey designed for Radio City Music Hall. Small magazine stands and coffee tables create abstract sculptures of planes and volumes, using asymmetrically placed circles, rectangles, and angular cut-outs.

Pieces were offered in high-gloss natural finishes over exotic veneers. Desks and tables were accented with green formica, swirled plastic, ivory leather, or mirrored glass tops. Several color combinations produced with stains, lacquers, and enamel paints predominated in shades of green, coral, mauve, black, gold, and silver. Most were sparsely decorated, although the silver was often used in repeating leaf patterns on small stools and book-

Clark Gable's Home, featured in *The Stylist*, Early Fall, 1936.

out he was saying, 'I'll take two of those and two of those and two of those. . . .' I'll never forget it. He ordered $20,000.00 of Victorian furniture in about 45 minutes—the largest single sale I ever made. He was from Warner Brothers, and he wanted the furniture for the set of 'Gone With the Wind.' Clark Gable and Vivian [sic] Leigh sat on Vander Ley furniture."

In some ways this was the ultimate triumph for Grand Rapids' reproducers of antiques. Whereas one might expect that the logical place to buy Southern Victorian antiques during

Vander Ley Brothers Victorian armchair, ca. 1940. Courtesy, Mrs. Esther Vander Ley.

the Depression would have been in the South, where set designers could have bought the real things at bargain prices from financially strapped plantation owners, they instead thought first of Grand Rapids.

German-born, Los Angeles-based architect and industrial designer Kem Weber was contracted to design Moderne lines for a number of Grand Rapids manufacturers. The Grand Rapids Chair Co. introduced "The Kem Weber Group" in 1928, which featured light horizontal planes divided by thin dark bands, rounded corners, and striking combinations of color. A group of all-over upholstered pieces designed by Weber was shown by Baker Furniture, Inc. in its 1936 showrooms. That year Weber also produced designs for a line of multi-planed coffee tables, end tables with radios, and waterfall nesting tables for Berkey & Gay Furniture Co., but the line was never produced.

Perhaps the most significant of Weber's Grand Rapids contracts was for the Fleetwood Line, introduced by the Mueller Furniture Co. in 1936. The line included tables, desks, chairs, and sofas, either fully upholstered with geometric print fabrics or made of plywood with mahogany, maple, and applewood veneers. Also included was a production version of Weber's classic "Airline Chair," which he originally designed for the Airline Chair Co. of Los Angeles in 1934. Its design is streamlined and aerodynamic, giving the impression that the form was shaped by the flow of air in a wind tunnel. Whereas the Airline chair featured a contoured plywood seat and backrest, the Fleetwood chair had a straight back and seat. The Airline Chair was sold in a box, its simple design allowing for easy assembly. The Fleetwood Chair was likely sold assembled, though its long, sliding dovetail construction was also easy to put together.

Mueller's Fleetwood line, from the Summer, 1936 *Market Ambassador.*

stands. Upholstery fabrics ranged from gold and silver satins to cubist geometric prints. New designs were continuously introduced from 1928 through 1935.

Johnson's Dynamique furniture was sumptuous and daring, but not universally appreciated. For those who found its sleek lines too severe, Johnson continued to produce and sell traditional Colonial Revival designs concurrently with its Moderne group, as did most Grand Rapids factories. The daughter of company owner Carl Gustav Johnson was one such customer. Pauline (Johnson) Heggie was a young girl in 1928 when her father took her to the factory showroom one day to select a suite of furniture for her bedroom. She remembered how he told her on the way that she could choose any set she saw, confident that she would be mesmerized by his stunning new Dynamique designs. But when she picked one of the oldest and least expensive Colonial Revival suites instead, her father could not bear to keep his promise. When Mrs. Heggie donated to the Public Museum the bedroom suite she had received but never liked as a young girl, she recalled:

Dynamique gentleman's dresser, 1928.

> I didn't get the one I wanted. [Father] was so proud of his new line that I got this instead. It was a heck of a thing to put in a little girl's room!

As the Depression dragged on, some manufacturers sold the idea that life would become easier in the near future, using modern furniture and advancements in technology. In 1936 the Grand Rapids Gas Light Company built the "All Gas Wonder House" to promote its products. The display house's large glass windows and International styling contrasted with its suburban East Grand Rapids neighborhood of Tudor and Colonial homes. Local manufacturers provided futuristic furnishings, to give the impression that someday all homes would be improved with natural gas as their energy source. The dining suite selected for the house may have been produced by the Hastings Table Company. Its angular silhouettes, striking green and red colors, and industrial-looking chrome-plated steel hardware were all intended as symbols of a brighter, more efficient future.

Until 1927, the Herman Miller Furniture Company and its predecessor, the Michigan Star Furniture Company, had produced ornate, wooden, period revival bedroom suites, like most of the other companies in West Michigan. But after company president D. J. DePree saw an exhibition of French Art Deco furniture in 1927, the conservative son of Dutch immigrants began to think more about the virtues of modernism. Herman Miller introduced its first "Modern French" suite that same year, made from Honduran mahogany and sequoia burl with ivory inlay.

But the company's real conversion to modernism came in the summer of 1930, when, faced with falling sales, DePree was approached in his Market showroom by a young New York industrial designer named Gilbert Rohde. Rohde suggested that DePree change his company's entire attitude toward design. Looking ahead, DePree saw that Herman Miller was underfinanced, and no more than a year away from bankruptcy, so he accepted the proposal.

Rohde's first designs for Herman Miller debuted at the Chicago Century of Progress Exhibition in 1933. The pieces were sleek, simple, and aerodynamic, with chromium-plated hardware and inlaid horizontal stripes as the only decoration. Through Herman Miller, Rohde was able to reach an audience with his ideas for improved living. Through Rohde, Herman Miller was able to offer products that were different from those of other manufacturers.

Rohde also designed the first modern clocks offered by the Howard Miller Clock Company, the "next-door neighbor" of Herman Miller in Zeeland, Michigan. Made of glass and chrome-plated steel, and battery-operated, they were also introduced in Chicago in 1933. In his designs for Herman Miller, Rohde was one of the first American designers to combine wood with such industrial materials as steel, chrome, glass, plastic, and bakelite. By 1934 Rohde had also convinced the company to begin manufacturing upholstered goods. He invented the concept of the modular sofa, with upholstered sections that could be strung together as a single unit.

Modern-style furniture gradually gained acceptance with consumers. According to Ransom, fully one-third of the Hekman Furniture Company's factory was turned over to the production of modern designs by 1939. For some, the percentage was much higher. Herman Miller continued to decrease its traditional production in favor of modern until 1945, one year after Gilbert Rohde's death, when all traditional designs had been phased out. By the end of the 1940s, a veritable "Who's Who" of modernists had created lines for Grand Rapids companies. Grand Rapids had, in turn, taken modernism to the masses.

Colonial Traditionalism Symbolizes Security

The Colonial Revival style also struck a chord with Americans during the difficult years of the Depression and second World War. Where Modernism had pointed the way to an easier future through technology and change, Colonial Revival provided comfort through timeless tradition and continuity. Colonial furniture and its first cousin, Early American, convinced buyers that since their hardy forefathers had endured hardships through a life of rugged yet honest simplicity, so could they. The economy of the furniture's construction and its lack of non-essential ornamentation reassured buyers that the purchase was not frivolous. The Colonial Revival of Grand Rapids manufacturers from the 1930s and '40s focused narrowly on eighteenth-century American versions of Georgian furniture.

Two important projects during the 1930s had a tremendous impact on the buying public's interest in Colonial Revival. The first was John D. Rockefeller Jr.'s restoration of the entire city of Colonial Williamsburg to its eighteenth-century appearance. The restoration was extensively pictured in print media, inspiring a generation of Americans to create their own Williamsburg interiors. According to David Gebhard's article, "The American Colonial Revival in the 1930s" from vol. 22 of *Winterthur Portfolio*, consumers could, by the mid-1930s, purchase Williamsburg-inspired furniture, china, silver, paints, fabrics, wallpapers, and lighting.

The HOUSE *of* TOMORROW

INTRODUCING the All Gas Wonder House—the first pre-fabricated steel house of its type to be built in Michigan.

Designed by Howard T. Fisher, architect and pioneer developer of this type of home, with General Homes, Inc., of Chicago—the All-Gas-Wonder-House has been erected at Alexander Road and Cambridge Boulevard by Owen-Ames-Kimball, builders, employing Grand Rapids labor and using Grand Rapids supplied materials.

In plan, construction and treatment throughout, the house is an interesting example of authentic modern architecture and the successful use of new and special materials. It is completely insulated against cold, heat and noise—it is fire-proof, termite-proof, gas heated and air conditioned and equipped throughout with all modern gas conveniences.

The dwelling contains eight rooms, three baths and a two-car garage—recreation room and complete laundry in basement. All of the closets are lined with cedar—no plaster is used, all walls and ceilings are of sheet-rock—a Grand Rapids product.

It is open for public display for a period of one year.

Architects drawings and floor plans are shown in this issue—a full description of the interior with actual photographs will be shown in the next issue (Spring, 1936) of the Grand Rapids Mirror.

ABOVE: Intersecting cubist planes of walnut, bird's-eye maple, and glass, with circular shapes of brushed steel and bakelite, made this bedroom dressing table, designed by Gilbert Rohde for Herman Miller in 1936, a radical departure from the furniture to which consumers of Grand Rapids furniture had become accustomed. BELOW: During the first three decades of the twentieth century, much was learned by designers, architects, and the general public about authentic attributes of historical styles. Books and magazines provided a great body of examples. Designers at Johnson Furniture Co. clipped hundreds of images from printed sources and placed them on the pages of scrapbooks like the one below according to form categories such as tables, chairs, beds, desks, and sideboards. Designers consulted these scrapbooks in their attempts to represent details accurately.

A feature article from the Early Fall, 1937 issue of *The Stylist*, entitled "Pictures from the Past: Colonial Williamsburg," demonstrates that once again, Grand Rapids was quick to turn this consumer interest into a marketing opportunity. Photos show reproduction furniture in room settings at Williamsburg's Colonial Capitol, Governor's Palace, and Raleigh's Tavern. The article stresses the American-ness and authenticity of the restoration:

> *Not even our severest critics can deny that North Americans have imagination of a sort it is difficult to match anywhere else. And the restoration of Williamsburg, seat of government of the Colony of Virginia during the 18th Century, evidences that this trait can be put to practical use. . . . No detail has been overlooked, no matter how minute, to make this restoration faithful and authentic in every important respect.*

The feature article in the preceding Summer issue, "About Time YOU Changed YOUR Dining Room Furniture," focused on several eighteenth-century mahogany and walnut dining suites made in Grand Rapids. The following Autumn issue's feature article, "A Delightful Living ROOM in Traditional Style and Feeling," gave hints on eighteenth-century principles of proportion. Its illustrations showed Grand Rapids-made wing chairs, Sheraton and Chippendale occasional tables, a Duncan Phyfe sofa, and a gilded looking glass. A direct connection between the article on Williamsburg and those on Grand Rapids furniture was never made, but was left to the readers' "ability to recognize that which is beautiful and fine."

The second project was Henry Ford's creation of Greenfield Village in Dearborn, near Detroit, Michigan. By purchasing and moving to a single site historic American buildings, and creating new replicas of such icons as Independence Hall, he created a romanticized ideal of a colonial village. Inside the houses, and the cavernous Edison Institute, Ford displayed literally acres of early American antiques. These were accessible to the visiting public, and also to Grand Rapids furniture designers who lived just a few hours to the west.

Colonial furniture reminded Americans of a simpler lifestyle, and it could be very simple to produce. The sparing use of ornamentation in American versions of William and Mary, Queen Anne, Chippendale, Federal, and Duncan Phyfe furniture meant that manufacturers could still make durable, high-quality pieces, but at a lower production cost than highly ornamented European revival styles. Some companies, like the Robert W. Irwin Furniture Company, made uncharacteristic forays into producing inexpensive furniture based on more costly Colonial lines. Irwin's "Pendleton Line," launched in 1940, provided simplified versions of traditional, eighteenth-century furniture at a reduced price. It also offered its furniture as patriotic symbols, at a time when America stood on the brink of war.

Other companies, like Baker, built their reputations almost entirely on high-quality, eighteenth-century mahogany reproductions. Baker's catalogs from the 1930s and '40s listed the provenance for every single reproduction. While many were from England or from Hollis Baker's famous collection, many others came from American museums like the Essex Institute in Salem, Massachusetts, the Cooper Union Museum and the Metropolitan Museum of Art in New York City, Israel Sack's galleries in Boston, and private collections in Virginia, Pennsylvania, and New York. Others were adapted from illustrations in Wallace Nutting's *Furniture Treasury*, or L.V. Lockwood's *Colonial Furniture in America*.

The Furniture City Goes to War

Just as the nation's economy and the outlook for the Grand Rapids furniture industry were beginning to improve, both were thrust into preparation for World War II. According to Richard Harms and Robert Viol's *Grand Rapids Goes to War: The 1940s Homefront*, Grand Rapids residents began enlisting for military service in November of 1940. By the end of the war, more than 30,000 residents of the Grand Rapids region would leave their homes and jobs for military service. As had been the case during World War I, most of the individuals who went off to fight were men, and many of those who took their places in the factories were women.

As early as the 1880s some factories had hired women to do decorative painting, caning, finishing, and sewing of upholstery. During World War I, when many male employees were called to serve in the military, factories hired women to fill their positions, but the factories were not welcoming places for women to work. Some companies were reluctant to add separate bathrooms and changing areas for women, or believed their presence would be too distracting for the men. Long dresses, loose blouses, and high heels were ill-suited for operating woodworking machinery, so women had to alter their wardrobes for factory work.

As World War I progressed, factory owners found, to their delight, that their factories ran as smoothly with largely female work forces as they had with mostly men. And, since women were routinely paid less than men, owners obtained the same quality of work for less money. When the men came home after the war, most were able to return to their jobs, and most of the women resumed their roles at home. But some female employees who chose to stay on were permitted to do so. Women had gained a foothold in the male-dominated factories.

When America began to increase its homefront production during World War II, Grand Rapids' women again stepped into their husbands' and brothers' jobs in the furniture factories. Berkey & Gay even opened a recruiting station downtown, to hire women for assembly line positions in its factory. Most companies continued to produce furniture, particularly firms like American Seating Company, The Macey Company, and the Metal Office Furniture Company (Steelcase), which had to add employees and shifts to fill large contracts for metal drafting tables, desks, folding chairs, file cabinets, and bunk beds for various branches of the military. But as the war languished, the use of wood for civilian manufacturing was curtailed and the use of metal prohibited. For those companies that depended on metal, government contracts became their only sources of income.

In 1943 the city's furniture industry began to reconvert to civilian production. By the end of 1945, it became clear that the pent-up need to buy furniture after fifteen years of depression and war, combined with the increased number of marriages and new homes under construction, meant prosperity for furniture makers. *Census of Manufactures* figures show that the number of Grand Rapids furniture companies nearly doubled, from forty-

Grand Rapids Industries

Companies that made wooden furniture continued limited civilian production during the war. But most plants stopped making traditional residential furniture and converted to wartime production. According to Harms and Viol, this conversion began in 1940; by the end of the next year, local firms had received $10 million in government contracts. In 1942, Grand Rapids factories were awarded contracts worth another $96 million.

Because the largest companies received the largest government contracts for wartime production, seventeen medium-sized Grand Rapids furniture factories joined together to form Grand Rapids Industries. GRI handled contract bidding, ordered materials, and allocated production among its plants. This new organization represented thousands of workers and millions of square feet of production capacity, so its firms were awarded more government contracts, and GRI was upheld as a model for factories in other cities.

GRI plants made a host of wooden products that were necessary for the war effort. Using existing woodworking machinery, they made ship furniture, airplane propellers, mortar shell boxes, gunstocks for M-1 carbines, and even portable housing. Much of GRI's production was devoted to making components for aluminum and wooden glider planes, which were used to land troops during the 1944 D-Day invasion.

BELOW: A female wartime worker assembles a glider wing in one of the Grand Rapids Industries plants. From *The Furniture Capital of America Goes to War*, published by Grand Rapids Industries, ca. 1943.

ABOVE: So many male workers left Berkey & Gay to fight during World War II that the company had to open this recruiting station to attract female workers. Courtesy, Grand Rapids Public Library. BELOW: When metal became restricted for military use, it could no longer be used to make upholstery springs. Local furniture designer Guido Alessandrini invented a solution in 1942. Manufactured by Waddell Manufacturing Co. and marketed by the Wood Spring Corp. as the "Victory Spring," his patented chair bottom substituted flexible bentwood strips, similar to old wooden carriage springs, instead of the usual coiled wire springs.

seven in 1940 to eighty-eight in 1947. Though some of the old giants had fallen, newer, medium-sized companies like Baker, Brower Furniture Company, Kindel Furniture Company, and Hekman emerged as important players in the industry.

Still, results of the long-awaited recovery were mixed. Though Grand Rapids sales rose dramatically, Southern companies saw even greater increases. Grand Rapids stuck to its pre-war tactic, stressing high-end design and quality craftsmanship. A 1947 article in *Business Week* entitled "Grand Rapids Bets on Quality" proclaimed:

> *Grand Rapids furniture makers would like the world to think that their goods are in a class with Rolls Royce. They grant that more and more Fords are bobbing up in their industry. But they stubbornly insist that Grand Rapids won't follow suit.*

Unfortunately for Grand Rapids, returning G.I.s and families moving into their first homes were more likely to buy inexpensive furniture. The more costly Grand Rapids furniture was something many of these young buyers could only hope to purchase someday.

The optimistic mood of the post-war era and the young age of many furniture buyers swung public interest decidedly toward the modern. Many Grand Rapids manufacturers introduced lines that had been commissioned in the late 1930s or early '40s, but postponed in production until after the war. These lines reflected the growing preference for designs from Scandinavia, and the reality of smaller, less formal living spaces. The "Scandinavian Modern" style, which combined wood craftsmanship with functionalism to create lightweight, graceful forms, became so popular that a number of Grand Rapids companies hired Scandinavian designers. Danish architect and designer Finn Juhl created a line of chairs for Baker in 1945, which consisted of sleek wooden frames that supported the seat and back by means of hidden crossbars, giving the illusion that they floated independently in space.

Americans and American innovation also played a tremendous role. After the death of Gilbert Rohde in 1944, Herman Miller president D. J. DePree looked for a successor who could wield the same degree of influence as Rohde had with architects and interior designers. DePree found his champion in George Nelson, the managing editor of *Architectural Forum*. Though he had no experience with furniture, his vision and design sense would prove to be a perfect match with Herman Miller's penchant for progressive experimentation. As design director for the company from 1945 through the early 1960s, Nelson did more than just create new forms of furniture. He affected corporate philosophy, standardized manufacturing techniques, and introduced new marketing strategies. His ability to articulate his thoughts in writing helped to define the company, and to communicate the virtues of its products to the architects who would recommend them to their clients. Even products that sold poorly were seen as significant design developments by this elite group of taste makers, furthering Herman Miller's leadership in defining the modern interior.

Like his predecessor, Nelson also designed several lines of clocks for the Howard Miller Clock Company. The most famous is the "Ball and Spoke Clock," sometimes called the "Atom Clock," designed and introduced in

1947. This wall clock featured twelve metal rods radiating from a circular metal dial, and terminated in painted wooden balls that took the place of numbers. Looking like a chemistry class model of a molecule, this clock's design was inspired by the nation's fascination with the Atomic Age.

George Nelson's influence went beyond his own designs: he also hired other notable designers to add to Herman Miller's offerings of innovative furniture. Japanese-American sculptor Isamu Noguchi designed his famous biomorphic "Noguchi coffee table" for Herman Miller, which introduced it in 1947. Manufactured until 1972, then re-introduced in 1984, its rounded triangular plate-glass top appears to rest precariously atop a two-piece walnut base. Like his abstract sculptures, it displays Noguchi's attempt to imitate the moods of nature, stripped down to bare, almost primitive forms. Danish designer Verner Panton, known for his single-form chair designs, devised the stackable "Cantilever Chair," which was molded as a single, continuously flowing form of fiberglass-reinforced polyester. Introduced by Herman Miller in 1967, the Cantilever Chair was sold in a variety of brilliant colors until production ceased in 1975.

But the most significant, and longest-lived, of these contractual design arrangements between Herman Miller and outside design talent was with the American husband-and-wife team of Charles and Ray Eames. Though Charles receives much of the credit for the designs, most were actually collaborations with his wife, Ray, and other designers. During World War II, he applied his knowledge of molding and bending plywood to the design of equipment for the U.S. Navy.

In 1946, shortly after the war ended, Eames's biomorphic, molded plywood furniture was exhibited in a one-man show at the Museum of Modern Art in New York City. The exhibition featured his molded plywood chair, sometimes nicknamed the "potato chip chair," which consisted of a bent molded back, joined to a molded seat by bent plywood or chrome-plated steel legs. These chairs were produced by Eames's own company, Evans Manufacturing, in California and Grand Haven, Michigan until 1949, when he reached an agreement for Herman Miller to assume production.

In 1950 Herman Miller also began to produce Eames's molded plastic chairs, which had won a prize in a different Museum of Modern Art competition for low-cost furniture designs. The chairs, which were strengthened by impregnating the plastic with fiberglass, left the texture of the fibers exposed to create an unusual surface treatment. Over the years, many variations of the basic molded plastic chair were manufactured with and without upholstery, as interlocking auditorium seating, and with a variety of bases. Another variation was made by molding wire mesh into the same form, then adding a two-piece upholstery sleeve, which inspired its nickname, the "Bikini Chair." In 1956, Herman Miller introduced the "Eames Lounge Chair and Ottoman" live, on national television. It featured laminated rosewood "petals" with black leather upholstery, joined by metal connectors, and mounted on a swivel base. In 1958, Herman Miller debuted the first of a number of Eames seating lines that used tension-stretched leather or fabrics on cast aluminum frames.

Eames's furniture designs were frequently introduced for residential use, but later adapted for commercial applications. Their unusual shapes and

Widdicomb French Provincial chest of drawers and mirror, from *The Stylist*, Summer, 1948. Stylistically, most companies continued the trend of producing both modern and traditional lines. Though traditional residential furniture continued to be popular, it took on new characteristics. Companies like Baker and Kindel had continued success with formal, eighteenth-century mahogany furniture. But the increasingly open plans of suburban homes in the 1950s, and the trend towards informal living, prompted some firms to produce Early American forms in pine. Pine-tique Furniture, Inc. in Grand Haven produced both reproductions and original designs based on American rural or folk furniture. The Pine Shops in nearby Big Rapids made reproductions and close adaptations of Colonial American pieces, with turned legs, straight, un-carved panels, and pie-crust aprons or brackets. Catalogs explained how the designs were adapted for today's living.

The John Widdicomb Co. updated its long-selling French Provincial line, which it now made in fruitwood and finished in a nut brown tone or painted antique white with gold highlights. Chairs and bed headboards were upholstered with fabrics in new bold shades of green, blue, gold, and even orange and purple. Imperial and Hekman continued to make Sheraton, Regency, and Chippendale tables from mahogany. But they also made less formal French and Italian Provincial tables with a fruitwood finish.

When designing furniture, George Nelson was always concerned with finding solutions to complex problems. ABOVE: Nelson's Basic Storage Components line was composed of residential modules supported on platform benches and included components that housed the latest home conveniences such as television sets and hi-fi equipment. The Comprehensive Storage System, produced between 1959 and 1973, blurred the lines between furniture and architecture. By hanging shelving, lighting, storage units, and desk components on floor-to-ceiling uprights along the walls of a room, Nelson took advantage of vertical space and gave interiors a more open feeling. Many of his freestanding tables, desks, and chairs had a lightweight appearance, created by the use of blond woods, delicate lines, and fine tubular metal legs. Several of his seating designs, including the Coconut Chair (1955 - 1978), which resembled a wedge-shaped slice taken from a hollow sphere, and the Marshmallow Sofa (1956 - 1965), made from orange, pink, and purple naugahyde-covered foam disks attached to a steel frame, quickly became pop-culture classics (BELOW). Courtesy, Herman Miller, Inc.

functional materials received lukewarm acceptance by the general public, who wanted furnishings for their own homes. But they were often the perfect complement to the architecture of post-war schools, airports, offices, and auditoriums.

One of the most influential design critics of the 1940s and '50s, London-born architect and designer Terrence Harold Robsjohn-Gibbings, was hired to design modern furniture for the Widdicomb Furniture Company in 1943, though production was delayed until 1946. He served as the principal designer of Widdicomb's modern lines until 1956. Much to the disdain of traditionalists, Gibbings authored in 1944 a satirical critique of Americans' love affair with European antiques entitled *Good-bye, Mr. Chippendale*. But just as modernists were grinning with satisfaction, he attacked their world in 1947 with *Mona Lisa's Moustache*, which debunked modern art.

Gibbings was himself fascinated with antique furniture from ancient Greece. He designed a line of seating for Widdicomb with upholstered cushions supported on a woven web of fabric straps, an idea adapted from an ancient Greek klismos chair at the British Museum. The legs of his Colosseum coffee table mimicked the repeating arcade of the famous Roman arena. Other pieces can best be described as Scandinavian Modern with classical elegance. The slender rectangles of upholstery on his chairs were supported by blond frames with swelled organic legs. Widdicomb also produced several of Gibbings's designs for amoeboid, or biomorphic, coffee tables, one with a walnut top on three metal legs which tapered to a point, and another with a plate-glass top over a three-point walnut base.

George Nakashima, an American-born studio craftsman of Japanese descent, designed the "Origins" line, which Widdicomb produced in the late 1950s and early '60s. The line featured his distinctive styling, which was consistent with the principles of Scandinavian Modern, but derived more from Japanese simplicity and Shaker craftsmanship.

In 1939, the Johnson Furniture Company began a collaboration with Finnish architect and designer Eliel Saarinen, who had become president of the Cranbrook Academy, and his Cranbrook colleagues, J. Robert F. Swanson and Pipsam Swanson. They designed the Flexible Home Arrangements line, a system of modular furniture for the entire home. F.H.A. units displayed the characteristic functionality, lightweight appearance, and blond finish typical of Scandinavian Modern design. But their chief feature was the flexibility of different-sized units to fit any room dimensions, and the interchangeability of utility cabinets from living room to dining room to bedroom. F.H.A. was so successful that it expanded to include sixteen manufacturers, plus fabrics, floor coverings, lighting, and objets d'art.

From Bedroom Suites to Office Suites

Grand Rapids' strategy to position itself as America's "Paris of Furniture Design" in the face of declining market share showed some signs of success. As the furniture industry emerged from the post-war boom era, a number of companies had become firmly established as some of the finest manufacturers of residential furniture in America. The reputations of firms like Baker, Kindel, John Widdicomb, Hekman, Sligh, Howard Miller, Forslund, Superior, LaBarge, and others as makers of limited production, design-oriented, quality crafted furniture were widely known among those who could afford their furniture.

Unfortunately, there was room at the top for only a limited number of companies. The decades following the end of World War II witnessed a tremendous consolidation of furniture manufacturers in Grand Rapids. When smaller firms lacked the money to update their plants, or weaker companies began to falter, they were purchased by stronger manufacturers at an unprecedented pace. Between 1945 and 1970, the William A. Berkey, Vander Ley Brothers, Widdicomb Furniture, and Grand Rapids Bookcase & Chair Companies were merged into the John Widdicomb Company. Bergsma Brothers, a newcomer to Grand Rapids in 1945, purchased Gunn Furniture and Imperial Table Companies. Trend Clock Company and, for a period of time, the Grand Rapids Chair Company, were merged with Sligh. Baker acquired Williams-Kimp, Barnard & Simonds, and Kozak Studios, and bought Grand Rapids Chair from Sligh. Howard Miller expanded beyond the manufacture of grandfather clocks by turning Hekman and Alexis Manufacturing into wholly owned subsidiaries.

Some companies changed the types of furniture they made, in response to changes in the market. A number of prominent residential manufacturers switched completely to the production of furniture ordered in large contracts by corporations, schools, or governmental organizations. The Mueller Furniture Corporation continued to manufacture lines of upholstered seating, but for use in offices, meeting rooms, and reception areas. Through a series of mergers, Johnson dropped its residential lines to manufacture hotel, dormitory, and eventually office furniture. The most significant company to change its paradigms from residential to contract was Herman Miller, whose innovations for the office became so successful in the 1950s and '60s that it devoted all its efforts to their production. Still other traditional, wooden furniture manufacturers like Sligh, Baker, and Hekman added dormitory or executive office furniture divisions while retaining their residential lines.

Finally, the rapid expansion of contract furniture manufacturers helped to offset the loss of jobs in the residential industry. Grand Rapids became the center for a new type of industry, making furniture in large contracts for schools, churches, universities, libraries, airports, hospitals, and most importantly, offices. The huge government and military contracts awarded during World War II to Grand Rapids' contract furniture manufacturers were but one reason for this industry's meteoric rise. After the war, the construction of thousands of new schools, churches, and offices created an enormous new market for manufactured furniture. And once again, Grand Rapids was ready to supply it.

RIGHT: Eames's Molded Plywood Dining Chair (DCW) was originally manufactured by Herman Miller, Inc. between 1946 and 1958, before being re-introduced by Herman Miller Products for the Home in 1994. BELOW: Vienna-born designer Paul Frankl, best known for his early Art Deco work in New York, contracted with Johnson Furniture Co. to create several modern lines in 1950 and '51. His "Contemporary" line was described in Johnson catalogs as a group of "classic simplicity," which conveyed a feeling of "informal luxury." Included in the group were a number of amoeboid-shaped cocktail tables with bleached cork tops, on darkly stained tapering legs of pearwood or mahogany. The line also included suites for the bedroom and dining room. The dining set came with Frankl's "plunging neckline" chairs, like the one shown below, which featured upholstered trapezoidal backs with "V" shaped cut-outs resembling the low-cut neckline of a Christian Dior dress!

Changing conditions forced Grand Rapids to re-invent its principal product. Today, West Michigan's titans of industry lead the world in the production of a new kind of furniture made from metals and plastics, for use in offices and public spaces.

A New Industry: Grand Rapids Contract Furniture

The manufacture and sale of furniture to fill a large order, according to a contract with a single client, is far from a new concept in Grand Rapids. Even the earliest factories, like Powers & Ball, produced pieces on contract for businesses in big cities, and most of the residential furniture companies also made some contract furniture. Early in Grand Rapids' history, companies emerged that made contract furniture exclusively, and for places other than residences. Since the public never purchased this furniture, they never knew these companies existed. Some contract furniture makers became giants in their markets, but conducted their business in the shadow of the more visible residential furniture companies. When Grand Rapids' residential industry appeared to falter, many people assumed that the city no longer made furniture. But when the contract furniture companies became style innovators and joined the ranks of America's largest corporations, Grand Rapids' new identity began to come forth.

Since Grand Rapids' early residential production was based on bedroom "suits," it was logical to contract with hotels, which needed large quantities of beds, dressers, and washstands. Berkey & Gay supplied hotels in Washington, D.C. and New York City. An article in the October 11, 1875 issue of the *Grand Rapids Eagle* proudly announced the award of large contracts to Grand Rapids firms for hotels at the 1876 World's Fair in Philadelphia:

> *It is reported that the hotels in course of erection upon the Centennial grounds, are to be furnished with furniture from Grand Rapids, Mich., and other cities of the West. The reason assigned is that [since] they have employed large capital in producing special articles, they can furnish them at lower prices. . . . The report is certainly a high compliment to this city, and one which our manufacturers are entitled to. . . .*

More recently, the Sligh-Lowry Contract Furniture Company, a subsidiary of Sligh Furniture between 1953 and circa 1974, produced room furniture for hotels, motels, and nursing homes. During this same period, when America's universities were experiencing unprecedented growth, Sligh-Lowry also made more college dormitory fur-

OPPOSITE: Installation of 65,000 stadium seats by American Seating Co. at Soldier Field, Chicago, ca. 1980. American Seating seats endure the spills of food and drink and the pounding of crazed fans at nearly every stadium in the nation. Courtesy, American Seating Co. BELOW: The "Equa" Chair, designed for Herman Miller, Inc. by Don Chadwick and William Stumpf in 1984. Innovations in ergonomic seating by a number of Grand Rapids manufacturers have improved the comfort and health of office workers in the twentieth century. Courtesy, Herman Miller, Inc.

niture than any other manufacturer. Timberline, Inc. began in 1959 as a manufacturer of contract furniture for hotels and motels. After Timberline merged with Johnson Furniture Company in 1963, Johnson began to manufacture Timberline furniture for hotels, motels, and college dormitories. This attracted the interest of Holiday Inns of America, Inc., which purchased Johnson and operated it as a subsidiary until 1975. Johnson received a steady flow of contracts to install its furniture in Howard Johnson motels and Holiday Inns nationwide, and in special projects like the Aladdin Hotel in Las Vegas.

Today, a number of Grand Rapids companies sell furniture to restaurants and dining rooms. Charter House, Inc. of Holland, Michigan, founded in 1988, carved a niche for itself in a profitable growth industry: fast food. Charter House manufactures wood and fiberglass tables and cabinets, condiment counters, and planters for family-oriented and fast food restaurants. Its clients include Big Boy, Arby's, Wendy's, McDonald's, Burger King, Denny's, and International House of Pancakes restaurants in the United States, Canada, Latin America, Europe, and the Middle East. Some of the company's products are custom-made according to the dictates of the client's culture, like booths for fast food establishments in Saudi Arabia with higher-than-normal partitions to segregate male and female customers.

While the Grand Rapids furniture industry was rising, so was the country's retail industry. During the late nineteenth and early twentieth centuries, Americans had more money to spend on consumer goods than ever before. Stores became larger and spent more on their interiors. Several Grand Rapids companies manufactured furniture for these retailers to use. The Chocolate Cooler Company manufactured "The Grand Rapids" ice cream cabinets and refrigerators, florists' refrigerators, and confectioners' tables between circa 1895 and 1919. The Grand Rapids Showcase Company, organized in 1901, could entirely furnish drug, confectionery, clothing, and department stores. The company also designed store layouts for its clients. By 1913 Grand Rapids Showcase claimed that it manufactured more retailing furniture by volume than the combined total of its three leading competitors, and that it shipped more furniture than any other manufacturer in Grand Rapids.

After Grand Rapids Showcase's success, other companies followed. The Wilmarth Showcase Company, founded in 1908 as Wilmarth & Wilmarth, manufactured high-end showcases, counters, and wall cases for stores. In 1909 the Welch Folding Bed Company dropped the products it had manufactured since 1886 and became the Welch Manufacturing Company, makers of retail showcases and equipment. These two companies merged in 1926 to form Welch-Wilmarth Corporation. A year later Welch-Wilmarth merged with its rival, Grand Rapids Showcase, to become the Grand Rapids Store Equipment Company. Its design departments provided layouts and furnishing plans for stores, with elaborate paneling, lighting, and furniture in Colonial, Sheraton, Moderne, and other popular styles of the day. Products included showcases, counters, shelving, wardrobes, cabinets, wrapping tables, and desks. Grand Rapids Store Equipment became the world's largest designer and manufacturer of furniture for dry goods, department, and specialty stores, and remained a major player in the commercial furnishings industry until it closed in 1955.

Elijah Haney began his Empire Iron Works foundry in Grand Rapids in 1872. In 1875 Empire received a large contract to cast iron components for school desks for the Beckley-Cardy Company of Chicago. By 1878 Empire had become the exclusive producer of complete school desks for the Chicago firm, and changed its name to Haney Manufacturing Company. In 1888 Haney improved the product, and patented the "combination school desk with moveable seat." Its success was phenomenal: Haney produced fifty thousand combination desks for the Chicago School District in 1893 alone, and sold millions more throughout the United States, Europe, South America, China, and India.

As thousands of one-room schoolhouses opened across the country, Haney's design quickly became the industry standard. Other companies devised combination desks, though not always legally. In 1891 Haney won a lawsuit against the Grand Rapids School Furniture Company for infringing on its patent. Relations between the two companies improved, and in 1900 Haney produced thirty-five thousand desks on contract for Grand Rapids School's successor, American School Furniture Company. The next year, American School bought annual rights to use Haney's patents.

American School was formed in 1899 when Grand Rapids School, founded in 1886, merged with eighteen other school, church, and seating furniture manufacturers across the country. Headquartered first in New York, then in Chicago, the company changed its name to American Seating Company in 1906, and moved its headquarters to Grand Rapids in 1931. American Seating revised its own school desks in 1911, with a tubular steel rather than cast iron base.

The Steel Furniture Company, founded in 1907 by Earle, Eber, and Robert Irwin, made school furniture and theatre, church, lodge, and public seating. As early as 1911 the company was selling large contracts of school furniture in North, Central, and South America, as well as Africa and China. In 1932 the company's name was changed to Irwin Seating Company.

When the post-World War II baby boom resulted in an incredible need for new schools, Haney, American Seating, and Irwin Seating provided much of the school furniture. They produced new lines with space-age designs in laminated plywood, tubular steel, fiberglass, Formica, and plastics. Haney turned its attention to library furniture in 1966 and ceased production altogether in 1978. American Seating sold its line of classroom seating to Irwin in 1986, in order to concentrate on stadium and theatre seats and open office systems. Irwin increased its school furniture production to fill more than two thousand orders annually, and continues as a major manufacturer of school furniture today.

Many of these same companies also became producers of fixed mass seating. Haney expanded into opera and church seating before the turn of the century. Grand Rapids School, even before its consolidation into

ABOVE: Illustration of Wilmarth "500 Line" of soda booths for drug stores, from the Wilmarth Showcase Co. 1920 drug store catalog. This deluxe line featured monogrammed mahogany veneers, brass fittings, marble bases and counters, plush tufted upholstery, fern brackets, and artistic scenery panels. BELOW: Grand Rapids School Furniture Co. combination desk, ca. 1890. Each unit featured a fold-up seat in front and a writing surface in back. Students used the writing surface attached to the seat in front of them. The desk tops were fashioned from Michigan maple, while the legs and frames were cast iron. With fewer parts than separate desks and chairs, combination desks were simpler and cheaper to produce.

Installation of chairs by the Irwin Seating Co. in New York City's famous Carnegie Hall, 1987. Irwin leads the nation in the manufacture of auditorium and theatre seats, producing more than half a million annually. Some of Irwin's other recent installations include De Vos Hall and Van Andel Arena in Grand Rapids, Arthur Ashe Stadium in New York City, The Palace at Auburn Hills, Market Square Arena in Indianapolis, the National Holocaust Museum in Washington, D.C., and Roy Thompson Hall in Toronto. Courtesy, Len Allington.

American Seating, made cast iron and laminated plywood theatre and opera seats, which were replaced by more opulent upholstered seats with elaborate Rococo decorations for the motion picture palaces of the 1920s. Notable installations of American Seating Theatre lines have included the U.S. Senate and House Galleries in Washington, D.C., and Radio City Music Hall and Lincoln Center in New York. Having added stadium seating to its product line in 1951, American Seating today boasts that it has furnished seats for most major-league ballparks in the United States, including Houston's Astrodome, Denver's Mile-High Stadium, and Baltimore's Camden Yards.

Irwin Seating produced cast iron and bent plywood theatre and auditorium seating from its beginning. After World War II, Irwin introduced new lines such as "The Comet," a streamlined seat available with or without upholstery. New lines of arena seating made from steel and injection-molded plastic were added in the 1970s and '80s. By the mid-1980s, Irwin had become the leading manufacturer of indoor seating for auditoriums, movie theatres, and arenas in the nation, furnishing between eight hundred and nine hundred facilities each year. Combined, Irwin and American Seating today control most of the country's fixed seating market.

Manufacturers applied much of what they learned in the production of folding chairs and upholstered theatre seats to other areas. American Seating's Transportation Division manufactured the first all-tubular-steel-framed seats used in urban buses in 1931. It introduced to furniture-making many of the assembly-line techniques, such as overhead conveyor systems, that were developed by the automotive industry. The division expanded to claim a ninety percent share of the market for seating in cross-country buses, subways, and mass-transit systems, and drivers' seats for trucks and locomotives. Clients of American Seating have included the San Francisco Bay Area Transit System and the New York City Transit Authority.

Grand Rapids Furniture Goes to Work

The largest and most significant segment of Grand Rapids' contract furniture industry is its office furniture manufacturers. The office as we know it was a result of the industrial revolution, and so was furniture making in Grand Rapids. In the 1820s, American factories grew so large that they needed office workers. New inventions like the telegraph, typewriter, telephone, dictaphone, carbon paper, and duplicating machine became standard office equipment by the late nineteenth century. These inventions made offices into centers of communication. They also cluttered work surfaces, and created an explosion in the amount of paperwork to be processed and stored.

Before the 1870s, little attention had been paid to developing specialized office furniture. Most desks and chairs used in offices were the same as those used at home, so they were made by residential furniture companies. But by the 1870s, the Phoenix Furniture Company had begun manufacturing one of the earliest specialized forms of office furniture: the high, sloping clerk's desk. Its height allowed clerks to work while standing, or sitting on a stool. Its simple design featured a slanted writing surface, and several slots beneath for storing ledgers. By the 1880s Phoenix had developed a special order department, which designed and manufactured woodwork and furniture to order, primarily for large government contracts. The Phoenix Special Order department supplied the office furnishings for such major structures as the Grand Rapids and Chicago City Halls, and the Michigan and Texas State Capitol Buildings.

By the 1890s companies like the Gunn Furniture Company, Z.E. Allen Company, and Grand Rapids Desk Company in Grand Rapids, and the Moon Desk Company of nearby Muskegon, Michigan, were manufacturing a more sophisticated form: the roll-top desk. Beneath the writing surface were two pedestals, separated by a kneehole in the center. One pedestal included slots for ledgers, while the other contained drawers for filing papers and storing smaller office accessories. Above the writing surface were various shelves, slots, drawers, and pigeonholes, designed to organize papers. The roll-top closed over the writing surface and pigeonholes, reducing the appearance of clutter, and restricting access.

Gunn continued to experiment with storage solutions. Gunn's "Coronet Desk," introduced in the mid-1940s, represented the ultimate attempt at organization. Designed for executives, the Coronet Desk was wired for electricity and came equipped with radio, electric razor, cigarette lighter and ashtray, built-in fluorescent lights, electric clock, slide-out telephone and dictating equipment, refrigerator, bar with decanters and stemware, and a combination safe!

Early in its history, American Seating Co. made wooden folding chairs for use with folding bridge tables or in meeting halls. These were replaced in 1930 by the "Folding Forty" chair, which combined a laminated plywood seat with a rounded frame of tubular steel (ABOVE). This form and its successors (BELOW, Courtesy, American Seating Co.) proved immensely popular: more than five millon were made for the American armed forces during World War II alone, and millions more are still in use in gymnasiums, cafeterias, church basements, and schools throughout the world. Though they may not realize it, most Americans have sat on a folding chair from Grand Rapids at some point in their lives.

Several producers of church furniture were merged into the American Seating Co., and consolidated in Grand Rapids as the Church Division between 1927 and 1969. Most church furniture was made from wood, often with considerable symbolic and figural carving. Under the direction of Bavarian master carver Alois Lang, a wide range of furniture was made for churches across the country, like the pulpit, lectern, altar, reredos, communion rail, and carving of Da Vinci's "Last Supper" seen here in Grand Rapids' Trinity Lutheran Church, ca. 1946. Courtesy, Trinity Lutheran Church. The Morgan Manufacturing Co., which moved to Grand Rapids from Chicago in 1946, continues to make church furniture and other religious articles in wood today, and American Seating and Irwin Seating have installed their theatre-style seats in church sanctuaries nationwide.

As the amount of office paper continued to increase, new forms of furniture were designed for its storage and retrieval. In 1893 Otto H. L. Wernicke of Minneapolis invented "elastic cabinets," a stacking system of wooden compartments that interlocked vertically and horizontally to create flexible storage. In 1897 he moved his Wernicke Furniture Company to Grand Rapids, where elastic cabinets were manufactured under the Wernicke name until the company merged with the Fred Macey Furniture Company in 1905.

Fred Macey was founded in 1892 as a mail-order business, selling desks, file cabinets, and other office furnishings made by other manufacturers. When the success of its mail-order sales began to undercut traditional sales, area manufacturers refused to produce finished goods for Macey to sell. In response, Fred Macey built his own factory in Grand Rapids, and a national system of warehouses for distribution. A. W. Shaw and L. C. Walker, former Fred Macey employees, incorporated the Shaw-Walker Company in 1899 in Muskegon to manufacture and sell oak filing boxes for 3 x 5 file cards, which were advertised as a "complete office system." By 1903 Shaw-Walker had expanded to manufacture multi-drawer filing cabinets, desks, and office chairs.

When roll-tops were added to desks, users had to remove typewriters, adding machines, and books from the writing surface, and place them on new, specialized pieces of furniture. The Hetterschied Manufacturing Works, founded in Grand Rapids in 1883, and the Adjustable Table Company, founded in 1905, manufactured revolving bookstands, typewriter stands and tables, tripod tables for office machines, dictionary stands, and drafting tables. Because of the weight of early office equipment and books, both companies produced their stands with heavy iron bases. All this weight made them difficult to move, so they were placed on casters, allowing workers to create their own arrangement of office equipment. Swivel office chairs permitted workers to turn easily from their desks to equipment stands. These stands were some of the first office furnishings produced in iron instead of wood, and helped workers to become used to the aesthetic of metal in the office.

Despite this use of iron, office furniture was still overwhelmingly wood. The Stow & Davis Furniture Company was founded in 1885 as a manufacturer of wooden kitchen and dining extension tables. But by 1889 the company had begun to manufacture its first boardroom tables, which became a company specialty for more than a century. By the 1910s Stow & Davis had abandoned residential tables altogether, and expanded into furniture for financial institutions. This clientele required furniture that projected an image of durability, and was impressive yet conservative. The company's large Adam or Colonial Revival desks, in oak or mahogany, and oversized leather swivel chairs established the look of the American executive office. In 1928 Stow & Davis introduced the first wooden desk with steel framework. This innovation further improved furniture assembly and durability, but lines still carried names like Nottingham, Baronial, Georgian, Jacobean, and Gothic, indicating that traditional period revival styles were still popular in the upper echelons of corporate America.

Although most office workers preferred wood, metal office furniture found a new market because of the threat of fire. Offices in the early twentieth century were still mostly furnished with wood and cluttered with paper. Cigar and pipe ashes were emptied into wicker wastebaskets, which often ignited and caught fire. The Metal Office Furniture Company was founded in Grand Rapids in 1912 to make furniture that would reduce the risk of fire. It manufactured metal safes and wastebaskets under the brand names "Victor" and "Steelcase," and tested them to prove that they could resist prolonged exposure to fire. But people were still used to the look of wood, so Metal Office purchased machines that the Grand Rapids Panel Company had used a decade earlier to create hardwood grains on softwood furniture. Metal Office mechanically grain-painted most of its early products, to make them look like oak or mahogany.

Illustration of "Quaint Office Furniture" by Stickley Brothers Furniture Co., from the June, 1905 issue of *The Grand Rapids Furniture Record*. Stickley Brothers manufactured this line of Mission oak office furnishings in addition to its primary offerings for the home. Other companies, including The Macey Co., Gunn Furniture Co., and Grand Rapids Desk Co., sold Mission-inspired office furniture for years after the style had waned in popularity for home use. Their practical appearance and affordability made Mission oak desks frequent choices for lower-level clerks.

Metal Office also began to manufacture wood-grained metal filing cabinets and safes under the brand name "Inter-Inter," to be sold by Macey, whose plant was next door. Shaw-Walker introduced its first steel filing units in 1913. A prophesy by Thomas Edison, published during the infancy of steel furniture manufacturing in the January, 1911 *Furniture Manufacturer and Artisan*, predicted:

> *All furniture will soon be made of steel. . . . The babies of the next generation will sit in steel high chairs, and eat from steel tables. They will not know what wooden furniture is.*

When the height of skyscrapers began to exceed the capabilities of fire fighting equipment, the U.S. government began to require fireproof furniture in all its new buildings. When the government requested proposals to furnish desks for its new twenty-story Boston Customs House Tower in 1914, the small, one-year-old Metal Office Furniture Company submitted a bid, though it had never manufactured a single desk. The company won its first major order, for two hundred "601 desks," because its products were fireproof.

Large office buildings and metal furniture became inextricably linked. Shaw-Walker compared the steel framework of its filing cabinets to the structure of the Woolworth Building in New York City and sold them with the slogan, "Built like a skyscraper." As the wood furniture industry began to decline in the 1920s, government and corporate contracts for metal office furniture became increasingly important to Grand Rapids' economy.

"The Great Workroom," S.C. Johnson & Son headquarters, Racine, Wisconsin, ca. 1939. Courtesy, Steelcase, Inc.

Despite their innovation with new materials, Metal Office's 601 line was conservative in design. This reputation for producing durable but conventional furniture changed in 1937, when Metal Office received a contract to custom-manufacture furnishings for the new corporate headquarters of S.C. Johnson Wax. The forty different forms were designed by the building's famous architect, Frank Lloyd Wright. Wright insisted on complete control over the interior appearance of the building, which he exercised by designing all of its furnishings, as well as carpets, windows, and lighting. The stream-lined, modern Johnson Wax Building called for the same rounded shapes, cantilevered planes, colors, and materials in its furniture as in its walls and ceilings.

Wright first contacted Stow & Davis, by then the producer of as much as sixty percent of America's corporate executive furniture. But the designs required a combination of wood, sheet metal, and tubular metal, and Stow & Davis lacked the metalworking capabilities to submit a bid. So Wright turned to metal furniture manufacturers, among them Metal Office. Because of its location in Grand

Real estate banker Stuart Williamson argued this point in an unidentified Grand Rapids newspaper article in March, 1934:

Metal trades now employing more than 10,000 men in Grand Rapids, will outstrip the [wooden] furniture industry's palmiest days if present activity is continued for a short time. . . . Much has been said in regard to the decline of the furniture industry . . . and not nearly enough about the progress in the metal trades in this city.

In the 1920s and '30s, Metal Office expanded its "Steelcase" line, entering into a cooperative venture with Grand Rapids-based Terrell Manufacturing Company. Terrell made steel cabinets, lockers, and shelving to complement the desks, safes, wastebaskets, and file cabinets.

The more designers created furniture for organizing office work, the more they thought about how their furniture fit into the work place. They began to think about furniture as cubes or modules that occupied measurable units of space. If a piece of furniture required three modules of space to perform its function, then they designed it to occupy only three modules of space. The significant space saved with modular furniture could be used to house more workers.

Wernicke's elastic cabinets were some of Grand Rapids' first experiments with modularity. The ability to combine different units allowed customers to custom-fit their cabinets to their offices. Wernicke's use of both horizontal and vertical space created more storage with less floor space. Stacking bookcases, made in Grand Rapids by Macey, Gunn, and Metal Office, also provided flexibility. Rather than buying entire pieces of rigid furniture, customers bought only the size and quantity of units they needed, then put them together like building blocks. If they outgrew the number of modules they had, they just ordered more, and combined them with the ones already in use.

Office desks also became subjects for study and improvement. Gilbert Rohde, the New York designer who served as Herman Miller's chief of design from 1931 to 1944, began to design desks for modern office spaces in the late 1930s. His Executive Office Group (EOG), which was introduced by Herman Miller in 1942, attempted to offer clients maximum flexibility with minimum components. According to Ralph Caplan's *Design of Herman Miller*, Rohde's EOG had only fifteen basic components, but could be configured to make over four hundred different furniture forms.

Some customers preferred standardized sizes and shapes. During World War II, Metal Office Furniture Company made "Shipboard" office furniture according to specifications provided by the U.S. Navy. The Shipboard line included desks, captain's chairs, bunk beds, and chaplain's pulpits. The official signing of surrender documents by the Japanese on board the *U.S.S.*

Missouri took place atop a Steelcase mess hall table! In logical military fashion, the Navy required all of its desks and file cabinets to conform to standard sizes, which it calculated in multiples of fifteen inches. After the war, Metal Office designers applied this standard to a new civilian line named "Multiple-15." Former company officer David D. Hunting, Sr. relayed the story of the Multiple-15 desk:

> *The big problem after World War II was office space. By 1949, millions of veterans had returned to civilian jobs, but we still had a serious shortage of building materials so offices were really crowded. Office desks had always come in odd sizes like 62" x 34," and they wasted space. We made some tests to see how far the average person could reach, and we found that a 60" x 30" desk was just about ideal. This was the start of our "Multiple 15" principle. . . . We just converted the dimensions of all our office furniture to multiples of fifteen inches. It made office space easier to plan, and we could get six desks in the space usually required for five. So it made more room. . . . It worked very well, and six months later everyone in the industry switched over to the 60" x 30" desk.*

Similar studies by Shaw-Walker determined that the optimal height of writing surfaces for the greatest number of people was twenty-nine inches. In 1946 it began to make all its desks twenty-nine inches high, establishing the industry standard height for desk tops.

The grey metal Multiple-15 desk proved to be so popular that it became an icon of post-war prosperity. Fashionable movies like *The Apartment* in 1960, and early '50s TV series like *Dragnet*, used Multiple-15 desks to represent the organized world inhabited by masses of white-collar office workers. The image of a large rectangular room filled with rows of Multiple-15 desks and illuminated by artificial ceiling lights came to epitomize the large and sometimes impersonal American corporation. The middle manager seated behind his Multiple-15 desk, amid a sea of other middle managers seated at their Multiple-15 desks, became the Everyman of the 1950s.

Science Changes Rules of Design

The concern for greater efficiency in the office led furniture makers into a new scientific field. The study of how people do their work and respond to their environment, known as "ergonomics," became the driving force in design. The term comes from the Greek *ergon*, which means work, and *nomos*, which means law. Furniture companies set up research departments headed by a new breed of designer-engineer-scientists, who believed people would be healthier and more productive if furniture properly supported their bodies. They watched people sit, communicate, and circulate around the office. They measured people to determine typical body sizes. Then they experimented with new forms of furniture based on their research.

Much ergonomic study was, and continues to be, devoted to designing better places to sit. In 1946 Shaw-Walker introduced the "Correct Seating Chair," which it later claimed to have been the first ergonomically designed chair. A number of Charles Eames's and George Nelson's seating designs for Herman Miller from the 1940s through the 1960s incorporated head, back, and seat sections that could move independently to conform to and support

Rapids, in close proximity to so many other furniture companies, and because of the city's long history of companies cooperating, Metal Office won the contract. The company sub-contracted with Stow & Davis to produce the elliptical, oil-polished wooden desk tops, and with American Seating Co. to manufac-ture all the tubular steel com-ponents. Metal Office made all the  sheet metal parts, finished the metal compo-nents in "Cherokee red," and completed assembly.

The traditional office pool area was named "The Great Workroom." Its open plan, which Lance Knoebel describes in his *Office Furniture: Twentieth Century Design* as "a modern-day cathedral for workers," offered "light, space, air, and inspiration." Instead of sitting on heavy pedestals, Wright's desks hov-ered above the floor, with long horizontal wings supported by slender legs. Drawers and wastebaskets were detachable components that hung from horizontal grilles and swiveled out for use. Pigeonholes could be placed above the writing surface on a floating shelf. The chair backs had a swivel mechanism and identical upholstery on both sides, so they could be rotated to decrease wear. Wright also gave the chairs only three legs, to force users to either sit with good posture, or fall off! In an undated oral interview in the Steelcase, Inc. archives, David D. Hunting, Sr., first salesman and former officer of Metal Office, recalled his conversation with Wright about the chairs:

> *. . . He [Frank Lloyd Wright] also wanted that 3-legged chair and I told him one time, "Mr. Wright I'm concerned about that chair. Somebody will lean out to reach for something on the desk and he'll tip over!" Wright said, "Yes, maybe. They'll do it once, but not a second time."*

Steelcase representatives eventually con-vinced Wright to allow the chairs to be retro-fitted with four legs, just by persuading him to sit in one of the chairs himself.

ABOVE: Interior scenes like this, depicting a sea of Steelcase "Multiple 15" desks reaching back toward the horizon, became symbols of corporate organization during the post-World War II boom period. Courtesy, Steelcase, Inc. In 1954 Steelcase took a step toward making offices more varied and inviting with "Sunshine Styling," which gave customers a choice of colors for their metal office furniture, based on the natural hues of the American Southwest. New acrylic paint shades with names like "Autumn Haze," "Blond Tan," and "Desert Sage" (BELOW, Courtesy, Steelcase, Inc.) made metal furniture more acceptable to style-conscious clients. Beginning in 1952, Herman Miller, Inc. made its own move to brighten office interiors with fabrics designed by Alexander Girard. By placing certain colors in repeating patterns on seating upholstery and wallpaper, Girard made surfaces seem to move or vibrate, and offices seem less formal, even playful.

the body. When the Industrial Designers Society of America named Eames the "Most Influential Designer of the 20th Century" in 1985, it announced that he had "changed the way people store things, sit, build, play, communicate, teach, learn, and think."

In 1966, William Stumpf began to perform time-lapse photography to study people's sitting habits at work. His research confirmed his assumption that people rarely sit still. Yet, by the 1970s, many office workers were spending much of their work day sitting in front of a computer terminal. Stumpf began to experiment with an ergonomic chair that would properly support all the positions in which office workers sat. In 1976 Herman Miller introduced his "Ergon" chairs, named for the Greek root of ergonomics. Their design was meant as a solution to "seating equity," meaning that everyone, regardless of their rank in a company, was entitled to proper support by their chairs. The Ergon and its later replacement, the "Ergon 2," were manufactured so that users could adjust the seat height and the backrest height, angle, and depth to fit their body proportions. Ergon's contoured shape and tilt-and-swivel mechanisms were designed to adjust as the body moved. Steelcase's "ConCentrx" chair, introduced in 1980, was created specifically for electronic office workers. It quickly became the most successful seating product in company history.

Recognizing that ergonomic chairs helped only those who could properly adjust them, Chadwick and Stumpf created the "Equa" Chair, introduced by Herman Miller in 1984. The Equa was simpler to operate: users adjusted only the seat height and tilt tension, and the chair did the rest. Manufactured with a special shell of glass-reinforced polyester, the chair was designed to flex automatically with the movements of a person's body. Steelcase introduced the "Sensor" chair in 1986, the industry's first office chair to be sold in three distinct sizes. The 1994 "Rapport" line featured an adjustable lumbar support pillow and controls that adjusted with the touch of a fingertip.

Significant as these seating groups were, it was Grand Rapids' role in the invention of open office systems furniture that may have impacted society more than any other single development in the city's history. Open office systems furniture synthesized many of the traits that designers had sought to incorporate into their furniture: it provided solutions for clutter, accommodated new technologies, maximized vertical space, offered flexibility through modular components, and responded to the ways people worked.

A number of experiments in office systems during the 1950s and '60s paved the way for the systems revolution of the 1970s and '80s. George Nelson's 1959 "Comprehensive Storage System" lifted individual pieces of furniture off the floor into a single, flexible system hung from floor-to-ceiling metal uprights. The "Eames Storage Units" (ESU) was another early modular system, designed by the Eameses in 1948 and sold by Herman Miller beginning in 1951. ESU consisted of a variety of building blocks like panels, uprights, and struts, designed so that anyone with a screwdriver could take pieces apart and put them together in new combinations. The materials, including masonite, molded plywood, perforated aluminum, plated steel, and glass, were strong yet lightweight, colorful, and easy to clean. Like many Herman Miller products, ESU was developed for residential use but found greater success when adapted for the office.

Steelcase brought more flexibility to its metal office furniture in 1955 with the introduction of its "Convertibles" line: a variety of file cabinets, shelving units, and credenzas that could be arranged in custom combinations with different work surfaces. The addition of "convertiwalls" made the line popular with fast-growing companies, because it allowed them to reconfigure work spaces without knocking out walls. Slotted posts could be fitted with panels of steel or glass to create dividers between desks, and accessories like shelves and chalkboards could be added without tools. By 1965 Steelcase's sales exceeded all others in the office furniture industry.

Producing flexible wall systems became a growth industry. Modern Products, founded in Holland, Michigan in 1948 and renamed Haworth, Inc. in 1975, began producing modular office partitions under the brand names "Soundex" and "E-Series" in 1954. Nucraft, which began as a manufacturer of wooden accessories to complement Stow & Davis lines in the 1940s, introduced a series of walnut and colorful plastic room partitions called "UnitWall" in 1967. Architectural Systems, Inc., forerunner of Westinghouse Furniture Systems and now part of Knoll, Inc., was founded in 1960 to manufacture movable floor-to-ceiling partitions. Trendway Corporation was established in Holland in 1968 to make "TrendWall," a gypsum-based, steel-framed, floor-to-ceiling panel system used to create interior walls.

Research by Herman Miller designer George Nelson, and Robert Propst, head of the Herman Miller Research Corporation, brought modular furniture and wall panel systems together in a breakthrough that influenced office design for the next two decades. The Research Corporation was set up in Ann Arbor, Michigan, in 1960, with a simple but lofty mission: to identify problems and find solutions for them. Propst and his team conducted experiments to see how they could improve all sorts of work and living environments.

The climate was ripe for change in office furniture. Propst's tests resulted in the publication of landmark studies like *The Office: A Facility Based on Change*. Based on its findings, Herman Miller launched the "Action Office I" line in 1964, which featured freestanding units supported by T-shaped cast aluminum sled frames, which could be arranged to form individualized work stations. Action Office I was a reaction against the rectilinear, sterile offices of the 1940s and '50s. It allowed configurations with odd angles and individual expression, and face-to-face communications and accidental encounters among workers. Files were suspended from the backs of desks, and roll-tops covered clutter, but the absence of drawers prevented the pile-up of too much paperwork. Work surfaces were raised above the standard twenty-nine inches, so workers could stand, lean, or sit on stools. Action Office I foreshadowed the coming Information Age with built-in electrical outlets and channels for wiring. Telephones were built into free standing "communication units," which held Dictaphones and tape recorders.

Action Office I was not a big seller for Herman Miller. Its pieces were

In 1971, the Herman Miller Research Corp. designed a new form of furniture called "Sapiens" for college dormitories. Researchers had found that students often did not use furniture in the way it was intended. Because of their simple "U" and "V" shapes, light weight, and rounded edges, Sapiens could be used as chairs, head rests, floor pillows, or lap desks. The bright colors and strange shapes were intended to be playful. Though prototypes such as this tested favorably, the new forms were never produced commercially.

expensive to produce, and the concepts it promoted were too radically different for most users. But it prepared the way for its replacement, Action Office II, introduced in 1968, which had many of the same features, but mounted vertically on free-standing panels. The use of panel space for storage, bookshelves, lighting, bulletin boards, and writing surfaces used floor space efficiently. The panels allowed for greater privacy and sound control between work stations, but still created an open environment for communication among workers. Action Office II eliminated expensive castings and so was cheaper to produce. But most of all, it marked a fundamental shift away from free-standing units of furniture placed within fixed spaces, and towards a series of components that combined to create the furniture and define the space.

Action Office II gave managers efficiency and economy, restored a sense of territory to workers, and met with tremendous commercial success. Herman Miller moved from a medium-sized manufacturer to a fast-growth company, and catapulted into the ranks of the Fortune 500 by 1986. Action Office II reached over $2.5 billion in sales by 1990, creating the largest base of open-plan office furniture installed around the world.

With the lines between office furniture and room partitions now fully blurred, a revolution occurred in the Grand Rapids office furniture industry. Steelcase introduced "Movable Walls" in 1972, its first office system that hung work surfaces and storage units from hinged panels. This was followed by another panel-based system the next year, "Series 9000," which won national design awards in 1973, 1974, and 1976. Steelcase took the basic concepts and made them solid, affordable, and the standard in the industry. Series 9000 sales grew steadily, making it the top-selling office system in history, and Steelcase the largest manufacturer of furniture in the world.

The still-moderately sized Modern Products Company joined the revolution in 1971 with "Modern Office Modules." This system included acoustical panels and the "universal panel hinge," which increased flexibility of panel set-up. In 1976 Modern Products, renamed Haworth, Inc., began to sell "ERA-1," the industry's first pre-wired, panel-based office system, which gave workers access to power for electronic equipment without extension cords or hard wiring. ERA-1 was later re-designed as "UniGroup," Haworth's flagship office system product. In 1984 the company produced its millionth UniGroup panel, and in 1986 introduced a more sophisticated electrified system, "Power Base," which allowed for multiple dedicated circuits in the same work station. By dedicating power to specific uses, workers reduced electrical interference. Haworth sustained a sales growth rate between twenty and sixty percent annually, surpassing $1 billion in 1994.

By the mid-1980s systems furniture had become a multi-billion-dollar-a-year industry for West Michigan. Though most corporate and governmental offices now installed panel-based systems, many workers felt indifferent about their new surroundings. Popular cartoons like "Dilbert" poked fun at panel-based work stations, nicknamed "cubicles." Workers were comically shown as lab mice trying to find their way through mazes of office panels, while ergonomic technicians with stopwatches looked on.

Manufacturers looked for fresh ways to give office systems more creature comforts and aesthetic appeal, while still providing the functional advantages of panel systems. Herman Miller's "Ethospace Interiors," introduced in 1984, was designed by William Stumpf and Jack Kelley to provide an architectural alternative to panels. Ethospace used a frame-and-tile structure, into which could be slotted an assortment of tiles made of powder-coated steel, fabric, glass, plastic, wood laminates, or tack board. "Rail Tile Work Tools" resurrected the concept of pigeonholes in a modern vocabulary, with slotted "rails" accommodating every kind of desk-top accessory imaginable.

Bruce Burdick's panel-less Burdick Group was produced by Herman Miller for risk-taking, techno-savvy executives. Burdick believed that sitting behind a Burdick desk should give the owner the same sense of control and performance as sitting behind the wheel of a Porsche 911. Steelcase's "Contex" system, introduced in 1989, and Haworth's "Places: New Views," launched in 1991, replaced rectilinear cubicles with curving work surfaces, on stations that flowed into each other to facilitate team interaction.

A New Life for Wood

Another alternative to metal, plastic, and fabric-wrapped panels was Grand Rapids' old friend, wooden furniture. Throughout the systems revolution, companies like Stow & Davis, Baker, Sligh, Hekman, and Nucraft continued to make traditional wooden desks, seats, boardroom tables, and other office furniture. But some manufacturers created open office systems in wood. In 1971, Nucraft introduced "Nuspace," a line of acoustical screens with fabric panels and walnut posts and components that was produced until the mid-1980s. Stow & Davis offered its first open office line, known as the "Free-Dimensional furniture and wall system," in 1974. This system was finished in a combination of wood veneers, plastic laminates, metals, and fabrics. Rose/Johnson, Inc., the result of a merger between Johnson Furniture Company and Rose Manufacturing, produced several lines of wooden panel systems from 1980 until it became La-Z-Boy Contract, Inc. in 1993.

During the 1980s, the race to introduce open office systems became a race for market share. The largest companies began gobbling up smaller ones, to round out their lines and increase their production and distribution capacities. Steelcase purchased Stow & Davis in 1985 to increase its wood and design-oriented production. Herman Miller bought Spring Lake, Michigan-based Meridian, Inc. in 1980, to add Meridian's lines of file cabinets and metal furniture to its own. Haworth purchased Mueller Furniture Corporation in 1990, to make seating to complement its open office systems. And Knoll International, a furniture industry innovator with no previous Grand Rapids presence, became The Knoll Group in 1990 when it was purchased by Westinghouse Electric Corporation of Pittsburgh, and consolidated with Westinghouse Furniture Systems Division in Grand Rapids and Shaw-Walker in Muskegon. Nationally and internationally, these companies purchased or entered into cooperative agreements with dozens of companies. These new subsidiaries and partners created entries into worldwide markets across Europe, South America, and the Pacific Rim.

By 1997, contract furniture manufacturing had become a six-billion-dollar-a-year industry in West Michigan alone. Long the center of the resi-

Because of the rapid rate of change for businesses in the twentieth century, Grand Rapids' office furniture companies have continued to seek new innovations. Large companies institutionalized this search with new spaces for think tanks, test labs, and creative teamwork. Herman Miller opened its informal, playful "Design Yard" in 1988, created to blend in with the barns and silos of rural Zeeland, Michigan (ABOVE). Courtesy, Herman Miller, Inc. BELOW: In 1989 Steelcase dedicated its Corporate Development Center, a futuristic-looking pyramid that appears to have just landed on a restored prairie outside Grand Rapids. Courtesy, Steelcase, Inc.

Though expensive to build and operate, these temples to design will pay for themselves if they produce just one idea with as much growth potential as the panel-based system.

dential furniture industry, Grand Rapids was now the global center for office furniture manufacturing. Steelcase, Herman Miller, and Haworth, known locally as "The Big Three," became the top three manufacturers of office furnishings in the country. Combined, they now produce approximately forty-five percent of the nation's office furniture.

Office furniture manufacturers' products have become so different from those made for residential use that they have become an entirely separate industry. Some leading manufacturers don't even use the word "furniture" anymore, preferring new phrases like "systems," "office environments," or "intelligent workplaces." This separation into two furniture industries was made more apparent in 1973, with the organization of the Business and Institutional Furniture Manufacturers Association (BIFMA), headquartered in Grand Rapids. The organization was established to develop safety and performance standards and provide statistics for the contract furniture industry in the United States. After the adoption of the North American Free Trade Agreement, it became BIFMA International in 1995, with members from Canada and Mexico.

What new innovations will Grand Rapids' office furniture industry devise next? Greater mobility marks one recent trend in the invention of new office furniture forms. Haworth's "Crossings" line is lightweight, with modestly sized, free-standing components that are easy to move. New forms called "work planes," "perimeters," "stow-aways," and "organizers" are mounted on large wheels, allowing workers to transport part or all of their work stations for team collaboration. Crossings' residential scale, quirky angles, and finishes with names like "Bumpy Martian" and "Mystic Pumpkin" appeal to creative, high-tech, design-oriented businesses. Its tubular legs and repeating horizontal stretchers, combined with sheet metal and rounded wooden surfaces, are strikingly reminiscent of Frank Lloyd Wright's 1930s designs for Johnson Wax. But its innovative power and communications components clearly set the line in the late 1990s.

One manufacturer took the mobile office to its logical extreme. The

"Mobile Office Vehicle," or "MO-V," was introduced by the Lippert Furniture Company of Zeeland in 1994. Conceptualized by Southfield, Michigan inventor George Landry and designed by Grand Rapids designer Thomas Hazzard, the MO-V was part office and part conversion van. The rear of the van was outfitted with a permanently mounted desk and swivel chair, and lateral file cabinets and desk drawers were placed so that they could be reached from the fixed seat. The on-board cellular telephone, computer, printer, and fax machine could be tucked safely in the desk during travel. The van's back door opened to reveal a flip-up drawing board for engineers and architects who could use the mobile office at a job site.

After almost two centuries of separating the home from the office, many people are moving their work back into their homes. In 1959, Grand Rapidian Vennice Mark invented the "Little Home Office," made and sold by his company. But despite its intriguing name, Little Home Office was primarily a high-grade typewriter table disguised as a lamp or end table. The objective was to provide utility, with the appearance of residential furniture.

Traditional quality manufacturers like Sligh and Hekman continue to make not only wooden executive suites for the office, but also richly veneered kneehole, writing, and computer desks for use in the home.

Some companies have found success manufacturing new forms of furniture invented for specific Information Age professions. Interior Concepts Corporation of Spring Lake, Michigan has made modular computer furniture for classrooms and training facilities since 1982. It also makes work stations for catalog, reservation, and telemarketing centers and travel agencies. Nucraft's "Duomo" line of conference room furniture, introduced in 1994, includes a number of accommodations for information technology, including tables wired for phone and data networks, video conferencing cabinets, visual presentation boards, pre-wired lecterns, and "rollabout" computer presentation carts. Its 1997 "Satellite Collection" is specifically designed to accommodate information technology in intensive computer training areas.

Fast-tracked and forward-looking, Grand Rapids' office furniture industry now depends upon change. As headquarters for the industry's top three manufacturers, and producer of nearly half of the industry's output, Grand Rapids has emerged with a new self-image. The radically different nature of its products has even caused some to question whether Grand Rapids can still call itself "The Furniture City"!

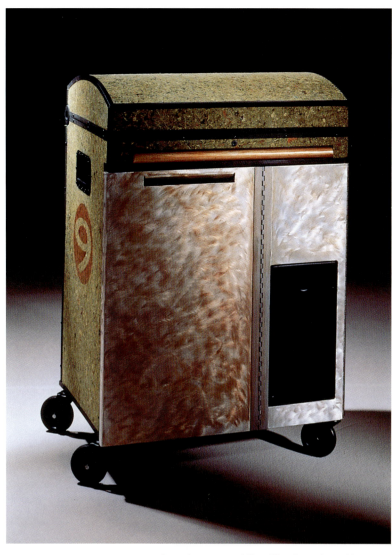

A temporary mobile office introduced by Haworth in the mid-1990s is "Correspondent." Based on an experimental prototype, which Haworth designers dubbed "Office-in-a-Box" (ABOVE), the entire Correspondent work station closes into a compact, refrigerator-sized cube with wheels and handles for easy movement. Designed to be a worker's short-term office while away from home base, Correspondent unfolds to reveal privacy panels, writing and keyboard surfaces, and bulletin and marker boards. Courtesy, Haworth, Inc.

While radical changes created one new furniture industry, skillful hands and adherence to tradition preserve the other. Today's Grand Rapids artisans still make fine wooden residential furniture in some of the nation's oldest operating factories.

Does Grand Rapids Still Make Furniture?

After the jarring revolution that overtook the contract furniture industry beginning in the 1960s, you might logically ask if Grand Rapids still makes wooden, residential furniture. Didn't that severe paradigm shift away from history, decoration, and even wood write the final epitaph for traditional Grand Rapids furniture? The simple answer is that Grand Rapids still makes a lot of furniture, in many of the same ways it always has.

It's true today that some of the old companies' names are remembered only by museums, libraries, and antique collectors. It's also true that the High Point Furniture Market in North Carolina now wields as much influence on the design community as the Grand Rapids Market once did. It's even true that Grand Rapids gave up most of its share of the market for medium- and lower-priced residential furniture to newer companies in other parts of the country. In fact, Grand Rapids' residential output today accounts for less than one percent of the nation's total. But of that small amount, most is purchased by the top two percent of the market.

Residential furniture makers have succeeded in West Michigan by making the most of the perception and reality that the Grand Rapids furniture industry is steeped in tradition. Locals point with pride to the continued operation of the Grand Rapids Area Furniture Manufacturers Association and the Grand Rapids Furniture Designers Association, both the oldest organizations in their fields in the United States. Graduates of the furniture design program at Kendall College of Art and Design populate furniture companies throughout the country, and look back to Grand Rapids as the place where they learned their craft. Some Grand Rapids manufacturers take pride in their long lineages, some dating back more than 140 years. Savvy advertisers make the most of romantic images from the factories, of furniture being made by the gnarled but skillful hands of "Old World craftsmen."

The longevity of some Grand Rapids furniture makers, and the success of their high-end marketing strategies, have resulted in tremendous continuity of certain product lines. Several manufacturers are selling pieces that have been in their catalogs for decades. These pieces are being produced from the same patterns as in the past, often on the same machines, in the same fac-

OPPOSITE: **This room setting was designed to capture the exclusivity of the Devonshire Hall, a one-thousand-piece limited edition grandfather clock by the Howard Miller Clock Co., 1996. With Howard Miller and Sligh Furniture Co. occupying the nation's number one and three spots respectively in the production of grandfather clocks, the Grand Rapids area today dominates that segment of the industry. Courtesy, Howard Miller Clock, Co.** ABOVE: **Students of the furniture design program at Kendall College of Art and Design review technical drawings with Bruce Mulder, an assistant professor who also maintains his own design practice in Grand Rapids. According to the College's own statistics, its graduates account for 90% of all U.S. residential furniture designers! Courtesy, Kendall College of Art and Design.**

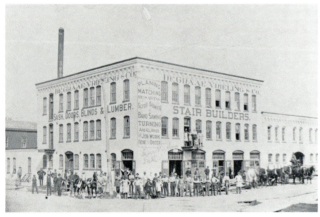

tory buildings, and by successive generations of the same families! Baker Furniture, Inc.'s "789" chair, a pierced-splat Chippendale chair, was first introduced as part of the "Georgian Mahogany Group" in 1933, when the company's factory was still located in Allegan, Michigan. More than six decades later, Baker still produces the same design at its factory in Holland, Michigan. The "W-80 Bombé Commode," a small French Provincial chest of drawers designed by Ralph Widdicombe for the John Widdicomb Company and made there since 1957, is still one of the company's top sellers.

Many techniques and procedures are handed down from one generation of worker to the next, and from one company to its successor. The Brothers Forslund moved in 1966 into the former Paalman Furniture Company plant, which had originally been constructed circa 1873 for DeGraaf, Vrieling & Co., a manufacturer of sash and blind as well as furniture. As each new firm moved into the factory, it adopted some of the original nineteenth-century equipment. Paalman had developed a production tracking system based on colors rather than words, since many of its workers spoke different languages. A different-colored box representing a style of furniture in production was placed over the corner handles of the heavy lugger carts, which were used to move stock through the factory. The box colors corresponded to tags on a production chart in the center of the factory. By looking for the appropriate colored box, workers could instantly tell which cart they should be working from, and foremen could take a quick visual inventory. When Forslund took over the factory, it continued to use the same system. Though most of its workers read English by then, there was no compelling reason to change, so the technique became a tradition.

Companies like Baker, John Widdicomb, Hekman, and Kindel have occupied the same factory buildings for long periods, and use old machinery and equipment. Some machines, like the Dodds Dovetailer, are much the same today as when they were invented, so there is no need to replace them. High traffic has worn depressions in the maple factory flooring around the machines. Durable tools like lugger carts often outlive several companies, and bear the stenciled names of their multiple owners to prove it.

Some changes have occurred in this atmosphere of tradition. West Michigan companies still produce high-end residential furniture, but portions of the work are completed in distant factories. The decorative residential mirrors and related accent tables manufactured by La Barge, Inc. are built in American factories outside the Grand Rapids area, and in Italy, Germany, Mexico, and the Pacific Rim. The plant at La Barge's Holland, Michigan headquarters simply assembles, warehouses, and distributes the completed pieces.

Other companies now utilize laser cutters for inlay veneers, because they are faster and more precise than hand cutting. But the laser-cut pieces are still ultimately joined with other machine- and hand-cut pieces, following Grand Rapids' heritage of combining labor-saving techniques with highly skilled, labor-intensive work.

The Herman Miller Clock Company of Zeeland, Michigan began making clocks in 1926 and changed its name to the Howard Miller Clock

Company in 1937. The company began to concentrate on tall, eighteenth-century case, or "grandfather," clocks after 1950, when the nation's families saw an increase in income, allowing more consumers to afford such a luxury. Today Howard Miller is the largest producer of clocks in America. It also reigns as the largest manufacturer of grandfather clocks in the world, with thirty to forty percent of the world market.

The Grand Rapids area is also home to one of the smallest clock makers in America, though its size only adds to its exclusivity. The American Heritage Clock Company of Grand Rapids began in 1990, employing a few highly skilled, highly paid craftsmen who had previously worked for other local manufacturers that are now defunct, like Colonial Clock Company of Zeeland. American Heritage's production is extremely limited: the company produces only about three hundred eighteenth- and nineteenth-century revival mantel, wall, and grandfather clocks per year, in cherry, yewwood, mahogany, curly maple, rosewood, and burled oak. Some of American Heritage's clocks are sold for more than $8,000, primarily through the Klingmans Furniture store in Grand Rapids, and by direct sales through the *Wall Street Journal*.

The clock division of the Sligh Furniture Company is also located in Zeeland. Founded as the Trend Clock Company in 1937 and acquired by Sligh in 1968, the Sligh Clock Division is one of the top three manufacturers of grandfather clocks in America today. Its eighteenth-century American reproductions of a cherry Goddard and a mahogany Aaron Willard grandfather clock were selected for Blair House, the presidential guest quarters in Washington, D.C., during its 1990 restoration.

Traditional Furniture: Museum Reproductions

Because mere reference to eighteenth-century style is insufficient proof of authenticity, Grand Rapids manufacturers have used museum specimens with impeccable provenance as inspiration for new lines of furniture since the 1920s. The efforts of several companies in this market niche have gained them exclusive relationships with some of Britain's and America's most prestigious historical institutions. It may seem ironic that the nation's finest reproductions of Colonial furniture come from factories in this second-tier Midwestern city. But to museums, Grand Rapids' high concentration of skilled carvers and finishers make it the only logical choice.

Baker's first direct connection with the great country estates of England for the purposes of furniture reproduction came in 1969, with its introduction of the "Woburn Abbey Collection." According to Sam Burchell's *A History of Furniture: Celebrating Baker Furniture 100 Years of Fine Reproductions*, the approximately twenty-five pieces of eighteenth-century English furniture, reproduced from the residence of the Duke of Bedford, were personally selected by the Duke and Hollis M. Baker. Measured drawings were made of each piece by Margaret Stephens Taylor of London's Royal College of Art, to record even the most minute details for reproduction. Literature for the collection carried a version of the distinctive coat of arms from the stone gate at the entrance to Woburn Abbey.

Sir Humphrey Wakefield, Bt., an authority on the history of British furniture, made the first selections of originals to be reproduced for Baker's

Master carver Lloyd Van Doornik uses hand chisels to carve a table leg at Baker Furniture, Inc.'s plant in Holland, Michigan, where he has worked for 43 years. Courtesy, Baker Furniture, Inc.

Some employees have worked in the same departments for long periods of time, and multiple family members stay at one plant through successive generations. Baker conducted a survey in 1952 to determine how many of its employees were related to at least one other person in the company and discovered an incredible 125 relatives! In the 1990s, the wood lathe operations at Zeeland Wood Turning Works were still controlled by three generations of men from the same family. Even giants like Steelcase, Inc. use institutionalized nepotism to keep good workers happy and "in the family."

Several companies still employ significant numbers of foreign-born workers. Today, just as a century ago, many languages are spoken in some Grand Rapids factories. Some well-trained workers are still recruited to leave their native lands to work in Grand Rapids. Others begin as hard-working, low-wage, unskilled workers, just as immigrants did in the nineteenth century.

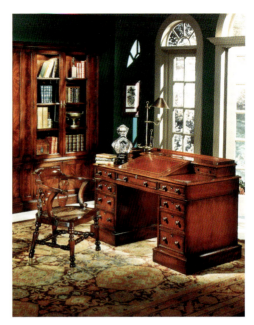

In 1991 the Hekman Furniture Co. introduced reproductions of furniture owned by the descendants of English novelist Charles Dickens. The line includes this sloped mahogany desk and cane seat smoker's bow chair. Because of the famous provenance of the original furniture, Hekman faithfully reproduced every detail, down to the impressions Dickens made tapping his ring on the desktop. Courtesy, Hekman Furniture Co.

1981 introduction of the "Stately Homes Collection." Distinctive pieces that could be adapted to the company's combination of machine production and skilled hand work were selected from some of the great homes of the British Isles, including Burghley House, home of the Marquess of Exeter; Chatsworth, home of the Duke of Devonshire; Floors Castle, home of the Duke of Roxburghe; Barons Court in Tyrone County, Ireland, home of the Duke of Abercorn; Blenheim Palace in Oxfordshire, home of the Duke of Marlborough; and Stratfield Saye House, home of the Duke of Wellington. The range of styles includes William and Mary, George II, Regency, Adam, Victorian, and Edwardian. Some of the most striking pieces from the collection are Chinese- or Roman-influenced Regency-style pieces, reproduced in mahogany with gilt, chinoiserie, and ebonized finishes.

The Hekman Furniture Company has also become known for its English adaptations and reproductions. Through the 1960s, Hekman remained largely a manufacturer of tables, in a wide range of styles including Neoclassical, Italian Provincial, French Provincial, and Danish Modern, as well as various English styles from the eighteenth century. In 1970 Grand Rapids native and Kendall College graduate Raymond K. Sobota designed the "English Yewwood Collection" for Hekman. When this traditionally styled group became one of the company's top sellers, it was quickly followed by other English Provincial collections with names like "Charing Cross," "Wind Row," and "Bambu Regency."

Before the 1980s, Kindel Furniture Company had a good reputation for furniture made in a range of English, Italian, Oriental, and French Provincial styles, but it could claim no particular niche. So in 1980 the company aggressively pursued the official license to reproduce furniture from the Henry Francis DuPont Winterthur Museum in Delaware, which holds one of the nation's largest and finest collections of Early American antiques. Kindel designers and crafts persons thoroughly studied and recreated every detail, even imperfections, of a 1660 Philadelphia Queen Anne mahogany chair from the museum's collections. Then company president Robert Fogarty took the chair to Delaware, and asked Winterthur curators to inspect it. Twenty-seven other manufacturers were also vying for the position, but Kindel was awarded the contract.

Over the next two years, Kindel designers and engineers spent an incredible 13,200 hours drawing every component of eighteen pieces. On a 1982 visit to the Kindel factory, *Connoisseur Magazine* editor Thomas Hoving was amazed to see 386 architectural drawings for one piece of furniture. He humorously remarked that there were skyscrapers in New York City that were not so well documented. According to the contract between Kindel and Winterthur, each drawing and prototype had to pass inspection by the museum's curators. Designs were designated as reproductions, adaptations, or variations, depending on the degree to which they followed the lines and measurements of the originals. Woods of the originals were analyzed by a botanist to ensure that the proper species were used, and castings ensured faithfulness to all the original hardware.

Today the Winterthur Reproduction Program is one of the most extensive in the country, with licensees for lamps, wallpapers, paintings, rugs, clocks, needlework, ceramics, fabrics, silver, and even playing cards, in addition to furniture. A select group of authorized Winterthur dealers retails the reproductions. Kindel reproduces almost exclusively in mahogany, with occasional inlays of satinwood and rosewood. Major pieces, which can retail for more than $30,000, include reproductions of a Philadelphia Chippendale high chest of drawers, a New York Federal sideboard, and a Newport, Rhode Island block-front secretary by Townsend and Goddard.

Kindel soon entered into a similar licensing contract for pieces from the historic properties owned by the National Trust for Historic Preservation, and in 1984 became the exclusive licensee for the Irish Georgian Society. Local carvers received training in hand carving, and a master carver was recruited from England. The company's sales and work force rose steadily, until by the late 1980s it claimed the nation's largest hand carving operation.

The distinctive flavor of eighteenth-century American furniture has been a feature of Baker's "Historic Charleston Reproductions" since 1976. The originals reproduced for this group reside in various public and private collections in Charleston, South Carolina. Many were made in England or France and exported to the wealthier residents of the Southern Colonies; others are reproduced from known Charleston cabinetmakers such as Thomas Elfe.

The Colonial Williamsburg Foundation was a pioneer in licensing manufacturers to reproduce its collections in the 1930s, though the Williamsburg furniture reproductions were made by Buffalo, New York-based Kittinger Company, Inc. But when Kittinger began to liquidate in the late 1980s, Williamsburg was besieged by more than twenty top manufacturers, all seeking to be the new licensee for the Williamsburg Collections. In 1990 the Foundation announced that, because of the craftsmanship of its factories and its marketing capabilities, Baker Furniture, Inc. of Grand Rapids would produce the "Williamsburg Line." Baker's long-standing commitment to reproducing seventeenth- and eighteenth-century English and American furniture suited Williamsburg's collections. The company's veneering and finishing also made possible the reproduction of pieces beyond Kittinger's abilities.

Baker introduced its first Williamsburg pieces in the spring of 1991. Half of the line were revivals of top-selling Kittinger pieces, while the other half were pieces that had never before been reproduced. In 1995 the line was broadened to include not only formal mahogany furniture, but also informal, folk, and painted pieces from the Abby Aldrich Rockefeller Folk Art Center, a sister institution of Colonial Williamsburg. These pieces included a painted cupboard made in Ohio, a Providence Hall cane sofa, and a pier table from the Virginia Piedmont. This attempt at "tradition with a twist" was aimed at younger buyers with more relaxed tastes.

Though much of Grand Rapids' wooden reproduction furniture has been English or American eighteenth-century, this is not exclusively the case. Because of the trade relationships between China and Europe in the eighteenth century, Chinese or chinoiserie (made to look like Chinese) furniture was frequently used alongside more conventional English, French, and American pieces. Baker's "Far East Collection," first marketed in 1949, provided designs drawn from the Tang, Ming, and Ch'ing dynasties and less

Kindel Furniture Co. reproduction of a rare, mahogany Townsend & Goddard block-front secretary, from an original in the collections of the Henry Francis DuPont Winterthur Museum, 1994. Courtesy, Kindel Furniture Co.

ABOVE: Baker "Norfolk Chair" reproduction, from an original owned by the Colonial Williamsburg Foundation, 1994. BELOW: This secretaire, made in 1996 as part of the John Widdicomb Co. "British India" line, combines the familiarity of English classical furniture forms with the exotic materials and motifs of Colonial India.

formal bamboo furniture. These pieces were compatible with Baker's English reproductions. The line's long life has allowed for the introduction of a wide range of forms over the decades, including bunching and console tables, chests, dining and bedroom suites, armoires, and entertainment centers. Far East finishes based on traditional lacquer techniques have included Celadon, Poppy Red, Gray-Gunmetal, Straw-Bone, and Tabasco-Mecassar. The "Tansu," or "Chests of Old Japan" collection, begun in the late 1970s, offered a modular system of cabinets for the home, made of American ash with antiqued iron hardware. The Kohler Company purchased Baker in 1986 and introduced the "Far East Vanity Ensemble," which incorporates Kohler sink and bathtub fixtures into Baker Far East altar tables.

Much of the 1980s and '90s production of the John Widdicomb Company, which specializes in custom and unusual finishes, has been traditional with an exotic flair. Chad Womack, a Detroit native who moved to Grand Rapids to attend Kendall College and pursue a design career, created several successful lines of exotic furniture for John Widdicomb. Womack began with the company in 1980, but his big break came in 1986 when the new owners decided to produce a line based on the nineteenth-century German neoclassic style known as Biedermeier. As Womack began to research the Biedermeier style, he occasionally ran across pieces made in Russia during the same period that were similar, but with a distinctly Russian flavor. The pieces were strongly masculine, with rich wood veneers, marble, and glass, and exotic figural carvings and hardware of eagles, lions, and mythical creatures like griffins, sphinxes, and Chimerae. Though Womack became more interested in these "Russian Empire" pieces than in the German Biedermeier, company officials were skeptical. After decades of Cold War opposition to Russia, would Americans buy Russian furniture?

Recognizing the beauty of Womack's designs, the company gave him the go-ahead to produce several pieces, and planned to market them under the generic moniker "Biedermeier" rather than the politically risky "Russian Empire." But after seeing the strength of character in his initial samples, the company decided to accept the risk and introduce the pieces at the High Point Market under the Russian name. Their timing couldn't have been better. The undoing of Communism and spirit of *glasnost* in current news headlines created a strong consumer interest in Russian art. John Widdicomb's Russian furniture was one of the hottest items at Market, and within a few years, the Russian Empire line accounted for fifteen percent of the company's production.

With a sudden demand for his Russian designs, Womack scoured antique shops, museum collections, and auction houses across the country in search of other rare examples. After the Iron Curtain was lifted, he traveled to Leningrad (now St. Petersburg), to study and sketch more pieces at the Hermitage and other palaces of the czars. One of the most distinctive pieces in the line was a reproduction from the period of Czar Alexander I, circa 1820, of a regal-looking wooden chair with a scrolled crest decorated in black with a two-headed eagle design. A console table blended a Gothic arched apron with neoclassical fluted legs and ormolu rosettes and lion mask pulls. A black frieze contrasted sharply with the cherry and Circassian walnut solids, and Russian Karelian birch and rosewood veneers.

Womack's exotic flair met new success in 1994 with the introduction of John Widdicomb's "British India" Collection, which also combined a bit of the familiar with a touch of the foreign. The line recreated the staid English forms of Regency, Chippendale, Adam, and Sheraton as they were enlivened by cabinetmakers in the Indian sub-continent during its colonial occupation. Because they were essentially Western forms, the occasional tables and secretaries in the British India Collection blended well with other English eighteenth-century reproductions in American homes. But their flamboyant Eastern decoration, based on Islamic and Saracenic motifs, and exotic materials such as faux ivory inlay and faux tortoise shell veneers, made them colorful room accents. Other companies also mixed the comfortable and the unusual in British Colonial furniture. In 1994 Baker's Milling Road division began to produce a line of mahogany armoires, campeche chairs, and four-poster beds based on British Colonial furniture from the West Indies.

Renowned New York interior designer Mario Buatta created a romantic line for John Widdicomb in 1989. With a passion for flowers and yards of fabrics, which earned him the nickname "Prince of Chintz," Buatta reproduced English Country antiques, some from his own home. The company's special talents in creating painted finishes were put to work, creating soft, pastel surfaces decorated by chinoiserie scenes or floral garlands with pink bows. Overstuffed chairs featured his trademark chintz, and pleated ottomans were given deep fringe skirts. Buatta's reputation as a designer for celebrities placed John Widdicomb in the national spotlight, and the Buatta Collection grew to nearly a quarter of the company's total sales.

A Tradition of Modernism

Not all of the residential furniture made today in Grand Rapids is traditional in its styling. Some lines play off of Grand Rapids' equally impressive heritage of modern designs. After nearly thirty years in which Herman Miller's products were absent from the residential furniture market, the company re-introduced fifty of its classic Nelson and Eames designs in 1994. Renewed interest in "Fifties Modern" furniture had become so great by the early 1990s that collectors were gobbling up originals from antique stores and auctions. Herman Miller decided to manufacture new pieces to meet the demand, and marked them with special medallions so that collectors could distinguish them from the 1950s originals. Though more affordable than the originals, the new pieces still ranged in price from $125 for a child's clothing rack to an $8,000 sofa.

Designers continued to experiment with bent plywood into the 1990s. Canadian architect Frank Gehry designed a sculptural line of scrolled, bent maple laminate furniture in 1991, which was introduced by The Knoll Group and manufactured on contract by Davidson Plyforms, Inc., of Grand Rapids. The paper-thin curves and basket weave design of the pieces give the illusion that they are fragile and lightweight, disguising their true structural strength. Because some of the forms resemble the padding of ice hockey players, each was given a name derived from a hockey term, such as the "High Sticking" and "Hat Trick" side chairs, and "Power Play" and "Cross Check" armchairs.

This "Power Play" chair, designed by Frank Gehry for The Knoll Group and produced in 1991 by Davidson Plyforms, Inc. of Grand Rapids, demonstrates the city's continuing role in the production of sculptural furniture shapes in bent plywood.

A newer Grand Rapids company, Bexley Heath, Ltd., creates lines that its owner, Jim DeVries, describes as "contemporary furniture with historic roots." Its 1997 cherry and maple "Beba Collection" (from "bed" and "bath"), conceived by Grand Rapids designer Mary Witte, shows the influence of 1930s French Art Deco. In 1998 the company introduced the "Widdicomb Collection," a series of re-issues of biomorphic and modern pieces designed by T. H. Robsjohn-Gibbings for the Widdicomb Furniture Company from the 1940s through the 1960s.

Carl Forlsund, Inc. was somewhat unique among Grand Rapids manufacturers, in that the company both made and retailed furniture. Its direct-mail catalog featured furniture made in the Brothers Forslund Manufactory, and lamps, glassware, china, and accessories by other manufacturers, which complemented the catalog's informal Early American personality. The conversational style of the catalog text was geared less toward wealthy clients of professional interior designers, and more toward middle-class buyers who drew personal satisfaction from designing their own interiors.

The "Background For Fashion" in Carl Forslund's *Quaint American Portfolio of Unusual Furniture* from the Summer of 1950 illuminates the catalog's folklorish charm:

> When our forefathers moved westward from the coastal colonies they took with them only the necessities that could be carried by pack, or at best packed into a single wagon. But very frequently such necessities included one or two prized pieces of beloved furniture. Because even in those days a spark of beauty was an essential to pioneer women to set-up **home**, as the rudiments of shelter and comfort.
>
> Today many of these originals are prized collection pieces, enviously sought for at old homestead auctions; inaccessible or priceless for the average.
>
> From such originals our "Quaint American" collection has been developed, piece by piece, over many years. It is as traditionally American as the flintlock squirrel gun and coon skin cap.
>
> It will be forever **good**, growing more treasured and fashionable with the passing years. . . . You can start your collection **now**, and add piece by piece until you have furnished as much of your home as you desire with these "Quaint American" authentic designs in solid cherry.

Forslund gave each item a colorful name, associated with an historical place or figure from Colonial or Victorian America, or a Forslund family member or acquaintance. For instance, "Grandma Castle's Pleasant Bedroom Furniture" was named after a ninety-two-year-old neighbor of the Forslunds. The "Trudy Dunwell Footstool for Needlepoint" was named for the woman who lent the family her original footstool for reproduction.

In addition to the catalog, the company operated its own store, which was originally located on Fulton Street in downtown Grand Rapids. Later the downtown store was moved to Pearl Street on the Grand River, and branches were opened in Ann Arbor, Michigan, and on Grand Rapids' 28th Street. One strategy that Forslund stores used to lure people through its doors also endeared the company in customers' hearts. A Forslund employee would send a personal note of congratulations to each bride-to-be listed in the newspaper engagement announcements, along with a certifi-

One of Forlsund's signature pieces was the "Rip Van Lee" chair, shown here in the library of Carl Forslund, Sr.'s home in a 1959 catalog. Owners of Rip Van Lee chairs proudly told anyone who would listen about their generous proportions and slipper-soft leather upholstery. According to Jon Forslund, when golfer Byron Nelson once played golf with President Gerald R. Ford, their conversation turned toward Ford's hometown of Grand Rapids. They realized they had more in common than their love of golf: they both also loved their Forlsund Rip Van Lee chairs.

cate for a free vase or bowl. Many of those young couples went to Forslund's to accept their gift, and became loyal customers.

Another marketing technique that Forslund stores used beginning in the 1950s was to place humorous, quaint signs along the highways of Michigan. Each featured a different colorfully painted cartoon of people making their way to Forslund's. One depicted a man trying to get his Model T up a steep hill; another showed a boy in a tug-of-war with an equally determined donkey. These large, wooden roadside signs, the regional version of Burma Shave signs, were instantly recognized and fondly remembered by those who passed them. The signs were taken down when the last Forslund store closed in 1992, but many people remain personally attached to the company's name and products.

Baker developed a national network of showrooms. In 1972 the company merged with Chicago-based Knapp & Tubbs to create Baker, Knapp & Tubbs. Their showrooms were established in key design centers of major American cities, including Atlanta, Chicago, Cleveland, Dallas, Detroit, Houston, Los Angeles, Miami, New York, Philadelphia, San Francisco, Seattle, and Washington, D.C. The company also operates a showroom in High Point, North Carolina, but the one in Grand Rapids, one of the final vestiges of the Grand Rapids Furniture Market, was closed in 1980. Baker, Knapp & Tubbs Showrooms are filled with Baker furniture, but they also display that old Grand Rapids predisposition toward cooperative marketing, selling the products of other high-end Grand Rapids manufacturers, such as Kindel and John Widdicomb.

Though Baker no longer maintains a Grand Rapids showroom, for several years its loyal customers were afforded a special opportunity to buy directly from the factory. Baker would advertise factory sales of closeout and discontinued merchandise. By the time these sales took place, news would have spread by word of mouth throughout the Midwest. Hundreds of people from Michigan and nearby states would travel to Grand Rapids or Holland where the sales were held, and line up early in hopes of finding a good deal on high-quality Baker furniture.

Grand Rapids' furniture manufacturers close the twentieth century as vibrant participants in the West Michigan economy and the global marketplace. As the nature of the products has changed, so has the identity of the region. No longer one united industry but several specialized industries make furniture in Grand Rapids and its surrounding communities.

But what about the future? Will Grand Rapids' identity continue to be associated with the products it makes? What will those products look like, and what will be their impact on society? Will manufacturers, laborers, designers, inventors, sales people, and crafts people continue to change to meet the new demands of their market? Will there be new advantages for them to exploit, like the ones that allowed the industry to thrive in the past? The future of Grand Rapids furniture is one chapter of this story that will have to be written by the furniture makers of tomorrow. But when they do write it, I'll bet it will be atop a desk from The Furniture City!

ABOVE: Bexley Heath, Ltd. reproduction of a "Fifties Modern" coffee table, originally designed by T. H. Robsjohn-Gibbings for the Widdicomb Furniture Co. Courtesy, John Widdicomb Co. BELOW: The humorous roadside signs of Carl Forslund Furniture Stores counted down the miles for auto travelers on their way to Grand Rapids. They stood along Michigan's highways from the late 1950s until the early 1990s, and served as a visible reminder that Grand Rapids was a place that made furniture. When the last Forslund store closed in 1992, many people viewed the removal of the familiar signs from the landscape as a symbol of irreversible change in the furniture industry. Courtesy, David and Karen Custer.

Directory of Grand Rapids Area Furniture
Makers and Marks

The following pages contain detailed information about nearly 800 companies that have made furniture in Western Michigan over the past 160-plus years. They range from one-person cabinetmaker shops to multi-national corporations employing tens of thousands of workers: makers of residential and contract furniture, pianos, clocks, lamps, refrigerators, stoves, wooden novelties, and movable architectural elements. I have also included some manufacturers or purveyors of finishes, upholstery, wood, and other accessories and supplies, if the company also sold some furniture under its name, or if the company's label might appear somewhere on a piece of furniture, and thus make identification of the actual maker confusing. A few of these related companies merit inclusion simply because of their long-standing connection to the industry.

Geographically, the directory covers roughly the western third of the state of Michigan centering on Grand Rapids, and extends from Traverse City in the north to Sturgis in the south. This area generally thinks of itself as one distinct region: historically, most of the furniture makers within this area advertised in Grand Rapids furniture journals, or had owners, suppliers, or a showroom located in Grand Rapids.

Working with the research staff of the Public Museum of Grand Rapids, I compiled this information with the needs of collectors, antique dealers, auctioneers, curators, archivists, librarians, and designers in mind. I hope that other furniture manufacturers, decorative arts historians, Michigan residents, and families who have had a member work in the area's furniture industry will also find it informative. We drew from a great number of sources, including period furniture journals and newspapers, furniture market guides, city directories, company histories and press releases, trade catalogs, community library vertical files, published articles and histories of Grand Rapids, and actual pieces of furniture. While most of the trademarks and labels pictured probably did appear on a piece of furniture, they were taken from all of the sources listed above, and not just from the undersides of furniture. Because of the size of the region covered and the great number of companies that have operated in it, there is little doubt that some companies have been inadvertently overlooked, and some facts that were taken from single sources might be disputable. With that in mind, I offer this directory to you as the best attempt to date to document the furniture makers of this region, with the hope that it will inspire further research into the history of countless cabinetmakers and manufacturers.

Christian G. Carron, Curator of Collections
The Public Museum of Grand Rapids

OPPOSITE: Sometimes the clue that identifies the maker of a piece of furniture turns up unexpectedly. Knowing where to look and what to look for can occasionally unravel the mystery. The origin of this ca. 1860 dresser was unknown until the drawers were removed, and a flashlight revealed the faint pencil signature "Thomas Bonnett Maker/Grand Rapids" on the inside of the case back.

A.B. CHAIR CO.
1927 - 1928

Charlotte, Michigan
Manufacturer of living room chairs. Listed in *The Buyer's Guide* for 1927 and 1928.

A-B STOVE CO.
1909 - 1945

1915   1922

Battle Creek, Michigan
Manufacturer of free-standing stoves, ranges, and furnaces.
COMPANY HISTORY
1909: Company founded.
1945: Merges with the Michigan - Detroit Stove Co.
1953: All manufacturing operations are moved to Detroit.

AMI

SEE Automatic Musical Instrument Co.

ACE TABLE CO.
1928

Greenville, Michigan
Manufacturer of folding tables. Listed in *The Buyer's Guide* for 1928.

ACME BEDDING CO.
1954 - 1996

Grand Rapids, Michigan
Manufacturer of bedroom furniture and mattresses.

ACME CHAIR CO.
1928

Reading, Michigan
Manufacturer of folding chairs and tables. Listed in *The Buyer's Guide* for 1928.

ACME MANUFACTURING CO.
1922

Niles, Michigan
Manufacturer of Red Cedar Chests.
Advertised in the *Furniture Record*.

1922

ADAMS, ZEPHANIAH
ca. 1835

Grand Rapids, Michigan
Chair maker.

ADJUSTABLE TABLE CO.
1905 - 1949

Grand Rapids, Michigan
Manufacturer, under the brand name "Satellite," of stands and tripod tables for office machines, card files, scientific equipment, reference books and ledgers; student and factory sketching tables.
SEE ALSO Karl Manufacturing Co.; White Steel Sanitary Furniture Co.

ALASKA REFRIGERATOR CO., THE
ca. 1913 - 1929

1913

Muskegon, Michigan
Advertised in *The Grand Rapids Furniture Record* and *Good Furniture* as "exclusive refrigerator manufacturers."

1918   1922-29

ALEXIS MANUFACTURING CO.
(A Howard Miller Company)
1945 - present

Grand Rapids, Michigan
Manufacturer of custom furniture; wood and upholstered chairs and chair frames by contract for other furniture manufacturers.

Alexis The chair manufacturer's chair manufacturer
ca. 1990

ALLEGAN FURNITURE CO.
1917

Allegan, Michigan
Manufacturer of furniture. Cited in a general listing of furniture manufacturers.

ALLEGAN WOOD CRAFT SHOPS
1928

Allegan, Michigan
Manufacturer of wood novelties. Listed in *The Buyer's Guide* for 1928.

ALLEN, Z. E. CO.
1870 - 1900

Grand Rapids, Michigan
Manufacturer of carpet sweepers from 1870 - 1882; manufacturer of tables, chairs, bedroom suites, and office desks from 1883 - 1900.
SEE ALSO Grand Rapids Table Co.
COMPANY HISTORY
1870: Company begins manufacture of carpet sweepers.
1883: Sweeper line sold to Bissell Carpet Sweeper Co. of Grand Rapids. Company begins production of furniture.
1900: Company purchased by Grand Rapids Table Co.

ALT & BATSCHE MANUFACTURING CO.
1914 - 1916

Grand Rapids, Michigan
Manufacturer of furniture. Cited in a general listing of furniture manufacturers.

AMERICAN CABINET CO.
1921 - 1928

1927

Holland, Michigan
Manufacturer of period revival bedroom furniture with decorative painting.

AMERICAN CARVING & MANUFACTURING CO.
1893 - 1918

Grand Rapids, Michigan
Manufacturer of carvings and moldings for the furniture and construction industries.

AMERICAN HERITAGE CLOCKS
1990 - present

Grand Rapids, Michigan
Manufacturer of approximately 300 high-end, hand-crafted mantel, wall, and grand-father clocks per year, in cherry, yewwood, mahogany, curly maple, rosewood, and burled oak. Distributed primarily through Klingmans Furniture Co. in Grand Rapids, and direct sales through the *Wall Street Journal.*

COMPANY HISTORY
1990: American Heritage Clocks founded by Charles Curtis.
1996: Purchased and operated by Minnesota-based Kuempel Chime Works & Studio, Inc.

AMERICAN PATENT DRESSING CASE CO.
ca. 1883 - ca. 1891

Grand Rapids, Michigan
In 1883 a patent was granted to inventor Joseph Penney for his American Eastlake-style combination dressing case and sanitary washstand. Its patented action allowed the above-drawer counter top with mirror to pivot, revealing a second marble counter top with inset sink, and a faucet pipe attached to its own water reservoir.

AMERICAN SCHOOL FURNITURE CO.
1899 - 1906

New York, New York
Manufacturer of school desks, church pews, and opera or theater seating.
SEE ALSO American Seating Co.; Grand Rapids School Furniture Co.

COMPANY HISTORY
1899: Formed when Grand Rapids School Furniture Co. was merged with eighteen other school, church, and seating manufacturers from across the country. Local plant was then known as the Grand Rapids School Furniture Works of the American School Furniture Co.
1906: Name changed to American Seating Co.

AMERICAN SEATING CO.
1906 - present

Grand Rapids, Michigan (also New York, New York and Chicago, Illinois)
SEE ALSO American School Furniture Co.

COMPANY HISTORY
1886: Grand Rapids School Furniture Co. (GRSFCo.) founded.
1899: GRSFCo. merges with eighteen other school, church, and seating manufacturers to form the American School Furniture Co., headquartered in New York.
1906: Name changes to American Seating Co. Offices move from New York to Chicago.

ca. 1895

1931: Offices move from Chicago to Grand Rapids.
1941 - 1945: Converted to 100% wartime production, including tank seats, mortar shell boxes, and bomber and glider parts.
1983: Company is purchased by Georgia-based Fuqua, Inc.
1987: Management-led buy-out returns headquarters to Grand Rapids.

PERSONNEL
Through most of its history American Seating has been served by presidents of unusual longevity, most notably Thomas Boyd (1906 - 1929), and H.M. Talliaferro (1929 - 1958). Probably the names most associated with American Seating were the master carvers in its Church Division. Alois Lang, who learned woodcarving in his home town of Oberammergau, Bavaria, began in the American School Furniture (later Seating) Co. carving studios in 1902. Joseph F. Wolters, who began as an apprentice carver in Germany, came to American Seating's Church Division in 1923. Both were known for their carved statuary, plaques, and architectural details, including "Last Supper" altar pieces, memorials, and special commissions that grace many churches and public buildings throughout West Michigan and the nation.

PRODUCTS
Since it began with the union of nineteen varied companies, American Seating always operated with multiple divisions and plants, and several lines of products. In its early years, the company produced school desks, church pews, and opera or theater

Sanding school desk tops with floor sander, American Seating Co., date unknown.

1915   1915

1930-56

1964

1964

1964   1964

1978

1986

1990

AMERIWOOD INDUSTRIES INTERNATIONAL CORP.
1991 - 98

1994

ANDERSON, JAMES A. & CO.
ca. 1886 - ca. 1901

seating. At different times it added stadium bleachers, folding chairs, transportation seating, and hospital and office furniture to that list. Most Americans have at some point sat in an American Seating product.

SCHOOL PRODUCTS: American Seating inherited production of the wood and cast iron "Combination" chair/desk from GRSFCo. In 1911 an updated Combination known as the "101" made use of tubular steel. Other models introduced such features as adjustable height, swivel seats, and bases that didn't need to be bolted to the floor. All of these elements were incorporated into the 1921 "Universal," which was scientifically designed to promote good posture, and stayed in production for decades. Post-WWII designs made use of new materials such as plywood, plastic, and plastic laminate.

SEATING PRODUCTS: Various wooden folding chairs for bridge tables or meeting halls were replaced in 1930 by the "Folding Forty" chair and its successors. More than five million of these were made for the armed forces during WWII alone, and millions more are in use every day throughout the world.

OFFICE PRODUCTS: While American Seating had long been making seating for public use, directories first list open office plan furniture among the company's products in 1973. Some concentration was placed on specialty offices in factories or laboratories, for which they already produced more conventional furniture.

STADIUM AND THEATER PRODUCTS: The plywood and cast iron opera seats made by their predecessors were replaced by more opulent, upholstered seats with elaborate Rococo decorations for the motion picture palaces of the 1920s. Streamlined designs culminated in the 1938 "Bodiform" chair, which required two years of research and testing. Notable installations of various lines can be found at Radio City Music Hall and Lincoln Center in New York, and the U.S. Senate and House Galleries in Washington D.C. Although American Seating first listed stadium seating among its products in 1951, it today boasts that most major league ballparks in the country, including the Houston Astrodome, Denver's Mile High Stadium, and Baltimore's Camden Yards, are outfitted with its products. At this writing they hold an approximately 50% share of the market in stadium and theater seating.

TRANSPORTATION PRODUCTS: the first all-tubular steel-framed seat for use in city buses was introduced in 1931. From that beginning, American Seating's Transportation Division expanded to claim a 90% market share at the time of this writing. Their products included seating for cross-country buses, subways and mass-transit systems, and driver's seats for trucks and locomotives. Larger clients have included the San Francisco Bay Area Transit System and the New York City Transit Authority.

CHURCH PRODUCTS: The Church Division, which was consolidated from other plants to Grand Rapids in 1927, provided a wide range of architectural and furniture designs, pews, altars, and special carvings for church interiors. Grand Rapids city directories last list the Church Division in 1969.

MARKS AND LABELS

Grand Rapids School Furniture Co. desks carried a casting of the company name and sometimes a "GRSFCo" monogram on the leg trestles. A scrolled monogram "ASCo" surrounded by a circle served as American Seating's early logo. In 1930 the company began to literally brand or wood-burn of a "lamp of knowledge" to wooden desks. This was replaced in 1956 by an impressionistic row of chair seats called the "modern chair row," which was applied or molded onto all products. In the 1970s the company logo was simply the sans-serif letters, "Am Se Co". In the 1980s the company used a square with rounded corners, surrounding a single line bent to represent a seat. By the 1990s the trademark had changed to a five-point star surrounding a stylized "S".

Grandville, Michigan
Factory for Ameriwood Furniture Division in Dowagiac, Michigan, one of the nation's largest manufacturers of "RTA" (Ready to assemble) home, home entertainment, and office furniture, under the brand names "Affordable," "Members Only," and "Portfolio." Purchased by Dorel Industries, Inc. in 1998. Successor to Rospatch, Inc. in 1991.
SEE ALSO Rospatch, Inc.

Grand Rapids, Michigan
Manufacturer of "machine and hand carvings."

ANDERSON MANUFACTURING CO.
1934

Grand Rapids, Michigan
Manufacturer of occasional tables. Listed in the *Grand Rapids Market Ambassador* for 1934.

ANWAY CO.
1912 - 1925

Grand Rapids, Michigan
Manufacturer of upholstered furniture.
Successor to Keil - Anway Co.
SEE ALSO Keil - Anway Co.

ARCADIA FURNITURE CO.
1906 - 1952

Arcadia, Michigan
Manufacturer of low- to medium-priced bedroom furniture. Pieces were made from native hard maple or "printed oak," a veneer which was stained, then mechanically roller-printed with a wood grain pattern to simulate more expensive solid oak. Early pieces carried a printed, rectangular paper label. Pieces from the 1940s are known to have been designed by Carl Eggebrecht of Grand Rapids.
SEE ALSO Arcadia Mirror Co.

ARCADIA MIRROR CO.
at least 1925 - 1927

Arcadia, Michigan
Manufacturer of mirrors, in association with the Arcadia Furniture Co.
SEE ALSO Arcadia Furniture Co.

ARCHITECTURAL SYSTEMS, INC. (ASI)
1960 - 1961

Grand Rapids, Michigan
Manufacturer of store fixtures and movable floor-to-ceiling partitions.
COMPANY HISTORY
1960: Company founded.
1961: Company is purchased and name changes to Architectural Systems Division of Westinghouse Electric Corp., eventually renamed Westinghouse Furniture Systems, Inc.
SEE ALSO Westinghouse Furniture Systems, Inc.

ASCOT FURNITURE BY DEVIN INDUSTRIES, INC.
1988 - present

Kaleva, Michigan
Manufacturer of furniture.

ASSID, ALFRED CABINETMAKERS
at least 1959 and 1960

Okemos, Michigan
Listed in the Grand Rapids Furniture Market guides as manufacturers of 18th-century reproduction candle sconces, table planters, small cabinets, chests, and drop lid desks in pine, walnut, and fruit woods.

1960

ATKINS & SOULE

1866 - 1868

Grand Rapids, Michigan
Manufacturer of furniture. Assets purchased by Phoenix Furniture Co. in 1870.
SEE ALSO Phoenix Furniture Co.

AULSBROOK & JONES FURNITURE CO.
1908 - 1922

Sturgis, Michigan
Manufacturer of mahogany and oak bedroom furniture.
Successor to Aulsbrook & Sturges Manufacturing Co. Predecessor to Aulsbrook-Jones-Grobhiser Co.
SEE ALSO Aulsbrook-Jones-Grobhiser Co.; Aulsbrook & Sturges Manufacturing Co.

AULSBROOK - JONES - GROBHISER CO.
1922 - 1933

Sturgis, Michigan
Manufacturer of bedroom suites and tables.
COMPANY HISTORY
1922: Company formed by merger of Grobhiser Co. and Aulsbrook & Jones Co.
1933: Reorganizes as the Sturges-Aulsbrook-Jones Corp.
SEE ALSO Aulsbrook & Jones Furniture Co.; Sturges-Aulsbrook-Jones Corp.

1927

AULSBROOK & STURGES MANUFACTURING CO.
1882 - 1908

Sturgis, Michigan
COMPANY HISTORY
1882: Founded by Albert Sturges and Martin Aulsbrook.
1908: Becomes Aulsbrook & Jones upon the death of Sturges.
SEE ALSO Aulsbrook & Jones Furniture Co.

AUTOMATIC MUSICAL INSTRUMENT CO. (AMI)
1909 - 1962

Grand Rapids, Michigan
COMPANY HISTORY
1909: Founded as National Automatic Music Co. Separate divisions handle manufacturing of nickelodeon pianos, and placement of the nickelodeons in

AMI "Streamliner" jukebox, 1939.

MANUFACTURED BY

Automatic
INSTRUMENT
GRAND RAPIDS,

1938

AMI *Incorporated*

1950

AMI
1971

Rowe **AMI**
1963

B & B FRAME CO.
1942 - 1949

B & B MANUFACTURING CO.
1946 - 1949

BAINES & MOSIER
1917 - 1918

BAKER & CO.

BAKER FURNITURE FACTORIES, INC.

BAKER FURNITURE, INC.
1903 - present

public facilities.

1925: Piano manufacturing division becomes the National Piano Manufacturing Co. and the Automatic Musical Instrument Co. (AMI) handles both the manufacturing and distribution of the automatic players and later jukeboxes.

1962: AMI is purchased by Rowe AC Services, a division of the Automatic Canteen Co. of America.

PRODUCTS

AMI's first products were electric pianos. Most notable was the "National Nick-elodeon," a coin-operated player piano without a keyboard. For a time cabinets for these player pianos were built by Bush & Lane, while other components were made by AMI in Grand Rapids. In 1927 AMI introduced the National Automatic Selective Phonograph, the first jukebox. Cabinets were wooden, and resembled other phonograph cabinets of the day. In 1930 styling was revamped, and the (still wooden) cabinet took on a more streamlined appearance. In 1932 AMI also came out with the first selective remote control wall boxes, which were miniature jukeboxes used in booths of diners.

Beginning with the "Top Flight" model introduced in 1936, which was made in part of plastics and had fluorescent lights, styling closely mirrored developments in popular culture and industrial design. The "Singing Tower" models of the early 1940s looked like science fiction robots. The "Model-A's," the first post-World War II models, resembled the front grilles of cars. The "Continental" models produced in the early 1960s looked like flying saucers with radar dishes. "Phono-Vue" was added in 1968, which showed 8mm films with the music, forerunners of music videos. The 1984 introduction of the "Video-Music Entertainment Center" made the merger of audio and video complete. Many of the cabinets for these machines were sub-contracted by another Grand Rapids manufacturer, RoseJohnson. In 1987 records were replaced with compact discs.

OTHER SOURCES

Rowe-AMI maintains a museum of its own products at its offices in Grand Rapids, which is not open to the general public. In 1988 a history was authored by Frank Adams, Ph.D., entitled *Rowe-AMI Jukeboxes, 1927-1988: Those Magnificent Juke-boxes*.

MARKS AND LABELS

The nickelodeons of the 1920s had stencils or metal plates which read "Property of Automatic Musical Instrument Company, Grand Rapids, Michigan". The stylized monogram "AMI" appeared on the 1938 "Streamliner," and continued with slight variations through the 1962 "Continental." In 1963, with the change in ownership, came the addition of "Rowe" to the AMI monogram.

Grand Rapids, Michigan
Manufacturer of upholstery frames.

Grand Rapids, Michigan
Manufacturer of furniture.

Allegan, Michigan
Manufacturer of furniture. Cited in general listing of furniture manufacturers .

SEE Baker Furniture, Inc.

SEE Baker Furniture, Inc.

Allegan, Holland, and Grand Rapids, Michigan
SEE ALSO Barnard & Simonds Co.; Cook, Baker & Co.; Grand Rapids Chair Co.; Kozak Studios; and Williams-Kimp Furniture Co.

COMPANY HISTORY

1903: Name changes from Cook, Baker & Co. of Allegan, Michigan, to Baker & Co.

1927: Name changes again to Baker Furniture Factories, Inc.

ca. 1929: Baker is sold to Peck & Hills, a national furniture wholesaler.

1933: Factories move from Allegan to Holland, Michigan.

ca. 1934: Peck & Hills declares bankruptcy; Hollis S. Baker buys company back.

1941: Baker Museum for Furniture Research established in Grand Rapids' Keeler Exhibition Building.

1948 - 1967: Baker purchases Grand Rapids manufacturers Williams-Kimp Furni-

Miniature Baker sales-sample table in oak, ca. 1910.

1927-ca. 1935

Baker Furniture Factories Inc.

Allegan, Michigan

1927-33

1940

CABINET MAKERS

1930s - present

1930s - present

ture Co., Grand Rapids Chair Co., Barnard & Simonds Co., and Kozak Studios.

1969: Baker sold to Magnavox, Inc.

1972: Baker, Knapp & Tubbs formed as design showrooms subsidiary.

1986: Baker sold to Kohler Co. Continues to operate as Baker Furniture, Inc.

PERSONNEL

Through most of its history, Baker Furniture was controlled as a family business. Siebe Baker was a founder of Cook, Baker & Co. in 1890, and became sole owner in 1915. Upon his death in 1925, presidency fell to his son Hollis S. Baker, Sr., who expanded the company and the number of factories, and made frequent trips abroad to collect books and furniture pieces as style examples for his designers. These formed the nucleus of the Baker Museum and Library for Furniture Research. Under his presidency Baker established the Milling Road Shops and later the Manor House in New York, exclusive showrooms of reproduction furniture. Frank Van Steenberg became president in 1953, and was succeeded by third-generation president Hollis M. Baker, Jr. in 1961.

William Millington, an Englishman with credentials from Waring & Gillow and W.& J. Sloane, became head designer in 1927. Millington designed the Millington Road shops, and many lines of authentic Georgian period reproductions. Millington Roads Furniture operated as a division of Baker Furniture, Inc. Well-known Modernists who designed for Baker include Finn Juhl and T.H. Robsjohn-Gibbings.

PRODUCTS

The earliest lines of Baker and its predecessors were bookcases and desks in Golden Oak, with vague Mission or Art Nouveau influences. By the 1920s bedroom and living room suites had been added to the inventory. Authentic period reproductions of Duncan Phyfe designs were made from pieces at the Metropolitan Museum of Art as early as 1923, and soon afterwards Baker became established in its niche of mahogany, walnut, and maple period reproductions from 18th-century England and France, and Colonial and Federal America. In 1949 the "Far East Collection" was introduced, followed in the 1950s and '60s by a series of reproductions and adaptations from Italy, France, England, and the Netherlands. The "#789 Chippendale" ribbon-back chair, introduced during this period, remained in production for decades.

Baker departed into Modernism with its Art Deco "Twentieth Century Shop," which was introduced in 1925 and produced in rosewood and olive burl, as well as several pieces designed by Donald Deskey. Later Modern designs included several Danish pieces by Finn Juhl in 1951, and a Modern Neo-classical dining and bedroom group by T.H. Robsjohn-Gibbings in 1961.

A renewed commitment to reproduction came with the "Stately Homes (of Great Britain and Ireland) Collection" in 1981. In 1990 Baker became the licensed manufacturer of the furniture reproduction line from Colonial Williamsburg. Baker entered the contract market in its early days with large runs of bedroom furniture for hotels and ocean liners. Traditional and modern styled office furniture is today made by the Baker contract furniture division.

OTHER SOURCES

The Public Museum of Grand Rapids and the Grand Rapids Public Library have collections of Baker trade catalogs. For further company history, SEE ALSO *A History of Furniture: Celebrating Baker Furniture, 100 Years of Fine Reproductions*, by Sam Burchell, 1991.

MARKS AND LABELS

"Baker Furniture Factories" was printed in a distinctive Gothic script from the late 1920s through the early 1930s, and furniture from the same period (post-1927) carried an octagonal "shopmark." The company name "Baker Furniture, Inc." appears in a script with flourishes as early as 1937, a variation of which is still used. In the 1940s Baker adopted the logo of a crown (signifying tradition) and tulip (signifying Dutch craftsmanship) over a "B" which is also in use today. Milling Road Furniture bore its own mark consisting of an upper case "M" and "R" divided by a tree sapling.

BAKER LAPBOARD CO., THE
1896

Buchanan, Michigan
Manufacturer of folding sewing tables. Advertised in *The Michigan Artisan*.

BALKE MANUFACTURING CO.
1903 - 1904

Grand Rapids, Michigan
Manufacturer of the "Combination davenport and billiard table."

BALL, NOYES & COLBY
1855 - 1856

Grand Rapids, Michigan

Supplier of lumber; manufacturer and retailer of bureaus, bedsteads, tables, stands, rocking chairs, chairs, sofas, ottomans, cribs, cradles, and looking glasses; hair, cotton and straw mattresses, and coffins.

Successor to Powers & Ball.

SEE ALSO Powers & Ball.

COMPANY HISTORY
1855: Company founded.
1856: Name changes to Ball & Colby.

BARBER BROTHERS CHAIR CO.
1903 - 1911

Grand Rapids and Hastings, Michigan

SEE ALSO Grand Rapids Bookcase & Chair Co.

COMPANY HISTORY
1902: Addison A. Barber and John W. Shank form Barber & Shank Co., sales agents for several local manufacturers.
1903: Barber Brothers Chair Co. is organized, with main office and salesrooms in Grand Rapids, and factory in Hastings.
1910: Barber Brothers products are cooperatively marketed under the names "Hastings Lines" and "Lifetime Furniture" with products of neighboring Grand Rapids Bookcase Co.
1911: Barber Brothers and Grand Rapids Bookcase Co. merge to form the Grand Rapids Bookcase & Chair Co.

PERSONNEL
Prior to forming his own companies, Addison A. Barber worked for many years in the sales departments of several Grand Rapids companies. In 1901 he organized the Grand Rapids Bookcase Co. in Hastings, Michigan. In 1902 he formed Barber & Shank Co. with John W. Shank. This firm represented the Welch Folding Bed Co. and Grand Rapids Brass & Iron Bed Co. as sales agents. A.A. Barber & Shank were joined by J.C. Barber in the formation of Barber Brothers Chair Co., which was represented by Barber & Shank. E.E. Dryden is known to have designed in the Mission style for the Barber Brothers.

PRODUCTS
Advertisements listed among its products high grade dining chairs, desk, reception and hall chairs, fancy rockers in oak and mahogany, Colonial and Mission chairs and novelties, rockers, settees, couches and Morris chairs, hall furniture and stools, and stained glass table and floor lamps. Most pieces shown in their ads are in the Mission style, and are generally in oak. Finishes included Golden Oak, Fumed Oak, Early English, Wax Golden, Weathered, and Tuna Mahogany. Forms are rather boxy, even stout, with repeating combinations of vertical or horizontal slats which are sometimes bent or set at dramatic angles. Most chairs and settees are upholstered with coarse grained leather hides, which are attached with exposed tacks, leather straps and oversized hand stitching. The #260 chair has a tall back with leather-covered crest, and the #575 arm chair has a tooled design on the leather back cushion, which are reminiscent of Mackintosh and the Glasgow School. Much of the seating was made to complement the case pieces made by Grand Rapids Bookcase Co.

MARKS AND LABELS
A simple rectangular paper label was used which read "Barber Brothers Chair Co., GRAND RAPIDS, MICH." Look also for the name of sales agents "Barber & Shank" or for the trademark names "Hastings Lines" and "Lifetime Furniture."

Mission-style rocking chair by Barber Brothers, from the *Grand Rapids Furniture Record*, Jan., 1904.

BARNARD & SIMONDS CO.
1898 - 1967

1963

Grand Rapids, Michigan

Manufacturer of "American and English Country" reproductions and adaptations, upholstered furniture and novelties.

SEE ALSO Baker Furniture Co.; Michigan Furniture Shops; Stratford Shops.

COMPANY HISTORY
1898: Company founded in Rochester, New York.
1959: Moves to Grand Rapids and merges with Michigan Furniture Shops and Stratford Shops.
1967: Purchased by Baker Furniture.

BART, J. UPHOLSTERING CO.
1936 - 1937

Grand Rapids, Michigan

Manufacturer of suites and chairs.

BARTON CABINET CO.
1926 - 1933

Grand Rapids, Michigan
Manufacturer of furniture.
Predecessor to Barton Furniture Co.
SEE ALSO Barton Furniture Co. of Grand Rapids.
COMPANY HISTORY
1926: First listed in Grand Rapids City Directory.
1933: Name changed to Barton Furniture Co.

BARTON FURNITURE CO.
1933 - 1934

Grand Rapids, Michigan
Manufacturer of novelties, tables, upholstered chairs, and furniture.
Successor to Barton Cabinet Co.
SEE ALSO Barton Cabinet Co.

BARTON FURNITURE CO.
1936 - ca. 1971

Grandville, Michigan
Manufacturer of living room furniture.

BATES TURNING CO.
at least 1925 - 1927

Manistee, Michigan
Manufacturer of candle sticks and art furniture in various woods, including maple, poplar, and walnut.

BATES, W. A. WOOD TURNING CO.
1905 - at least 1920

Grand Rapids, Michigan
Wood turners supplying the furniture industry. Listed in *The Furniture Manufacturer and Artisan* for February, 1920.

BAXTER & BEMIS
ca. 1849

Grand Rapids, Michigan
Maker of chairs.
SEE ALSO Bemis, Cyrus E.

BAY PARLOR FURNITURE MFG. CO.
1927

Grand Rapids, Michigan
Manufacturer of furniture.

BAY VIEW FURNITURE CO.
1898 - 1934

Holland, Michigan
Manufacturer of dining room extension tables, folding beds, spinet desks, library tables, and occasional tables.
OTHER SOURCES
The Joint Archives of Holland have significant archival collections relating to this company.

1928

BEAR FURNITURE MANUFACTURING CO.
ca. 1975 - 1985

Bear Lake, Michigan
Manufacturer of upholstery frames and custom upholstered furniture.

BECHTOLD BROTHERS UPHOLSTERING CO.
1916 - 1977

Grand Rapids, Michigan
Manufacturer of Oriental decorated, lacquered floor and table lamps, tables, and desks; upholsterers of period chairs and sofas.

1928

ca. 1960

BEERS MANUFACTURING CO. LTD.
1903 - 1904

Grand Rapids, Michigan
Manufacturer of high-grade mantel and hall clocks in mahogany.

BELDING MANUFACTURING CO.
1884 - 1895

Belding, Michigan
Manufacturer of Belding "New Perfection" Ice Boxes (refrigerators).
SEE ALSO Belding-Hall Manufacturing Co.; Hembrook Manufacturing Co.
COMPANY HISTORY
1884 : Formed as a reorganization of The Richard T. Hembrook Manufacturing Co., headquartered in Chicago with a plant in Belding.
1895: Merges with Hall Brothers to become Belding-Hall Manufacturing Co.

BELDING - HALL MANUFACTURING CO.
1895 - 1908

Belding, Michigan
Manufacturer of wooden ice boxes (refrigerators).
Successor to Belding Manufacturing Co.; Hall Brothers Manufacturing Co. Predecessor to Gibson Refrigerator Co.
SEE ALSO Belding Manufacturing Co.; Gibson Refrigerator Co.; Hall Brothers Manufacturing Co.
COMPANY HISTORY
1895: Formed as the result of a merger of the Hall Brothers Manufacturing Co. and the Belding Manufacturing Co.

ca. 1903

ca. 1903

ca. 1903

1908: Merges with the Skinner & Steenman Furniture Co. to form the Gibson Refrigerator Co.

BEMIS, CYRUS E.
ca. 1849

Grand Rapids, Michigan
Chair maker.
SEE ALSO Baxter & Bemis.

BENNETT MILLS CO.
1931 - 1935

Grand Rapids, Michigan
Manufacturer and supplier of fabrics and upholstery supplies to the furniture industry.
Successor to A. F. Burch Co. Predecessor to John K. Burch Co.
SEE ALSO Burch, A.F. Co.; Burch, John K. Co.

BENNETT, WILLARD J. CO.
1943 - 1951

Grand Rapids, Michigan
Manufacturer of upholstered furniture.

BENTON HARBOR FURNITURE CO.
1865 - at least 1880

Benton Harbor, Michigan
Manufacturer of "general household furniture."
COMPANY HISTORY
1865: Company founded.
1880: Listed in *History of Berrien and Van Buren Counties, 1880.*

BERGELIN, ROBERT CO.
ca. 1962 - 1964

1962

Big Rapids, Michigan
Manufacturer of furniture, clocks, brackets, and wood novelties.

BERGSMA BROTHERS, INC.
1940 - 1985

Grand Rapids, Michigan
Manufacturer of novelties and furniture initially.
SEE ALSO Gunn Furniture Co.; Imperial Furniture Co.
COMPANY HISTORY
1940: Company founded in Denver, Colorado.
1945: Begins manufacturing furniture. First listed as furniture manufacturers.
1953: Purchases Gunn Furniture Co.
1954: Purchases Imperial Furniture Co.
1976: Becomes a division of Norlin Music, Inc.
1985: Company closes.
PRODUCTS
After 1954 Bergsma added tables to their line. During the 1970s and 1980s they made furniture and cabinetry on contract for other companies, including stereo speakers, armories, and entertainment centers, as well as case clocks for Hamilton, and organ cabinets for Lowry Organ Cabinets.

BERKEY BROTHERS & CO.
1863 - 1866

Grand Rapids, Michigan
Manufacturer of furniture, including the scalloped walnut "Berkey Table," and window sash, doors, and blinds.
SEE ALSO Berkey & Gay Furniture Co.; Berkey & Hamm; Berkey & Matter Co.; Berkey, William A. Furniture Co.
COMPANY HISTORY
1863: Berkey & Matter becomes Berkey Brothers & Co.
1866: George Gay joins as a partner, name is changed to Berkey Brothers & Gay.

BERKEY & GAY FURNITURE CO.
1866 - 1931; 1935 - 1948

Grand Rapids, Michigan
Successor to Berkey Brothers & Co.
SEE ALSO Berkey Brothers & Co.; Berkey & Hamm; Berkey & Matter; Grand Rapids Upholstering Co.; Oriel Cabinet Co.; Wallace Upholstering Co.
COMPANY HISTORY
1866: George W. Gay becomes partner in Berkey Brothers & Co.; name is changed to Berkey Brothers & Gay.
1872: William Berkey withdraws from leadership of company.
1873: Company is incorporated as Berkey & Gay.
1874: New six-story factory, with wholesale and retail showrooms, becomes one of Grand Rapids' most prominent structures.
1875: Salesroom opens in New York City.

1876: Berkey & Gay is one of three Grand Rapids companies to win an award for its display at the Philadelphia Centennial Exposition.

1885: Firm advertises nationally, and ships over a half million dollars in goods throughout the U.S. and Europe.

1895: Company name immortalized by Eugene Field's poem "In Amsterdam."

1900: Retail operations discontinued.

1911: Berkey & Gay acquires Oriel Cabinet Co.

1923: Wallace Upholstering Co. and Grand Rapids Upholstering Co. are merged with Berkey & Gay as the Consolidated Furniture Companies.

1929: Simmons Co. of Chicago acquires Berkey & Gay's $10 million in assets, including 5 Grand Rapids plants with 1.5 million square feet of space, and $8 million in annual sales.

1931: Sales decline sharply; Berkey & Gay forced to declare bankruptcy.

1934: Stockholders win $2,000,000 judgement in suit against Simmons, then the largest civil award in history.

1935: Berkey & Gay re-opens under new management.

1948: Company declares bankruptcy; name is purchased by Harvest Furniture Co. of Louisville, Kentucky and production ceases.

PERSONNEL

Many prominent names were associated with this largest of Grand Rapids' residential furniture manufacturers. Brothers William and Julius Berkey were among the first to make the transition from sash and blind milling to furniture production. William H. Gay, the son of an early partner in the business, George Gay, became a prominent leader of both the company and the community, and sat on the boards of many banks and civic organizations. After his death in 1920, George Whitworth and five members of the Wallace family, led by Winfred J. Wallace, took the reins of the company. Under their management several plants were merged into the giant Consolidated Furniture Companies, which had its own newsletter, gymnasium, Americanization classes, sports leagues, and farm. They advertised aggressively directly to consumers in the most highly circulated journals of the day.

Cabinetmaker John Frohberg (or Froburgh) may have created designs for Berkey & Gay in the early 1870s. John Keck of Ann Arbor, Michigan, designed Renaissance Revival, Neo-Grec, and Eastlake-style pieces on contract for Berkey & Gay in the 1870s. Louis Bornemann became the company's chief designer some time after the Centennial Exposition, and left to work for Phoenix and finally on his own in 1886. Frederick Koskul and John Mowatt designed for Berkey & Gay between 1877 and 1879. Arthur Kirkpatrick, who grew up in Grand Rapids, received formal art training before he became a designer at Berkey & Gay. He went on to found the Grand Rapids School of Furniture Designing in 1904. Adrian Margantin designed pieces in Golden Oak and Colonial styles for Berkey & Gay from 1898 until his death in 1914. Several designers, including Lachlan MacLachlan in the 1910s and Frank C. Lee in the 1920s, came to Grand Rapids via a sort of "pipeline" from the prestigious Waring & Gillow in London and W. & J. Sloane in New York. They brought with them considerable knowledge of classical decoration and period styles, which is reflected in the company's products of the time.

Many Berkey & Gay designs required a considerable amount of hand craftsmanship, so the company cultivated large departments of carvers and decorators. Some, including Fred Weber and Chris Haraldstadt, grew up in America but came from regions of Germany and Norway that were known for their carving traditions, and worked for forty years or more at Berkey & Gay. Others, like Florentine master carver Leopold Baillot, and Japanese decorator Fugi Nakamiso, were recruited through American foreign embassies to bring their experience overseas, to work for Berkey & Gay.

PRODUCTS

Because of the company's size and longevity, collectors seem to encounter Berkey & Gay products more frequently than those of any other Grand Rapids company. Its inventory of lines was quite large and varied over time; only a brief overview is included here.

1866 - 1890: From its very first machine-made, scalloped, walnut and cherry "Berkey Tables," the company's products were made for wholesale shipment and sale to the masses. Berkey & Gay capitalized on the public's interest in whole suites or "suits" of furniture, which included everything needed for bedrooms and dining

Berkey & Gay settee from a parlor suite, ca. 1895.

1905-29

1929-35

1929-48

rooms. Pieces were also manufactured for the hall and office. Much of the company's early production was likely shipped "in the white" (unfinished), to be finished by the retailer upon arrival. Some pieces, however, were given painted faux burl panels at the factory. Large contracts for bedroom suites were supplied to hotels in Washington, and in New York at Coney Island and Manhattan Beach.

With its introduction to the country at the 1876 Philadelphia Centennial Exposition, it became known for production of massive Renaissance Revival beds and secretaries. Typically of walnut and walnut burl, with lower-end suites in ash, they were decorated with multiple layers of geometric and architectonic panels and carvings. In fact, Berkey & Gay's products of this period have become synonymous with the term "Grand Rapids furniture" in the minds of many collectors.

An 1878 article in the *American Cabinetmaker* says the company "makes a specialty of bevel plate mirrors in their finer work." The article revealed that sides and ends of drawers were produced in red cedar to prevent moths. It also noted that Berkey & Gay did not make its own parlor frames, but purchased them from Holton & Hildreth of Chicago, then completed the upholstery for its own retail trade.

Eastlake style suites from the late 1870s and '80s were equally massive. Some at the higher end demonstrate keen knowledge of Eastlake's principles of design, and stand apart from the company's other medium-grade lines.

1890 - 1915: As consumer style preferences changed, so did Berkey & Gay, but the feeling of massiveness and strength in its furniture remained. The company continued to produce whole suites for the parlor, bedroom, and dining room. Pieces were in Golden Oak or mahogany. Berkey & Gay's Golden Oak pieces have very high relief in their carving, which ranged from grottoesque fantasy creatures to swirling French flourishes.

A few Arts and Crafts style suites were introduced in the first decade of this century under names like "English Modern," but generally speaking Berkey & Gay passed on the whole movement.

1915 - 1931: The era between World War I and the Great Depression was Berkey & Gay's zenith of production. Upholstering was spun off to subsidiaries like Wallace Upholstery and Grand Rapids Upholstery, so Berkey & Gay concentrated on living room and bedroom suites. Although designs ran the gamut of freely translated European and American revival styles, most tended toward larger, heavier periods like Elizabethan, William and Mary, and American Empire.

Pieces were well constructed. A variety of woods was used, mostly dark mahoganies and walnuts, with occasional accents of lighter woods, painted decoration, or exotic materials like turquoise. These were further darkened by the application of stains wiped around edges and carvings, to give the appearance of age.

One interesting novelty was the "Old Ironsides Table," of which only about 100 were produced. Its scalloped apron and block-turned legs and stretchers were adapted from an illustration in a Wallace Nutting book on American antiques. An eagle medallion on the single drawer front was carved in wood taken from the *U.S.S. Constitution*, during its restoration in Boston Harbor.

1934 - 1948: Berkey & Gay had ventured into Modern or Art Deco designs before it was closed in 1931, and continued to produce both "traditional and modern" lines when it re-opened. Kem Weber contracted to design a Modern line, but his relationship with the company turned sour over its financial difficulties.

Popular frenzy over the novel and movie *Gone With the Wind* inspired Berkey & Gay's "Old South Line" in the late 1930s. It featured Victorian Revival parlor chairs, and full and half-tester beds.

OTHER SOURCES

Both the Public Museum of Grand Rapids and the Grand Rapids Public Library have large collections of advertising pieces and company histories, as well as trade catalogs from Berkey & Gay.

MARKS AND LABELS

A Berkey & Gay table, circa 1875, in the collections of the Public Museum bears a black stencil of the company name on the underside of its stretchers. The underside of marble tops from the same period were sometimes scored with the initials "B&G" by the local marble supplier. Paper labels that read "From Berkey & Gay Furniture Co. Grand Rapids, Mich." were used in the 1880s and '90s, and have been found on the backs of case pieces, and under the upholstery on chair armrests. Specific methods for attributing and dating Berkey & Gay furniture based on other markings and methods of construction are described in detail in the chapter by Joel Lefever.

By 1905 Berkey & Gay had adopted a new trademark consisting of a series of concentric rings. A circular line surrounds the words "BERKEY & GAY FURNI-TURE" which surround a "C" with the "O" as the center. This mark appeared as an inlaid wood tag or paper label for a short time, then was replaced by a brass tag. When the company changed owners in 1929, "DIVISION OF SIMMONS CO." was added between the "C" and the company name. From as early as 1929, the Simmons line was sometimes replaced by "TRADE-MARK-REG. U.S. PAT OFF".

BERKEY & HAMM
1861

Grand Rapids, Michigan
Predecessor to Berkey & Matter.
SEE ALSO Berkey Brothers & Co.; Berkey & Gay Furniture Co.; Berkey & Matter.
COMPANY HISTORY
1859: Julius Berkey establishes a sash and blind mill with James Eggleston.
1861: Julius Berkey and Alphonso Hamm begin making their signature scalloped walnut "Berkey Table" at the sash and blind mill of William A Berkey, but the partnership closes in less than a year.
PRODUCTS
The partners made and marketed "Berkey Tables," simple occasional and sewing tables in cherry or walnut. One had turned legs, a plywood lift-up top, and lower shelf with scalloped edges. Others had legs and tops made from plywood and band sawed to shape, also with scalloped edges, and center finials or drop pendants.

BERKEY & MATTER
1862 - 1863

Grand Rapids, Michigan
Manufacturer of the scalloped "Berkey Table" and other furniture for wholesale trade in the Chicago and Milwaukee markets.
Successor to Berkey & Hamm. Predecessor to Berkey Brothers & Co.
SEE ALSO Berkey Brothers & Co.; Berkey & Gay Furniture Co.; Berkey & Hamm.
COMPANY HISTORY
1862: After his partnership with Hamm dissolves, Berkey forms a new partnership with Elias Matter.
1863: Company becomes Berkey Brothers & Co.

BERKEY, JULIUS TABLE CO.

SEE Berkey Brothers & Co.; Berkey & Hamm; Berkey & Matter.

BERKEY - WIDDICOMB CO.

SEE Berkey, William A. Furniture Co.; Widdicomb, John Co.

BERKEY, WILLIAM A. FURNITURE CO.
1859 - 1976

Grand Rapids, Michigan
SEE ALSO Berkey Brothers & Co.; Phoenix Furniture Co.; Widdicomb, John Co.
COMPANY HISTORY
1859: William A. Berkey manufactures window sashes and doors for building construction.
1882: After years as a director of various other furniture companies, Berkey opens his own factory.
1885: Company incorporates as William A. Berkey Furniture Co.
1950: Company is purchased but continues to operate as a division of John Widdicomb Co.
1976: Company ceases to operate as a separate division.
PERSONNEL
William A. Berkey spent years as a part owner of Berkey Brothers & Co. and the Phoenix Furniture Co. before he severed his ties to furniture making in 1863. But in 1882 he returned to furniture, with the organization of his own company. He served as his company's president until his death, when he was succeeded by his son-in-law W.H. Jones. He, in turn, was succeeded as head of the company by his son, E. Berkey Jones. He ran the company until it was purchased by Lewis T. Peck and A.G. Green in 1940. In 1950 ownership of the company passed to the John Widdicomb Co.
PRODUCTS
The first products of the William A. Berkey Furniture Co. were fine- and medium-grade wood-top center tables in native oak, ash, maple, and "bay wood." By 1886 the factory was producinf 20,000 tables and pedestals a year. By the 1890s its line had expanded considerably, to include upholstered parlor furniture and fancy cabinets. Its offerings for the parlor included fancy chairs and rockers, couches, rattan chairs and rockers, and center tables. By 1900, William A. Berkey was offering dressers, chiffonniers, bookcases, parlor and music cabinets, and library, work, toilet,

Wm. A. Berkey dresser, with Empire Revival and Art Nouveau influences, from the *Grand Rapids Furniture Record*, June, 1904.

1909

1935

and bedroom tables, mostly in mahogany.

In the 1910s and '20s William A. Berkey Furniture Co. established itself as a producer of mahogany period revival furniture for the dining room, library and living room in various American Colonial and 18th-century European styles, including Empire, Jacobean, Oriental lacquer, Adam, Sheraton, Hepplewhite, and Chippendale. During the 1930s the company manufactured mostly tables, as well as some desks and secretaries, corner china cabinets, bookcases, chests of drawers, highboys and lowboys, dining room suites, and a few bedroom pieces, in mahogany only.

Beginning in the 1950s the company began producing furniture to complement John Widdicomb Co.'s other lines. A William A. Berkey catalog circa 1972 shows the "Interlude" line of bedroom furniture in matching French poplar veneers, and the "Beta Group" of contemporary bedroom and dining room furniture. Both were nearly identical in styling to the "Wellington Group" produced by Berkey's parent company, John Widdicomb.

OTHER SOURCES

An archival collection relating to the formation of the William A. Berkey Furniture Co. is in the collections of The Public Museum of Grand Rapids.

BERRY FURNITURE CO. 1934 - 1935	Grand Rapids, Michigan Manufacturer of "Fancy furniture."
BEXLEY HEATH, LTD. 1996 - present	Grand Rapids, Michigan Manufacturer of "functional and stylish home furniture in wood," described by its designer, Mary Witte, as "contemporary furniture with historic roots." Lines include the "Beba" (Bed and Bath Collection) inspired by the French Art Deco Movement, and the "Victoria and Albert Collection" consisting of inspirations from Viennese Modern pieces in the museum's collections. Also manufacturers of reproductions of T. H. Robsjohn-Gibbings' modern designs from the 1940s - 1960s, sold as the "Widdicomb Collection." Established as a sister company to Designers Workshop and John Widdicomb, Inc. SEE ALSO Designers Workshop/DW2; John Widdicomb, Inc.
BIG RAPIDS FURNITURE MANUFACTURING CO. between 1917 and 1928	Big Rapids, Michigan Cited in various sources as a manufacturer of dining room furniture.
BILTWELL UPHOLSTERING CO. 1928	Grand Rapids, Michigan Manufacturer of upholstered furniture. Listed in *The Buyer's Guide* for 1928.
BIRGE & SHATTUCK 1890	Grand Rapids, Michigan Manufacturer of and wholesale dealer in parlor furniture, upholstered goods, and upholstered bed springs.
BISHOP FURNITURE CO. 1895 - present	Grand Rapids, Michigan Bishop had its beginnings as a manufacturer and retailer of furniture, both through its retail outlet in downtown Grand Rapids, and through a direct mail-order-consumer catalog. Correspondence from the first decade of the 20th century claimed that Bishop was "the largest exclusive furniture house in the world shipping to the consumer direct." Catalogs from the same period show a range of oak and mahogany tables, chairs, commodes, dressers, couches, and cabinets in Empire Revival, Golden Oak, and Mission styles, but do not distinguish which pieces are made by other Grand Rapids manufacturers. The company later dropped both its manufacturing and mail-order operations, but continues as a home furnishings retailer.
BLACK, H. S. 1871 - 1875	Buchanan, Michigan Manufacturer of bedsteads and lounges. Predecessor to Black & Willard Furniture Co. SEE ALSO Black & Willard Furniture Co.
BLACK & WILLARD FURNITURE CO. 1880	New Buffalo and Buchanan, Michigan Manufacturer of "Furniture of all kinds, bedsteads principally. Goods sold West and South." Listed in *The History of Berrien and Van Buren Counties*, 1880. SEE ALSO Black, H. S.
BODART FURNITURE CO. 1949 - 1973	Grand Rapids, Michigan Manufacturer of high-end antique reproduction upholstered and case pieces in Louis XV, Louis XVI, and Directoire styles.

1960

BONNETT, THOMAS
ca. 1865

BORROUGHS CORP.
1939 - 1991

SEE ALSO Colonial Furniture Co.
COMPANY HISTORY
1949: Moves from New York to Grand Rapids.
1973: Company is purchased by Colonial Furniture Co. of Zeeland, Michigan.
OTHER SOURCES
The Public Museum of Grand Rapids has a significant collection of Bodart trade catalogs.

Grand Rapids, Michigan
Cabinetmaker, known to have made Empire - Rococo Revival transitional case pieces in mahogany and walnut.

Kalamazoo, Michigan
COMPANY HISTORY
1938: Walter Borroughs founds the Probar Co.
1939: Name changes to Borroughs Corp.
1950: Borroughs Co. becomes a part of American Metal Products.
1966: Borroughs Co. becomes a division of Lear Siegler, Inc. of Grand Rapids.
1987: Forstmann Little purchases parent company Lear Siegler.
1988: Forstmann Little acquires the Andrew Wilson Co., and transfers manufacture of its products to Borroughs.
1991: Tyler family purchases Burroughs from Forstmann Little.
PERSONNEL
The company's namesake, Walter Borroughs, started the Probar Co. in 1938, but changed the name to the Borroughs Co. in 1939. After several decades of outside ownership between 1950 and 1991, Borroughs was purchased by its own management and members of the Tyler family, who had a long relationship with Borroughs as industrial distributors.
PRODUCTS
Borroughs' first products were metal retail display furniture and automotive manufacturing storage equipment, which it fabricated on contract for other firms. During World War II Borroughs developed the "Flexi-bin," the first parts bin for use in automotive manufacturing. Its success prompted the expansion of Borroughs' line of metal equipment for automotive manufacturing to include shop desks, benches, and cabinets. Borroughs introduced clip-assembled industrial shelving in 1954. Rivet-Span, a frame shelf product for archival and general storage, entered production in 1992.

In 1952 Borroughs widened its range of offerings by modifying the successful Flexi-bin into a series of open-faced and sliding door metal storage cabinets for offices, and a line of metal bookcase shelving for libraries. The "Adaptafile" line of lateral file cabinets was introduced in 1965. "Sigma 2000," a free-standing office system with C-leg furniture, pedestals, and other accessories, was introduced in 1984. "Unimetrics," a companion product, was introduced the following year. Sales remained small, and both lines were discontinued by 1991. When the Andrew Wilson Co. was acquired in 1988, its multi-level "Wilsonstak Cantilever Library Shelving" and "Record Master" shelving case goods were added to Borroughs' offerings for libraries and offices. During the 1990s Burroughs partnered with PIPP, Inc. to develop "Easy-Trak Lateral Movable Systems" for high-density storage.

Borroughs' first retail display products included metal shelving for shoes and liquor, and point of purchase display racks. In 1975 Borroughs collaborated with RCA to create the retail scanning checkout system. Borroughs became the leading producer of these systems in America. In 1992 Borroughs contracted with Wal-Mart, the nation's largest retailer, to produce more than 1,000 custom steel checkstands.
MARKS AND LABELS
Cabinets by Borroughs sometimes carry a rectangular metal tag reading "BORROUGHS" or "BORROUGHS CORP / KALAMAZOO, MICH." in uppercase italics. Some shelving parts may be stencil painted with the name "Borroughs" and the part type number. Retail checkout systems may be identified with the tradename "X-series" or a rectangular trademark with rounded ends which reads, "SERIES 90 / BORROUGHS / SYSTEMS / KALAMAZOO, MICHIGAN".

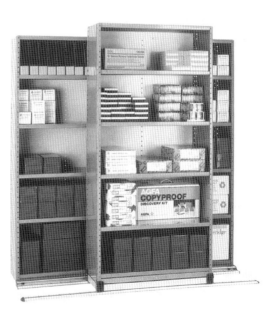

Borroughs "Easy-Trak" movable filing system, from 1996 catalog, Courtesy Borroughs Corp.

BOYCE BROTHERS 1915 - 1926	Grand Rapids, Michigan Cabinetmakers, Ernest and Robert Boyce.
BOYNS & MORLEY FURNITURE CO. 1895	Grand Rapids, Michigan Manufacturer of library book cases and insurance, catalogue, and file cases. Listed in *Furniture Buyers Record*, 1895.
BOYNTON & CREQUE ca. 1867 - 1872	Grand Rapids, Michigan Dealers in parlor, bedroom, dining and "common furniture," looking glasses, and picture frames. They may also have manufactured some of the products they sold. Predecessor to J.P. Creque. SEE ALSO Creque, J.P.
BRADFIELD FOLDING TABLE CO. 1878	Grand Rapids, Michigan Manufacturer of "Bradfield Folding Tables" in ash, walnut, or both; with or without chess-board tops. Described in *The American Cabinetmaker, Upholsterer and Carpet Reporter*. Predecessor to McCord & Bradfield. SEE ALSO McCord & Bradfield.
BRANDT, JAMES C. FURNITURE CO. 1960 - ca. 1967	Grand Rapids, Michigan Manufacturer of furniture.
BRANDT OF GRAND RAPIDS, INC. 1949 - 1985	Grand Rapids, Michigan Manufacturer of upholstered furniture designed for "high-style appeal and high-value sales," including the Sturbridge Collection of Casual Colonial.

Brandt
1960

BRANDT, RUSSELL CO. 1935 - 1937	Grand Rapids, Michigan Manufacturer of upholstered furniture. Predecessor to Lazard-Brandt. SEE ALSO Lazard-Brandt.
BRASS & IRON BED CO. 1895 - ca. 1899	Grand Rapids, Michigan Manufacturer of brass-trimmed, enameled-iron bedsteads and cribs.
BRILL FURNITURE CO. 1946 - present	Ludington, Michigan Manufacturer of pine and oak restaurant and residential furniture.
BROCKMEIER PIANO CO. 1908 - 1910	Grand Rapids, Michigan Small maker of pianos, sold in Milwaukee and Grand Rapids.
BROTHERS FORSLUND CO.	SEE Forslund, Brothers Co.
BROWER FURNITURE CO. 1919 - 1977	Grand Rapids, Michigan Originally, makers of chairs "in the white" to match tables and case goods of other local manufacturers, principally Imperial, Grand Rapids Chair, and Hekman. **COMPANY HISTORY** 1919: Company is founded by John M. Brower (son of designer John E. Brower) and the heads of several local firms, to supply them with chairs. 1974: Becomes a division of the Great Western Group, Inc. 1927: Adds a contract furniture line, for which it manufactured, upholstered, and finished chairs, tables and companion pieces for retail stores, hotel dining rooms, clubs, school dormitories, and ships.

Brower
1956

BROWNE - MORSE CO. at least ca. 1920 - 1950	Muskegon, Michigan Manufacturer of steel file cabinets, book shelves, card files, waste baskets, wardrobes, map cabinets, and desks. SEE ALSO Grand Rapids Desk Co.
BRUNSWICK - BALKE - COLLENDER CO. 1904 - present	Grand Rapids and Muskegon, Michigan Manufacturer of billiard and pool tables, bar fixtures, bowling alleys, and supplies. **COMPANY HISTORY** 1904: Moves to Grand Rapids from Chicago. 1911: Moves to Muskegon from Grand Rapids. The successor company, Brunswick Corp., continues to operate in Muskegon.
BUCHANAN CABINET CO. 1892 - 1921	Buchanan, Michigan Manufacturer of Golden Oak sideboards and desks.

Successor to Buchanan Manufacturing Co.
SEE ALSO Buchanan Manufacturing Co.

BUCHANAN MANUFACTURING CO.
1872 - 1892

Buchanan, Michigan
Manufacturer of bedsteads, lounges, carriages, and wagons for shipment to "all parts of the west and south."
Predecessor to Buchanan Cabinet Co.
SEE ALSO Buchanan Cabinet Co.

BUDINGTON & TURNHAM
1859 - 1866

Grand Rapids, Michigan
"Wholesale and retail dealers in and manufacturing of all kinds and styles of Cabinet Furniture."
Successor to Hamm & Turnham.
SEE ALSO Hamm & Turnham.

BUITEN, DOEZEMA & CO.
1909 - 1911

Grand Rapids, Michigan
Cited in general listing of woodworking and furniture manufacturers.

BUITEN & SHANK FURNITURE CO.
1928 - 1933

Grand Rapids, Michigan
Manufacturer of bedroom and dining furniture.
Successor to The Cabinet Shops.
SEE ALSO Cabinet Shops, The.

BURCH, A. F. CO.
1895 - 1931

1922

Grand Rapids, Michigan. Branches: Kansas City, Missouri; Cincinnati, Ohio; and Oakland, California
Furniture repairers; supplier of interior decorating, furniture, and upholstery materials to the industry.
Predecessor to Bennett Mills Co. and John K. Burch Co.
SEE ALSO Bennett Mills Co.; Burch, John K. Co.

BURCH CO.

SEE Burch Fabrics

BURCH FABRICS
1950 - present

BURCH
The John K. Burch Co.
Upholstery Fabric
Panel Fabric
Supplies
1989

Grand Rapids, Michigan
Manufacturer and national distributor of upholstery fabrics, panel fabrics, and upholstery supplies to the furniture industry.
Successor to John K. Burch Co.
SEE ALSO Burch, John K. Co.
COMPANY HISTORY
1950: John K. Burch Co. changes name to Burch Co.
1980: Burch Co. changes name to Burch Fabrics.

BURCH, JOHN K. CO.
1935 - 1950

Grand Rapids, Michigan
Manufacturer and supplier of fabrics and upholstery supplies to the furniture industry.
Successor to Bennett Mills Co. Predecessor to Burch Co.
SEE ALSO Bennett Mills Co.; Burch, A. F. Co.; Burch Fabrics.

BURG BROTHERS & CO.
ca. 1928 - 1945

Grand Rapids, Michigan
Manufacturer of upholstered furniture.

BURNETT & VAN OVEREN
1903 - 1907

Grand Rapids, Michigan
Cited in a general listing of woodworking and furniture manufacturers from *The Furniture Manufacturer and Artisan*, February, 1920.

BURWOOD PRODUCTS CO.
1981

Burwood.
1981

Traverse City, Michigan
Manufacturer of home furnishing accessories, including New Haven clocks and weather stations. Advertised in the *Merchandise Mart Buyer's Guide*.

BUSH & LANE PIANO CO.
1905 - 1929

Holland, Michigan
Manufacturer of pianos.
OTHER SOURCES
The Joint Archives of Holland have significant archival collections relating to this company.

BUTLER, SAMUEL F.
ca. 1841 - 1856

Grand Rapids, Michigan
Cabinetmaker.

CABINET SHOPS, THE
1922 - 1928

1928

Grand Rapids, Michigan
Manufacturer of "Better dining room and living room furniture," with "new ideas" in Chippendale, Duncan Phyfe, and other period revival styles.
Predecessor to Buiten & Shank Furniture Co.
SEE ALSO Buiten & Shank Furniture Co.

CABINETMAKERS CO.
1904 - 1908

Grand Rapids, Michigan
Manufacturer of tables and library suites.
Predecessor to Johnson Furniture Co.
SEE ALSO Johnson Furniture Co.

1905

CADILLAC CHAIR CO.
1911 - 1916

Cadillac, Michigan
Manufacturer of inexpensive rocking and dining chairs, "for the bread and butter business."
Predecessor to Great Northern Chair Co. in 1916.
SEE ALSO Great Northern Chair Co.

CALORIC FIRELESS COOKSTOVE CO.
1905 - 1909

Grand Rapids, Michigan
Manufacturer of fireless cookers.

The Company
1905

CALVIN FURNITURE CO.
1953 - 1973

Grand Rapids, Michigan
Manufacturer of Scandinavian Modern-influenced furniture known as the "Irwin Collection," designed by Paul McCobb.

CARLTON-SURREY, INC.
1946 - 1997

ca. 1965

Grand Rapids, Michigan
Manufacturer of Scandinavian Modern and traditional desks and seating for office or home, upholstered in leather and fabric; special order conference tables, and other furniture by contract.

CAROLAC CO.
ca. 1948

Grand Rapids, Michigan
Operated for only a short time "on the side" by several Robert W. Irwin employees. Decorated inexpensive Oriental raised lacquer bookcases, commodes, and mirrors for wholesale. Case goods were made for Carolac by Stiles Lumber Co.

CARROM CO., THE
1889 - present

Ludington, Michigan
Manufacturer of folding card tables, Carrom game tables, banquet tables, piano benches, and Drueke game boards and sets.
Successor to the Ludington Novelty Co.
SEE ALSO Drueke, William F. & Co.

CENTRAL FURNITURE CO.
ca. 1893 - 1904

Grand Rapids, Michigan
Manufacturer of bookcases, music cabinets, ladies' desks, and buffets including a rectilinear Mission Oak line with leaded and stained art glass.
Predecessor to Shelton & Snyder Furniture Co.
SEE ALSO Shelton & Snyder Furniture Co.

CENTURY FURNITURE CO.
1900 - 1942

Hand-decorated chinoiserie chair, Century Furniture Co., ca. 1935.

Grand Rapids, Michigan
SEE ALSO Murray Furniture Co.

COMPANY HISTORY
1900: Founded by partners David S. Brown and J.C. Rickenbaugh.
1905: Incorporates as the Century Furniture Co. upon Rickenbaugh's death.
1940: Century is purchased by R.J. Murray, President of Murray Furniture Co., and designer David L. Evans.
1942: Century declares bankruptcy. A reorganization attempt fails by 1944 due to lack of demand during WWII.
1945: Century factory and name are purchased by Murray Furniture Co. of Grand Rapids. Century ceases production.

PERSONNEL
Century's founders were both veterans of the Grand Rapids furniture scene, Brown having worked for Nelson & Matter, and Rickenbaugh having held interests in the Royal Furniture Co. Edgar Somes became an officer in 1906 after leaving his position as designer at Michigan Chair Co. David L. Evans, who participated in the 1940 company buy-out, served as staff designer at Century from 1917 to 1928. His name appears on design drawings in the Museum's Century Archival Collection.

PRODUCTS
Unlike many of the companies started a generation earlier, which began making

cheap goods and later upgraded, Century strived from its onset "to manufacture the best possible line of the particular kind of goods made by the company." Century furniture was well built, with expensive materials and lavish details and decoration. It began primarily as a producer of upholstered goods. Fabrics were rich silks or hand-woven needlework pictorials imported from France.

By the early 1930s it had expanded production to include furniture for the living room, dining room, library, hall, bedroom, and office. Case pieces were heavily carved, inlaid with marquetry panels, or painted with elaborate floral and pictorial motives.

While the company maintained a large line of pieces, only a small number of any single item needed to be produced in a year to keep it in the catalog. Manufacturing followed "batch production," meaning pieces were not made until enough orders, perhaps 25 or 50, were received to run a "batch." Each piece could then be custom-finished to order. Records show that some pieces remained active in the catalog for years, even though no more than a single batch of that piece had been run in an entire year.

Century was the earliest and perhaps most significant promoter of the antiques reproduction movement in Grand Rapids. A 1911 *Grand Rapids Herald* article credits Edgar Somes with cultivating a collection of antiques for reproduction in the factory. Not satisfied with producing new designs in the manner of historical styles, Century presented their reproductions as "correct" and "authentic," and consequently superior. Lines covered the range of acceptable European and American styles from the Renaissance to the early 19th century. Provenance of originals was often included in ads as a favorable selling point. Pieces were reproduced from such famous locales as Knole House in England, and the Massachusetts "Wayside Inn" immortalized by Longfellow.

Century went beyond the exact duplication of historical pieces in their production of new antiques. Many techniques were used in manufacturing to give the finished piece an appearance of great age. Fabrics were woven with threads missing to give the appearance of slight moth damage. Foot rails were planed to simulate centuries of wear. Beautiful woods were beaten with "distressers," rings of keys, nuts and bolts, to approximate nicks and powder beetle damage. Dark stains were applied around edges and in deep carvings to look like dirt build-up.

OTHER SOURCES
The Public Museum of Grand Rapids has a large collection of business records for the Century and Murray Furniture Companies. The Museum has a major collection of Century furniture manufactured from the 1910s through the 1930s. Both the Museum and the Grand Rapids Public Libraries have significant collections of Century trade catalogs.

MARKS AND LABELS
Early Century pieces often had square, white paper labels on the underside of a chair seat or table top, with no logo, but the company name, and lines which sometimes carry the product number or finish and upholstery information. A number of fanciful monograms were used in advertisements from circa 1905. Some 1910s and '20s pieces in the Museum's collection are marked with a pyrotechnic (burn or brand) of the word "Century" with the "u" in a distinctive Roman "v" shape. Most commonly, pieces from the 1910s through the 1920s have a small circular brass tag which can be found almost any place inconspicuous. The tag bares the logo of a squat Greek cross, with a triangle over the names of the company and city. Beginning around 1928 the company adopted the use of a rectangle with rounded corners, surrounding the words "CENTURY / GRAND RAPIDS" with the "U" again in Roman "v" shape.

1905

1905

1915

1925

1928

CHAIR CRAFT CO., THE
at least 1911 - 1914

1928

Traverse City, Michigan
Manufacturer of tufted leather and oak Morris chairs, with reclining backs and hinged footrests, under the names "Comfort Chair" and "Rest Fest Reclining Chair." Cited in *The Grand Rapids Furniture Record.*

CHALLENGER CORN PLANTER CO.
1882 - ca. 1904

Grand Haven, Michigan
Manufacturer of refrigerators and combination buffet/refrigerators for homes, hotels, and grocers.

Predecessor to Challenger Refrigerator Co.
SEE ALSO Challenger Refrigerator Co.
COMPANY HISTORY
1882: Company founded.
Prior to 1904: Name changed to Challenger Refrigerator Co.

CHALLENGER REFRIGERATOR CO.
ca. 1904 - 1929

1928

Grand Haven, Michigan
Manufacturer of refrigerators with charcoal-lined walls to eliminate odors, under the brand names "Challenger," "Iceberg," "Grand Victor," and "Triumph."
Successor to Challenger Corn Planter Co.
SEE ALSO Challenger Corn Planter Co.
COMPANY HISTORY
Prior to 1904: Name changed from Challenger Corn Planter Co.
1929: Company closed.

CHARLES OF GRAND RAPIDS
1955 - 1969

Grand Rapids, Michigan
Manufacturer of furniture.

CHARLOTTE CHAIR CO.

SEE Charlotte Co., Inc., The.

CHARLOTTE CO., INC., THE
1912 - present

Charlotte and Belding, Michigan
Manufacturer of wooden upholstered seating and case goods for the office, health care, hospitality, and institutional markets.
Founded as the Charlotte Chair Co., which made upholstered antique reproduction seating. Currently called The Charlotte Co. and located in Belding.
OTHER SOURCES
The Public Museum of Grand Rapids has a significant collection of trade catalogs from this company.

1930

1970

1971

CHARLOTTE CHAIR COMPANY
1971

CHARLOTTE
1994

CHARLOTTE FURNITURE CO.
1919 - at least 1932

1927

1929

1929

Charlotte, Michigan
Manufacturer of antique reproductions and adaptations under names like "Provincial Group" and various other "Charlotte Historical Groups" for the bedroom, living room, and dining room. Company founded with assets of Charlotte Manufacturing Co. Listed in various sources until at least 1932.
Successor to Charlotte Manufacturing Co.
SEE ALSO Charlotte Manufacturing Co.

CHARLOTTE FURNITURE COMPANY CHARLOTTE, MICHIGAN
1929

CHARLOTTE MANUFACTURING CO.
1894 - 1919

Charlotte, Michigan
Manufacturer of tables, pedestals, and plant stands.
Predecessor to Charlotte Furniture Co.
SEE ALSO Charlotte Furniture Co.

CHARTER HOUSE, INC.
Subsidiary of Stainless, Inc.
1988 - present

charter house
1989

Holland, Michigan
Formerly a division of Holland Stitchcraft.
Manufacturer of wood and fiberglass custom tables and cabinets, condiment counters, and planters for family-oriented and fast food restaurants. Clients include Big Boy, Arby's, McDonald's, Burger King, Denny's and International House of Pancakes in the United States, Canada, Latin America, Europe, and the Middle East.

CHASE BROTHERS OF MUSKEGON

SEE Chase Brothers Piano Co.

CHASE BROTHERS PIANO CO.
1858 - 1893

Grand Rapids and Muskegon, Michigan
Manufacturer of grand and upright pianos, with patents for double repeating action, convex sounding board, folding desk, and duplex damper.
COMPANY HISTORY
1858: Company founded in Ripley, Ohio.
1867: Moves to Richmond, Indiana.
1884: Moves to Grand Rapids, Michigan.
1889: Moves to Muskegon, Michigan. Name changes to Chase-Hackley Piano Co.
1893: Company declares bankruptcy and ceases operations.

CHASE CHAIR CO.
1896 - 1901

Grand Rapids, Michigan
Manufacturer of chairs.

CHASE - HACKLEY PIANO CO.	SEE Chase Brothers Piano Co.
CHASE, W. H. FURNITURE CO. 1913 - 1927	Grand Rapids, Michigan Manufacturer of library tables; home furnishings retailer.
CHERRYMASTERS OF GRAND RAPIDS, INC.	SEE Grand Rapids Dinette Co.
CHOCOLATE COOLER CO. ca. 1895 - 1919	Grand Rapids, Michigan Manufacturer of "The Grand Rapids" ice cream cabinets and refrigerators, special ice cream and confectioners' tables, and refrigerators for florists. "Fritz & Goedel" and "Fritz Manufacturing Co." often appear associated with Chocolate Cooler Co.
CHOCOLATE ICE CREAM CABINET CO.	SEE Chocolate Cooler Co.
CHURCH, MELVIN B. BEDETTE FURNITURE CO. 1883 - 1885	Grand Rapids, Michigan Manufacturer of Church's Folding Spring Cot, a mattress-less camping bed.
CINNEY & BINLY TABLE CO. at least 1902	Chicago, Illinois and Grand Rapids, Michigan Manufacturer of oak Arts and Crafts-style tables and desks with cut-outs. *The Cinney & Binly Table Co.* 1902
CLARK & HODGES FURNITURE CO. 1886 - ca. 1888	Grand Rapids, Michigan Manufacturer of hardware tables and stands; contract supplier of machine carvings and turnings. Predecessor to Valley City Table Co. SEE ALSO Valley City Table Co.
CLAY STEEL FURNITURE CO. OF GRAND RAPIDS, THE 1933	Grand Rapids, Michigan Manufacturer of "Cape Cod" furniture, chairs, tables, and sofas in flat and chrome-plated tubular steel, for summer homes, beauty parlors, hotel lobbies, and auto showrooms.
COLLINS, HUGHES & CO. founded 1885	Grand Rapids, Michigan Manufacturer of mattresses.
COLONIAL ART FURNITURE SHOP 1941 - 1967	Grand Rapids, Michigan Manufacturer of French Provincial living room tables.
COLONIAL CUSTOM UPHOLSTERING CO. 1936	Grand Rapids, Michigan Manufacturer of high-grade upholstered living room furniture. Advertised in the *Grand Rapids Furniture Festival Program* for 1936. TRADE MARK 1936
COLONIAL FURNITURE CO. 1910 - 1949	Grand Rapids, Michigan Manufacturer of carvings, chairs, and upholstery frames. 1920
COLONIAL MANUFACTURING CO. 1906 - 1983 1937 1957 1966	Zeeland and Grand Rapids, Michigan Manufacturer of hall or "Grandfather" clocks, library and living room furniture in solid mahogany, and spinet desks in Mission, Colonial Revival, and oriental lacquered styles. **COMPANY HISTORY** 1906: Company incorporates. 1908 - 1935: Herman Miller is General Manager. 1979: Company is purchased by Thomas Industries. 1983: Company closes. **PERSONNEL** Designers include John Kemp, John Zeiss, William Balback, John Boukma, Ray Sabota, Stanley Green, and Henry Glass. **OTHER SOURCES** The Public Museum of Grand Rapids has a significant number of trade catalogs, as well as a collection of clock face decoration patterns from this company. 1957
COLONIAL RUSH SEAT CO. 1935 - 1944	Grand Rapids, Michigan Manufacturer of cane seats for chairs.
CONREY - BIRELY TABLE CO. ca. 1889 - 1909	Grand Rapids, Michigan Manufacturer of tables.

Predecessor to Davis - Birely Table Co.
SEE ALSO Davis - Birely Table Co.

CONSOLIDATED FURNITURE COMPANIES
founded 1923

Grand Rapids, Michigan
Umbrella corporation for several companies.
SEE Berkey & Gay Furniture Co.; Grand Rapids Upholstering Co.; Wallace Upholstering Co.

CONTEMPRA, INC.
1946 - 1947

Grand Rapids, Michigan
Manufacturer of store fixtures. Operated by the owners of Grand Rapids Store Equipment Co.

CONTI , TIMOTHY A. & CO.
1905 - 1937

Grand Rapids, Michigan
Designers and producers of inlay, marquetry, and scrollwork in gold, silver, brass, copper, mother of pearl, tortoise shell, and natural and stained woods.
SEE ALSO Stickley Brothers Furniture Co.
COMPANY HISTORY
Before 1905: Designer, Stickley Brothers Co.
1905 - 1907: T.A. Conti & Co.
1908 - 1915: T.A. Conti & Son.
1916 - 1937: Conti Marqueterie Manufacturers.

CONTRACT FURNITURE CO.
1956 - 1968

Grand Rapids, Michigan
Manufacturer of furniture.

CONVERSE MANUFACTURING CO.
1889 - 1898

Grand Rapids and Newaygo, Michigan
Manufacturer of oak, ash, and "imitation" wood chamber suites, sideboards, bookcases, chiffonniers, tables, and beds for the Grand Rapids Folding Bed Co., with English Aesthetic or Arts and Crafts, and Mission or Art Nouveau influences.
SEE ALSO Newaygo Furniture Co.

CONVERTA SOFA CO.

SEE Robinson Furniture Co. of Grand Rapids.

COOK, BAKER & CO.
1890 - 1903

Allegan, Michigan
Manufacturer of Golden Oak combination bookcases, buffets, china cabinets, and desks.
SEE ALSO Baker Furniture, Inc.
COMPANY HISTORY
1890: Company founded to make sash and blind and other architectural wood products.
1893: Produced its first combination bookcase.
1903: Name changed to Baker & Co.

COOKERETTE CO.
1909 - 1910

Grand Rapids, Michigan
Cited in a general listing of woodworking and furniture manufacturing institutions.

COTTAGE CHAIR CO.
1913 - 1914

Grand Rapids, Michigan
Cited in a general listing of woodworking and furniture manufacturing companies.

COTTAGE FURNITURE CO., THE
ca. 1912

1912

Grand Rapids, Michigan
"Manufacturer of furniture and novelties for cottage, sun parlor, porch, and lawn."
SEE ALSO Grand Rapids Bungalow Furniture Co.

The Cottage Furniture Company
Manufacturers of Furniture & Novelties for Cottage, Sun Parlor, Porch and Lawn
1912

COUFFIELD, H.L. CO.
1907 - 1911

Grand Rapids, Michigan
Manufacturer of furniture.

COUNTRY ROADS, INC.
1974 - present

Belding, Michigan
Restorer and manufacturer of vintage seating for theaters, auditoriums, and churches.

COX & WOLTERS WOODCRAFTERS
ca. 1983 - 1992

Wyoming, Michigan
Manufacturer of home game-room furniture and reproductions of Frank Lloyd Wright-designed furniture and lighting.

COY, ANDREW & CO.
1901 - 1912

Grand Rapids, Michigan
Manufacturer of automatic lathe turnings and furniture novelties.

Predecessor to W. C. Hammond Wood Turning Co.
SEE ALSO Hammond, W. C. Wood Turning Co.

CRATER & HOLT
1914

Crater and Holt GRAND RAPIDS MICHIGAN
1914

Grand Rapids, Michigan
Designers of "Easy-to-make" furniture in the Mission style. Designs sold through Grand Rapids Furniture Record Co. to manual instructors, students, and home craftsmen. Advertised in *The Grand Rapids Furniture Record*, January, 1914.

CRAWFORD CHAIR CO.
1902 - 1929

Grand Ledge, Michigan
Manufacturer of dining chairs on contract for other furniture factories in Grand Rapids.
Predecessor to Jones-Hoerner-Guest Co.

CREQUE, J.P.
1866 - 1883

Grand Rapids, Michigan
Manufacturer and retailers of lounges, mattresses and upholstered goods.
Successor to Boynton & Creque.
Predecessor to Kent Furniture Manufacturing Co.
SEE ALSO Boynton & Creque; Kent Furniture Manufacturing Co.

CRESCENT CABINET CO.
at least 1890

Grand Rapids, Michigan
Manufacturer of tables, easels, and fancy furniture. Advertised in 1890 issues of *The Michigan Artisan*.

CRESCENT FURNITURE & MANUFACTURING CO.
1888

Big Rapids, Michigan
Manufacturer of bedroom suites with incised and chip carving, in ash or maple. Advertised in issues of *The Michigan Artisan*.

CRISWELL FURNITURE CO.
1910 - 1922

Grand Rapids, Michigan
Manufacturer of Classic reproductions in English, Italian, and American period styles for the library, living room, and bedroom. Specialties included mirrors, carved tables, and upholstered seating.
Successor to The Criswell-Kepler Co.
SEE ALSO Criswell-Kepler Co., The.

CRISWELL - KEPLER CO., THE
1907 - 1909

Grand Rapids, Michigan
Manufacturer of "correctly executed" classic reproductions, upholstered furniture, Davenports, chairs, settees, and rockers.
Predecessor to Criswell Furniture Co.
SEE ALSO Criswell Furniture Co.

CROCKETT & HOPPINS MANUFACTURING CO.
1885 - ca.1890

Grand Rapids, Michigan
Retailer and refinisher of "all kinds of furniture"; manufacturer of parlor furniture, couches, and special orders.

CURTIS & SON
at least 1894

Charlotte, Michigan
Manufacturer of bedroom suites. Advertised in 1894 issues of *The Michigan Artisan*.

DANKER MARQUETERIE, INC.
1923 - 1955

Grand Rapids, Michigan
Manufacturer of inlay borders, metal stencils, and panels of fine marqueterie for furniture manufacturers.

DANKER
MARQUETERIE COMPANY
251 Market Ave., S.W.   Grand Rapids, Mich.
1930

DANLYNN CO., THE
1987 - present

Grand Rapids, Michigan
Designer and maker of furniture samples and prototypes, and contract hand decorators for other manufacturers. Manufacturer of music stands, podiums, and Shaker-style game tables, and custom home furnishings under its own name.

D'ARCANGEL , J.N. UPHOLSTERING CO.
ca. 1965 - 1985

Grand Rapids, Michigan
Manufacturer of upholstered furniture.

DAVIDHAZY FURNITURE STUDIO
1956 - 1988

Grand Rapids, Michigan
High-end, custom and contract designers, decorative painters and finishers of furniture in various European painted and Oriental lacquer styles. Operated by Frank J. Davidhazy, who came to Grand Rapids to head the decorating department of the Robert W. Irwin Furniture Co. in 1922, and his son Frank C. Davidhazy.
SEE ALSO Irwin, Robert W. Furniture Co.

DAVIDSON FURNITURE CO.

SEE Davidson Plyforms, Inc.

DAVIDSON PLYFORMS, INC.
1927 - present

davidson plyforms inc.
1989

Grand Rapids, Michigan
Founded as Davidson Furniture Co., a manufacturer of upholstery frames. Now a manufacturer of bent, curved, and molded plywood furniture, components, frames, and shells for other manufacturers, including some of Charles and Ray Eames's molded plywood designs for Herman Miller, Inc., and Frank Gehry's series of bentwood "hockey" chairs for Knoll, Inc.

DAVIES FURNITURE CO.
ca. 1926 - 1957

Grand Rapids, Michigan
Manufacturer of upholstered furniture.
Started by the former owners of Davies-Putnam Co.

DAVIES - PUTNAM CO.
1912 - 1922

DP
1917

The Gift Line
1915

Grand Rapids, Michigan
Manufacturer of "The Gift Line" vases, stands, and other novelties; the "Tape-O-Lite" match holder ash tray; and occasional tables, tea carts, desks, and dining sets in period revival styles.
Predecessor to Stuart Furniture Co.
SEE ALSO Stuart Furniture Co.
OTHER SOURCES
The Public Museum of Grand Rapids has a significant collection of trade catalogs of this company.

DAVIES - WHEELER, INC.
1943

Allegan, Michigan
Cited in a Grand Rapids Furniture Market list as a manufacturer of upholstered chairs and Victorian reproductions.

DAVIS - BIRELY TABLE CO.
1909 - at least 1911

Grand Rapids, Michigan
Manufacturer of tables.
Successor to Conrey - Birely Table Co.
SEE ALSO Conrey - Birely Table Co.

DEGRAAF, VRIELING & CO.
1873 - 1894

Grand Rapids, Michigan
Mostly a manufacturer of sash and blind, doors, stairs, lumber, and other architectural wood products. However, they also made pulpits, church pews, bank desks, and counters.

DEKORNE & LINDHOUT
1912 - 1923

Grand Rapids, Michigan
Manufacturer of furniture.

DELLENBAUGH - ALTON MANUFACTURING CO.
ca. 1902 - 1905

Portland, Michigan
Manufacturer of Morris chairs exclusively.
Predecessor to Ramsey-Alton Manufacturing Co.
SEE ALSO Ramsey-Alton Manufacturing Co.

DELUXE UPHOLSTERING CO., INC.
ca. 1921

Grand Rapids, Michigan
Manufacturer of upholstered furniture for the living room, hall, solarium, bedroom; and special furniture for hotels, lodges, and houses.
Cited in *The Grand Rapids Furniture Record*, June, 1921.

DENNETT, DAVID A.
ca. 1984 - present

Wyoming, Michigan
Custom maker of traditional wooden home furnishings including jewelry boxes, breakfronts, blanket chests, side tables, and custom curio cabinets in bird's-eye and quilted maple, cherry, and various other woods.

DENTON MANUFACTURING CO.
at least 1917 - 1918

St. Joseph, Michigan
Manufacturer of furniture. Cited in a general listing of furniture manufacturers.

DENUIT, JOHN H.
ca. 1865

Grand Rapids, Michigan
Upholsterer of furniture.

DESIGNERS WORKSHOP/DW2
1969 - 1997

designers workshop
DW2
1994

Grand Rapids, Michigan
Custom manufacturer of conference, reception, occasional, and residential furniture; interior designers/fabricators for restaurants and businesses.
Predecessor to Jeup, Inc.
SEE ALSO Jeup, Inc.

DEWEY FURNITURE CO.
1941 - 1949

Grand Rapids, Michigan
Manufacturer of dining room and bedroom furniture.

DEWEY & PUGH
1890

Grand Rapids, Michigan
Manufacturer of "The Boss Lawn Chair," a classic sling canvas deck chair on a folding wooden frame. Advertised in issues of *The Michigan Artisan* from 1890.

DOEZEMA FURNITURE CO.
1917 - 1955

Grand Rapids, Michigan
Manufacturer of "exquisitely" carved furniture, dining and bedroom furniture, end tables, and occasional furniture, including several pieces that were placed in the White House.
SEE ALSO Furniture Arts Co.

DOLPHIN DESK CO.
at least 1908 - 1920

Grand Rapids, Michigan
Manufacturer of desks. Cited in a list of manufacturers from *The Furniture Manufacturer and Artisan*, February, 1920.

DONNELLY MIRRORS, INC.

SEE Hart Mirror Division, Donnelly Corp.

DONOVAN - WELCH
1945 - 1953

Grand Rapids, Michigan
"Wood products manufacturer."

DRUEKE, WILLIAM F. & CO.
1919 - 1991

Grand Rapids, Michigan
First manufacturer of chess sets in the United States. Drueke also made wooden chess boards, chess tables, cribbage boards, poker chip racks, backgammon sets, dominoes, checkers, card boxes, and other wooden accessories in walnut, cherry, and maple. Drueke expanded into manufacture of injection mold plastic pieces for its wooden boards around 1940. Drueke's name and product lines were assumed by The Carrom Co. of Ludington, Michigan in 1991.
SEE ALSO Carrom Co., The.

The Drueke Company
1990

DRY - KOLD REFRIGERATOR CO.
ca. 1918 - 1935

Niles, Michigan
Manufacturer of refrigerators and refrigerated cases for hotels, hospitals, florists, grocers, and meat markets.
SEE ALSO Tyler Refrigeration Corp.
COMPANY HISTORY
1918: Company founded as Vyking Refrigerator Co.; name later changes to Dry-Kold.
1935: Company is purchased by Tyler Refrigeration Corp.

DRYDEN - ANNIN - ROSE CLOCK CO.
1893 - ca. 1898

Grand Rapids, Michigan
Advertised in the October, 1893 issue of *The Michigan Artisan* as a manufacturer of high-grade, Colonial Revival hall clocks.
Predecessor to Grand Rapids Clock & Mantel Co.
SEE ALSO Grand Rapids Clock & Mantel Co.

DUNHAM, THOMAS N.
ca. 1855

Greenville, Michigan
Cabinetmaker.

DUTCH WOODCRAFT SHOPS, INC.
at least 1928 - early 1940s

Zeeland, Michigan
Manufacturer of library, living room, hall, and bedroom furniture, occasional tables, and telephone stands, with crotch mahogany veneers. From the late 1930s through the early 1940s, the company jointly manufactured the "Calvert Line" of colonial reproductions with the Holland Furniture Co.
SEE ALSO Holland Furniture Co.

Dutch Woodcraft Shops
1930   1930

DUYSER UPHOLSTERY CO.
1928

Grand Rapids, Michigan
Manufacturer of upholstered furniture, which was also retailed directly from the factory. Cited in *The Buyer's Guide*, July, 1928.

EAGLES - PULLMAN CO.
1850 - 1854

Grand Rapids, Michigan
Manufacturer of furniture to order, and retailers of furniture made in New York City. A carved and veneered mahogany, Rococo Revival sideboard with etagere in the collections of The Public Museum of Grand Rapids is attributed to Eagles - Pullman Co. George M. and A.B. Pullman later moved to Chicago, where they manufactured George's signature invention, the Pullman Palace railroad cars.

EAST SHORE FURNITURE CO.
1888 - 1891

Oak Hill, near Manistee Michigan
Manufacturer of hardwood furniture.

EATON FURNITURE SHOPS
1946 - ca. 1949

1948

Grand Rapids, Michigan
Manufacturer of upholstered furniture with Honduran mahogany frames, sold through Carl Forslund's store and mail order. Carl V. Forslund was president.
SEE ALSO Forslund Brothers Co.

EHRLICH OF GRAND RAPIDS

SEE Grand Rapids Leather Furniture Co., Inc.

ELFERDINK, HAROLD
1938 - 1949

Grand Rapids, Michigan
Manufacturer of upholstered furniture.

ELLIS, P.M. CO.
1928

Grand Rapids, Michigan
Manufacturer of upholstered furniture. Cited in *The Buyer's Guide*, July, 1928.

EMPIRE FURNITURE CO.
1912 - 1922

Grand Rapids, Michigan
Founded by George M. Haney when he parted ways with the Haney School Furniture Co. Contract manufacturer, for Steel Furniture Co. and others, of components for school desks and seats.
SEE ALSO Haney School Furniture Co.; Steel Furniture Co.

ENGSTROM & JOHNSON NOVELTY SHOP
1915 - at least 1918

Grand Rapids, Michigan
Small manufacturer of wood novelties and occasional furniture.

ERSTEIN, BERNARD CO.
1928 - 1962

ERSTEIN
1960

Grand Rapids, Michigan
Manufacturer of upholstered furniture and occasional chairs.

ESTEY, D.M. FURNITURE CO.
1875 - ca. 1940

1902   1919   1928

Owosso, Michigan
Throughout its early history, Estey was a large manufacturer of inexpensive beds and chamber suites. By the 1920s its listings include bedroom and dining room furniture. During the mid-1930s Estey produced bedroom sets with very severe Modern lines, with sharp contrasting white holly against dark burl walnut. These avant garde pieces were designed by Donald Deskey.

ESTEY MANUFACTURING CO.

SEE Estey, D.M. Furniture Co.

EUREKA CABINET CO.
1894

Grand Rapids, Michigan
Manufacturer of cabinets. Listed in the 1894 *Business & Professional Directory of Kent County, Michigan*.

EUROPEAN UPHOLSTERING CO.
1925

Grand Rapids, Michigan
Manufacturer of upholstered mohair davenports and wing chairs. Cited in *The Furniture Blue Book*, September, 1925.

EVART FIBER FURNITURE CO.
at least 1928 - 1935

Evart, Michigan
Small operation, maker of "fine fiber furniture."

EXCELSIOR FURNITURE CO.
ca. 1882

Grand Rapids, Michigan
Manufacturer of parlor furniture, lounges, easy chairs, and center tables.

EXTENSOLE CORP.
ca. 1946 - 1978

1968

Sparta, Michigan
Successor to Fine Arts Studio.
SEE ALSO Worden Co.
COMPANY HISTORY
1936: Company founded in Holland, Michigan as Fine Arts Studio.
1937: Moves to former Grand Rapids Store Equipment Co. plant in Sparta. Name changes to Michigan Artcraft Co. Also known as Sparta Furniture Shops, Inc.
ca. 1946: Name changes to Extensole Corporation.
1978: Company is purchased by Worden Co. of Holland, Michigan.
PRODUCTS
As Fine Arts Studio the company made occasional pieces, wall brackets and some desks. As Michigan Artcraft they expanded the line to include dining suites, occasional chairs, and tables. After World War II, the company built its size and reputa-

tion on the manufacture of console extension and drop leaf extension tables, which featured T.E. McFall's patented devices for extending, lowering and raising surfaces.

FALCON MANUFACTURING CO.
at least 1917 - 1934

Big Rapids, Michigan
An ad from *The Buyer's Guide*, July, 1928, describes Falcon as a manufacturer of Art Moderne style living room and library tables, breakfast suites, and kitchen furniture.

FALKEL, A. & SON
1913 - 1917

Grand Rapids, Michigan
Manufacturer of novelties. Cited in a list of manufacturers from *The Furniture Manufacturer and Artisan*, February, 1920.

FALKEL RATTAN WORKS
1897 - ca.1901

Grand Rapids, Michigan
Manufacturer of woven wicker furniture.
Successor to Valley City Rattan Works.
SEE ALSO Valley City Rattan Works.

FICK & INGERSOLL
1884

Grand Rapids, Michigan
House and furniture carvers.

FILER TOWN MANUFACTURING CO.
1888 - 1890

Oak Hill, near Manistee Michigan
Manufacturer of furniture.

FINE ARTS FURNITURE CO.
1925 - 1977

Fine Arts Furniture Co.
GRAND RAPIDS. MICHIGAN
MAKERS OF DISTINCTIVE TABLES
1929   1954

Grand Rapids, Michigan
Manufacturer of occasional tables and chairs.
Combined with Ralph Morse Co. after 1966.
SEE ALSO Morse, Ralph Co.
OTHER SOURCES
The Public Museum of Grand Rapids has a significant collection of trade catalogs from this company.

Fine Arts   Ralph Morse
802 Monroe N.W.   1134 Freeman S.W.
Grand Rapids, Michigan
1970

FINE ARTS STUDIO

SEE Extensole Corp.

FINNEY, JAMES T.
ca. 1835

Grand Rapids, Michigan
Chair maker and decorator.

FISHER SHOWCASE CO.
1912 - 1914

Grand Rapids, Michigan
Manufacturer of showcases for retail stores. Cited in a list of manufacturers in *The Furniture Manufacturer and Artisan* from February, 1920.

FLEETWOOD FURNITURE CO.
1955 - present

Grand Haven, Zeeland, and Holland, Michigan
Manufacturer of educational and business furniture, audio-visual equipment, audience-reply electronics, dormitory furniture, bookcases, cabinets, and tables.
Moved from Grand Haven to Zeeland in 1958, and to Holland Township in 1986.

FOLDING TABLE & CHAIR CO.
1881 - ca.1889

Grand Rapids, Michigan
Manufacturer of folding chairs; bookcases and farmers' secretaries; and breakfast, kitchen extension, and folding tables. American Eastlake and faux bamboo styles, in maple, oak, and ash.

FOOTE-REYNOLDS CO.
1919 - 1926

1922

Grand Rapids, Michigan
Manufacturer of four-post beds and day beds in Colonial Revival style. Purchased by Kindel Furniture Co. in 1926.
SEE ALSO Kindel Furniture Co.

FORD FURNITURE CO.
founded 1881

Grand Rapids, Michigan
Manufacturer of tables.

FOREST CRAFT GUILD
1903 - at least 1914

Grand Rapids, Michigan
SEE ALSO Stickley Brothers Furniture Co.
COMPANY HISTORY
1903: Company founded by Forrest Mann to make Arts and Crafts jewelry, metalwork, and ceramics.
1912 - 1914: Cited in a general listing of woodworking and furniture manufacturers.
MARKS AND LABELS
The undersides of decorative objects produced by Mann were sometimes stamped with the words "FOREST CRAFT GUILD."

FORSLUND, BROTHERS CO.
1935 - 1991

Grand Rapids, Michigan
SEE ALSO Eaton Furniture Shops; Forslund, Carl V., Inc.; Nucraft Furniture Co.

COMPANY HISTORY

1935: Carl Forslund Sr. quits as a salesman for Stickley Bros. to begin his own retail consignment store.

ca. 1948: Carl V. Forslund, Inc. adds catalog and mail order sales.

1968: Brothers Forslund Co. established to succeed Eaton Shops and Grand Rapids Custom Shop in manufacturing furniture for sale through Carl Forslund retail and mail order. Name is later reversed to Forslund Brothers.

1989: Forslund Brothers Co.'s manufacturing division sold to Nucraft Furniture Co. of Comstock Park.

1990: Carl Forslund retail division sold to Custer Office Environments of Grand Rapids.

1991: Manufacturing plant closed.

1992: Retail stores closed.

1993: Limited production of selected Forslund pieces is resumed for a short time through an arrangement with Swartzendruber Hardwood Creations of Goshen, Indiana.

PERSONNEL

The manufacturing, retailing, and mail-order divisions of Forslund were all established by Carl V. Forslund, Sr., who remained in charge of the company from its inception until his retirement in 1972. He was succeeded by his sons, who joined the business in the 1940s and '50s. Carl Forslund, Jr. headed the manufacturing operations, Jon Forslund the retail, and Blake Forslund the overall administrative and financial management of the companies.

PRODUCTS

Forslund specialized in the manufacture of cherry, oak, and walnut furniture, in revivals of various Victorian and Early American styles. The mail-order business adopted a "folksy" style of advertising which influenced its product line, and had great appeal to its customers. Reproductions and adaptations were made from originals associated with colorful historical figures. Forslund catalogs were filled with pieces named for famous individuals, and lively histories of their namesakes. Such pieces as the "Rip Van Lee Chair" and the "Aunt Lucy Ball's Chair" were produced for decades, and became popular favorites for local residents and devoted mail-order customers.

OTHER SOURCES

The Public Museum of Grand Rapids has a significant collection of trade catalogs as well as business records from this company.

MARKS AND LABELS

Forslund adopted the silhouette of a Merry-Go-Round horse as its trademark, and the phrase "Timeless Furniture" as its motto.

1988

1988

FORSLUND, CARL V., INC.
1935 - 1992

Grand Rapids and Ann Arbor, Michigan
Retail arm of Forslund Brothers Co.
SEE ALSO Forslund Brothers Co.; Grand Rapids Custom Shop.

COMPANY HISTORY

1935: Company begun by Carl Forslund, Sr.

1992: Company closes.

FORSYTHE PRODUCTS CO.
ca. 1943 - 1950.

Grand Rapids, Michigan
Manufacturer of desks.

FOX, DORUS M.
ca. 1858

Grand Rapids, Michigan
Cabinetmaker.

FRANKS CARVING
1969 - present

Grand Rapids, Michigan
Manufacturer of carvings, multiple carvings, spindle carvings, and embossings on contract for furniture makers.

FREMONT FURNITURE CO.
1890 - 1896

Fremont, Michigan
Manufacturer of hotel suites, bedsteads, bookcases, and desks in oak, ash, and maple. Also maker of beds on contract for other companies.

FRITZ & GOEDEL MANUFACTURING CO.	SEE Chocolate Cooler Co.
FRITZ MANUFACTURING CO. 1915 - 1918	Grand Rapids, Michigan Manufacturer of furniture. Cited in general listings of furniture manufacturers.
FRITZ MANUFACTURING CO.	SEE Chocolate Cooler Co.
FROBACK, JOHN	SEE Frohberg, John.
FROHBERG, JOHN ca. 1859 - 1877	Grand Rapids, Michigan German-born cabinetmaker, known to have made American Empire furniture, some in the manner of John Hall. Frohberg may have worked both independently and for larger manufacturers, including Winchester Brothers Co., and Nelson, Comstock & Co. SEE ALSO Nelson, Comstock & Co.; Winchester Brothers Co.
FROBURGH, JOHN	SEE Frohberg, John.
FURBISH, FRANK L. CO. 1875 - 1885	Grand Rapids, Michigan Manufacturer of "Fancy cabinetware and brackets." Successor to Roberts & Furbish. **COMPANY HISTORY** 1875: Roberts & Furbish becomes Frank L. Furbish Co. 1885: Frank L. Furbish Co. closes. **PRODUCTS** Products included a small work table with scroll sawn legs and a turned sewing basket which was patented in 1875. Furbish also made Aesthetic-style easels, side cabinets, "dwarf sideboards," work tables, foot rests, and music racks in walnut and ebony. The company also produced a small line of toys in ash. However, most of their products were parts produced on contract for Phoenix; Nelson, Matter; Berkey & Gay; Widdicomb; and others. **OTHER SOURCES** The Public Museum of Grand Rapids has the business records of this company.
FURNITURE ARTS CO. 1942 - 1965	Grand Rapids, Michigan Manufacturer of furniture, operated by members of the Doezema family. Predecessor to the Rausch Furniture Co. SEE ALSO Doezema Furniture Co.; Rausch Furniture Co.
FURNITURE CAPITAL SHOPS 1923 1923	Grand Rapids, Michigan Advertised in the June, 1923 issue of *Good Furniture* magazine as a manufacturer of period revival wooden tables and spinet desks for the hall, library, and living room.
FURNITURE CITY CABINET CO. 1949 - ca. 1956	Grand Rapids, Michigan Manufacturer of tables.
FURNITURE CITY CARVING CO. 1905 - 1910	Grand Rapids, Michigan Cited in a listing of manufacturers from *The Furniture Manufacturer and Artisan*, February, 1920.
FURNITURE CITY NOVELTY CO. ca. 1945	Grand Rapids, Michigan Manufacturer of wood novelties.
FURNITURE CITY UPHOLSTERY CO. 1920 - 1977	Grand Rapids, Michigan Manufacturer of "The Quality Line" of informal upholstered living room sofas and chairs.
FURNITURE CRAFTSMEN 1955 - 1958 1957	Grand Rapids, Michigan Manufacturer of custom furniture and custom stereo cabinets in walnut, cherry, and "knotty pine."

FURNITURE SHOPS OF GRAND RAPIDS
1923 - 1933

1928

Grand Rapids, Michigan
"Manufacturer of living room, library, and hall furniture at moderate prices," in Colonial Revival styles.
SEE ALSO Grand Rapids Furniture Shops; Raab, John D. Chair Co.

FURNITURE STUDIOS, INC.
1918 - 1929

Grand Rapids, Michigan
Manufacturer of high-quality screens, cabinets, tables, seating, lamps, and covered boxes, and finished in Antique Polychromed Italian, Spanish, English, and French Renaissance, or Oriental styles.

G & P CARVING WORKS
1942 - 1951

Grand Rapids, Michigan
Contract carvers for other manufacturers.

G & T DISTRIBUTORS, INC.

SEE G & T Industries, Inc.

G & T INDUSTRIES, INC.
1954 - present

Grand Rapids, Michigan
Suppliers of seat cushions to manufacturers of office furniture and recreational vehicles.
COMPANY HISTORY
1954 - 1975: Company operated under the name G & T Distributors, Inc.
1975 - present: Operates under the name G & T Industries, Inc.

GALLMEYER & LIVINGSTON CO.
1928

Grand Rapids, Michigan
Contract spindle carver for other manufacturers. Listed in *The Buyer's Guide*, July, 1928.

GIBSON REFRIGERATOR CO.
1908 - 1975

Greenville, Michigan
Manufacturer of refrigerators and household appliances.
Successor to Belding-Hall Manufacturing Co.; Skinner & Steenman Furniture Co.
Predecessor to White-Westinghouse Corp.
SEE ALSO Belding-Hall Co.; Gibson Refrigerator Co.; White Consolidated Industries, Inc.; White - Westinghouse Corp.
COMPANY HISTORY
1908: Frank Gibson purchases assets of Skinner & Steenman Furniture Co. and Belding-Hall Manufacturing Co. and begins to manufacture refrigerators under the name Gibson Refrigerator Co.
1967: Becomes a subsidiary of White Consolidated Industries, Inc.
1975: Name changes to White-Westinghouse Corp.
1989: Name changes to Frigidare Co.

GILBERT FURNITURE CO.
1949 - 1950

Grand Rapids, Michigan
Manufacturer of furniture frames for upholstering.

GILMORE, S.F. FURNITURE, INC.
1983 - present

Grand Rapids, Michigan
Manufacturer of office and custom furniture, veneer and laminate-wrapped cylinders, custom conference tables, receptionist stations on contract.

GLEASON, H.B. & B.H.
ca. 1865

Greenville, Michigan
Cabinetmakers.

GLEASON WOOD ORNAMENT CO.
1880 - 1891

Grand Rapids, Michigan
Manufacturer of artificial and natural wood ornaments.
Predecessor to Widdicomb Mantel Co.
SEE ALSO Widdicomb Mantel Co.

GRAFF FURNITURE MANUFACTURING CO.
1945 - 1950

Grand Rapids, Michigan
Manufacturer of furniture.
Name changed in 1949 to "Graff of Grand Rapids."

GRAND LEDGE CHAIR CO.
1883 - 1981

Grand Ledge, Michigan
SEE ALSO Grand Ledge Table Co.
COMPANY HISTORY
1874: Small carpentry mill opens along Grand River.
1883: Company founded.
1973: Company becomes a division of the Holabird Co.
1981: Company closes.

Empire Revival piano stool by Grand Ledge Chair Co., early twentieth century.

1968

1958

GRAND LEDGE CHAIR CO.

GRAND LEDGE, MICH.

date unknown

1988: Old 1906 factory is remodeled as the Riverwalk Apartments.

PERSONNEL

Grand Ledge Chair Co. was founded by Thomas Garrett, Harry Jordan, and Edward Crawford, all of Grand Rapids. In 1893 they sold the company name and factory to their financier, Edward Turnbull, while they returned to Grand Rapids to start the Michigan Chair Co. During Turnbull's tenure, Grand Rapids designers, including John Brower, designed for Grand Ledge under contract. Upon Edward Turnbull's death in 1916, his wife Emma became sole owner of the company until she died, in 1944. An unattributed newspaper article from the period claimed that she had become "the only woman so far as is known to own a furniture factory in the United States."

PRODUCTS

Grand Ledge's primary product was always chairs, for use in the dining room and bedroom, as well as rockers and occasional chairs. Turnbull founded the Grand Ledge Table Co. in 1902 to expand to entire suites, but the new factory mostly handled overflow from the Chair Co. Styles ran the gamut for the period when the company was in business, including Golden Oak, Mission, Jacobean, Colonial Revival (including some very nice ladder back chairs). Women were especially employed to do hand-painted cottage and fancy designs, and to weave rush seats. In its later years Grand Ledge also produced chairs for large contracts, for clients including the Library of Congress, Marshall Fields Dept. Store, and area universities.

OTHER SOURCES

A collection of Grand Ledge chairs is owned by the Grand Ledge Area Historical Society. They also maintain an archive of catalogs and factory photographs, which is housed at the Grand Ledge Public Library.

MARKS

Paper labels were applied around the mid-20th century, which are white and include the names "Grand Ledge Chair Co." and "Grand Ledge, Mich." in blue ink. In 1958 the company used a special diamond anniversary logo with a flourished "GLC" monogram in the center. After this date the monogram was still used, without the additional anniversary designs.

GRAND LEDGE FURNITURE CO.
1919 - 1938

Grand Ledge, Michigan
Manufacturer of upholstered leather chairs, living room suites, children's rockers, sofa beds, and mattresses.

GRAND LEDGE INDUSTRIES
ca. 1945

Grand Ledge, Michigan
Manufacturer of tables, cabinets, and radio cabinets for Wilcox-Gay Co. of Charlotte, Michigan.

GRAND LEDGE MANUFACTURING CO.
1936 - ca. 1945

Grand Ledge, Michigan
Manufacturer of desks and occasional tables.

GRAND LEDGE TABLE CO.
1902 - ca. 1905

Grand Ledge, Michigan
Manufacturer of tables and chairs.
SEE ALSO Grand Ledge Chair Co.

GRAND RAPIDS AMERICAN ART FURNITURE CO.
1912 - 1916

Grand Rapids, Michigan
Manufacturer of furniture. Cited in a general listing of manufacturers from *The Furniture Manufacturer and Artisan*, February, 1920.

GRAND RAPIDS AUTOMATIC CHAIR CO.
ca. 1900

Grand Rapids, Michigan
Manufacturer of mechanical reclining Morris chairs.

GRAND RAPIDS BEDDING CO.
1914 - 1970

Grand Rapids, Michigan
Manufacturer of springs, mattresses, bedding, and daybeds. A 1937 advertisement showed the company's "Spring-Air" mattress trademark as belonging to the Charles Karr Co. of Holland, Michigan.
Successor to Hot Blast Feather Co.
SEE ALSO Hot Blast Feather Co.

COMPANY HISTORY

1898 - 1914: Operates under the name Hot Blast Feather Co.
1914 - 1970: Operates as Grand Rapids Bedding Co.

1925

GRAND RAPIDS BEDROOM FURNITURE CO.
1924 - 1928

Office and Showroom: Grand Rapids, Michigan
Factory: Grand Ledge, Michigan
Manufacturer of bedroom furniture.

GRAND RAPIDS BOOKCASE CO.
1897 - 1911

Grand Rapids and Hastings, Michigan
SEE ALSO Grand Rapids Bookcase & Chair Co.

COMPANY HISTORY

1897: Grand Rapids Bookcase Co. founded in Grand Rapids.
1899: Fire destroys Grand Rapids factory; new factory site found in Hastings.
1901: New building erected; company reorganizes with A.A. Barber as president.
1910: Grand Rapids Bookcase Co. products are cooperatively marketed under the names "Hastings Lines" and "Lifetime Furniture" with Barber Brothers Chair Co.
1911: Grand Rapids Bookcase Co. and Barber Brothers Chair Co. merge to form the Grand Rapids Bookcase and Chair Co.

PRODUCTS

Manufacturer of "medium priced" Mission and Colonial bookcases, desks, ladies' desks, china closets, side tables, gentlemen's chiffonniers, buffets, and parlor cabinets, in oak and mahogany.

GRAND RAPIDS BOOKCASE & CHAIR CO.
1911 - 1960

Hastings, Michigan
SEE ALSO Barber Brothers Chair Co.; Grand Rapids Bookcase Co.; Hastings Corporation of the Medallion, Ltd.; Hastings Table Co.

COMPANY HISTORY

1911: Company begins as a result of a merger between the Grand Rapids Bookcase Co. and Barber Brothers Chair Co.
1956: Grand Rapids Bookcase and Chair Co. and Hastings Table Co. come under ownership of Alexander Stuart.
1960: Both companies sold to Medallion Ltd. of New York, and are operated as the Hastings Corporation of the Medallion, Ltd.
ca. 1975: Factory closed.

PERSONNEL

The merger of Grand Rapids Bookcase Co. and the Barber Brothers Chair Co. was the work of owners Addison A. Barber and James C. Barber, who ran the new company until their separate but nearly simultaneous deaths in 1915. Keller Stem, an officer and possibly designer of pieces under the Lifetime trademark, took control of the company after this. The company went through a succession of other owners until it was sold to Alexander Stuart (son of John Stuart, who owned the John Widdicomb Co. of Grand Rapids) in 1956.

Living Room with "Lifetime" Mission furniture, from the *Grand Rapids Furniture Record*, April, 1911.

PRODUCTS

The Grand Rapids Bookcase & Chair Co. is best known for their Mission-style "Cloister Line," which was introduced in 1911 under the "Lifetime" trademark, and included pieces for the library, den, bedroom, hall, and dining room. The line was marketed using images of monks and Spanish Southwestern mission churches in its catalogs, several of which have been reprinted for collectors. Pieces are unadorned, with massive, straight lines and occasional arched front rails. Joints are mortise-and-tenon, and finishes are mostly frequently fumed oak. A variation of Cloister was introduced in 1913 as the "Jacobean" line, which included essentially the same pieces with turned period revival stiles and legs. Cloister received another "makeover" when it was reintroduced around 1917 as the "Puritan" line, which retained the same forms, but lines were more slender, with slight arches and attenuated curving brackets.

During the 1920s and '30s, as the market for Mission plummeted, the company reinvented its product, establishing itself as a maker of heavily carved suites for the dining room, living room, and private office. These oak reproductions and adaptations were heavily antiqued and came in various European period styles, and were sold with names like "Dr. Samuel Johnson's Dictionary Table" and "Prince Arthur's Dole Cupboard."

The company continued to produce pieces in oak under the name "Oakmaster" through the 1940s, and in 1952 introduced a new line called "Hastings Square."

OTHER SOURCES

The Catalog for the "Cloister" Line of Lifetime Furniture, circa 1910, has been

1928

1951

reprinted by Turn of the Century Reproductions.

MARKS AND LABELS
The distinctive black and white "LIFE TIME FURNITURE" trademark was used on paper labels for several decades, and is more commonly known to today's collectors of Mission furniture than the name of the company it represents.

GRAND RAPIDS BRASS CO. 1888 - 1956	Grand Rapids, Michigan Manufacturer of brass and bronze goods and artistic furniture trimmings.
GRAND RAPIDS BRASS & IRON BED CO., LTD. 1900 - 1905	Grand Rapids, Michigan Manufacturer of Mission and ornate scrolled brass and enameled iron beds and bed-stands.
GRAND RAPIDS BUNGALOW FURNITURE CO. 1911	Grand Rapids, Michigan Manufacturer of furniture and novelties for cottages, sun porches, and lawns. SEE ALSO Cottage Furniture Co., The.
GRAND RAPIDS CABINET CO. 1921 - 1954	Grand Rapids, Michigan Manufacturer of refrigerators, ice-cream refrigerators, ice-cream cabinets, soda fountains, and stove equipment.
GRAND RAPIDS CABINET FURNITURE CO. 1908 - 1912	Grand Rapids, Michigan Manufacturer of "the American Line," consisting of Jacobean Revival pieces in oak and cane, with carving and rope turning, for the living room.
GRAND RAPIDS CARVED MOULDING CO. 1897 - 1905	Grand Rapids, Michigan Manufacturer of "Art Moldings." Predecessor to Superior Carved Moulding Co. SEE ALSO Superior Carved Moulding Co.
GRAND RAPIDS CARVERS 1953 - 1955	Grand Rapids, Michigan Manufacturer of architectural, furniture, and hand carvings.
GRAND RAPIDS CASE GOODS CO. 1928 - 1932	Grand Rapids, Michigan Manufacturer of trunks, bags, leather goods, automobile trunks, salesman cases, veneer trunks, and carrying cases.
GRAND RAPIDS CASE WORKS 1922 - 1923	Grand Rapids, Michigan Manufacturer of medium-priced bedroom furniture.

GRAND RAPIDS CHAIR CO.
1872 - 1973

Grand Rapids, Michigan
SEE ALSO Baker Furniture Co.; Imperial Furniture Co.; Sligh - Lowry Furniture Co.

COMPANY HISTORY
1872: Company founded; incorporated the following year.
1945 - 1957: Company operates as a subsidiary of Sligh-Lowry, but continues to produce furniture under the Grand Rapids Chair name.
1957: Firm is purchased by Baker Furniture Co., but furniture is still produced under the Grand Rapids Chair name.
1973: Factory and assets fully integrated into Baker; furniture no longer made under the Grand Rapids Chair name.

PERSONNEL
The company was founded by a partnership that included local lumber, sawmill, and furniture baron Charles Carter Comstock as president, along with officers Elisha Foote, Henry Fralick, and S. W. Worden. Elisha Foote ascended to the presidency of the company in 1900, followed by Roger Butterfield in 1920. He was succeeded by Elisha's son F. Stuart Foote, who ran the firm until its sale to Charles R. Sligh, Jr.

Elisha Foote was responsible for bringing John E. Brower, Sr. from New York to Grand Rapids sometime in the 1890s. He served as the company's chief designer until his death in 1915. His son, John M. Brower, started the Brower Furniture Co. in 1919, to manufacture unfinished chairs for Grand Rapids Chair and its sister company, Imperial.

Brower was succeeded in the 1920s by George Fletcher and Carl Hammarstrom, who designed a full range of historical revival lines. Renowned designer Kem Weber created an Art Deco dining and living room group for Grand Rapids Chair Co. in 1928. Grand Rapids Chair Co. designs between 1945 and 1973 often came from staff designers of its parent companies Sligh and Baker. Herbert Ten Have

Armchair by Grand Rapids Chair Co., with Glasgow Art Nouveau influences, ca. 1900.

1927   1947

1942

designed the "Cross Country" line.

PRODUCTS

From its founding until 1880, the company produced chairs and sold surplus logs and lumber. In 1878, they boasted more than 450 styles of chairs. More than 300 boys and girls were employed at the State Reform School in Lansing to cane the seats. In that same year, they began production of upholstery frames for parlor furniture. In 1880 Elisha Foote expanded the styles of furniture made and began manufacturing complete suites. An 1883 article about Grand Rapids Chair Co. mentions that ash is their popular wood for that season, with "carved panels and heavier moldings." By the late 1880s their product lines had expanded to include medium-grade chamber suites, tables, bookcases, sideboards, and chiffoniers of maple, birch, cherry, and walnut, as well as chairs. Ads by the turn of the century stated emphatically that "we make no chairs."

Early 20th-century ads show both Golden Oak case pieces with serpentine fronts and cabriole legs referencing French historical styles, as well as Mission oak pieces. A 1900 article also lists mahogany, birch, maple, and bird's-eye maple in their lines. Ads from the 1910s and '20s show dining room, living room, and hall furniture, and spinet desks in a wide range of period styles, including Spanish Renaissance, Spanish Gothic, Elizabethan, Jacobean, Georgian, Adam, and Early American. Favored woods were walnut and mahogany. A Tudor line called "Castle Oak" seems to have been a flagship product in the early twenties.

In 1928 Grand Rapids Chair introduced the "Gaylady" Group, which may have been the name for its first modern line by Kem Weber. Its pieces featured the soft lines of French Art Deco, with light and dark contrasting woods and "artistic color treatments." During the 1950s the company made the "High-Lo Table," aimed at newly married couples with small apartments. It featured an adjustable height mechanism which allowed it to transform from cocktail table to card or dining table. The "Cross Country" line was a modular unit ensemble introduced in 1950 and marketed by Sligh. Its Scandinavian Modern styling and flexibility made it particularly suitable for ranch-style homes. The entire factory was eventually devoted to production of the Cross Country line.

MARKS AND LABELS

Beginning sometime in the 1910s or early 1920s, Grand Rapids Chair Co. adopted a logo which was basically a square frame of molding with chamfered corners that surrounded the words "GRAND RAPIDS CHAIR COMPANY / GRAND RAPIDS / MICHIGAN." These were printed in a distinctive block type which used triangular shapes for the rounded letters. An elliptical trademark was adopted for the "Dexter" line in the 1940s. The original rectangular logo was updated as a rectangular chiseled plaque in the late 1940s.

GRAND RAPIDS CLOCK & MANTEL CO. 1898 - 1916	Grand Rapids, Michigan Manufacturer of high-grade art mantels and hall clocks in Mission, Colonial, and Dutch Revival styles. Successor to Dryden-Anin-Rose Clock Co. SEE ALSO Dryden-Anin-Rose Clock Co.
GRAND RAPIDS CRAFTSMAN CO. 1946 - 1964	Grand Rapids, Michigan Manufacturer of traditional residential upholstery frames. Division of Rose Manufacturing Co. SEE ALSO Rose Manufacturing Co. *Grand Rapids Craftsman Co.* 1960
GRAND RAPIDS CUSTOM BUILT CHAIRS 1936	Grand Rapids, Michigan Manufacturer of custom furniture.
GRAND RAPIDS CUSTOM SHOP 1948 - 1967	Grand Rapids, Michigan Established by Carl V. Forslund, Inc. to manufacture upholstered furniture for its retail and mail-order operations. SEE ALSO Carl V. Forslund, Inc.
GRAND RAPIDS DESK CO. 1893 - ca. 1956	Grand Rapids and Muskegon, Michigan Manufacturer of office furniture, roll-top and pedestal desks in Golden Oak, mahogany and mission oak. SEE ALSO Browne - Morse Co.; Stow & Davis Furniture Co.

1903

COMPANY HISTORY
1893 - 1898: Company operates in Grand Rapids, Michigan.
1898: Moves to Muskegon, Michigan after factory burns in Grand Rapids.
1907: Purchased and operated by Browne - Morse Co. of Muskegon.
1928: Purchased by Stow & Davis Co. of Grand Rapids and operates until circa
       1956.

GRAND RAPIDS DINETTE FURNITURE CO.
1901 - 1902

Grand Rapids, Michigan
Manufacturer of dinettes.

GRAND RAPIDS DINETTE FURNITURE CO.
1948 - 1959

Grand Rapids, Michigan
Manufacturer of living room and dining room furniture
in solid cherry under the name "Cherrymasters of
Grand Rapids," and dining groups in cherry and mahogany.

1955

GRAND RAPIDS DOWEL WORKS
1913 - present

Grand Rapids, Michigan
Manufacturer of dowels for joining furniture components, and
turnings and carvings for other furniture manufacturers. The
company also made lamp parts, picture frames, and do-it-
yourself home oak spiral staircases.

1960

grand rapids
DOWEL
W O R K S

1960

GRAND RAPIDS ENAMELED FURNITURE CO.
1890

Grand Rapids, Michigan
Manufacturer of fancy tables and cabinets, gilt and decorated with pure gold leaf, in
white-and-gold, ivory-and-gold, gold, or silver finishes.
Advertised in 1890 issues of *The Michigan Artisan*.

GRAND RAPIDS FANCY FURNITURE CO.
1898 - 1939

1936

Grand Rapids, Michigan
Manufacturer of oak and mahogany benches, bookcases, cabinets, desks, and tables
in Mission and revival styles.
Acquired in 1940 by Metal Office Furniture Co. (Steelcase, Inc.).
SEE ALSO Steelcase, Inc.

GRAND RAPIDS FIBRE FURNITURE CO.
1917 - 1927

Grand Rapids, Michigan
Manufacturer of high grade fibre furniture, chairs, settees, chaise lounges, hotel
hampers, waste buckets, and ferneries.
Successor to Valley City Chair Co.
SEE ALSO Valley City Chair Co.

GRAND RAPIDS FIRELESS COOKSTOVE CO.
1909 - at least 1920

Grand Rapids, Michigan
Manufacturer of stoves. Cited in a list of manufacturers in *The Furniture Manufacturer and Artisan* for February, 1920.

GRAND RAPIDS FIXTURE CO.
1898 - 1908

Grand Rapids, Michigan
Manufacturer of patented wood and plate glass show cases.
Predecessor to Wilmarth Showcase Co.
SEE ALSO Wilmarth Showcase Co.

GRAND RAPIDS FURNITURE CO.
1877 - 1891

Grand Rapids, Michigan
Manufacturer of bedsteads.

GRAND RAPIDS FURNITURE CO.
1902 - 1957

1927

Grand Rapids, Michigan
Manufacturer of combination school desks, and tables, chairs, sideboards, and china
closets for dining rooms, in Austrian Arts and Crafts, and various English revival styles.
Successor to New England Furniture Co.
SEE ALSO Brower Furniture Co.; New England Furniture Co.
COMPANY HISTORY
1902: Name changes from New England Furniture Co. to Grand Rapids
       Furniture Co.
1957: Acquired by Brower Furniture Co.

GRAND RAPIDS FURNITURE MANUFACTURING CO.
1874 - 1943

Grand Rapids, Michigan
Manufacturer of furniture.
Successor to Moore, Richardson & Co.

Grand Rapids Furniture Mfg. Co.
Grand Rapids, Mich.
1905

GRAND RAPIDS FURNITURE SHOPS
1921 - 1923

Grand Rapids, Michigan
Manufacturer of radio cabinets and library, living room, hall, and occasional furni-

1923

ture in Colonial Revival styles.
Successor to John D. Raab Chair Co.
SEE ALSO Furniture Shops of Grand Rapids; Raab, John D. Chair Co.; Stone-Hoult Furniture Co.

GRAND RAPIDS IRON BED CO., LTD.
SEE Grand Rapids Brass & Iron Bed Co., Ltd.

GRAND RAPIDS JUVENILE FURNITURE, INC.
1959 - 1966
Grand Rapids, Michigan
Manufacturer of furniture for children.
Predecessor to Grand Rapids Wood Products Co.
SEE ALSO Grand Rapids Wood Products Co.

GRAND RAPIDS LAMP CO.
1916 - 1920
Grand Rapids, Michigan
Manufacturer of lamps. Cited in a list of manufacturers in *The Furniture Manufacturer and Artisan* from February, 1920.

GRAND RAPIDS LEATHER FURNITURE CO.
1946 - 1978
Grand Rapids, Michigan
Manufacturer of leather furniture. "Ehrlich of Grand Rapids" was an apparent trademark of the same company.

Ehrlich of Grand Rapids
1923

GRAND RAPIDS LOUNGE CO.
1933 - 1946
Grand Rapids, Michigan
Manufacturer of upholstered living room furniture.

GRAND RAPIDS MARBLE & FIREPLACE CO.
1912 - 1970
Grand Rapids, Michigan
Manufacturer of fireplace equipment.

GRAND RAPIDS MATTRESS CO.
founded 1882
Grand Rapids, Michigan
Manufacturer of mattresses and spring beds.

GRAND RAPIDS MATTRESS CO.
1941 - 1975
Grand Rapids, Michigan
Manufacturer of mattresses and box springs.

GRAND RAPIDS METAL CABINET CO.
1945 - 1949
Grand Rapids, Michigan
Manufacturer of cabinets.

GRAND RAPIDS PANEL CO.
1898 - 1960
Grand Rapids, Michigan
Manufacturer of graining plates and graining machines that printed various hardwood grains on wood or sheet metal. Products were used by a wide variety of West Michigan manufacturers, including Arcadia Furniture Co. and Metal Office Furniture Co. (Steelcase).

GRAND RAPIDS PARLOR CHAIR CO.
1891 - ca. 1892
Grand Rapids, Michigan
Upholsterers of parlor suites and lounge frames for wholesale only.
Successor to Strahan & Long.
Predecessor to Mueller & Slack Co.
SEE ALSO Mueller & Slack Co.; Strahan & Long.

GRAND RAPIDS PARLOR FRAME CO.
1922 - 1945
Grand Rapids, Michigan
Manufacturer of upholstery frames and wood carvings.

GRAND RAPIDS PHONOGRAPH CO.
1919 - 1925
Grand Rapids, Michigan
Manufacturer of the "L'Artiste" phonograph and nine other models in period revival styles.
Associated with the Grand Rapids School Equipment Co.
SEE ALSO Grand Rapids School Equipment Co.

L'Artiste
1919

GRAND RAPIDS PIANO CASE CO.
1891 - 1925
Grand Rapids, Michigan
Manufacturer of parlor desks, music cabinets, and piano cases.

GRAND RAPIDS OFFICE CHAIR CO.
1923
Grand Rapids, Michigan
Manufacturer of office chairs.

GRAND RAPIDS REFRIGERATOR CO.
1883 - 1926
Grand Rapids, Michigan
SEE ALSO Kelvinator-Leonard-A.B.C.
COMPANY HISTORY
1883: Company founded.
ca. 1901: Some refrigerators are manufactured under the name Northern Refrigerator Co. of Grand Rapids.

"Leonard" Refrigerator, ca. 1890.

1926: Company merges with Kelvinator; name changes to Kelvinator-Leonard Co.

1958: Kelvinator-Leonard Refrigerator acquires Altorfer Brothers Co. (A.B.C.) of Peoria, Illinois, and changes its name to Kelvinator-Leonard-A.B.C.

PERSONNEL

The founding members of the Grand Rapids Refrigerator Co. were Charles Leonard, president; Frank Leonard, vice-president; and Fred H. Leonard, secretary and treasurer.

PRODUCTS

Manufacturer of the "Leonard Cleanable," "Northern Light," and "Challenge" Refrigerators. In the 1890s the company also manufactured "catalogue cabinets," "shoe wardrobes," shaving cabinets, and folding boot racks. These featured porcelain-lined steel inner compartments and solid ash exteriors. The company held patents for a number of other features, including removable interior walls which could be washed, air-tight locks, solid iron shelves, and an interior designed to preserve ice. In 1909 the company advertised combination refrigerators with a table surface on top, which could be substituted for a kitchen table in small kitchens, or combined with a "kitchen cabinet set" on top, to create a refrigerator/Hoosier cabinet. In 1910 the company innovated seamless inner compartments in its refrigerators.

In 1914 the company began an association with Kelvinator, which made electric, mechanical refrigeration systems, and introduced its own electric refrigerators. After the merger with Kelvinator, the company phased out ice box production. After the merger with A.B.C., the company diversified into production of electric ranges, washers, dryers, home freezers, and refrigerated cabinets for commercial use, in addition to refrigerators.

GRAND RAPIDS SAMPLE CASE CO.
1933 - 1949

Grand Rapids, Michigan
Manufacturer of trunks, bags, leather goods, automobile trunks, salesmen cases, bread containers; also general repair work.

GRAND RAPIDS SCHOOL EQUIPMENT CO.
1919 - 1926

Grand Rapids, Michigan
Manufacturer of vocational school equipment.
SEE ALSO Grand Rapids Phonograph Co.

GRAND RAPIDS SCHOOL FURNITURE CO.

SEE American Seating Co.

GRAND RAPIDS SHOWCASE CO.
1901 - 1926

Headquarters and main factory: Grand Rapids, Michigan. Branch factory: Portland, Oregon. Branch offices and showrooms: Chicago, Illinois; Boston, Massachusetts; and New York, New York.
SEE ALSO Grand Rapids Store Equipment Co.; Welch - Wilmarth Co.

COMPANY HISTORY

1901: Grand Rapids Showcase Co. organizes.

1913: Grand Rapids Showcase Co. claims to manufacture more retail furnishings by volume than the combined total of its three leading competitors. Company also claims to ship more furniture than any other manufacturer in Grand Rapids.

1926: Merges with Welch - Wilmarth Co.; name changes to Grand Rapids Store Equipment Co.

PRODUCTS

Manufacturer of furniture and equipment for drug, confectionery, cigar, clothing, and department stores, including showcases for hats, gloves, and dress goods; dress form cases, cash register stands, vestibule display cases, cloak and suit cases, tables for clothing, dry goods, bargains, cashier's desks, and clothing cabinets. The company also maintained a special store planning department, which provided custom design and layout services to its retailer customers.

GRAND RAPIDS STORE ENGINEERING

SEE Grand Rapids Store Equipment Co.

GRAND RAPIDS STORE EQUIPMENT CO.
1926 - 1955

Main offices and factory: Grand Rapids, Michigan. Additional factories: Portland, Oregon; Baltimore, Maryland; New York, New York; Los Angeles, California.
SEE ALSO Grand Rapids Showcase Co.; Welch - Wilmarth Co.

COMPANY HISTORY

1926: Company organized with the merger of Grand Rapids Showcase Co. and Welch - Wilmarth Co.

1948

1955: Company is purchased by Weber Showcase Co. of California.

PRODUCTS

Claimed to be the largest designer and manufacturer of dry goods, department, and specialty store furniture and equipment in the world, including showcases, counters, shelving, wardrobes, cabinets, wrapping tables, and desks.

MARKS AND LABELS

During the 1940s the trademark was simply the elongated block letters "GR".

GRAND RAPIDS STORE FIXTURE CO.
1915 - 1940

Grand Rapids, Michigan
Suppliers of store sales equipment and fixtures, restaurant, soda fountain, and pool-room supplies; re-builder and manufacturer of special-order fixtures.

GRAND RAPIDS STUDIO FURNITURE CO.
1918 - 1927

Grand Rapids, Michigan
Manufacturer of polychrome painted and decorated furniture.
Associated with Shear-Maddox Furniture Co.
SEE ALSO Shear-Maddox Furniture Co.

GRAND RAPIDS TABLE CO.
ca. 1890

Grand Rapids, Michigan
Predecessor to W.P. Leffingwell. Successor to W.P. Leffingwell.
SEE Leffingwell, W. P.

GRAND RAPIDS TABLE CO.
1900 - 1904

Grand Rapids, Michigan
Manufacturer of oak and mahogany tables, chairs and office desks in Venetian and Colonial Revival, and Austrian Modern styles.
Successor to Z. E. Allen Furniture Co.
SEE ALSO Allen, Z. E. Furniture Co.

GRAND RAPIDS TEA TRAY CO.
1907 - 1920

Grand Rapids, Michigan
Manufacturer of tea trays and stands. Cited in a listing of manufacturers in *The Furniture Manufacturer and Artisan*, February, 1920.

GRAND RAPIDS TURNING CO.
1926 - 1939

Grand Rapids, Michigan
Manufacturer of occasional tables and novelties.

GRAND RAPIDS UPHOLSTERING CO.
1906 - 1930; 1938 - 1979

Grand Rapids, Michigan
Begun as upholsterers of seating frames for Berkey & Gay Furniture Co. During the 1910s frames were made from mahogany exclusively.
SEE ALSO Berkey & Gay Furniture Co.; Wallace Upholstering Co.

COMPANY HISTORY

1906: Company founded as a subsidiary of Berkey & Gay.
1930: Closes when Simmons closes Berkey & Gay.
1938: Reopens under new management.
1979: Company closes.

1917

1969

GRAND RAPIDS WOOD PRODUCTS CO.
1966 - 1968

Grandville, Michigan
Successor to Grand Rapids Juvenile Furniture, Inc.
SEE ALSO Grand Rapids Juvenile Furniture, Inc.

GRAND RAPIDS WOOD FINISHING CO.
1901 - 1990

Grand Rapids, Michigan
Manufacturer of furniture finishes, veneers, and stains for the furniture industry.

OTHER SOURCES

The Public Museum of Grand Rapids has an extensive archival collection for this company, which includes recipes of finishes it mixed for furniture manufacturers in Grand Rapids and nationwide.

1930

1941

GRAND RAPIDS WOODCARVING CO.
ca. 1890 - 1912

Grand Rapids, Michigan
Manufacturer of ornamental wood carvings and relief carvings; also carved novelty wall shelves and plate racks.
Associated with Charles A. Greenman Co. and Greenman & Dosch.
SEE ALSO Greenman, Charles A. Co.; Greenman & Dosch.

GRAND RAPIDS WOODCRAFT CORP.
1946 - 1951

Grand Rapids, Michigan
Manufacturer of radio cabinets.

GREAT LAKES FOREST PRODUCTS
1983 - present

Grand Rapids, Michigan
Manufacturer of components for other furniture manufacturers.

 GREAT LAKES FOREST PRODUCTS
1989

GREAT NORTHERN CHAIR CO.
1916 - 1919

Cadillac, Michigan
Manufacturer of chairs.
Successor to Cadillac Chair Co. Predecessor to Northern Chair Co.
SEE ALSO Cadillac Chair Co.; Northern Chair Co.

GREAT WESTERN NOVELTY WORKS
1903

Zeeland, Michigan
Advertised in *The Grand Rapids Furniture Record* as a manufacturer of dressing
stands, commodes, and china racks.

GREEN, JONATHAN J.
ca. 1865 - 1888

Grand Rapids, Michigan
Cabinetmaker and wagonmaker. The 1886 Grand Rapids City Directory lists Green
as an upholsterer. Known work includes a maple folding campaign chair with hand-
carved bulldogs and an American eagle crest.

GREENMAN, CHARLES A. CO.
1905 - 1910

Grand Rapids, Michigan
Manufacturer of Arts and Crafts tables, tabourets, pedestals, writing tables, maga-
zine stands, and palm stands.
Associated with Grand Rapids Woodcarving Co.
Successor to Greenman & Dosch.
SEE ALSO Grand Rapids Woodcarving Co.; Greenman & Dosch.

GREENMAN & DOSCH
1898 - 1905

Grand Rapids, Michigan
Manufacturer of wood and furniture carvings.
SEE ALSO Grand Rapids Woodcarving Co.; Greenman, Charles A. Co.

GREENVILLE PRODUCTS CORP.

SEE White Consolidated Industries.

GREENWAY FURNITURE CO.
1905 - 1907

Grand Rapids, Michigan
Manufacturer of furniture.
Predecessor to Michigan Desk Co.
SEE ALSO Michigan Desk Co.

GRELICK, J.E. CO.
at least 1914

Traverse City, Michigan
Advertised in *The Grand Rapids Furniture Record* in June, 1914, as a manufacturer of
Golden Oak and Mission-style library tables.

GROBHISER FURNITURE CO.
at least 1922

Sturgis, Michigan
Merged with the Aulsbrook & Jones Furniture Co. to form the Aulsbrook-Jones-
Grobhiser Co.
SEE ALSO Aulsbrook-Jones-Grobhiser Co.

GROENLEER FURNITURE CO.
1933 - 1934

Grand Rapids, Michigan
Manufacturer of bedroom furniture.
Predecessor to Groenleer-Vance Furniture Co.
SEE ALSO Groenleer-Vance Furniture Co.

GROENLEER - VANCE FURNITURE CO.
at least 1935 - 1936

Grand Rapids, Michigan
Manufacturer of Sheraton and Hepplewhite-style furniture in mahogany.
Successor to Groenleer Furniture Co.
SEE ALSO Groenleer Furniture Co.

GUARDSMAN PRODUCTS
1915 - present

GUARDSMAN
1996

1985

Grand Rapids, Michigan
Manufacturer of varnish, coatings, and consumer products.
COMPANY HISTORY
1915: Company founded as Grand Rapids Varnish Co.
1966: Changes name to Guardsman Chemicals, Inc.
1986: Changes name to Guardsman Products.

GUEST, M. A. CO.
ca. 1934

Big Rapids, Michigan
Manufacturer of bedroom furniture.

GUILD OF SHAKER CRAFTS, INC.
1965 - 1984

1971

Spring Lake, Michigan
Manufacturer, distributor, and retailer of exact, hand-crafted reproductions of origi-
nal Shaker designs for clocks, furniture, textiles, small household accessories in
wood with a variety of lacquer or tung oil finishes, and books on Shaker history.
Sales were by catalog or, beginning in 1969, through the Guild's "Portfolio" store in
Spring Lake.

A collection of catalogs and other records resides at the Tri-Cities Historical Museum in Grand Haven, Michigan.

MARKS AND LABELS

Pieces were marked with a pyrotechnic mark of a tree in full bloom.

GUNN FOLDING BED CO.

SEE Gunn Furniture Co.

GUNN FURNITURE CO.
1893 - 1953

Advertisement for Gunn "Lino" desks, from *Good Furniture Magazine*, Feb., 1922.

1905   1914

1927   1935

Grand Rapids, Michigan
Successor to Gunn Folding Bed Co.
SEE ALSO Bergsma Brothers, Inc.

COMPANY HISTORY

1874: William S. Gunn adds a retail furniture department to his hardware business.
1890: Gunn Folding Bed Co. is established and incorporated.
1893: Company changes name to The Gunn Furniture Co.
1949: Company purchased by Edsko Hekman and a group of associates.
1953: Company acquired by Bergsma Brothers, Inc.

PERSONNEL

William S. Gunn served as the company's founder and first president. After his death in 1909, the general management of the company passed to his son, William A. Gunn.

PRODUCTS

The company's initial products were folding beds. As early as 1893 folding beds began to decline in popularity, so the company changed its name and its products to roll-top desks, sectional bookcases, letter filing devices, and similar goods. By 1896 the company boasted that it produced 80 styles of desks. In the 1910s and '20s the company produced sectional bookcases which included a module with pigeonholes and a fold-down desk top. Cases were made in walnut, mahogany, imitation mahogany, and quartered oak. In the mid-1920s Gunn introduced its trademark "Lino" desks and cafeteria tables, which had wood frames and black linoleum top surfaces.

MARKS AND LABELS

As early as 1914, Gunn began to mark its furniture with the word "GUNN" in upper-case block letters, underlined on the bottom and slightly concave in their alignment on top. Desks and tables in the "Lino" line also are marked with the word "LINO" in block letters, with the foot of the "L" underlining the other letters. In the 1930s the trademark was modernized with a large uppercase "G," with part of the "G" underlining the "UNN".

HALDANE, WILLIAM "DEACON"
1836 - ca. 1859

Grand Rapids, Michigan

COMPANY HISTORY

1836: Haldane comes to Grand Rapids from Ohio to open one of the city's first cabinet shops.
1848: Haldane installs the first power machinery in his Canal Street shop.
1854: Haldane forms a partnership with Enoch W. Winchester, which dissolves after one year.
ca. 1859: Haldane closes his shop.
1936: Grand Rapids celebrates "Centennial of Furniture Making" one century after Haldane's arrival, and enshrines Haldane as "The Father of the Furniture Industry."

PERSONNEL

William Haldane was born in Dehli, New York in 1807, the son of poor Scottish immigrants. William's first important job was reported to be carpentry for the construction of a church in Panesville, Ohio in 1831. Here he met and married Sarah Tomlinson, the niece of the minister. In 1836 they traveled by horse and wagon to Grand Rapids. Haldane's first shop was in the back of their small frame residence. Built in 1837, it stood at the corner of Pearl and Ottawa Streets downtown, until it was torn down in 1888.

William "Deacon" Haldane.

William "Deacon" Haldane was chosen to be venerated in 1936 as "Father of the Furniture Industry" by 20th-century promoters of the Grand Rapids Furniture Market. While he does seem to be one of the first white settlers to set up a furniture shop in Grand Rapids, he made few lasting contributions toward birthing an industry. Most frontier towns had a cabinetmaker, along with a blacksmith, tinsmith, wheelwright, and other assorted tradespeople. Their shops and homes were generally one and the same, and their markets were usually limited to the local village.

If the success of Grand Rapids' furniture industry was built on large factories with many unskilled and semi-skilled workers producing furniture in assembly line fashion for wide distribution, then Haldane was the antithesis of a typical Grand Rapids furniture maker. Haldane was trained in a pre-industrial system of apprentices, journeymen, and master craftsmen. His shop employed only seven men, and presumably made most of his furniture for local buyers. Haldane reportedly led his workers in prayer and Bible reading every morning before they began their work, one of the activities that earned him the nickname "Deacon."

Haldane is also sometimes credited as the first to use power machinery to make furniture in Grand Rapids. In 1848 he added a circular saw, which he brought from Ohio, and a power lathe to his shop. But by 1859, about the time Grand Rapids' first actual factories were being set up, Haldane had abandoned furniture-making to his larger competitors and began selling real estate. He continued to reside in Grand Rapids until his death in 1898.

PRODUCTS

Haldane's product range is known to have included case pieces, beds, chairs, tables, and coffins. In his first year in Grand Rapids, he also made several sleighs or cutters to earn extra money. A hoop-back Windsor arm chair attributed to Haldane circa 1840 is in the collections of The Public Museum of Grand Rapids. Made from a combination of Michigan woods including oak, hickory, maple, and poplar, this chair appears to have been finished originally with a dark red-brown wash. Interestingly, though Haldane is known to have had a lathe in his shop, the spindles in this chair back were crudely fashioned with a spoke shave. The Public Museum's collection of Haldane's tools includes a number of wood planes and two spoke shaves.

In 1855 Haldane was awarded two prizes at the annual fair of the Kent County Agricultural Society for a bedstead and a bureau. The Public Museum also owns a circa 1880 walnut sewing table attributed to Haldane, and donated by a distant relative. While it is conceivable that he made it as a present for a relative, the sewing table dates stylistically from a time considerably later than when Haldane is known to have quit the furniture business.

OTHER SOURCES

Haldane is chronicled in most histories of early Grand Rapids, although many incorporate some amount of myth building about his furniture career. In 1936 his niece recorded her recollections for a newspaper feature on Haldane for the Century of Furniture Celebration. A copy of these reminiscences is in the collections of the Grand Rapids Public Library.

The Public Museum of Grand Rapids owns two pieces of furniture attributed to Haldane, and a collection of his tools.

MARKS AND LABELS

No piece currently attributed to Haldane is signed or marked, making attribution of other pieces without clear provenance difficult.

HALL BROTHERS MANUFACTURING CO.
1890 - 1895

Belding, Michigan
Manufacturer of stove boards, sewing and card tables, and sideboards.
Predecessor to Belding-Hall Manufacturing Co.
SEE ALSO Belding-Hall Manufacturing Co.
Absorbed by the Belding Manufacturing Co. in 1895, and reorganized to become the Belding-Hall Manufacturing Co.

HALL, H.N. CABINET CO.
ca. 1895 - 1896

Grand Rapids, Michigan
Manufacturer of ladies' desks, music cabinets, parlor tables, fancy stands, dressers, combination desks, and cheval mirrors in birch and mahogany with inlay.

HAMM & TURNHAM
ca. 1855 - 1859

Grand Rapids, Michigan
Manufacturer of cabinetware.
Predecessor to Budington & Turnham.
SEE ALSO Budington & Turnham.

HAMMERSCHMIDT, INC.
1946 - 1960

Grand Rapids, Michigan
Manufacturer of furniture.

HAMMOND, W. C. WOOD TURNING CO.
1906 - 1923

Grand Rapids, Michigan
Manufacturer of automatic wood turnings and furniture novelties.

Sometimes cited as successors to Andrew Coy & Co., although Coy continued operation for some years after Hammond began operation.
SEE ALSO Coy, Andrew & Co.

HANEY EQUIPMENT CO.

SEE Haney School Furniture Co.

HANEY MANUFACTURING CO.

SEE Haney School Furniture Co.

HANEY SCHOOL FURNITURE CO.
1889 - 1978

Headquarters and factory: Grand Rapids, Michigan. Sales offices:London, England; Chicago, Illinois; New York, New York.
Successor to Empire Iron Works.
SEE ALSO American School Furniture Co.; Empire Furniture Co.; Grand Rapids School Furniture Co.

COMPANY HISTORY
1872: Elijah Haney founds Empire Iron Works.
1875: Empire receives large contract to cast iron components for school desks.
1878: Company begins production exclusively of complete school desks for the Beckley - Cardy Co. of Chicago; company name changes to Haney Manufacturing Co.
1886: Haney ends contract with Beckley - Cardy and begins producing desks under its own name.
1888: Elijah Haney receives patent for his automatic folding seat desk.
1889: Company reorganizes as Haney School Furniture Co.
1891: Haney wins suit against Grand Rapids School Furniture Co. for infringing on its automatic folding seat desk patent.
1900: Haney produces 35,000 desks on contract for American School Furniture Co.
1901: Haney reaches an agreement allowing American School Furniture Co. to buy annual rights to use Haney's patent in its own lines.
1912: George M. Haney leaves the company and begins Empire Furniture Co.
1919: Haney School Furniture Co. declares bankruptcy.
1922: George M. Haney is awarded a patent for his pedestal desk and begins a new Haney School Furniture Co. under his control.
1966: Company is purchased by Joseph Kiraly and its name changes to Haney Equipment Co.
1978: Haney Equipment Co. ceases production.

PERSONNEL
Elijah Haney was the company's founder and first president. An inventor and mechanic at heart, he initially had his foundry produce small agricultural implements. After switching to school furniture, he received patents for his improvements, which eventually became standard in that segment of the industry. Control of the company rested solidly in family hands, with Elijah as president, Ida Haney vice-president, Alberta Haney as secretary, and George M. Haney as treasurer. Elijah remained president until the company's bankruptcy in 1919.

George M. Haney left the firm in 1912 because of disagreement over how the company was being managed, but restarted the bankrupt company after its original charter expired in 1922. Stricken with a sudden illness in 1923, George M. Haney was forced to turn over management to his wife Rose, and two sons Elijah William Melvin (Mel) Haney and George Francis (Fran) Haney. After George died in 1926, Rose served as president until her death in 1949. Fran succeeded his mother as president until the company was sold in 1966.

At that point control of the company for the first time moved out of the hands of the Haney family. It was purchased by Joseph Kiraly, formerly a sales representative for another company.

PRODUCTS
Although the legs, frames, and other parts were cast iron, the desk tops and seats were fashioned from Michigan maple. Elijah's automatic folding seat desk featured a fold-up seat in the front, and a writing surface in back. Each seated student used the writing surface attached to the desk unit in front of him or her. This innovation allowed for easy cleaning of floors and rearrangement of the desks. Its success was phenomenal. Haney produced 50,000 of the desks for the Chicago school district in 1893 alone, and sold millions more throughout the United States, Europe, South America, China, and India. As the company grew, so did its product line, to include teachers' desks, office desks, opera seating, and church seating.

Haney Combination School Desk, ca. 1888.

In 1922 George M. Haney received a patent for his modernized "pedestal school desk." It too featured a seat on the front of the unit, but it was mounted to a cylindrical pedestal that allowed for adjustment in the height of the seat. During World War II Haney produced desks for American military training centers.

After the war, light aluminum table and chair units with hard maple tops and chair backs were introduced. In 1960 "The Coloramic Line," with free standing desks and chairs in soft colors, went into production. "Coloramic" desks were constructed of tubular steel, with plastic over hard maple tops.

With the sale of the company in 1966 came changes in the product line to mostly library furnishings. With a heavy emphasis on metals and plastics, the new line included check-out desks, library tables, lecterns, study centers, book carts, and newspaper racks. An innovation for the classroom was the "Selectern," a teacher's desk with a pop-up lectern.

OTHER SOURCES
A detailed history of the company including a finding aid of papers relating to the company was compiled by descendant David Haney in an unpublished thesis in 1972.

MARKS AND LABELS
School desks made after 1889 were marked with "PAT'D SEPT 18, 1888 / HANEY SCHOOL FURNITURE CO. GRAND RAPIDS, MICH." cast on the side of the leg or trestle. Even if Haney produced a desk for another company and another name is stamped in the ironwork, you can tell it was actually produced by Haney if the tongue and groove joints between the boards in the seat form a zig-zag pattern. During the period following WWII, the company trademark included the name "Haney school furniture" in script, surrounded by a rectangular shape with concave sides. Pieces after 1966 will be marked simply "Haney" or "Haney Equipment Co."

1890

HARDING PARLOR FRAME CO.
1951 - 1962

1958

Grand Rapids, Michigan
Manufacturer of fine residential upholstery frames.
Purchased by Timberline, Inc. around 1960.
SEE ALSO Timberline, Inc.

HART MIRROR DIVISION, DONNELLY CORP.
1958 - 1962

1959

Holland, Michigan
Manufacturer of decorative residential mirrors.
Successor to Hart Mirror Plate Co. Predecessor to La Barge, Inc.
SEE ALSO Hart Mirror Plate Co.; La Barge, Inc.

DONNELLY MIRRORS INC.
1961

HART MIRROR PLATE CO.
1901 - 1958

1952

1902

Grand Rapids, Michigan
Manufacturer of mirrors. Predecessor to Hart Mirror Division - Donnelly Corp.
SEE ALSO Hart Mirror Division - Donnelly Corp.

HASTINGS CABINET CO.
1900 - 1916

Hastings, Michigan
Manufacturer of free-standing kitchen cabinets.

HASTINGS CORPORATION OF THE MEDALLION LTD.
1960 - ca. 1975

Hastings, Michigan
Manufacturer of furniture.
Successor to Grand Rapids Bookcase & Chair Co.
SEE ALSO Grand Rapids Bookcase & Chair Co.

HASTINGS FURNITURE CO.
1889 - 1895

Hastings, Michigan
Manufacturer of furniture.

HASTINGS KITCHEN CABINET CO.

SEE Hastings Cabinet Co.

HASTINGS RUSTIC FURNITURE CO.
at least 1897

Hastings, Michigan
Manufacturer of wicker furniture.

HASTINGS SCHOOL FURNITURE CO.
1895 - 1897

Hastings, Michigan
Manufacturer of school furniture.
Successor to Hastings Furniture Co.
SEE ALSO Hastings Furniture Co.

HASTINGS TABLE & CHAIR CO.
1890 - 1893

Hastings, Michigan
Manufacturer of tables and chairs.
Predecessor to Hastings Table Co.
SEE ALSO Hastings Table Co.

HASTINGS TABLE CO.
1893 - 1930

1918

Hastings and Grand Rapids, Michigan
Manufacturer of dining and pedestal exten-
sion tables, spinet desks, and tea wagons.
Successor to Hastings Table Co.
SEE ALSO Hastings Table Co.

1927   1927

HAWORTH, INC.
1975 - present

Headquarters and plants: Holland, Michigan. Manufacturing plants:
Allegan and Douglas, Michigan:
Successor to Modern Products Co.
SEE ALSO Mueller Furniture Corp.

COMPANY HISTORY

1948: G.W. Haworth founds company using name Modern Products.

1957: Company incorporates under name Modern Products Co.

1959: Modern Partitions organized as marketing arm for Modern Products Co.

1971: Company's first open office system, known as Modern Office Modules
(MOM), is introduced.

1975: Modern Products and Modern Office Partitions become Haworth, Inc.

1976: Floor-to-ceiling partitions line sold. First pre-wired panel system introduced.
Haworth concentrates on office furniture systems exclusively.

1988: Haworth begins aggressive program of acquisition of domestic and interna-
tional companies in order to offer a full range of design and products. Domestic acquisitions between 1988 and 1998 include Lunstead, Globe Business
Furniture, Myrtle Desk Co., Anderson Hickey, United Chair, and the RACE
system from Sunar Hauserman. International acquisitions include Comforto
(Germany); Kinetics (Canada); Ordo (France); Cortal-Seldex (Portugal);
Castelli (Italy); Mobilier International (France); Omni Office Interiors
(Australia); and COM (Italy). Sales offices and joint ventures expand
throughout Europe, the Middle East, Mexico, and the Pacific Rim.

1990: Haworth acquires Mueller Furniture Corp. of Grand Rapids.

PERSONNEL

In 1948 G. W. Haworth founded Modern Products, which he operated out of his
garage. He continued as its president until 1976. G.W. Haworth continued as chairman of the board until 1994, when he was named founding chairman.

He was succeeded by his son, Richard G. Haworth, who was elevated to the position of president and C.E.O. Richard Haworth joined the company in 1964 and
was named vice-president of research and development in 1966. He was responsible
for developing the company's first open office system, and the office furniture industry's first pre-wired panel system. He holds ten patents for his office furniture innovations. While president, he oversaw a program of rapid employment and sales expansion. This explosive growth rapidly raised the company from barely over 200
employees to more than 10,000, and the rank of third in the nation in office furniture sales. In 1994 Richard Haworth became chairman and C.E.O. In 1997 Jerry Jo-
hanneson was named C.E.O.

Over the years, members of the Haworth family and corporation have been
strong supporters of Western Michigan University (WMU), G.W. Haworth's alma
mater. In 1991 a donation toward a new home for the business school resulted in its
renaming as the Haworth College of Business at WMU.

PRODUCTS

Modern Products began as a small manufacturer of custom wood products. It made
retail display racks for neck ties and baked goods. In 1950 it began to produce bank
and floor-to-ceiling partitions. In 1954 Modern Products began making modular office partitions under the brand names "Soundex" and "E-Series." Product lines were
later expanded to include planters and room dividers (1955); language labs (1958);
study carrels (1962); and dormitory furniture (1965).

In 1971 Modern Products joined the open office system revolution with the introduction of "Modern Office Modules" It included acoustical panels and the universal panel hinge, which increased flexibility of panel set-up. In 1976, all non-of-
fice product lines were eliminated. Haworth began sales of "ERA-1," the industry's

1948-75

1975-93

1993

first electrical pre-wired, panel-based office system. It evolved into "UniGroup," Haworth's flagship product.

A line of office seating was added in 1981. A more sophisticated electrified system known as "Power Base," which allowed for multiple dedicated circuits, was introduced in 1986. After 1988 numerous new product lines and designs were also added through company acquisitions.

MARKS AND LABELS

From 1948 to 1975, Haworth was known as Modern Products. In this period its logo was a solid block "M" with the words "modern" and "products," all encircled by an oval outline. In 1975 the company name changed to Haworth, Inc. Its trademark became the name "Haworth" with double bars running beneath the name, and coming to a peak under the letter 'A'. In 1993 the logo was changed by dropping the double bars underneath the name, and placing a single red triangle inside the 'A'.

HEGEMAN & DRIEBORG, WOOD TURNERS

SEE Wood Products Corp.

HEGEMAN TABLE & SPECIALTY CO.
1926 - 1936

Grand Rapids, Michigan
Wood turners; manufacturer of occasional tables and furniture novelties.
Successor to Hegeman Wood Turning Co.
SEE ALSO Hegeman Wood Turning Co.

HEGEMAN WOOD TURNING CO.
1923 - 1926

Grand Rapids, Michigan
Successor to Hegeman & Drieborg.
Predecessor to Hegeman Table & Specialty Co.
SEE ALSO Hegeman & Drieborg; Hegeman Table & Specialty Co.

HEKMAN FURNITURE CO.
1922 - present

1927

1937

1943

1981

1949

1981

Offices and factory: Grand Rapids, Michigan. Additional factories: High Point and Lexington, North Carolina.
SEE ALSO Alexis Manufacturing Co.; Howard Miller Clock Co.; St. Johns, Inc.

COMPANY HISTORY

1922: Company founded by brothers Henry, Jelle, and John Hekman.
1942: Main showroom moves from Grand Rapids to Merchandise Mart in Chicago.
1964: Second plant acquired in Lexington, North Carolina.
1969: Hekman becomes a division of Beatrice Foods Co.
1974: Hekman acquires Alexis Manufacturing Co. of Grand Rapids.
1976: Hekman acquires H. Meulenberg & Son.
1977: Indiana Moulding & Frame Co. becomes a division of Hekman.
1978: St. Johns, Inc. of Cadillac, Michigan becomes a division of Hekman.
1983: Hekman is purchased by Howard Miller Clock Co. of Zeeland, Michigan, but continues to operate under its own name.
1994: Hekman purchases Woodmark Originals, Stanton-Cooper, and Dansen Contemporary Lines from Markwood, Inc. of High Point, North Carolina, adding new lines and three additional plants to Hekman.

PERSONNEL

Three sons of Dutch immigrants, Henry, Jelle, and John Hekman started the Hekman Furniture Co. along with experienced engineer and close friend James Boonstra in 1922. Henry served as company president from the time of its founding until he was succeeded by his brother Jelle in 1952. In 1936 Henry was elected president of the National Association of Furniture Manufacturers. Jelle, in turn, served as president of Hekman from 1952 until 1960. Adrian Vanden Bout was elected president in 1960, and served until succeeded by Harold Rodenhouse in 1974. Dan Henslee became president in 1989.

William Halstrick designed the company's first line of 30 tables. John F. Samuelson also served for a time as one of Hekman's designers. In 1970, Grand Rapids native Raymond K. Sobota designed the company's English Yewwood Collection, which became one of its most successful lines.

PRODUCTS

Hekman's first introduction was a line of 30 occasional tables. From there, the line grew to include occasional pieces for the living room, library, and hall. During World War II the factory was converted for production of glider bottoms and ammunition boxes. In 1960, pieces were offered in Neo-classical, Italian Provincial, French Provincial, and Danish Modern styles. Besides Sobota's "English Yewwood

Hekman Furniture Co., from 1924 catalog.

Collection," the company produced other wood occasional lines in 1970s, including the English Provincial "Charing Cross" collection, the sleek-lined, Mapa burl-veneered "Wind Row" collection, a series of entertainment centers, and the faux bamboo "Bambu Regency" collection.

During the early 1980s Hekman also began marketing desks and computer cabinets for home offices. At about that same time Hekman furnished several large hotels, including the Amway Grand Plaza in Grand Rapids, and the Ritz-Carlton in Chicago.

In 1991 Hekman introduced a line of reproductions of furniture owned by English novelist Charles Dickens, including a sloped mahogany desk and a cane seat smoker's bow chair. Hekman faithfully reproduced impressions made on the original desk by Charles Dickens, who nervously tapped his ring while he was writing.

MARKS AND LABELS

Beginning at least in the late 1920s, Hekman used a modified shield shape in red, surrounding a large white "H" inside which was written, "HEKMAN FURNITURE CO., GRAND RAPIDS, MICH." In the 1940s the company switched to a large "H" containing the name "HEKMAN," surrounded by a laurel wreath. In the 1960s the company used a solid circle surrounding a white block "H", with "HEKMAN" printed inside. By the 1970s the circle was dropped, leaving a dark block "H" surrounding the name "HEKMAN" in white.

HELMS PRODUCTS, INC. 1957 - 1975	Plainfield Township, Kent County, Michigan Manufacturer of furniture and wood products.
HEMBROOK MANUFACTURING CO. 1875 - 1884	Factory: Belding, Michigan. Offices and factory: Chicago, Illinois. Manufacturer of hall seats, school desks, railroad settees, lawn seats, office desks, and refrigerators. Reorganized in 1884 as the Belding Manufacturing Co. SEE ALSO Belding Manufacturing Co.
HEMBROOK, RICHARD T. MANUFACTURING CO.	SEE Hembrook Manufacturing Co.
HENDERSON - AMES CO. 1928	Kalamazoo, Michigan Listed in the July, 1928 issue of *The Buyer's Guide* as a manufacturer of lodge furniture and equipment.
HERRICK & LONG PIANO MANUFACTURER ca. 1896	Grand Rapids, Michigan Manufacturer of pianos.
HERRICK PIANO CO. 1908 - 1920	Grand Rapids, Michigan Manufacturer of pianos.
HETTERSCHIED MANUFACTURING WORKS 1883 - 1915	Grand Rapids, Michigan Manufacturer of drafting and typewriter tables, adjustable bedstands, and plant stands in iron, unfinished, or in Japan, copper bronze, or nickel plate finishes.
HEWITT, E. RUSH UPHOLSTERING CO. 1936 - 1937	Grand Rapids, Michigan Upholsterer of seating frames.
HEXTON FURNITURE CO. 1953 - 1960	Grand Rapids, Michigan Manufacturer of furniture.
HEYMAN CO. 1898 - 1953	Grand Rapids, Michigan Home furnishing retailer and showcase manufacturer between 1898 and 1926. The company continued as a retailer only from 1927 - 1953. Successor to Heyman, S. & Sons. SEE ALSO Heyman, S. & Sons.
HEYMAN, S. & SONS 1877 - 1898	Grand Rapids, Michigan Manufacturer of show cases; retail dealer of furniture.
HOENER FURNITURE CO. ca. 1934	Grand Rapids, Michigan Manufacturer of bedroom furniture, dining room furniture, and novelties.
HOLLAND CHAIR CO. 1926	Holland, Michigan Manufacturer of decorated telephone stands. Advertised in *The Furniture Blue Book*, October, 1926.

HOLLAND FURNITURE CO.
1894 - 1975

1927

1928-56

Holland, Michigan
Initially manufactured Golden Oak bedroom suites and sideboards. From the late 1930s through the early 1940s , the company jointly manufactured the "Calvert Line" of colonial reproductions with Dutch Woodcraft Shops in Zeeland, Michigan. Successor to Van Ark Furniture Co.
SEE ALSO Dutch Woodcraft Shops; Van Ark Furniture Co.

HOLLISTER, GEORGE C. & CO.
ca. 1915

Grand Rapids, Michigan
A company catalog advertised the "New All Oak Line," including dressers, princess dressers, chiffonniers, commodes, wood beds, and suites.

HOMESTEAD SHOP, THE
ca. 1971 - 1974

Wyoming, Michigan
Reupholsterer and maker of custom-made Victorian Revival furniture. Successor to Vander Ley Brothers Co.
SEE ALSO Vander Ley Brothers Co.

HOOD & WRIGHT
1901

Big Rapids, Michigan
Cited in a listing of manufacturers in a 1901 issue of *The Grand Rapids Furniture Record*.

HOOKER UPHOLSTERY
1948 - 1972

Grand Ledge, Michigan
Manufacturer of custom chairs; also refurbishers.

HOT BLAST FEATHER CO.
1898 - 1914

1911

Grand Rapids, Michigan
Manufacturer of mattresses, pillows, bed springs, and other bed products. Predecessor to Grand Rapids Bedding Co.
SEE ALSO Grand Rapids Bedding Co.

HOWARD CITY FURNITURE CO.
at least 1928

Howard City, Michigan
Listed in the July, 1928 issue of *The Buyer's Guide* as a manufacturer of chests of drawers, breakfast tables, and poster beds.

HUBBELL, H.L., INC.

SEE Hubbell, H.L. Manufacturing Co.

HUBBELL, H. L. MANUFACTURING CO.
at least 1929 - 1974

1947

Zeeland, Michigan
Originally manufacturer of "Fine Chests for the Home." In the 1970s the company manufactured metal components for file cabinets.

1974

HUIZINGH BROTHERS FURNITURE CO.
1927 - 1954

Grand Rapids, Michigan
Manufacturer of furniture.

IDEAL SEATING CO.
1938 - 1977

Grand Rapids, Michigan
Manufacturer of theater chairs.

IMPERIAL CHAIR CO.
1926

Holland, Michigan
Manufacturer of chamber, dining, and library suites. Advertised in *The Grand Rapids Furniture Record*, October, 1926.

IMPERIAL FURNITURE CO.
1903 - 1954

Grand Rapids, Michigan
SEE ALSO Grand Rapids Chair Co.; Bergsma Brothers.

COMPANY HISTORY
1903: Founded by F. Stuart Foote.
1904: Production of extension tables begins. Later other tables and bookcases are added.
1910: First dividend of 5% common stock declared.
1936: $80,000 showroom and dining hall built adjacent to factory.
1940s: Company builds airplane wings for the government.
1954: Company sold to Bergsma Brothers Co. after Foote dies.

PERSONNEL
F. Stuart Foote began at the Grand Rapids Chair Co., which his father, E.H. Foote, owned. There he learned about many aspects of the furniture business. In 1903, after ten years at the Grand Rapids Chair Co., he raised the money to found Imperial Furniture Co., with the help of Daniel McCoy, who was the president of Kent State Bank. McCoy was the first president of the company but Foote would soon take over and continue to be president for fifty years.

1910   1927   1939
TRADE MARK
ON EVERY PIECE

1953

1954

America's Proudest Name in Tables

1955

1956

1962

PRODUCTS

Imperial's primary product was tables, with the addition of bookcases to its line later in its history. Foote laid claim to inventing the "coffee table" after he helped his wife prepare for a party by lowering the legs on a table. Imperial made dining room tables to go along with buffets made by the Grand Rapids Chair Co. Imperial was the first factory to bring out Duncan Phyfe reproductions. They worked mostly in mahogany but also had pieces of cherry. In the 1940's, they made wood airplane wings for the government. Imperial was the first company to concentrate large-scale efforts on occasional furniture.

MARKS AND LABELS

Through most of its history, Imperial's trademark was a triangular shield with a crown on top. On the shield is written "Imperial, Grand Rapids, Michigan". The crown and the lettering vary only slightly by date.

INNER - BRACE CHAIR CO., THE
1911

1962

Schoolcraft, Michigan
Advertised in the June issue of *The Grand Rapids Furniture Record* as a manufacturer of "The Inner-Brace Chair." According to the ad, the patented invisible steel braces and steel joints hidden inside the wooden rails made it "the strongest wooden chair made."

INTEGRATED METAL TECHNOLOGY

SEE Miller, Herman, Inc.

INTERIOR CONCEPTS CORP.
1992 - present

Spring Lake, Michigan
Manufacturer of modular computer furniture for educational use and commercial fixtures for catalog, reservation, and telemarketing centers, and travel agencies. Formed by a merger of Interior Specialists and the office division of Structural Concepts.
SEE ALSO Interior Specialists; Structural Concepts.

INTERIOR SPECIALISTS
1982 - 1992

Grand Rapids, Michigan
Manufacturer of modular computer furniture for educational use and commercial fixtures for chain discount retailers. Combined with the office furniture division of Structural Concepts in 1992 to form Interior Concepts.
SEE ALSO Interior Specialists; Structural Concepts.

INTERNATIONAL FURNITURE TECHNOLOGIES, LIMITED PARTNERSHIP
1991 - present

Big Rapids, Michigan
First manufacturing source in the U.S. for Sweden-based IKEA ready-to-assemble furniture.

IONIA FURNITURE CO.
1893 - 1897

Ionia, Michigan
Manufacturer of low- and medium-priced chamber suites and dressers.

IRWIN, ROBERT W. CO.
1919 - 1953

Grand Rapids, Michigan
SEE ALSO Phoenix Furniture Co.; Royal Furniture Co.

COMPANY HISTORY

1900: Robert W. Irwin purchases a controlling interest in Royal Furniture Co. from Alexander Hompe and Ralph Tietsort.

1911: Irwin, Hompe, and Tietsort acquire Phoenix Furniture Co.

1919: Irwin buys Hompe's and Tietsort's shares in Royal and Phoenix. Royal and Phoenix are merged to form the Robert W. Irwin Co.

1931: Irwin purchases prestigious manufacturer Cooper - Williams, Inc. of Boston.

1951: Company is purchased by group of investors from Cincinnati.

1953: Company closes and discontinues production. Rights to the Irwin name sold to Sterling, Inc., of New York City.

PERSONNEL

At the age of only 23, Robert W. Irwin rose from office clerk to plant superintendent of the Grand Rapids School Furniture Co. In 1900, he and several associates purchased the Royal Furniture Co. He was instrumental in the founding of Irwin Seating Co. in 1905. Irwin was an active figure in business circles on both the local and national levels. In 1914, while still just the secretary of the Royal Furniture Co. and vice-president of Grand Rapids National City Bank, he was elected president of the Furniture Manufacturers and Fixture Manufacturers Association of the U.S. In the 1930s, he headed a national drive to eliminate elements of Roosevelt's "New Deal" legislation relating to price fixing and production control. His views were often published in trade journals as well as leading business periodicals such as *Forbes Magazine*, on everything from the history of the furniture industry, to the Red Cross, to selling life insurance. Having no direct heirs to inherit the company, Irwin sold his interest in the firm in 1951. He continued with the company as an unpaid advisor until its closure in 1953.

J. Stuart Clingman started as assistant designer at Royal in 1903, and stayed on after Royal became a part of Irwin in 1919. Clingman specialized in the "modernization" of designs by Sheraton and Hepplewhite. He eventually became head of design for Irwin, and also served on the Board of Directors as secretary and vice-president. Clingman stayed with the company until its sale in 1951.

Trained in architecture at Cooper Union in New York, William Hoffmann came to Grand Rapids in 1921 to work for Robert W. Irwin after designing furniture for several years at W. & J. Sloane in New York. He created designs for both the Phoenix and Royal lines, until he opened his own design studio circa 1933.

Frank J. Davidhazy was recruited to come from New York to Grand Rapids and head the Phoenix plant's decorative painting department in 1920. At its height the department employed thirty-five men and women, and hand-painted decoration became one of the signatures of Irwin furniture. Davidhazy created the decorative painting designs, which were copied by the other painters. Davidhazy worked for the company, and so eventually did his son Frank C. Davidhazy, until it closed in 1953.

PRODUCTS

An ad in a 1927 *Grand Rapids Press*, Market Edition, depicts a highly carved Georgian dining suite from the "Royal Division," with Oriental lacquer decoration on the doors of the china cabinet. In 1928 a special "Phoenix suite," with hand decoration by Davidhazy, was issued in commemoration of the 100th Grand Rapids Furniture Market. Both plants produced high-quality living room, dining room, and bedroom suites and occasional pieces in a large range of woods and period revival styles. In the 1930s many suites featured striking matches of veneers in French walnut, rosewood, mahogany, aspen, satinwood, and curly maple, with hand-painted, raised lacquer, or carved accents. Styles included Modern/Art Deco, Biedermeier, Georgian, Duncan Phyfe, and most 18th-century French and English influences.

In 1940 Irwin introduced its competitively priced, apartment-scaled "Pendleton" line, a departure from its tradition of larger, high-end suites. Pendleton pieces used less expensive woods and less hand work in Georgian, Regency and Federal styles. An entire coordinated line of Pendleton carpets, lamps, and fabrics was introduced at the same time. But the line was not particularly well received by consumers, and the conversion of Irwin's factories for wartime production brought an end to the line.

OTHER SOURCES

The Public Museum of Grand Rapids owns a large collection of tools, sample panels, papers, and oral interviews from the Davidhazys, relating to the Phoenix factory's decorating department and general factory operations. The Museum has a variety of Irwin catalogs, and also owns the contents of a scrapbook about Mr. Robert W. Irwin, maintained by his personal secretary.

MARKS AND LABELS

The Phoenix and Royal companies operated under their own distinct logos from 1920 through 1925; new versions were designed in 1926. Pieces from the Royal plant bore a metal tag with a bust of George Washington in relief, and "ROYAL FURNITURE / MADE BY / ROBERT W. IRWIN CO." Pieces made in the Phoenix plant were given a rectangular metal tag with a relief of the Phoenix bird rising from the fire, and "PHOENIX FURNITURE / MADE BY / ROBERT W. IRWIN CO."

A 1928 ad in *Good Furniture Magazine* shows a new circular logo with "ROBERT W. IRWIN COMPANY / GRAND RAPIDS" in the outer circle, which surrounds a shield topped by the Phoenix bird rising from the ashes. A sash across the shield reads "PHOENIX"; above the sash is a set of calipers, and below is a cabinet clamp. In 1931 the company discontinued the Royal name, calling those lines "Custom" instead. All other lines were placed under the "Phoenix" name.

At some point in the 1930s Irwin adopted another new trademark, which it continued to use until it closed in 1953. Seen as a brass tag on pieces of furniture, the logo consisted of an eye shape surrounding the name "IRWIN". In 1940, when the company launched its "Pendleton" line, a special logo was used, with the Irwin eye shape, topped with the name "Pendleton" in script.

1925

1928

1941

1950

IRWIN SEATING CO.
1932 - present

1950

Irwin Seating Company
1975

Grand Rapids and Walker, Michigan
Successor to Steel Furniture Co.
SEE ALSO American Seating Co.; Steel Furniture Co.

COMPANY HISTORY

1932: Steel Furniture Co. changes its name to Irwin Seating Co.

1973: Company establishes Irwin Seating Canada Limited in Ontario.

1984: Company establishes Irwin Telescopic Platform Co. of Harlingen, Texas.

1989: Company purchases Canadian Chair Co. of Ontario, a renovator of auditorium seating.

1991: Company purchases the Folding Bleacher Co. of Altamont, Illinois to manufacture telescopic bleachers. Telescopic platform production moves from Texas to the Illinois facility.

1996: Company creates a joint venture to manufacture theater seating in Port Klang, Malaysia.

PERSONNEL

The Steel Furniture Co. was organized by three brothers: Earle, Eber, and Robert Irwin (who later owned the Robert W. Irwin Furniture Co.), along with John Duffy, and R.P. Tietsort. Earle was president and head of operations. Earle's son William joined the company in 1933. During World War II William served as head of the purchasing department and production manager for the Irwin-Pedersen Arms Co., which manufactured M-1 Carbine rifles at the vacated Macey Co. plant, in which the Irwin family also had a financial stake. At the end of the war, William left Irwin-Pedersen and re-established the family business. He became president in 1946. The current head of the company is Earle S. "Win" Irwin, who joined the company in 1975 and became president in 1984 when his father William retired.

PRODUCTS

From its beginning, The Steel Furniture Co. and later Irwin Seating made classroom furniture and auditorium seating. During WWII production by Irwin was halted, and the factory was leased to Lear-Avia to make fractional horsepower motors. The company was outfitted with new machinery after the war, and by the end of 1945 restarted production of simple auditorium seats with bent plywood seats and backs.

From the 1940s through the 1960s, school furniture was made in bent plywood and steel. Movable combination chair/desks were made with slanted, lift-up tops, or tablet arm tops with book storage underneath the seat. "The Comet" and other auditorium chairs also utilized plywood and steel in streamlined designs, and came with or without upholstery. "The Comet" remained a part of the company's auditorium seating offerings for decades, with only minor revisions. New lines of stadium/arena seating were added in the 1970s and '80s including the more angular, injection-molded plastic and steel "Citation" and "Gladiator" models. These came in several options which could be screwed to the floor, or attached to the step-up behind the seat, allowing them to fold down for flexible seating requirements. In 1988 Irwin introduced a top-of-the-line theater seat called the "Marquee," which was ergonomically designed.

By the mid-1980s, the company had claimed as high as 60% of the nation's market share as the leading manufacturer of indoor seating for auditoriums, movie theaters, and arenas. It produced chairs for an average of 800 to 900 theaters and auditoriums a year. In 1994 Irwin ranked as the 97th largest furniture company of any kind in America. Irwin Seating installations include chairs for DeVos Hall and Van Andel Arena in Grand Rapids, New York City's Carnegie Hall and Arthur Ashe Stadium, The Palace in Auburn Hills, Market Square Arena in Indianapolis, Roy Thompson Hall in Toronto, and the Holocaust Museum in Washington D.C. Virtually all seating components, including solid wood and veneers, upholstery, and the die-forming of steel parts is done in the company's own facilities.

While approximately 80% of the company's sales now come from auditorium and theater seating, the remaining 20% comes from the sale of classroom furniture. New lines were developed using a tubular, nickel-plated steel frame onto which were attached contoured plastic, plywood, or upholstered seats and back rests. These seats were combined in a variety of ways with attached or free-standing desks or tablet arms with laminated writing surfaces. Other lines designed for lecture settings incorporated fiberglass shell chairs on fixed steel pedestals, and strip tables or folding tablet arms. In 1986 Irwin purchased the classroom furniture line of the American Seating Co. of Grand Rapids. By the late 1980s, it was filling approximately 2,000

Cover, "Modern School Furniture" catalog, Irwin Seating Co., ca. 1945.

orders for classroom furniture annually. Irwin also makes and sells seating for installation in church sanctuaries.

MARKS AND LABELS

In the 1940s and '50s, the Irwin Seating Co. used an "eye" shaped trademark, similar to that of the Robert W. Irwin Co. The Irwin Seating mark contains the word "IRWIN" in the center, surrounded by "SEATING COMPANY" on top and "GRAND RAPIDS, MICH" below. Beginning at least in 1970s, the corporate trademark became a rectangular, lower case "i" shadowed by repeats of the same character behind, and to the right the name "Irwin Seating Company".

JELTES, S. & SON
1914 - 1917

Grand Rapids, Michigan
Manufacturer of furniture. Cited in a listing of manufacturers in the February, 1920 issue of *The Furniture Manufacturer and Artisan*.

JENISON MANUFACTURING CO.

SEE Morgan Manufacturing Co.

JEUP, INC.
1997 - present

je**up** inc.
1997

Grand Rapids, Michigan
Manufacturer of high-end custom contemporary furniture designed by Joseph Jeup. Successor to Designers Workshop.
SEE ALSO Designers Workshop/DW2.

JOHNSON FURNITURE CO.
1908 - 1983

Grand Rapids, Michigan
Successor to Cabinetmakers Co.; Predecessor to RoseJohnson, Inc.
SEE ALSO Cabinetmakers Co.; La-Z-Boy Contract Furniture Co.; Rose Manufacturing Co.; RoseJohnson, Inc.; Timber-Line, Inc.; Uniline.

COMPANY HISTORY

1903: Johnson brothers begin Cabinetmakers Co.
1908: Cabinetmakers Co. sold; Johnson brothers begin Johnson Furniture Co.; Tom Handley hired as staff designer.
1913: Company completes a new factory at 1101 Godfrey Avenue SW.
1922: Johnson-Handley-Johnson organized as a companion company, utilizing the same factory, showrooms, and officers as Johnson Furniture Co.; plant expands to include former Grand Rapids Piano Case factory next door.
1942 - 1945: Johnson plant converts to wartime production of parts for Stinson Bomber aircraft.
1963: Last Johnson family member retires and company is sold; company merges with Timber-Line, Inc., while retaining Johnson name.
1968: Purchased by Holiday Inns of America, Inc.
1983: Merges with Rose Manufacturing Co. to become RoseJohnson, Inc.

PERSONNEL

Johnson Furniture was founded by three brothers who emigrated from Sweden in 1887: Carl (who had received a medal for his cabinetmaking skills from the King of Sweden), Hjalmar, and Axel. Tom Handley, who got his start at the prestigious firm of Waring and Gillow in London, became their in-house designer in 1908 and joined them as an officer in 1922. He continued to hold both positions until his untimely death in 1926. Handley established Johnson and Johnson-Handley-Johnson as major producers of high-quality, period revival, residential furniture. The nature of Handley's designs required the skills of hand craftsmen like Bohemian-born carver Joseph Heyda, and Austrian-born Frank Davidhazy. Sr., who created the floral, figural, and classical designs that were painted on the surfaces of some case pieces.

David Robertson Smith, designer of Stickley Brothers Arts and Crafts lines, led Johnson into the production of Art Deco and Modern lines in 1928. The company later claimed that this was the first complete line of "modern" furniture produced in the United States. Lorenzo (Renzo) Rutili served as head of design from 1933 into the 1960s. He personally designed groups in the Modern and Neoclassical repertoires, and oversaw the contracted design of lines by a "Who's Who" of famous Modern designers, including Paul Frankl, Eliel Saarinen, and J. Robert F. Swanson and Pipsam Swanson.

When Earl Johnson retired and the family sold the company in 1963, it was purchased by a group of investors led by James Van Oosten. Milo Baughman and Kipp Stewart designed lines of residential furniture which Johnson produced for Directional Industries between 1963 and 1968. After being owned by Holiday Inns, Inc.

Chest of drawers by Johnson-Handley-Johnson, ca. 1925.

1913   1927

1927

1951

1961

1972

between 1968 and 1975, the company returned to the ownership of Van Oosten and company.

PRODUCTS

Generally speaking, Johnson produced wood residential furniture for the bedroom, while the Johnson-Handley-Johnson label was used for dining suites, occasional tables, and case pieces for the hall and library. Pieces produced between 1908 and about 1920 were designed in period revival styles, especially Sheraton, Hepplewhite, and Empire, and in a combination of European and American Revivals including Colonial, William and Mary, Jacobean, Queen Anne, French Provincial, Chinese Chippendale, and painted Italian or Venetian, from circa 1920 to 1935. Most notable are pieces designed by Tom Handley, which feature intricate marquetry designs and elaborate carving. Some of his most unusual designs are adaptations of classical Egyptian furniture, introduced in the early 1920s to capitalize upon popular fascination with contemporary archeological discoveries.

The 1928 introduction of the Art Deco "Dynamique" line by D. Robertson Smith, with its exotic wood veneers and forms reminiscent of Frankl's "skyscraper" bookcases, began a long period in which the company concurrently produced both modern and revival lines. Renzo Rutili selected traditional master works from museum collections across the country for reproduction in the 1938 American Museum Group. A sharp contrast to these reproductions came only a year later, when Johnson introduced a modular system for the home known as "Flexible Home Arrangements" (FHA), designed by Eliel Saarinen and J. Robert F. Swanson and Pipsam Swanson of the Cranbrook Institute. In the early 1950s Johnson produced several lines by Paul Frankl, among them the "Contemporary" line, made from pearwood with bleached cork counter tops, and chairs with "plunging neckline" cut-out backs that mimicked women's fashions of the day. New lines referencing historical styles were also introduced in the 1950s and early 1960s, including the "Country Directoire," "Mediterranean," and "Riviera" lines designed by John Wisner.

In 1963 Johnson began to produce television and stereo cabinets and juke boxes on contract. Johnson also became the sole manufacturer of case goods and occasional furniture for Directional Industries. After Johnson merged with Timberline, Inc. it added furniture for hotels, motels, and college dormitories to its contract lines. Johnson produced and installed furniture in dormitories of many major state and private universities under the name "Uniline" as a subsidiary of Holiday Inn. Its hotel and motel furnishings were installed in most Holiday Inns and many Howard Johnson motels worldwide, and in special projects such as the Aladdin Hotel in Las Vegas.

OTHER SOURCES

The Public Museum of Grand Rapids has in its collections a large number of Johnson catalogs, original design drawings, and other archival materials ranging from the 1910s through the 1970s, as well as a good representation of its products from the same range of dates.

MARKS AND LABELS

Both Johnson and Johnson-Handley-Johnson used the same symbol as their logo: three teardrops spiraling around a common center, a sort of three-part yin and yang. This symbol commonly appears as a metal tag inside the right-hand drawer of case pieces, or on a paper label affixed to the back of a case piece or under the seat of a chair. Some paper labels between 1908 and circa 1930 also include a box with the printed signature "T.S. Handley". In the 1960s the company name was printed in uppercase serif letters, with a crown resting on the "J". During the late 1960s and early 1970s the trademark was a bold "J" over a small red dot.

JOHNSON - HANDLEY-JOHNSON FURNITURE CO.	SEE Johnson Furniture Co.
JOHNSON - RANDALL CO. at least 1928	Traverse City, Michigan Listed in the July, 1928 issue of *The Buyer's Guide* as a manufacturer of fiber furniture.
JONES, M. F. & CO. at least 1873	Grand Rapids, Michigan Manufacturer of "Jones Organs" in 35 different styles.

JONES - HOERNER - GUEST CO.	SEE Crawford Chair Co.

JULIEN MANUFACTURING CO. 1946 - 1978	Lamont, Michigan Manufacturer of unpainted deacon benches, Boston rockers, etc. in extra-fine quality.

JULIEN, RAY, WOOD TURNING	SEE Julien Wood Turning.

JULIEN WOOD TURNING 1950 - present	Lamont, Michigan Contract wood turner for other manufacturers. **COMPANY HISTORY** 1950: Company is founded as Ray Julien Wood Turning. ca. 1959: Name changes to Julien Wood Turning as Julien's three sons join the firm 1970: Company is operated by Jerry Julien.

KRT, INC. at least 1957	South Haven, Michigan Manufacturer of wooden furniture legs.

KALAMAZOO SLED CO. at least 1907 - 1928	Kalamazoo, Michigan Manufacturer of bentwood chairs, rockers, and swing sets; reclining lawn, beach, invalid, and parlor chairs; folding stools, chairs, and hammock stands; lawn and porch swings; and children's settees, folding beds, and hammock stands.

1907

KARL MANUFACTURING CO. 1932 - 1969	Grand Rapids, Michigan Manufacturer of office machine stands. Company is begun by an officer and former employees of the Adjustable Table Co. SEE ALSO Adjustable Table Co.

KARR, CHARLES CO.	SEE Grand Rapids Bedding Co.

KEIL - ANWAY CO. at least 1909 - 1912	Grand Rapids, Michigan Manufacturer of leather upholstered chairs and rocking chairs with movable cushions. Predecessor to Anway Co. SEE ALSO Anway Co.

KELVINATOR, INC. 1914 - 1958	Wyoming, Michigan Manufacturer of refrigerators, refrigeration equipment, electric ranges, clothes washers and dryers, and home freezers. SEE ALSO Grand Rapids Refrigerator Co.; Leonard Refrigerator Co.; White Consolidated Industries. **COMPANY HISTORY** 1914: Company begins manufacturing association with Leonard Refrigerator Co. 1926: Kelvinator merges with Leonard. 1955 - 1968: Company is a division of American Motors Corp. 1958: Division becomes Kelvinator - Leonard - A.B.C. with acquisition of Altorfer Brothers Co. of Peoria, Illinois. 1968 - 1981: Company becomes a division of White Consolidated Industries.

KELVINATOR - LEONARD - ABC	SEE Grand Rapids Refrigerator Co.; Kelvinator, Inc.; Leonard Refrigerator Co.

KENDALL MANUFACTURING CO. ca. 1892	Grand Rapids, Michigan Manufacturer of furniture ornaments.

KENT FURNITURE MANUFACTURING CO. at least 1880 - 1901	Grand Rapids, Michigan Manufacturer of medium- and low-priced bedroom suites, chiffoniers, sideboards, bureaus, and tables.

KENT OF GRAND RAPIDS 1949 - 1975	Grand Rapids, Michigan Manufacturer of furniture.

KENT UPHOLSTERY CO. 1933 - 1962	Grand Rapids, Michigan Manufacturer of upholstered furniture.

KINDEL BED CO.   SEE Kindel Furniture Co.

KINDEL FOLDING BED CO.   SEE Kindel Furniture Co.

KINDEL FURNITURE CO.   Grand Rapids, Michigan
1924 - 1978   SEE ALSO Valley City Furniture Co.; Foote-Reynolds Co.

COMPANY HISTORY

Hide-a-bed sofa sales-sample miniature, Kindel Bedding Co., ca. 1915.

1899: Kindel Bedding Co. is founded in Denver, Colorado.
1904: Company moves to St. Louis, Missouri.
1912: Company moves to Grand Rapids, Michigan, and is renamed Kindel Bed Co.
1915: Company is purchased by Kroehler Manufacturing Co. of Chicago.
1924: Charles Kindel buys company back; renames it Kindel Furniture Co.
1926: Company purchases Foote-Reynolds Co.
1959: Kindel purchases old Valley City Furniture Co. plant.
1965: Kindel family sells company to Ball Brothers of Muncie, Indiana.
1978: Company is purchased from Ball Brothers by Robert Fogarty.

PERSONNEL

The Kindel Bedding Co. was founded by Charles J. Kindel, Sr. From 1913 to 1915 he served as president of the National Association of Upholstered Furniture Manufacturers. When Charles J. Kindel, Sr. died in 1962, Charles M. Kindel, Jr. and Thomas G. Kindel assumed control of the company. With the sale in 1965 to Ball Brothers, Charles M. and Thomas continued as president and vice-president, with Robert Fogarty as the primary stockholder. Wendell Davis was named president in 1966, and was replaced in 1974 by David Shuart. Robert Fogarty purchased the company in 1978.

PRODUCTS

When the company moved to St. Louis in 1904, it was listed as a manufacturer of convertible davenport beds, which were protected by patent. The patent's primary improvement over other folding beds was that it allowed for conversion of a piece of furniture into a bed without the need to move it away from the wall. In 1911 the company made three convertible parlor beds: the "Senior davenport," the "Junior divanette," and the "Sophomore easy chair." Throughout the 1910s the company still manufactured davenport sofas that converted into beds, in various period reproduction styles including Sheraton, Adam, William and Mary, and Jacobean. It also made a Mission-style oak divanette with leather upholstery.

In 1924 the product line had expanded slightly, to include "fine Colonial reproductions" of beds and davenports. But by 1932 the line had grown to include whole suites of bedroom as well as dining room furniture. From the 1930s until the early 1980s the company produced traditional residential pieces in French Provincial and various English, Oriental, and Italian styles.

In 1982 Kindel became a manufacturer of authentic reproductions, when it was awarded the exclusive license to reproduce furniture from the extensive collections of the prestigious Henry Francis DuPont Winterthur Museum. These pieces are "line for line" copies of the 18th-century American originals, made from the same woods including mahogany, satinwood, sycamore, cherry, and solid poplar cores. A few pieces in the Winterthur Collection were adaptations, primarily when the original was too large to be reproduced for use in modern homes. Pieces in which the original design was used for another form were described as "variations." Pieces were chosen for reproduction based upon recommendations of both museum curators and Kindel representatives.

Kindel also became the exclusive licensee reproducing the collections of the National Trust for Historic Preservation, and in 1984 for the Irish Georgian Society. Special hardware for some of Kindel's museum pieces is created by Keeler Brass Co. of Grand Rapids. Pieces from these collections continue to be produced in low quantity production, and sell for as much as $15,000 to $20,000 per piece.

MARKS AND LABELS

In the 1910s and 1920s the name "Kindel" or "Kindel Beds" was used in a bold, Gothic script type style, surrounded by a rectangle with chamfered corners. By the 1930s the trademark was an oval frame surrounding a silhouette bust of George Washington. From the 1950s into the 1980s, the name "KINDEL" was printed in upper-case letters, over "Grand Rapids" in script, surrounded by an oval. Under Fogarty, Kindel adopted a carved scallop design over the name "KINDEL" as its trademark.

1927

1928-29

1937

1957

1998

KLINGMAN & LIMBERT CHAIR CO.
1889 - 1892

1889

Grand Rapids, Michigan
Sales agent for other manufacturers; manufacturer of English Arts and Crafts-style chairs and rockers.

KLISE MANUFACTURING CO.
1913 - 1985

1926

1928

Grand Rapids, Michigan
Manufacturer of wood carvings, fine moldings, turnings, wall paneling, and upholstery frames.

1939

1970

1980

KLOK CRAFTSMAN GUILD
1951 - 1964

Grand Rapids, Michigan
Manufacturer of furniture.

COMPANY HISTORY

1951 - 1961: Company operates under the name Klok Craftsman Guild.
1962 - 1964: Operates under the name Klok of Grand Rapids, Inc.

KLOK OF GRAND RAPIDS, INC.

SEE Klok Craftsman Guild.

KNAPE & VOGT
1898 - present

1951

Grand Rapids, Michigan
Manufacturer of specialty hardware, drawer slides, cabinets, store fixtures, and shelving and storage products.

1948

1957

KNOLL, INC.
1938 - present

Headquarters: East Greenville, Pennsylvania. Michigan facilities: Kentwood, Muskegon, and Norton Shores.
SEE ALSO Shaw-Walker Co.; Westinghouse Furniture Systems, Inc.

COMPANY HISTORY

1938: Company founded as Hans G. Knoll Furniture Co. in New York City.
1990: Westinghouse Electric Corp. of Pittsburgh, Pennsylvania purchases Knoll International, renames it The Knoll Group, and makes its Westinghouse Furniture Systems division in Kentwood, Michigan and Shaw-Walker division in Muskegon and Norton Shores, Michigan part of The Knoll Group companies.
1994: Knoll Group moves Muskegon operations to the Norton Shore facility.
1996: Name changes to Knoll, Inc.

PERSONNEL

Mike Gluhanich was named vice-president of operations for Knoll Group - Muskegon in 1991. He was succeeded by vice-president of manufacturing Ron Racle. At the time of this writing, the Kentwood facility was under the direction of vice-president for manufacturing Rick Vales.

PRODUCTS

Although Knoll has a long and distinguished history of products with famous modern designers and designs, most of that history did not involve the Grand Rapids area. Knoll only became a player in the region after 1990. Its local products since that time have been mostly panel-based metal office systems components, a strength inherited from Shaw-Walker and Westinghouse Furniture Systems, Inc. Systems produced in the Kentwood and Norton Shores facilities include "Equity," which can be configured as a panel-based or free-standing system; the more architecturally elegant "Reff System," which features modular panels and pedestals with wood laminates; and the "Morrison System," which can also be configured for use in open-plan spaces or private offices.

MARKS AND LABELS

"Knoll" or "The Knoll Group", in sans-serif upper- and lower-case letters, replaced the Westinghouse Furniture Systems and Shaw-Walker trademarks after the companies were consolidated after 1990.

1994

KOCH, WILLIAM
ca. 1865

Grand Rapids, Michigan
Upholsterer of furniture.

KOLVOORD, JAN & GRIETJE
1849 - 1856

Old Groningen settlement between Holland and Zeeland, Michigan
The Kolvoords were a Dutch immigrant married couple. Jan turned bedsteads and chairs which his wife Grietje assembled.

A maple rope bed in the collections of The Holland Museum by the Kolvoords is finished with a reddish stain.

KOMPASS & STOLL
at least 1928

Niles, Michigan
Manufacturer of tables and Hoosier cabinets.
Listed in *The Buyer's Guide*, July, 1928.

KOZAK STUDIOS
1929 - 1967

Grand Rapids, Michigan
Manufacturer of high-quality hand-decorated furniture in 18th-century English, French, and Italian styles. Purchased by Baker Furniture Co. in 1967.
SEE ALSO Baker Furniture Co.

KUCHINS FURNITURE MANUFACTURING CO.
1929 - 1940

Offices and factories: St. Louis, Missouri.
Factory and showrooms: Grand Rapids, Michigan.
Manufacturer of decorative painted kitchenette and dinette suites, tables, chairs, cabinets, and novelties in Spanish and Colonial Revival and Art Deco styles under the tradename "Color-Kist."

KUCHINS "Color-Kist"
1927

KUIPER CARVING CO.

SEE Kuiper Manufacturing Co.

KUIPER MANUFACTURING CO.
1936 - 1951

Grand Rapids, Michigan
Manufacturer of carving, turning, and millwork on contract, sporting goods supplies, dining and occasional chairs, and a special recliner designed to alleviate lower back pain.

COMPANY HISTORY
1927 - 1936: Company operated under the name Kuiper Carving Co.; produced carvings on contract for furniture manufacturers.
1936 - 1950: Name changes to Kuiper Manufacturing Co.
1951: Merged with Michigan Chair Co.
SEE ALSO Michigan Chair Co.

LFI
1969 - at least 1988

Grand Rapids, Michigan
Manufacturer of "site furniture" for malls, parks, and office buildings, including benches, picnic tables, planters, and trash and ash receptacles, in metal, wood, and fiberglass.

LA BARGE, INC.
1962 - present

Holland, Michigan
Successor to Hart Mirror Division, Donnelly Corp.
SEE ALSO Hart Mirror Division, Donnelly Corp.

COMPANY HISTORY
1962: Company founded from Hart Mirrors, the residential mirror division of Donnelly Corporation of Holland, Michigan.
1987: La Barge is purchased by Masco Corp. of Taylor, Michigan.
1990: Masco consolidates Los Angeles-based Marbro into La Barge.
1996: La Barge becomes a wholly owned subsidiary of Lifestyle Furnishings International.

PERSONNEL
La Barge, Inc. was started by William E. La Barge, Sr. from the former residential division of Donnelly Mirrors. He served as president until 1987 when he was succeeded by his sons Robert, as chief operational officer, and James as president. Their successor, Mike Peterson, gained experience in the home furnishings industry as publisher of *Colonial Homes* magazine before coming to La Barge in 1994. Dale Metternich serves as vice-president in charge of design.

PRODUCTS
La Barge's first products were high-end decorative residential mirrors, and in this category it is still considered the industry leader. Designed as room accents, they cover a large range of styles including American Southwest, Baroque, Hepplewhite, Chippendale, Georgian, Queen Anne, Louis XIV, XV, and XVI, Directoire, French Restoration, English Regency, Florentine, Bavarian, Edwardian, Art Deco, and others. Many feature beveled glass. The frames are made from highly carved wood or metals, including cast bronze, wrought iron, stainless steel, and brass.

Most of the company's occasional tables are either console or coffee tables with glass tops. Many are made to match as accents with the mirrors, and as such are made from gilded wood, brass, bronze, wrought iron, steel, and even lead crystal.

George II-inspired mirror by LaBarge, Inc., from 1997 catalog. Courtesy, LaBarge, Inc.

La Barge.
1962

La Barge
1997

LB
Mirrors
Inc.

1964

The "Hunt Club" collection includes tables and seating, made from belt straps of iron and aluminum. The "Nature" line features glass tops over lost wax cast bronze sculptures of deer, cranes, and Bonsai trees. Other accent pieces include metal wine and bakers' racks, tea carts, pedestals, and umbrella stands.

A hand-painted entertainment center armoire, designed by Dave Warren in 1989, was donated to the White House by La Barge in 1993 for use in President Clinton's private living quarters. The introduction of La Barge's "Magellan Collection" in 1997 further extended its offerings of case goods.

High profile celebrities such as Donald and Ivana Trump, Wayne Newton, and Leona Helmsley have been among the list of customers to purchase Marbro lamps. Pieces include high-end crystal chandeliers, and marble and crystal decorative lamps.

Much of La Barge's production is done on contract by other manufacturers; approximately 60% in the U.S. and the rest in Italy, German, Mexico, and the Asian Pacific region. The Holland plant completes assembly and inspection, then warehouses and distributes completed pieces.

MARKS AND LABELS

The company trademark since 1962 has been the name "La Barge" in a hand-written script. The styling of this signature was updated in 1997. The trademark "ENTREE" is used to mark La Barge mirrors and tables that retailed for lower prices than its other offerings. After 1990 the name "MARBRO" preceded by an Aladdin-style oil lamp was used on lighting fixtures. The Magellan trademark was introduced in 1997. It is topped by a compass directional pointer, over the words "MAGELLAN / COLLECTION BY La Barge".

LA-Z-BOY CONTRACT FURNITURE GROUP
1993 - 1997

LA·Z·BOY
BUSINESS FURNITURE

1964

Grand Rapids and Monroe, Michigan
Manufacturer of a line of wooden open office systems furniture called "RJ Plus II," under the name "La-Z-Boy Business Furniture." A division of LA-Z-BOY CHAIR CO.
SEE ALSO RoseJohnson, Inc.
COMPANY HISTORY
1986: La-Z-Boy Chair Co. acquires RoseJohnson, Inc.
1993: Name changes to La-Z-Boy Contract Furniture Group.
1997: Grand Rapids facility closed; production moves to North Carolina.

LAFAVE MANUFACTURING CO.
1949 - 1956

Grand Rapids, Michigan
Manufacturer of custom store fixtures, display units, showcases, wall cases, fixtures, and millwork.
COMPANY HISTORY
1946 - 1948: Company operates under the name LaFave Wood Products & Engineering.
1949 - 1956: Operates under the name LaFave Manufacturing Co.

LAFAVE WOOD PRODUCTS & ENGINEERING

SEE LaFave Manufacturing Co.

LAKESIDE FURNITURE MANUFACTURING CO.
ca. 1890 - 1900

Holland, Michigan
Manufacturer of desks, bookcases, and tables.

LARAWAY, WILLIAM & CO.
1865 - 1870

Grand Rapids, Michigan
Manufacturer of "Vermont, Italian, Egyptian and Grand Rapids" marble table tops for the furniture industry; manufacturer of marble and plaster mantels, paper weights, ornaments, monuments, and gravestones. Laraway is thought to have supplied much of the marble used by Grand Rapids manufacturers of this period, and to have inscribed the initials of the company placing the order on the underside of the table tops.
COMPANY HISTORY
1859: William Laraway founds Excelsior Marble Works.
1865 - 1870: Operates under the name William Laraway & Co.

LAUZON, C.A. FURNITURE CO.
1915 - 1926

Grand Rapids, Michigan
Manufacturer of upholstered and caned furniture, floor lamps, novelty stands, and desk-top accessories, in brown or antique mahogany, Chinese grey, imperial yellow, and black lacquer finishes. Pieces were designed by Francis Fry.
Company absorbed in 1926 by the Ralph Morse Furniture Co.

SEE ALSO Morse, Ralph Furniture Co.

LAWRENCE FREEDMAN CO.
1921 - 1923

Grand Rapids, Michigan
Manufacturer of furniture.

LAZARD - BRANDT
1938 - 1947

Grand Rapids, Michigan
Manufacturer of upholstered furniture and occasional living room tables.
Successor to Russell Brandt Co.
SEE ALSO Brandt, Russell Co.

LEFFINGWELL, W. P.
ca. 1889

Grand Rapids, Michigan
Advertisements in *The Michigan Artisan* in 1889 describe W. P. Leffingwell as successor to Grand Rapids Table Co. Ads in the same periodical for 1890 show the same illustrations, but again under the name Grand Rapids Table Co. Both described the company as a manufacturer of "Antique Oak, Sixteenth Century & Imitation Mahogany fancy tables and pedestals."
SEE ALSO Grand Rapids Table Co.

LENDE, JEFFREY
ca. 1972 - present

Lowell, Michigan
Designer and artisan of custom studio furniture, clocks, and furniture sculptures with unusual angles and a wide variety of materials, including black walnut and other cabinet woods, spalted wood, sassafras root, bone, copper, aluminum, epoxy, and leather. Sold through galleries and art museums in Michigan.

LENTZ TABLE CO.
1867 - 1943

1927

Nashville, Michigan
Manufacturer of occasional and extension tables, 18th-century reproductions, and novelties.
Purchased in 1943 by Plycoma Veneer Co.

1942

LEONARD MANUFACTURING CO.
1896

Grand Rapids, Michigan
Manufacturer of children's desks, sleighs, and novelties. Advertised in issues of *The Michigan Artisan* for 1896.

LEONARD REFRIGERATOR CO.

SEE Grand Rapids Refrigerator Co.

LETELLIER, F. & CO.
1898 - 1916

Grand Rapids, Michigan
Manufacturer of house interior millwork, special cabinets, and mantels.

LIFETIME FURNITURE

SEE Grand Rapids Bookcase & Chair Co.

LIMBERT, CHARLES P. CO.
1894 - 1944

Grand Rapids and Holland, Michigan
SEE ALSO Klingman & Limbert Co.

COMPANY HISTORY
Pre-1894: Klingman & Limbert Co. serve as sales agents for other manufacturers.
1894: Charles Limbert starts a new company to manufacture chairs, and continues as a sales agent for other manufacturers.
1902: Company begins production of its "Dutch Arts and Crafts" Line.
1906: Factory moves from Grand Rapids to Holland, but showrooms remain in Grand Rapids.
1923: Charles Limbert dies.
1944: Furniture no longer made under the Limbert name.

PERSONNEL
Prior to his entry into furniture manufacturing, Charles Limbert had extensive experience in the sale of furniture. His father had been a furniture dealer, and Charles worked as a salesman for a company in Indiana and the famous J.A. Colby Co. of Chicago. In 1889 Limbert formed a partnership with another salesman, Philip J. Klingman. Together they served as sales agents for several manufacturers, and leased showroom space to out-of-town companies at the Grand Rapids Furniture Market. While the partnership dissolved in 1892, Limbert continued to represent other manufacturers for more than a decade. Limbert made frequent trips to the centers of the European Arts and Crafts Movement, and to the Netherlands, to study historical furniture styles and modern furniture production.

The man who designed Limbert's most sophisticated pieces may have been Austrian-trained William J. Gohlke. According to Don Marek's *Arts and Crafts Design:*

Oak Arts and Crafts sideboard with copper hardware, Charles P. Limbert Co., ca. 1912.

The Grand Rapids Contribution, he designed for the company at least between 1909 and 1914, and became a vice-president in 1921. He was likely familiar with the Vienna Secessionist Movement, and its influence can be clearly seen in Limbert's Arts and Crafts designs.

D.B.K. Van Raalte appeared as part of the sales force at Limbert by 1916, and became one of the controlling officers upon Charles Limbert's death in 1923. Van Raalte apparently gained even greater control, because by 1927 ads and the company logo read "Limbert Furniture, By Van Raalte Craftsmen."

PRODUCTS

Little is known about the company's early designs. Oak chairs bearing the label of Klingman & Limbert surface occasionally, with straight slats and small cut-outs that indicate an early movement toward Mission and folk-inspired design.

In 1902 Limbert introduced its "Dutch Arts and Crafts" line which came in oak and ash, with fumed finishes and leather or woven hickory bark upholstery. It resembled other American Mission lines, but was influenced instead by Dutch peasant furniture. Limbert was also a sales agent for the Old Hickory Chair Co., and many of the outdoor and porch furniture designs in the Dutch Arts and Crafts "Summer Line" have that same rustic feel. This prompted use in many lodges and summer homes, including the hotels at Yellowstone. Though lines were simple, some earlier pieces included Art Nouveau-style leaded and colored art glass, inlay, pyrotechnics (burn marks), or cut-out decorations.

Between 1904 and about 1910, designs became more severe and innovative, reflecting more influence from the Austrian Secessionists and perhaps the Prairie School in Chicago. Pieces were devoid of decoration, except for geometric cut-outs set against strong, dramatic angles. From 1910 forward some refinement of these designs continued, but with less innovation. An exception is the Austrian-inspired "Ebon-Oak" line, introduced in 1915, which featured simple inlaid squares on crests and stiles.

Limbert began to produce "original interpretations" of period revival styles in 1916, though its Arts and Crafts line lasted at least through 1918. The company offered dining suites in the standard array of 17th- and 18th-century English styles, as well as an Italian Polychrome suite, which are indistinguishable from similar pieces by other manufacturers.

OTHER SOURCES

A number of Limbert catalogs have been reprinted in recent years, including the 1903 Catalog, published by Dover and the Public Museum; The Fall 1905 Catalog and "Catalog #100," published by The American Life Foundation; and "Catalogs #112 and 119," by Turn of the Century Publications.

MARKS AND LABELS

Klingman & Limbert made use of an elliptical white paper label with blue lettering. The famous insignia of a furniture worker at his bench appeared with the Arts and Crafts lines, as a burn mark or a paper label. Between 1902 and 1905 the mark mentions Grand Rapids as the sole location; from 1906 forward it reads "Grand Rapids and Holland." The logo that accompanied the 1915 ads for the "Ebon-Oak" line featured the same worker, but wearing Dutch wooden shoes instead of 20th-century footwear. With the change from Mission to Period Revival came a change on the logo, from the words "Arts and Crafts Furniture" to simply "Cabinet Makers." Sometime in the mid-1920s this was replaced by the words "By Van Raalte Craftsmen."

1902-05

1906-44

1920

1925

LINDQUIST, PETER
1913 - at least 1920

Grand Rapids, Michigan
Manufacturer of furniture. Cited in a listing of manufacturers in *The Furniture Manufacturer and Artisan* for February, 1920.

LINN-MURRAY FURNITURE CO. LTD.
1903 - 1905

Grand Rapids, Michigan
Manufacturer of living, dining, and bedroom furniture along with clocks.

LIPPERT FURNITURE CO.
1985 - present

LIPPERT FURNITURE
1989

Zeeland, Michigan
Major supplier of wood edged surfaces and conference tables to the office furniture industry. In 1994 Lippert introduced the "Mobile Office Vehicle," or "MO-V," an Astro mini-van converted into a fully functioning office on wheels.

LITTLE HOME OFFICE CO.
1959 - 1975

1965

Grand Rapids, Michigan
Manufacturer of a patented typewriter desk called the "little home office," and picture projection cabinet called the "little home theatre," both designed by Vennice E. Mark.

"little home theatre"™
1965

LOWELL FURNITURE CO.
at least 1908

Lowell, Michigan
Manufacturer of parlor tables. Advertised in *The Grand Rapids Furniture Record*, for December, 1908.

LOWERY PIANO CO.
1963 - 1968

Grand Rapids, Michigan
Manufacturer of pianos.

LUCE FURNITURE CO.
1896 - 1930; 1935 - 1938

Grand Rapids, Michigan
Successor to McCord & Bradfield.
SEE ALSO Furniture Shops of Grand Rapids; McCord & Bradfield Furniture Co.; Michigan Art Craft Co.; Michigan Chair Co.

COMPANY HISTORY
1880: Ransom C. Luce becomes president of McCord & Bradfield Furniture Co.
1896: McCord & Bradfield Furniture Co. changes name to Luce Furniture Co.
1910: Factory is enlarged and remodeled.
1912: Luce begins to claim in advertisements to be the world's largest manufacturer of bedroom and dining room furniture exclusively.
1925: In the largest merger of furniture manufacturers in Grand Rapids history, Luce consolidates with the Furniture Shops of Grand Rapids.
1926: Luce Furniture Corp. and The Furniture Shops purchase Michigan Chair Co.
1930: Company is purchased by Kroehler Manufacturing Co. of Naperville, Illinois, and operates as a division known as Furniture Shops of America, Inc.
1933: Company files for bankruptcy.
1935: Finances are reorganized and company re-opens.
1938: Luce Furniture Co. closes.

PERSONNEL
Luce's predecessor company, McCord & Bradfield, was founded by Thomas McCord, John Bradfield, and Fred R. and Ransom C. Luce. Bradfield invented and patented the company's original folding bed; R.C. Luce was a banker with National City Bank and often served as the company's treasurer. In the early 20th century a third family member, Gregory M. Luce, also served as company president. John C. Hoult was a cabinetmaker by training who became plant manager in 1894, and reached the position of president before his death in 1915. His son John H. Hoult was president of Luce at the time it was sold in 1930.

Thomas Handley, who received his training at Waring & Gillow of London, served as staff designer for a number of years prior to leaving Luce in 1915 to join the Johnson brothers in the formation of Johnson-Handley-Johnson. Handley was succeeded as designer in 1915 by another Waring & Gillow trainee, Stanley Holt Stirrup. Both held special interest and expertise in the design of English period styles. In 1920 Thomas Johnson, also from London, designed Luce's line of period revival bedroom and dining suites.

Glasgow-influenced mahogany dining chair with copper, pewter, and wood inlay, Luce Furniture Co., ca. 1905.

PRODUCTS
An 1897 ad in *The Michigan Artisan* lists Luce as a maker of chamber suites, sideboards, and chiffoniers, and claims that its factory has the largest capacity of any in the world. Its goods are listed in a 1900 *Grand Rapids Herald* article as medium- and cheap-grade chamber (bedroom furniture) and sideboards in oak, birch, ash, and other woods. In 1904 - 1906, Luce's bedroom and dining suites were in oak and mahogany, with a decidedly English Arts and Crafts feel. Leaded art glass windows were employed in vitrine and sideboard windows; geometric cut-outs in chair backs and back splashes, and sometimes unusual and beautiful Art Nouveau-influenced inlays of wood, copper, and pewter. In 1912 the company advertised itself as the largest shipper of Mission Dining Room furniture.

During the later 1910s and throughout the 1920s, the company continued to produce bedroom and dining suites, which ran the gamut of European period revival styles including Florentine, Italian Renaissance, Cromwellian, Jacobean, Eliza-

1920

1927

1936

1937

bethan, Georgian, Queen Anne, Adam, Hepplewhite, Chippendale, Louis XIII, XIV, XV, and XVI, American Colonial, and Duncan Phyfe. Pieces were veneered in walnut and mahogany, and many were enameled and painted.

With the reorganization of Luce in 1935, the company introduced a line of Art Deco furniture with bold geometric circular and rectangular shapes, and figured woods employed in unusual patterns and colors. These modern suites existed in catalogs alongside other, more traditional revival lines.

MARKS AND LABELS

The company trademark from at least 1909 through the 1920s was the word "LUCE" in slender, upper-case letters, shaped in a circle, and surrounded by a circle. After the reorganization in the 1930s, the name "Luce" was printed in script inside an oval, surrounded by the words, "GRAND RAPIDS/ CERTIFIED FURNITURE" and a second oval.

LUCE - REDMOND CHAIR CO.
at least 1904 - 1917

Big Rapids, Michigan
Manufacturer of Colonial Revival mahogany chairs, rocking chairs, and suites.

LUDINGTON NOVELTY CO.

SEE Carrom Co., The.

LUNDEEN & BENGSTON CO.
at least 1917

Grand Rapids, Michigan
Manufacturer of furniture.
Cited in a general listing of furniture manufacturers.

LUTHER & SUMNER MANUFACTURING CO.
1876 - 1884

Grand Rapids, Michigan
Manufacturer of furniture.

LUXURY CHAIR CO.
1908 - 1917

Grand Rapids, Michigan
Manufacturer of automatic reclining chairs, equipped with a unique see-saw fixture.

LUXURY FURNITURE CO.
1919 - 1962

Grand Rapids, Michigan
Manufacturer of furniture.
Purchased in 1962 by Norwalk Supply Co. and moved to Norwalk, Ohio.

MACEY CO., THE
1896 - 1940

Grand Rapids, Michigan
SEE ALSO Steelcase, Inc.; Wernicke Furniture Co.

COMPANY HISTORY

1892: Fred Macey begins selling furniture by mail order.
1896: The Fred Macey Furniture Co. is founded.
1905: Merges with Wernicke Furniture Co. to form Macey - Wernicke Co.
1908: Name is simplified to The Macey Co.
1916: Company goes into receivership but continues to operate, and eventually recovers.
1937: Company again files for bankruptcy.
1940: Company closes.

PERSONNEL

The Macey Furniture Co. was founded by Fred Macey, who served as its first chairman, along with his brother Frank, who also served as treasurer. In 1892 Fred began a mail-order business selling office desks made by other manufacturers, which were advertised in popular magazines as "the best $25 roll-top office desk in the world." His hefty advertising budget made the company a quick success, and other pieces of office and library furniture were soon added to the mail-order line. But as his mail-order sales began to cut into the traditional sales through retailers, Michigan retailers pressured area furniture manufacturers to prevent them from producing finished goods for Macey. To get around this obstacle, Fred Macey invested his mail-order profits in the construction of his own factory. He also expanded his mail-order business, with a national system of warehouses for distribution.

In 1905, when the Wernicke Furniture Co. merged with the Fred Macey Co., Otto H. L. Wernicke became an officer of the company. In 1906 the Globe - Wernicke Co. of Cincinnati sued Macey, for continuing to produce furniture using Wernicke's patents. After years of litigation, Macey won, then counter-sued to recover its court costs. Following Fred Macey's death from typhoid pneumonia in 1909, Otto Wernicke became company president, a position he held until his retirement from active involvement at Macey in 1916.

PRODUCTS

In addition to roll-top desks, Macey's early products also included oak card indexes

1896

1926

1905

Macey filing cabinet,
ca. 1910.

and file systems, and sectional bookcases and filing cases. Lines were expanded to include wooden library tables, swivel chairs, "ladies' desks," music cabinets, Morris chairs, Turkish and Colonial rockers, and couches. Filing card supplies were also sold to use in the card filing cabinets.

In 1912 the Metal Office Furniture Co. (later Steelcase), located next door to Macey's plant, produced the first metal filing cases and safes to be sold through Macey outlets. These pieces were sold with the Macey name until 1918, but were distinguished from the wooden products with the name "Inter-Inter" Line.

During the 1920s and '30s Macey produced wooden executive office suites in various period revival and even Art Deco styles.

MARKS AND LABELS

Pieces produced before 1908 may carry the name "Fred Macey Furniture Co." or simply "Macey" in an italic script, with the tail of the letter "Y" underlining much of the word. Pieces produced after 1908 will bear a modified version of the earlier mark, with "Macey" in simpler script, surrounded by a black or solid colored oval.

MACEY, FRED CO. LTD.	SEE Macey Co., The.
MACEY, FRED FURNITURE CO.	SEE Macey Co., The.
MACEY - WERNICKE CO.	SEE Macey Co., The; Wernicke Furniture Co.
MAK - KRAFT CREATIONS 1959 - 1977	Kaleva, Michigan Manufacturer of upholstered furniture, especially in large contracts for catalog companies.
MANISTEE ART FURNITURE CO. at least 1917	Manistee, Michigan Manufacturer of furniture. Cited in a general listing of furniture manufacturers.
MANISTEE CLOTHES RACK CO. at least 1919	Manistee, Michigan Manufacturer of clothes racks, hat trees, and clothes dryers. Advertised in *The Grand Rapids Furniture Record*, July, 1919.
MANISTEE MANUFACTURING CO. 1888 - 1976	Manistee, Michigan Manufacturer of Early American and Adam-style sideboards, hall trees, dressing tables, chiffoniers, dressers, four-poster beds, and other bedroom furniture, in bird's-eye maple, oak, ash, and maple stained to imitate mahogany or walnut.
MARBRO	SEE La Barge, Inc.
MARQUETTE UPHOLSTERY CO. 1931 - 1932	Grand Rapids, Michigan Upholsterer of seating frames.
MARSHALL CO., THE 1927 - 1928	Grand Rapids, Michigan Manufacturer of bed springs, mattresses, day beds, cots, porch swings, and baby walkers. A division of National Spring and Wire Co.
MARVEL MANUFACTURING CO. 1909 - 1911	Grand Rapids, Michigan Manufacturer of "rollseat" rockers and box set dining chairs. Successor to the Harrison Wagon Works Co.
MASTERCRAFT FURNITURE CO. at least 1947 - 1985	Grand Rapids, Michigan Manufacturer of fine traditional pieces, occasional tables in yewwood, fruitwood, and exotic woods and gold-tooled leather.
MATZDORF'S NOVELTY SHOP 1911 - 1913	Grand Rapids, Michigan Manufacturer of wood novelties.
McCORD & BRADFIELD FURNITURE CO. 1878 - 1896	Grand Rapids, Michigan This company's first products consisted of folding beds of a design patented by owner/partner John Bradfield. Its line was soon expanded to include other forms of medium-grade bedroom and dining furniture in ash and maple. SEE ALSO Bradfield Folding Table Co.; Luce Furniture Co. **COMPANY HISTORY** 1878: Company founded.

1928

1947   1954   1961   1985

1896: Name changes to Luce Furniture Co.

McDONALD, ARTHUR FURNITURE CO.
1932 - 1941

Grand Rapids, Michigan
Manufacturer of furniture.

McGRAW MANUFACTURING CO.
ca. 1894

Grand Rapids, Michigan
Manufacturer of "carvings and rosettes."

McINTYRE & GOODSELL PIANO MANUFACTURING CO.
1884 - 1885

Grand Rapids, Michigan
Manufacturer of Aesthetic style square, upright, and grand pianos.

McLEOD FURNITURE CO.
1919

Grand Rapids, Michigan
Manufacturer of furniture.

MENTZER - PIAGET FURNITURE CO.
ca. 1919 - 1923

MENTZER PIAGET CO.
IMPORTERS & BROKERS
1919

Grand Rapids, Michigan
Importer and broker of Chinese, Japanese, and Philippine furniture.
Predecessor to Mentzer-Read Co. and Piaget-Donnely Co.
SEE ALSO Mentzer-Read Co.; Piaget-Donnely Co.

MENTZER - READ CO.
1924 - ca. 1948

MENTZER REED FURNITURE CO.
IMPORTERS OF CHINESE FURNITURE
ca. 1925

Grand Rapids, Michigan
Manufacturer and importer of sea grass, cane, and decorated reed furniture.
Successor to Mentzer-Piaget Co.
SEE ALSO Mentzer-Piaget Furniture Co.

MERIDIAN, INC.
1970 - 1990

Spring Lake, Michigan
Manufacturer of design-oriented steel office furniture.
SEE ALSO Miller, Herman, Inc.
COMPANY HISTORY
1970: Company founded.
1990: Becomes a subsidiary of Herman Miller, Inc.

METAL OFFICE FURNITURE CO.

SEE Steelcase, Inc.

MICHIGAN ART CARVING CO.
1896 - 1911

Grand Rapids, Michigan
Manufacturer of carved wooden components and novelties.

MICHIGAN ART CRAFT CO.
1890 - 1926

Grand Rapids, Michigan
Manufacturer of occasional tables and wood novelties.
Merged with Luce Furniture Co. in 1926.
SEE ALSO Luce Furniture Co.

MICHIGAN ARTCRAFT CO.

SEE Extensole Corp.

MICHIGAN BARREL CO.
1890 - 1909

Grand Rapids, Michigan
Manufacturer of refrigerators.

MICHIGAN CABINET CO.
1910 - 1914

MICHIGAN CABINET CO.
KITCHEN CABINETS
THE LITTLE SALT SHAKER
GRAND RAPIDS MICH.
1913

Grand Rapids, Michigan
Manufacturer of kitchen cabinets.

MICHIGAN CHAIR CO.
1890 - 1938; 1946 - 1972

Venetian grottoesque scallop
chair by Michigan Chair Co.,
ca. 1900.

Grand Rapids, Michigan
SEE ALSO Grand Ledge Chair Co.; Michigan Furniture Shops, Inc.; Kuiper Manufacturing Co.
COMPANY HISTORY
1890: Owners of Grand Ledge Chair Co. in Grand Ledge, Michigan move to Grand Rapids and begin Michigan Chair Co.
1926: Company is purchased and operated as part of "Michigan Furniture Shops."
1930: Company is sold to Kroehler of Chicago; operates as part of Furniture Shops of America.
1938: Michigan Chair Co. closes.
1946: Michigan Chair Co. re-incorporates.
1951: Company absorbs Kuiper Manufacturing Co.
1972: Michigan Chair Co. closes.
PERSONNEL
The company was organized by Henry Jordan, Edward Crawford, and Thomas Garrett, all of whom had been previously involved with the Grand Ledge Chair Co. in Grand Ledge. After selling that business, they started Michigan Chair in Grand

Rapids. Garrett later bought out Jordan's interest in the company, and in 1913 handed over the presidency to his son Charles Garrett.

Some of the company's earliest designs were by Charles D. Thomson, who was also principal designer for the William A. Berkey Furniture Co. until his death in 1903. He was succeeded by Edgar R. Somes, an architect by training who was chief of design for Michigan Chair from 1901 until he left to work for Century in 1905. During this short period the company embarked on its most lively program of experimentation. Charles Nash took over as designer from 1905 until 1930.

PRODUCTS

The company initially made inexpensive chairs, which became more elaborate and of better quality over time. It introduced a line of stocky Mission chairs as early as 1898. Its catalogs from about 1900 included more than 1,500 chair designs in Grotto-esque, Medieval-folk, Mission, Prairie, Austrian Secessionist, Colonial, Empire, and Golden Oak styles, and produced in quarter-sawn oak, bird's-eye maple, mahogany, mahoganized curly birch, and Circassian walnut.

Michigan Chair also produced occasional pieces which could be used with its seating, including tabourets, tables, pedestals, and music cabinets. In 1903 it produced a line of carved oak figural novelty wall clocks with names like "Hans and Gretchen," "The Monk," "Mischief," "Rob Roy," "Miles and John," and "Contentment."

By circa 1909 Michigan Chair had already begun turning away from the Arts and Crafts styles, toward more ornamented period revival designs. While some were more austere examples in Adam, Windsor, and vaguely Colonial styles, the company seemed to specialize in executing chairs with a high degree of carving, in Elizabethan, Chippendale, and Louis V and XVI styles.

In the early 1930s Michigan Chair produced a line of stylish black lacquer enameled chairs and divans, with Art Deco lines and Cubist upholstery. When the company reopened following World War II the line was much smaller, consisting of only about fifty models in mid-century versions of Adam, white enameled "Venetian" and "Florentine," and French Empire.

MARKS AND LABELS

Michigan Chair's original label was circular, with the company name around the edge, the Grand Rapids-Made triangle, the words "Chairs and Tables" and sometimes space for a handwritten product number in the middle. Some time, perhaps in the mid-1920s, the logo was changed to a ribbon or banner with the company name in Old English script, surrounding a turned and caned chair on a circular medallion with the words "GRAND RAPIDS". Versions of this trademark were used until circa 1956. In the late 1950s the company used a logo of a banner with the company name in a simple, sans-serif type, over the shield-back of a chair with an "M" forming the back splat.

1927   1911

1905   1959

1956

MICHIGAN DESK CO.
1907 - 1918

Grand Rapids, Michigan
Manufacturer of desks.
Successor to Greenway Furniture Co.
SEE ALSO Greenway Furniture Co.

MICHIGAN FOLDING BED CO., THE
1889

Grand Rapids, Michigan
Manufacturer of combination folding beds in ash and maple. Advertised in *The Michigan Artisan*.

MICHIGAN FOLDING TABLE CO.
at least 1899

Grand Rapids, Michigan
Manufacturer of folding tables. Factory is listed in a Fire Department publication as having been destroyed by fire in 1899.

MICHIGAN FRAME CO.
1941 - 1962

1956

Grand Rapids, Michigan
Manufacturer of upholstery frames.
Purchased in 1962 by Rose Manufacturing Co.
SEE ALSO Rose Manufacturing Co.

MICHIGAN FURNITURE SHOPS, INC.
1936 - 1959

1956

Grand Rapids, Michigan
Manufacturer of upholstered living room furniture, Colonial tables, chairs, and occasional furniture. Merged with Barnard & Simonds Co. in 1959.
SEE ALSO Barnard & Simonds Co.

MICHIGAN ORDER WORK FURNITURE CO.
1902 - 1905

Grand Rapids, Michigan
Manufacturer of furniture of various kinds, made to order.

MICHIGAN PIPE ORGAN CO.
1943 - 1946

Grand Rapids, Michigan
Manufacturer and supplier of maintenance for pipe organs.

MICHIGAN SEATING CO.
1907 - 1960

Grand Rapids and Jackson, Michigan
Manufacturer of upholstered furniture.
COMPANY HISTORY
1907: Company founded in Grand Rapids.
1909: Moves from Grand Rapids to Jackson.
1955: Moves from Jackson back to Grand Rapids. Manufacturing is done on contract by Kent Manufacturing Co.
1960: Company closes.

MICHIGAN STAR FURNITURE CO.
1909 - 1923

Zeeland, Michigan
Manufacturer of walnut bedroom furniture in period revival styles.
Predecessor to Herman Miller, Inc.
SEE ALSO Miller, Herman, Inc.
COMPANY HISTORY
1905: Founded as Star Furniture Co.
1909: Name changes to Michigan Star Furniture Co.
1919: D.J. DePree becomes president.
1923: Ownership and name changes to Herman Miller Furniture Co.

MICHIGAN STORE & OFFICE FIXTURE CO.
1904 - 1916

Grand Rapids, Michigan
Manufacturer of office and store fixtures, showcases, typewriters, cash registers, and scales.

MICHIGAN TOY & NOVELTY CO.
1904

Holland, Michigan
Manufacturer of drop carvings, coach trimmings, embossed moldings, turned moldings, rope moldings, and rosettes. Advertised in *The Grand Rapids Furniture Record*, December, 1904.

MICHIGAN UPHOLSTERY CO.
1924 - 1932

Grand Rapids, Michigan
Manufacturer of upholstered furniture.

MICHIGAN WIRE GOODS CO.
at least 1928

Grand Rapids, Michigan
Manufacturer of the steel "aristocrat" and "popular" models of folding chairs for lawn and porch use, and Chinese red or Jade green enameled juvenile cribs, tables and beds. Listed in *The Buyer's Guide*, July, 1928.

MILCARE
1985 - present

Grandville, Michigan
Manufacturer of health-science systems for Herman Miller, Inc.
SEE ALSO Miller, Herman, Inc.
COMPANY HISTORY
1971: Herman Miller Health Care Group established.
1985: Milcare established as wholly owned subsidiary of Herman Miller, Inc.

MILLBROOK FURNITURE CO.
1960 - 1977

Grand Rapids, Michigan
Manufacturer of upholstered living room seats, chairs, sectionals, and sofa beds.

MILLER, HERMAN CLOCK CO.

SEE Miller, Howard Clock Co.

MILLER, HERMAN FURNITURE CO.

SEE Michigan Star Furniture Co.; Miller, Herman, Inc.

MILLER, HERMAN, INC.
1923 - present

Headquarters: Zeeland, Michigan. West Michigan factories: Zeeland, Holland, Grandville, and Spring Lake:
SEE ALSO Michigan Star Furniture Co.; Miller, Howard Clock Co.; Milcare; Meridian, Inc.
COMPANY HISTORY
1923: Michigan Star Furniture Co. changes ownership and name to Herman Miller Furniture Co.
1957: Herman Miller begins sales in Europe.
1960: Company incorporates and changes its name to Herman Miller, Inc.
1970: First offering of company stock to the general public.

1976: Star Industries, later called Integrated Metal Technology, becomes a wholly owned Herman Miller subsidiary.

1979 - 1986: Company operates training program for corporations, known as the Facility Management Institute.

1982: Tradex, Inc. becomes a Herman Miller Co. and changes its name to Phoenix Designs; Herman Miller acquires Vaughan Walls, Inc.

1983: Herman Miller acquires Miltech.

1985: Company's Health Science Division becomes a wholly owned subsidiary known as Milcare.

1986: Herman Miller purchases Helikon Furniture Co. of Connecticut; Milcare acquires Fairfield Medical Products.

1990: Herman Miller acquires Meridian, Inc. of Spring Lake, Michigan.

1992: Company begins Powder Coat Technology subsidiary in Spring Lake; Miltech dissolves and merges into Herman Miller.

1994: Herman Miller acquires Righetti of Mexico.

PERSONNEL

The company was named for its first major shareholder and president, Herman Miller. His son-in-law, D.J. DePree, who had been president of the Michigan Star Furniture Co. before it changed ownership, became general manager. In 1950 he changed the company's management by adopting the Scanlon Plan, still an important part of Herman Miller's corporate culture. DePree remained the primary corporate leader of the company until 1962, when he was succeeded by Hugh DePree, who served as president and CEO until 1980. Hugh took over the job of chairman of the board from D.J. in 1969, and was succeeded in that position by Max DePree in 1971. He served as CEO from 1980 until 1987, and president from 1982 until 1986. Glenn Walters became the first non-family member to serve as president from 1980 until 1982. Another non-family member, Ed Simon, served as president and chief operating officer from 1986 until 1990. Richard Ruch became CEO in 1987 and president in 1990. In 1992 Kerm Campbell became the company's 5th CEO and president, and the first from outside the company to assume those positions. In 1995 Mike Volkema became CEO and president.

Grand Rapids free-lance designers Edgar Cymes and Areal Bevelacqua created many of the Herman Miller Furniture Co.'s period revival residential designs in the 1920s. In 1931, New York designer Gilbert Rohde visited Herman Miller's Grand Rapids showroom, and sold D.J. DePree on the idea of switching the company's design emphasis to Modernism. DePree agreed to this gamble out of fear that the company would fail during the Depression without a new and compelling reason for it to thrive. Rohde became the company's design leader until his death in 1944.

Rohde's Modern design leadership was succeeded by George Nelson in 1945. Nelson remained a key design consultant for the company until his death in 1986. In 1958 Nelson served as principal architect for the first phase of the company's headquarters and factories, in Zeeland, Michigan. Charles and Ray Eames began to create designs for Herman Miller in 1946, and continued their relationship with the company until their deaths (in 1978 and 1988, respectively). In 1985, 2,000 designers from around the world named Charles Eames the most influential designer of the 20th century.

Alexander Girard directed the company's use of colors and textiles from 1950 into the 1970s. In 1952 he was made head of the newly formed Herman Miller Textile Division. Robert Propst was hired in 1960 to head the Herman Miller Research Division, which later became the Herman Miller Research Corporation. In 1961 he began scientific studies of human performance in the office environment.

PRODUCTS

The Michigan Star Furniture Co. made "Princess dressers" and other bedroom pieces which were sold by Sears, Roebuck & Co. and other retailers. The Herman Miller Furniture Co.'s first products were ornate, wooden, period revival bedroom suites for the home. After seeing an exhibition of French Modern furniture, DePree was inspired to produce his own version in 1927. Herman Miller's Art Deco-style "Modern French" furniture was made from Honduran mahogany and sequoia burl with ivory inlay. Herman Miller's Modern furniture by Rohde debuted at the Chicago Century of Progress exhibition in 1933. Rohde's residential designs included modular seating, and a number of lines of bedroom furniture in mahogany, walnut, birch, steel, and glass. By 1945 all traditional designs had been phased out of produc-

Wire shell chair with "bikini" upholstery, designed by Charles and Ray Eames for Herman Miller, 1953 - 1966.

tion.

By 1939 Rohde had begun to turn his attention to designing modern furniture for offices that matched the architecture of modern office buildings. In 1942 the company introduced its first office furniture, the modular Executive Office Group system, or EOG. The EOG utilized a minimum of components which could be configured in a variety of ways to create individualized work stations. The EOG was updated a number of times by George Nelson, and remained in production until 1978.

George Nelson's "Comprehensive Storage System" was produced between 1959 and 1973. This system hung various storage, surface, and lighting components from metal floor-to-ceiling uprights. He designed numerous lines of residential and office systems and seating for the company from the 1940s through the 1970s. Several of his seating designs, including the "Coconut Chair" (1955 - 1978) and the "Marshmallow Sofa" (1956 - 1965) are now considered pop culture classics.

In 1946 Charles and Ray Eames designed the award-winning molded plywood chairs, sometimes known by their nickname "potato chip chairs," for affordability and mass production. Manufacture of these chairs was done by Evans Manufacturing until 1949, when Herman Miller assumed production. In 1950 they began to produce Eames's molded fiberglass chair designs. In 1956 the leather and molded veneer "Eames Lounge Chair and Ottoman" were introduced live, on national television. The first of a number of seating lines designed by Eames and using tension-stretched fabrics on aluminum frames debuted in 1958.

Sculptor Isamu Noguchi designed his famous wood and glass-topped coffee table for Herman Miller in 1947. Verner Panton's "Cantilever Chair," which was molded as one continuous form of plastic, was introduced in 1967 and sold until 1975. The Poul Kjaerholm Group, which was produced in Denmark from 1955 - 1965, was made and sold in the U.S. as a Herman Miller product between 1973 and 1977. Many of Herman Miller's classic modern designs from the 1940s through the 1960s were reintroduced in 1994 as the "Herman Miller for the Home" collection.

In 1964 the company began production of a group of freestanding units supported by cast aluminum legs and frames, which was called "Action Office I." AOI was developed based on ergonomic studies by Robert Propst and George Nelson at the Herman Miller Research Corporation. In 1968 "Action Office II" was launched, by hanging work surfaces, storage compartments, and other components from open plan panels. AOII and the panel-based system revolutionized the office furniture industry. AOI was discontinued in 1970. In 1976 acoustical conditioners were added to the line, to create "white noise" or the sound of rolling surf in the office environment. A revision called AOIII was introduced in 1991.

The 1984 "Ethospace Interiors," designed by Bill Stumpf and Jack Kelley, was based on tiles of fabric, wood, laminate, window glass, bulletin board, and other materials hung on frames, rather than panels. The 1990 "Relay" office furniture system by Geoff Hollington was designed for use by people who work together in groups.

The "Coherent Structures," or "Co/Struc System," also developed based on Propst's research, was first marketed in 1971 for use in hospitals and other health and science settings. Co/Struc was replaced as the company's health and science product by Action Environments in 1981.

A modular seating group known as "Chadwick Seating" was designed by Don Chadwick and introduced in 1974. Based on five different forms of upholstered foam seating, Chadwick Seating could be configured in nearly any free-flowing, continuous shape. In 1976 Herman Miller began production of William Stumpf's Ergon Chair for use in offices. The company's next generation of ergonomically designed chairs came with the "Equa Chair" in 1984. The "Aeron Chair," introduced in 1994, was produced in multiple sizes to fit the demographics of office workers.

OTHER SOURCES

In 1989 a consortium of fourteen American museums was formed to receive more than five hundred pieces of Herman Miller furniture. Principal recipients were the Henry Ford Museum in Dearborn, Michigan (which also received a large archival collection), The Public Museum of Grand Rapids, and the Grand Rapids Art Museum. Herman Miller, Inc. continues to maintain an extensive photo and archive collection at its headquarters in Zeeland. *The Design of Herman Miller*, written in 1976 by Ralph Caplan, is an excellent source of information on Herman Miller products and designers. Numerous books, articles, and exhibition catalogs have been published about the designs of Herman Miller and its well-known designers.

1960

⊔ herman miller
1988

MILLER, HOWARD CLOCK CO.
1926 - present

"Ball and Spoke Clock," designed by George Nelson and introduced by Howard Miller ca. 1947. Courtesy, Howard Miller.

MARKS AND LABELS

According to an article in the May 24, 1994 issue of Herman Miller's newsletter *Connections*, the company adopted its first corporate logo in 1923, when the name changed from Michigan Star to Herman Miller. It featured a circle surrounding the monogram "HMFCo" written in script, with the "M" centered and about twice the size of the other letters. The name "The Herman Miller Furniture Company" was printed on the right side of the logo, and both were placed between horizontal lines.

In 1936 the logo changed to all upper-case letters with the words "HERMAN MILLER" printed above and twice as large as "FURNITURE COMPANY" below. Irving Harper, under the direction of George Nelson, conceived the current stylized capital "M" trademark, which looks like two sloping triangles, in 1946. Nelson also initiated the use of the company's distinctive "Herman Miller red."

Zeeland, Michigan
SEE ALSO Miller, Herman Inc.; Hekman Furniture Co.

COMPANY HISTORY

1926: Company founded as Herman Miller Clock Co.
1937: Name changes to Howard Miller Clock Co.
1964: Company builds modern headquarters and factory across the street from Herman Miller, Inc.
1981: Company establishes the "Hourglass Award," given each year to celebrity personalities for making outstanding use of their time.
1983: Company acquires Hekman Furniture Co. from Beatrice Co.
1994: Company acquires the Keininger company of Aldingen, Germany; Woodmark Originals of High Point, North Carolina; and Dimensional Products of Mobile, Alabama, and renames Dimensional Products as the Brookley Furniture Co.

PERSONNEL

According to a 1990 oral interview with Mr. Howard Miller, his father, Herman Miller, moved from Grand Rapids to Zeeland in 1910 to manage the Colonial Furniture Co., which made both furniture and clocks. In 1926 D.J. DePree formed the Herman Miller Clock Co. as a separate company from the Herman Miller Furniture Co. It operated under this name until it was placed under Howard's direction in 1937, and the name was changed to the Howard Miller Clock Co. According to company information, Howard Miller studied clock making in Germany's Black Forest region. Howard Miller remained associated with his namesake until his death in 1995. Since that time, leadership of the company has remained in Miller family hands.

New York designer Gilbert Rohde, who also created many designs for the Herman Miller Furniture Co., created Howard Miller's first Modern clock designs in 1933. George Nelson, another Herman Miller modern designer, also created clock designs for Howard Miller in the late 1940s and '50s. Arthur Umanoff of Umanoff & Huin Associates in New York City provided many of Howard Miller's designs between the 1950s and the mid-1980s. More than 40 clocks and collector's cabinets in the Howard Miller line have been designed by Larry Jaccoma and John LeShane of LeShane, Jaccoma & Associates in New York, who have been providing designs for the company since the early 1980s.

PRODUCTS

Though operated as a separate company, the Howard Miller Clock Co. has much in common with its neighbor, Herman Miller. Howard Miller's first products were chiming mantel clocks, but in 1933 Howard Miller introduced its battery-operated glass- and chrome-clock by Gilbert Rohde at the Century of Progress Exhibition in Chicago, the same place that Herman Miller introduced its first Rohde Modern furniture designs.

The Howard Miller Clock Co. makes the cases for its clocks and assembles them with works which, up until 1994, were imported from Germany, with some works for alarm clocks coming from Japan. With the acquisition of German clockworks maker Keininger in 1994, Howard Miller now makes many of its clocks' inside mechanisms as well. One of the Howard Miller Co.'s most famous products is the "Ball and Spoke Clock," sometimes called the "Atom Clock," which was designed by George Nelson and introduced around 1947. This wall clock featured a circular metal dial, from which extended twelve metal rods that terminated in painted wooden balls, which substituted for numbers. Looking like a chemistry-class model of a molecule, this clock has become a design icon for the "Atomic Age," and is much sought after by collectors. George Nelson also designed two lines of clocks known as the "Chronopak" series, which were produced throughout the 1950s. Nelson designed a number of items other than clocks, which were also manufactured by Howard Miller, including a line of fireplace accessories and lamps.

According to another taped interview with Howard Miller, the company's production of grandfather clocks greatly expanded after 1950, when family incomes increased, allowing many to buy what had previously been considered affordable only to the very rich. In the 1990s much of the company's production is in traditionally styled grandfather or tall case clocks in mahogany, cherry, oak, and walnut. Another line, introduced in 1989, incorporates the grandfather clocks into oak curio cabinets, and curio cabinets without clocks are also produced. Most of the grandfather clocks are cable-driven with Westminster or triple chime movements. In 1997 Howard Miller made over 70 styles of grandfather clocks, making it the largest clock manufacturer in America and the largest manufacturer of grandfather clocks in the world, with control of between 30% and 40% of the market.

Game and accent clock tables are produced in oak, and incorporate large clock faces under glass as the entire surface of the table. A line of traditional wall clocks produced since at least the early 1980s is named "Heritage Hill," after the historic neighborhood in Grand Rapids where many of the furniture company owners lived. The "Crystal Ice Collection" includes carved crystal table clocks and domed clocks. Other lines include mantel and tambour clocks, the "Gallery Collection" of wall clocks with oversized dials, neon and fluorescent glow wall clocks, battery-powered wall and institutional clocks, miniature and alarm clocks, and weather instruments.

OTHER SOURCES
Though there has never been an official corporate relationship between the two companies, the Herman Miller company archives nevertheless has several oral interviews of Howard Miller, as well as a number of Howard Miller price lists and catalogs from the 1950s.

MARKS AND LABELS
The well-known Howard Miller trademark is a stylized version of an hour glass. It generally appears on clocks in between the names "Howard" and "Miller," and was designed by George Nelson's design firm. In addition to the maker's mark, all grandfather clocks come with one brass plate engraved with the registration number, and the other with the buyer's name and date of purchase.

✗ Howard Miller
1980

✗ HOWARD MILLER®
1997

MILLER UPHOLSTERY CO.
1931 - 1936

Grand Rapids, Michigan
Manufacturer of upholstered furniture.

MILLING ROAD FURNITURE

SEE Baker Furniture, Inc.

MODERNIZE, INC.
1946 - 1949

Grand Rapids, Michigan
Manufacturer of furniture.

MODERN PRODUCTS CO.

SEE Haworth, Inc.

MOON DESK CO.
at least 1902 - 1914

The | Office Desk Line
1902

Grand Rapids and Muskegon, Michigan
Manufacturer of office desks.

1914

MOORE, RICHARDSON & CO.

SEE Grand Rapids Furniture Manufacturing Co.

MORGAN MANUFACTURING CO.
1936 - present

1989

Grand Rapids, Michigan
Manufacturer of church furniture and religious furniture.
COMPANY HISTORY
1936: Company incorporates in Chicago.
1946: Company moves to Grand Rapids.

MORRIS, F. E. BED & LOUNGE CO.
1888

Grand Rapids, Michigan
Manufacturer of beds and reclining couches.

MORRIS, F. E. CO.
1880 - 1889

Grand Rapids, Michigan
Manufacturer of lounges and reclining sofas which opened to convert into beds.
Predecessor to Star Furniture Co.
SEE ALSO Star Furniture Co.

MORSE, RALPH FURNITURE CO.
1913 - 1979

Grand Rapids, Michigan
Manufacturer of upholstered furniture
and occasional tables.
SEE ALSO Lauzon, C. A. Furniture Co.

1929   1945   1955

MOUW, ANDY, INC.
1921 - 1928

Grand Rapids, Michigan
Manufacturer of the "Davenola," a davenport sofa with a phonograph located in one
arm and a phonograph cabinet in the other.

MUELLER FURNITURE CORP.
1920 - 1992

Grand Rapids, Michigan
SEE ALSO Grand Rapids Parlor Furniture Co.; Haworth, Inc.; Mueller & Slack Co.;
Widdicomb Furniture Co.; West Michigan Furniture Co.

COMPANY HISTORY

1930

1949

1951

1958

1966

1980

1920: Name changes from Mueller & Slack Co. to Mueller Furniture Co.
1950: Mueller Furniture Co. merges with Widdicomb Furniture Co. to form the
    Widdicomb - Mueller Co.
1951: Company begins operation as Mueller Metals Co., a subsidiary of Widdicomb
    - Mueller.
1960: Mueller Metals separates from Widdicomb name as an independent company.
1962: Mueller Metals changes name to Mueller Furniture Corp.
1984: Mueller purchases West Michigan Furniture Co. in Holland, Michigan.
1990: Mueller is purchased by Haworth, Inc.
1992: Mueller is combined with another Haworth subsidiary, the Myrtle Desk Co.
    of High Point, North Carolina. Grand Rapids plant closes; product develop-
    ment and marketing move to Haworth in Holland, and manufacturing of
    some products under the Mueller name continues in High Point.

PERSONNEL

The company became Mueller Furniture Co. in 1920 when co-owner A.W. Slack
sold his interest in the Mueller & Slack Co. to his partner, Johann Frederick
Mueller. In 1920 his son, Frederick H. Mueller, joined the firm. The company continued in family hands when grandson Fritz Mueller went to work for the company
in 1946. In 1950 it was merged with Widdicomb Furniture Co., and became the division known as Mueller Metals. This division continued to be managed by Fritz
Mueller.

The company moved out of Mueller family hands in 1961 when it was purchased by G. Richard Bodkins. Partners David Lohr and Thatcher W. Rea, Jr. purchased the company in 1975. Rea became sole owner and operated Mueller until
1990, when it was sold and became a subsidiary of Haworth, Inc.

PRODUCTS

In the 1920s Mueller made high-grade, upholstered chairs, benches, ottomans, davenports, and sofas. Frames were mahogany and walnut, with patterned mohair, silk
brocade and tapestry fabrics that interpreted historical English and French styles.

The noted streamlined Modern designer Kem Weber designed the "Fleetwood"
line on contract for Mueller in 1936. The grouping included chairs, desks, and tables
made of lightweight plywood, cut into rounded and aerodynamic shapes similar to
his "Airline chairs" for a California company. Sofas and easy chairs in the Fleetwood
line were rectangular and boxy with rounded corners, and were all over upholstered
with leather or geometric patterned fabrics. At the same time Mueller continued to
advertise traditional lines which were adaptations of 18th-century English, French,
American Empire, Colonial and Victorian styles.

As Mueller Metals Co., the company manufactured tables, upholstered seating,
and other contract furniture for offices, especially sofas, lounge chairs, benches, occasional chairs, and table desks. When the company was purchased in 1961, the case
goods were dropped and the company concentrated just on upholstered furniture
and tables. Between 1963 and 1967, the company sub-contracted all of its manufacturing. It began to manufacture its own products again in 1967, after purchasing the
former Widdicomb factory.

The wooden component-based VARIA system was introduced in 1986, to provide flexible systems furniture for small office settings. According to a December,
1990 *Grand Rapids Press* article, Mueller was the first company to develop wooden
modular case goods for the contract market in the 1970s. A series of upholstered
wooden chairs named for Thatcher Rea's wife, Mary, and daughters Cara and Laura,

holster some pieces apparently made by other manufacturers.

Production in the 1880s favored the Aesthetic Movement. Pieces mixed elements of classical and Oriental form, with shallow geometric carving and stylized floral inlay. The wide range of forms offered included not only bedroom and dining room furniture but also parlor suites, onyx-top tables, couches, and lounges.

1900 - 1910: In 1900 the company made a complete line of fine- and medium-grade oak and mahogany furniture for the bedroom, dining room, and office. Nelson, Matter & Co. introduced its "Modern English" line in 1905. It featured Glasgow-influenced Arts and Crafts oak or mahogany bedroom and dining room suites. Though basically rectangular in form, the lines were softened by gently arching aprons, cut-outs, and leaded glass. A related bedroom suite was decorated with "Dutch marquetry," in sinewy Art Nouveau shapes and geometric patterns. At the same time, Nelson, Matter also produced a line of mahogany Colonial Revival furniture, which combined elements of the Empire, Queen Anne, and Chippendale styles.

1911 - 1917: The Empire - Colonial line was still listed in a 1911 *Grand Rapids Herald* article, along with mahogany Chinese Chippendale, satinwood Sheraton, and caned and white enameled Louis XVI. In addition to its residential furniture, Nelson, Matter was throughout its history a major furnisher of hotels. In 1916 it supplied the large new William Penn Hotel in Pittsburgh, Pennsylvania with white enameled furniture.

OTHER SOURCES

The Grand Rapids Public Library has in its collections some of the earliest Nelson, Matter photo catalogs.

MARKS AND LABELS

Nelson, Matter & Co. was the only Grand Rapids manufacturer to use a Knapp's Dovetailer to join its case pieces. This machine cut a distinctive semi-circular scallop instead of the more common trapezoidal dovetail shape, making the dovetail one possible means of identifying Nelson, Matter & Co.'s products. The underside of marble from early pieces may be inscribed "NM", signifying that the marble was cut by a contractor for Nelson, Matter & Co. Other specific methods of attributing and dating Nelson, Matter & Co. furniture based on marking and construction methods are described in detail in the chapter by Joel Lefever.

NEW ENGLAND FURNITURE CO.
1881 - ca. 1904

Advertisement for the New England Furniture Co., *Grand Rapids Furniture Record,* June, 1902.

Grand Rapids, Michigan
Predecessor to Grand Rapids Furniture Co.
SEE ALSO Grand Rapids Furniture Co.

COMPANY HISTORY

1880: Ward, Skinner & Brooks founded.
1881: Name changes to New England Furniture Co.
1902: Company is reorganized by owners of Grand Rapids Furniture Co.
ca.1904: Last production sold under the name of New England Furniture Co.

PERSONNEL

Company founder and president H.C. Brooks lived in Denver, Colorado, though he held part interest in several Grand Rapids firms. Company vice-president George Lewis supervised orders and the sales department. Secretary and Treasurer O.A. Ward ran the office and the company's financial affairs.

PRODUCTS

In the 1880s and '90s, New England Furniture Co. specialized in the production of "cheap and medium-grade" bedroom furniture and chamber suites decorated in a manner now referred to as "cottage" furniture. An inexpensive, domestic soft wood was machined in a form reminiscent of Aesthetic or Eastlake furniture, then painted all over to conceal the wood. The decorative painting often became quite busy, with several ground colors, a contrasting color in all the incising, and floral or scenery painting in central panels. Additionally, many pieces included faux marble or grain painting of mahogany or walnut burl. One of these cottage chamber suites was exhibited at the 1884 Cotton Centennial Exposition in New Orleans, and in 1893 the company won a medal for its "Baby Ruth Chamber Suite" at the World's Columbian Exposition in Chicago.

In the mid-1890s the company abandoned its earlier concentration on chamber suites, in favor of Golden Oak sideboards, buffets, and china closets. By 1903 it introduced a very boxy line of Mission dining suites, buffets, and sideboards, with ex-

1903

aggerated pegged mortise joints. At the same time New England continued to produce massive sideboards with highly figured carving of lions, mascarons, caryatids, and all manner of leafy flourishes.

MARKS AND LABELS

In 1903 New England Furniture Co. adopted a logo of an "N" connected to an "E", surrounded by a rectangular line. The hand-drawn character of this logo fit well with the company's introduction of its new Arts and Crafts line that same year.

NEWAYGO FURNITURE CO.
1880 - 1889

Factory: Newaygo, Michigan. Offices: Grand Rapids, Michigan.
Manufacturer of furniture.
Merged with Converse Manufacturing Co. in 1889.
SEE ALSO Converse Manufacturing Co.

NORMAN-WARD-BEECHER CO.
at least 1921 - 1924

1924

Grand Rapids, Michigan
Manufacturer of solid mahogany furniture named for American patriots, including the "Myles Standish" suite, and the "Dolly Madison," "Betsy Ross," and "Martha Washington" sewing cabinets. Advertised in 1921 issues of the *Grand Rapids Furniture Record*.

NORTHERN CHAIR CO.
1917 - 1955

Cadillac, Michigan
Manufacturer of chairs and rockers.
Operated under the name Wilcox Chair Co. between 1931 - 1937.

NORTHERN REFRIGERATOR CO. OF GRAND RAPIDS

SEE Grand Rapids Refrigerator Co.

NOVELTY FURNITURE CO.
1885

Grand Rapids, Michigan
Manufacturer of Japanese Eastlake-influenced tables, hat racks, towel racks, bookstands, pedestals, and whatnots in walnut, ash, oak, birch, and other domestic hardwoods. Advertised in *The Michigan Artisan*, January, 1885.

NOWACZYK HANDCRAFT FURNITURE CO.
1914 - 1918

Grand Rapids, Michigan
Manufacturer of furniture.

NUCRAFT FURNITURE CO.
1942 - present

Grand Rapids and Comstock Park, Michigan

COMPANY HISTORY

1942: Company founded in Grand Rapids.
1985: Plant and offices move to nearby Comstock Park, Michigan.

PERSONNEL

Nucraft was founded as a partnership between George William Schad and B.E. Richardson, both former employees of the Stow & Davis Furniture Co. Schad served as president until 1966, and as chairman after that. In that same year the Schad family purchased Richardson's interests in the company, and George Dewey Schad, son of George William, became president. He was succeeded as president by his son, Timothy O. Schad, in 1985. In 1997 Timothy Schad became chairman and Bob Bockheim president.

Most of the company's earlier designs were created by the Schads. Mitch Baker, a Nucraft employee, designed the company's first conference furniture line in 1988.

PRODUCTS

Nucraft's first products in the 1940s were walnut letter trays, followed by wastebaskets and costumers, made under the Nucraft name to match Stow & Davis office suites and sold through Stow & Davis dealers. The company continued production of letter trays and waste baskets until 1995.

In the late 1950s Nucraft introduced its first Danish Modern and International Modern style occasional tables in solid walnut or walnut and metal. From that time to the present a significant portion of Nucraft's production has been occasional tables, bookcases, sectional bookcases, and credenzas in walnut.

In 1967 the company introduced a modular walnut wall system called "Unit-Wall." The system was sold with colorful patterned plastic room partitions. A later version sold in the mid-1970s became an entire executive office system in walnut, known as "Group 4." In 1971 a line of straight and curved acoustical screens for open offices was introduced under the name "Nuspace." The Nuspace system evolved into a complete post-and-panel open office system with fabric panels and walnut components. Nuspace was discontinued circa 1985. Nucraft began production of traditionally styled computer desks in walnut or oak circa 1980, at the beginnings of the personal computer revolution. Newer versions of these desks are still in

Cover, Nucraft "UnitWall" Free Standing Office Units catalog, 1964. Courtesy, Nucraft Furniture Co.

NUCRAFT
NUCRAFT FURNITURE COMPANY
1985

NUCRAFT
1989

NUCRAFT
1997

production.

Nucraft's first line of conference room furniture was introduced in 1988. Produced in walnut with traditional styling, it included pieces required for special functions such as visual boards, computer cabinets, and utility carts, in addition to board tables and credenzas. A second conference line named "Duomo," introduced in 1994, included more accommodations for information technology, including tables wired for phone, data, and local area networks, and video conference cabinets. The 1997 "Satellite Collection" is designed for even more information technology in intensive computer training areas. Currently conference furniture constitutes about 60% of Nucraft's business.

MARKS AND LABELS

Even though their early trays, wastebaskets, and costumers were sold with Stow & Davis furniture, they were labeled with the Nucraft name. The company trademark, which appeared on labels by at least the early 1960s, was a circle overprinted with "Nucraft" in script over "OF GRAND RAPIDS" in block letters. A separate logo was devised for the Nuspace line and used in the early and mid-1970s. Circa 1975 the script trademark was replaced by the name "NUCRAFT" in Block Helvetica type. Between circa 1985 and 1995 a logo consisting of a round, square, and elliptical table top were used with the name trademark.

OCKER & FORD MANUFACTURING CO.
at least 1899

Grand Rapids, Michigan
Manufacturer of building exterior and interior millwork, mantels, church seats, and store and bank counters.

OLIVER & CO.
at least 1917 - 1928

Allegan, Michigan
Manufacturer of highboys, lowboys, and desks.

OMNI ALUMINUM EXTRUSIONS, INC.
at least 1968

Charlotte, Michigan
A catalog from 1968 describes Omni's product as "the original pole supported vertical spacemaker furniture system."

ORIEL CABINET CO.
1880 - 1912

Grand Rapids, Michigan
SEE ALSO Berkey & Gay Furniture Co.

COMPANY HISTORY

1880: Oriel Cabinet Co. founded.
1888: Original factory is expanded and remodeled.
1890: First factory burns; Oriel moves into former plant of McCord and Bradfield Furniture Co.
1893: Oriel's new factory is completed.
1912: Oriel's operations consolidated with Berkey & Gay's; Oriel plant becomes Berkey & Gay plant #1.

PERSONNEL

In 1887, Oriel's officers included two of the most prominent names in Grand Rapids' furniture industry: George Gay and Julius Berkey. George Gay served as president of Oriel until his death in 1899, when he was succeeded by his son William H. Gay, who was also the president of Berkey & Gay Furniture Co. Charles M. Black served as plant manager from 1884 until his death in 1910. He was credited with making the company profitable, and his death was the reason given for merging not only the boards but the operations of Oriel with Berkey & Gay in 1912.

John F. Samuelson is reported to have been hired as Oriel's designer in 1900 and 1901, at double the salary he received from his previous employer, Gimbel's Department Store of Philadelphia. Samuelson was trained as a cabinetmaker, but received a formal education through Drexel Institute, the Philadelphia School of Fine Art, and the University of Pennsylvania. Frenchman Rene Guenaux held the position of designer at Oriel from the time he came to America in 1906 until he took a position with Sligh because Oriel was absorbed into Berkey & Gay in 1912.

PRODUCTS

An image from *The Decorator and Furnisher* in 1882 shows one of Oriel's early products, a black walnut hall stand in the Oriental manner of Eastlake, with stylized floral and decorative carving and figured veneer panels. In Elstner's 1887 *Industries of Grand Rapids*, the company was described as "the largest manufactory of fancy and art furniture in the country." A 1900 list of the company's products in *The Grand Rapids Furniture Record* lists a large variety of forms, including standing and hanging hall racks, settees, China closets, buffets, chiffoniers and shaving stands, dressers,

The "Norman Suite" by Oriel Cabinet Co., *Grand Rapids Furniture Record*, Feb., 1909.

cheval mirrors, bookcases, desks, parlor and music cabinets, piano stools and benches, occasional tables, and dining and bedroom suites. It was also the only Grand Rapids factory producing tables, desks, pedestals, and music and parlor cabinets hand-painted with gold and vernis martin (French lacquer on white or colored ground).

In 1903 Oriel produced its Arts and Crafts "Dutch dining room suite" and Mission library suite, both in oak with leaded glass and legs, and stiles that flared as they descended. A 1907 article in *The Grand Rapids Furniture Record* describes Oriel's production as ranging from "simple, inexpensive Mission to the ornate Venetian Renaissance, including the most expensive Louis XV full chamber suites in Circassian walnut..." and continues to list gold and vernis martin among the company's special finishes.

The 1911 Norman Dining Room Suite featured massively carved mascarons, Chimerae, and putti, and Norman soldiers and griffins in full relief. A 1911 article in *The Grand Rapids Herald* sings the praises of Oriel's highly carved, high-end Renaissance furniture. Of Oriel's carved Gothic pieces, the article states that "its severely monastic ideas (are) represented so faithfully, one almost expects to hear the tolling bell summoning the worshippers to vespers..."

It also describes Oriel's Louis XV and XVI cabinets, colorfully decorated with "The Dancing Faun" and romantic French scenes by Jean Antione Watteau and others. French desks, bedroom suites, work tables, jardiniere stands, and dressing tables were decorated with elaborate floral marquetry. The list of novelties includes cellarets, liquor cabinets, cocktail wagons, and gaming tables. Pieces were produced using exotic and unusual woods such as French violet wood, amaranth, and chine verte. The reporter claims that Oriel's line of white enameled furniture in the manner of Hepplewhite is the only Hepplewhite in reproduction at that time in the United States.

Oriel also created what is described as "perfect reproductions" of historical pieces, including a cabinet owned by Jeanne Becu, Comtesse du Barry, mistress of Louis XV. Other exact reproductions from original pieces were produced in Elizabethan, William and Mary, Adam, Sheraton, and Chippendale styles. At the time of Oriel's merger with Berkey & Gay in 1912, market ads boasted a complete line of over 1,800 separate pieces. Berkey & Gay continued to call its specialty pieces the "Oriel Line" for a time, but eventually the name was dropped.

MARKS AND LABELS
An 1888 receipt shows a company logo reading "Oriel Cabinet Co.," with a piece of furniture surrounded by the oversized "O". In 1897 The name "ORIEL CABINET CO." appeared atop a log of wood.

1897

ORTH, BERNARD
ca. 1857 - 1866

Grand Rapids, Michigan
Cabinetmaker from Badendorf, Germany. The only known piece of his work is a faux oak grain painted sewing or work table with turned center pedestal resting on three serpentine scrolled legs. The piece is signed in pencil on the interior, making it the earliest marked piece of Grand Rapids furniture.

OSBORNE FURNITURE CO.
at least 1888

Buchanan, Michigan
Manufacturer of Eastlake-style fancy parlor tables, stands, etc. Advertised in 1888 issues of *The Michigan Artisan*.

OSGOOD & JORDAN
1872

Grand Rapids, Michigan
Manufacturer of extension tables. Listed in the 1872 *Grand Rapids Business Directory*.

OTSEGO CHAIR CO.
at least 1900 - 1901

Otsego, Michigan
Manufacturer of "cheap and medium grade chairs."

OTTAWA FURNITURE CO.
1887 - 1931

1917

Holland, Michigan
Manufacturer of medium-priced dining, breakfast, library, bedroom, and apartment suites in Mission, Colonial, Chippendale, Sheraton, and Adam Revival styles.

OVERSEAS REED & CANE CO.
1915 - at least 1934

Ionia, Michigan and Singapore
Manufacturer and importer of furniture in reed, fiber, rattan, and metal; operated as a division of the Ypsilanti Reed Furniture Co.

SEE Ypsilanti Reed Furniture Co.

OVERTON CO.
1906 - 1908

Grand Rapids, Michigan
Manufacturer of piano stools.

PAALMAN FURNITURE CO.
1916 - 1966

Paalman Furniture Company
GRAND RAPIDS   MICHIGAN

Makers of the "Drop-Handle" Line
1922

Grand Rapids, Michigan
Manufacturer of tea wagons, occasional tables, console sets, ferneries, and magazine stands in various European and Colonial Revival and Modern styles.
OTHER SOURCES
The Public Museum of Grand Rapids has an archival collection of business records of this company.

Paalman Tea Wagons
The "Drop-Handle" Line
1928

Paalman FURNITURE COMPANY Grand Rapids Michigan
1950

PAGE, LOREN
ca. 1841

Grand Rapids, Michigan
Chair maker and decorator.

PAINE BEDDING CO.
1895 - 1900

Grand Rapids, Michigan
Manufacturer of bedding and couches, reclining sofas, and davenports.
Name changed to C. S . Paine Co., Ltd. in 1901.
SEE ALSO Paine, C. S. Co., Ltd.

PAINE, C. S. CO. LTD.
1901 - 1924

PAINE
GRAND RAPIDS
1914

Grand Rapids, Michigan
Manufacturer of "Japanned" (Lacquered) furniture in Japanese, Chinese and European forms; oak furniture; davenports; couches; hall pieces; and living room, dining room, and breakfast room furniture. Some of the more intricate carved pieces may be the work of Italian immigrant carver Leopold Baillot.
Successor to Paine Bedding Co.
SEE ALSO Paine Bedding Co.

PARAMOUNT FURNITURE MANUFACTURING CO.
ca. 1945

Sturgis, Michigan
Occupied the former Sturges-Aulsbrook-Jones factory after WWII.

PEERLESS FURNITURE CO.
at least 1922 - 1923

Grand Rapids, Michigan
Manufacturers of the "Peerless Line" of davenport tables, book troughs, and console sets.

PENINSULAR FURNITURE CO.
1883 - ca. 1890

Grand Rapids, Michigan
Manufacturer of bedroom sets, bedsteads, bureaus, lounges, and simple, turned folding tables.

PENTWATER BEDSTEAD CO.
at least 1888 - 1896

Pentwater, Michigan
In the 1880s the company advertised cheap beds, "in the white" or finished. 1890s ads were for chamber suites, odd dressers, and chiffonniers with machine carving. Advertised in *The Michigan Artisan*.

PERIOD FURNITURE CO.
ca. 1960

Grand Rapids, Michigan
Manufacturer of upholstered Victorian Revival furniture.

Period Furniture Co.
ca. 1960

PERRY FURNITURE CO.
1953 - 1968

Grand Rapids, Michigan
Manufacturer of peg-legs, perri-legs, occasional tables, and contract woodwork for other manufacturers.

PETCO, INC.
1963 - present

Petco, Inc.
1989

Grand Rapids, Michigan
Manufacturer of upholstery seaming cord, frame edgings, spring edgings, and tucking strip for the furniture industry.

PETERSEN, RAY O.
1956 - 1991

Sand Lake, Michigan
Carver and cabinetmaker of Early American or Colonial-style cradles, curio cabinets, button box lamps, clothes hampers, cobbler's benches, butcher block tables, and sewing machine cabinets.

PETTIT, WILLIAM H. & CO.
1886 - 1906

Grand Rapids, Michigan
Manufacturer of fancy reed furniture and children's carriages.

PHOENIX DESIGN

SEE Miller, Herman, Inc.

PHOENIX FURNITURE CO.
1872 - 1953

Grand Rapids, Michigan
SEE ALSO Atkins & Soule; Berkey, William A. Furniture Co.; Davidhazy Studios;

Irwin, Robert W. Furniture Co.; Stow & Davis, Inc.

COMPANY HISTORY

1868: William A. Berkey becomes assignee for the property of cabinetmakers Atkins & Soule.

1872: Berkey combines residuals of Atkins & Soule with $200,000 new capital to form Phoenix Furniture Co.

1873 and 1875: Phoenix opens south, then north portions of its new four-story brick "model" factory at West Fulton and Summer Streets.

1876: Wareroom opens in New York City.

1883: Phoenix more than doubles its production space with construction of a large addition.

1911: Phoenix acquired by Robert W. Irwin, Alexander Hompe, and Ralph Tietsort.

1919: Robert W. Irwin buys out Hompe and Tietsort and consolidates Phoenix and Royal Furniture Companies into the Robert W. Irwin Co. Phoenix products continue to be labeled with the Phoenix name.

1926: Expansions are added to the north and west of the existing plant.

1953: Robert W. Irwin Co. closes; manufacturing complex is occupied for storage temporarily.

late 1950s: Complex becomes home to Stow & Davis, Inc.

1987: Manufacturing complex donated to Grand Valley State University by Steelcase and Stow & Davis.

1988: GVSU razes Phoenix factory complex; Public Museum of Grand Rapids salvages a 2000-square-foot section of the 1873 building.

1994: Factory section is reconstructed in the Van Andel Museum Center of The Public Museum of Grand Rapids.

PERSONNEL

The Phoenix Furniture Co. "rose from the ashes" of the Atkins & Soule partnership, with the help of its first president William A. Berkey, and a large investment of new capital. Berkey ran the company until 1879, when controlling interest was sold to J. W. Converse, a capitalist from Boston. Converse employed his friend and in-law from Massachusetts, Robert W. Merrill, to help manage the plant, which he did until 1912. In 1911 ownership of the company changed again, to Robert W. Irwin, who in 1919 consolidated Phoenix and the Royal Furniture Co. into the Robert W. Irwin Co. Because of the prominent reputation of Phoenix, pieces made in its plants were advertised and labeled as "Phoenix Furniture, by the Robert W. Irwin Co."

Born and trained as a furniture designer in Rochester, New York, David Wolcott Kendall first made his mark as a designer for the Wooton Desk Co. in Indiana. In 1879 John Strahan, superintendent and designer for the Phoenix factory, hired Kendall from an architecture firm in Chicago to work as a draftsman at Phoenix. But his talents were soon recognized and he was allowed to execute his own designs for the company. He left Phoenix for Berkey & Gay between 1883 and 1886, and formed the short-lived company of Kendall, Beardsley & Dey in Detroit in 1886. During this time Asa Lyon produced designs for Phoenix. Kendall returned to Phoenix as chief designer in 1888. At the time of his death in 1910, Kendall was not only chief designer, but an officer of the company and general manager of the factory.

Kendall traveled extensively throughout the Americas, Europe, and Asia, to collect artifacts and books as inspirations for his own designs. Kendall outfitted an entire chemistry laboratory at the Phoenix factory, in which he experimented with new finish colors for oak. In 1928 Kendall's widow founded the Kendall Memorial School of Art, now Kendall College of Art and Design, with funds from his estate.

J. Stuart Clingman designed special order furniture for the Tobey Furniture Co. in Chicago before becoming Royal's assistant designer under chief designer Alexander Hompe in 1903. Clingman made his mark in the modernization of forms by Hepplewhite and Sheraton. He remained with Robert W. Irwin Co. as designer and officer after the company's consolidation.

In 1917 William Millington became a designer for Phoenix. Millington was a native of England, and received his training from the Royal College of Arts. Like many of Grand Rapids' top designers of that period, Millington worked at Waring & Gillow in Lancaster and W. & J. Sloane in New York before coming to Grand Rapids.

PRODUCTS

An 1873 article in the *Grand Rapids Daily Eagle* described Phoenix's stock of furniture as "walnut and ash bedroom suits; parlor and divan suits; folding and reclining chairs; marble and wood top center tables; sideboards; pier and looking glasses; couches covered in terry and brussels carpet; hair, cotton, wool, palm leaf, husk, and excelsior mattresses... and office desks, tables and chairs." Phoenix was the only one of the "big three" Grand Rapids manufacturers in the 1870s to manufacture and upholster its own parlor furniture. Much of the company's 1870s production was probably shipped "in the white" (unfinished), to be finished by the retailer upon arrival.

In the 1880s the firm's products were listed as the finest grades of chamber suites, folding bedsteads, chiffoniers, ladies' desks, bookcases, sideboards, dining tables, hall stands, and every kind of furniture in mahogany, walnut, ash, oak, maple and cherry. David Kendall's designs in the mid-1980s included pieces that combined shallow stylized sunflower carving, reminiscent of Eastlake, with busy jigsawed architectural elements of late Victorian architecture. Phoenix began making "ebonized" furniture in the early 1880s, and produced substantial amounts until its popularity waned in the 1890s.

Phoenix opened its special order department in 1884, to produce furniture on contract for hotels, offices, city halls, statehouses, and federal buildings. Grand Rapids' elegant city hall opened in 1889, with furniture designed by Kendall and manufactured by Phoenix.

Catalogs from the mid-1890s show a whole series of hexagonal tabourets with concave and convex sides, and Moorish cut-outs and stenciling. Many of Kendall's designs incorporated exotic decoration, with Celtic, Byzantine, Japanese, Moorish, and Arabic origins. Though factory-produced for a mass market, some rested on the cutting edge of fantasy, and were contemporary with such avant garde designers as Carlos Bugatti and Charles Rohlfs.

Phoenix furniture from the 1890s through the first part of the 20th century also bears the innovative finishes developed by Kendall and widely copied by manufacturers and craftsmen across the country. One colorful tale relates that Kendall developed his "antique oak" stain after noticing how tobacco juice spit onto oak floor boards in the factory brought out the wood grain and gave it a pleasing darkened tone. Some of his other fumed and stained finishes transformed oak into hues of green (malachite), grey-black (Flemish), tan (cremona), and canary yellow. It has even been suggested by a number of sources that Kendall's finishes were responsible for popularizing oak as a cabinetmaking wood, at a time when oak was readily available and other hardwoods were becoming cost-prohibitive.

Phoenix's most successful line was undoubtedly its oak and cane McKinley Chairs, designed by Kendall in 1894. The chairs were so named because one was owned and used by President McKinley. Though the arm and seat rails incorporated delicately exotic Moorish arches, the use of oak, square spindles, and broad armrests, and absence of carved decoration have caused many researchers to anoint the McKinley chair as one of the first examples of the American Mission style. In his *The City Built on Wood*, historian Frank Ransom states that "the design for the McKinley Chair was supposedly achieved by having persons of varying size sit in snow banks, then transferring the curves left by the impression of their bodies onto the drawing board." Within a few years of its introduction, other manufacturers in Grand Rapids and elsewhere introduced their own versions of the McKinley chair, causing Kendall to patent the design in 1897. It remained in production into the early 1910s.

Some of Kendall's first designs for Phoenix were massive pieces in Jacobean, William and Mary, and other early English styles, as were some of his last. His many visits to cathedrals, castles, and museums in Europe reportedly made Phoenix one of the leaders in the development of "Period Furniture." A 1911 *Grand Rapids Herald* article about Phoenix's products, published not long after Kendall's death, claimed that some of its Colonial and Empire pieces were almost exact copies of actual antiques from those periods. Ads from the 1910s show high-end bedroom, dining room, and living room furniture in various period styles, including Elizabethan, Jacobean, Adam, Sheraton, and Louis XIV, made from oak, walnut, mahogany, imitation mahogany, and satinwood. One distinctive form produced in many styles by Phoenix during the mid-1910s was an approximately 8-foot-long sideboard, with cellaret pedestals on either end topped by urn-shaped knife boxes.

Stencil-painted taboret, Phoenix Furniture Co., ca. 1895.

1895

pre-1920

1925

(For more information on post-1920 products, SEE Irwin, Robert W. Co.)

OTHER SOURCES

The Public Museum of Grand Rapids owns a small collection of original drawings created for Phoenix by David W. Kendall. Many of the artifacts collected in Kendall's world travels were donated by his widow to The Public Museum and the Kendall College of Art and Design. Kendall College also owns his original photos and design drawings. An informative article on the designer, entitled "Progressive Designs in Grand Rapids," by Jane Perkins Claney and Robert Edwards, appeared in the September-October, 1983 issue of *Tiller Magazine*. A detailed adaptive reuse study of the Phoenix factory complex was completed in 1988 by preservation architect Richard Frank, prior to its demolition by Grand Valley State University. A series of Phoenix catalogs from the 1890s are in the collections of the Grand Rapids Public Library.

MARKS AND LABELS

During the 1870s Phoenix sometimes tacked rectangular paper shipping tags to the backs of furniture, with the recipient's name hand-written on the top portion, and "FROM / PHOENIX FURNITURE CO. / Grand Rapids, Mich." printed on the bottom. A rectangular metal plate with chamfered corners was used to mark furniture during the 1890s. It was textured to resemble hammer marks, and read, "Manufactured by / PHOENIX FURNITURE CO / GRAND RAPIDS Mich". Other specific methods for attributing and dating pieces according to marking and construction methods are described in detail in the chapter by Joel Lefever.

Ads from the 1910s often depict a Phoenix bird taking flight from a blazing fire. Even though Phoenix became part of the Robert W. Irwin Co. in 1920, ads continued to show lines from the "Phoenix Furniture Company" until at least 1926. Around this time, wording in ads and on a new, more rectangular logo of the phoenix bird rising from the flames changed to "PHOENIX FURNITURE/ MADE BY/ ROBERT W. IRWIN CO."

PHOENIX UPHOLSTERY CO.
at least 1928

Holland, Michigan
Manufacturer of upholstered furniture. Listed in *The Buyer's Guide*, July, 1928.

PIAGET-DONNELY CO.
1923 - 1937

1925

Grand Rapids, Michigan
Importer of Chinese reed and rattan furniture.
Successor to Mentzer-Piaget Furniture Co.
SEE ALSO Mentzer-Piaget Furniture Co.

PINE SHOPS
at least 1956 - 1973

1959

Big Rapids, Michigan
Manufacturer of Colonial reproductions in pine.

PINE-TIQUE FURNITURE, INC.
1955 - 1958

1955

Grand Haven, Michigan
Manufacturer of original designs and reproductions in "antique pine" for the bedroom, dining room, and living room; also accessories, wall pieces, and framed pictures. Listed in various market guides.

PLY-CURVES, INC.
1951 - present

Grand Rapids, Michigan
Manufacturer of molded plywood chairs and curved plywood parts for chairs and kidney desks. Founded by Charles R. Sligh Jr. and O.W. Lowry.
SEE ALSO Sligh - Lowry Furniture Co.

PORTLAND FURNITURE CO.
at least 1900 - 1901

Portland, Michigan
Manufacturer of furniture. Cited in an article in *The Grand Rapids Furniture Record* .

PORTLAND MANUFACTURING CO.
at least ca. 1902 - 1911

Portland, Michigan
Originally a manufacturer of tables; production later switched to washing machines.

POWDER COAT TECHNOLOGY

SEE Miller, Herman, Inc.

POWERS & BALL
1849 - 1855

Grand Rapids, Michigan
Manufacturer of bureaus, bedsteads, tables, stands, Windsor chairs, high chairs, sofas, ottomans, rockers, cribs, cradles, and looking glasses in black walnut, cherry, oak, and ash. According to Frank Ransom's *The City Built on Wood*, much of their

production went to the American Car Co. in Chicago. Powers & Ball also manufactured parts for McCormick Reapers assembled in Chicago.
Successor to William T. Powers. Predecessor to Ball, Noyes, & Colby.
SEE ALSO Ball, Noyes, & Colby; Powers, William T.

POWERS, WILLIAM T.
1847 - 1849

Grand Rapids, Michigan
Chair maker. Partnered with Ebenezer Ball in 1849 to form Powers & Ball.
SEE ALSO Powers & Ball.

PRATT MANUFACTURING CO.
1928

Coldwater, Michigan
Manufacturer of lawn and porch furniture, cots, and camp tables. Listed in *The Buyer's Guide*, July, 1928.

PRINCESS DRESSING CASE CO., THE
1890

Grand Rapids, Michigan
Manufacturer of the "Princess Dressing Case" and the "Princess Center Table." Ads claim the dressing case was a modern improvement over old-style commodes and washstands, with its swivel top that opened to reveal a sink. Advertised in 1890 issues of *The Michigan Artisan*.

PRITCHETT-POWERS CO.
1922 - 1927

Grand Rapids, Michigan
Manufacturer of furniture.
Merged with Charlotte Furniture Co. in 1928.
SEE ALSO Charlotte Furniture Co.

PROBAR CO.

SEE Borroughs Corp.

PROGRESSIVE FURNITURE CO.
1930 - 1962

Grand Rapids, Michigan
Manufacturer of frames.

PULLMAN FURNITURE CO.

SEE Eagles-Pullman Co.

QUAINT FURNITURE

SEE Stickley Brothers Furniture Co.

QUALITY FURNITURE CO.
1912 - 1916

Grand Rapids, Michigan
Manufacturer of roll-top desks and occasional tables.

RAAB, JOHN D. CHAIR CO.
1906 - 1924

Grand Rapids, Michigan
Manufacturer of occasional chairs in oak and mahogany.
Predecessor to the Furniture Shops of Grand Rapids.
SEE ALSO Furniture Shops of Grand Rapids.

RAMSEY-ALTON MANUFACTURING CO.
1905 - 1915

1905   1912

Portland, Michigan
Originally a manufacturer of Colonial Revival rocking chairs, oak Mission furniture, Morris chairs with leather or fabric upholstery, and matched suites for the living room, library, hall, and den under the tradename "Oak Craft." In 1914 the company introduced a selection of cane and Jacobean pieces alongside the Mission line. After 1919 the plant was occupied by a factory of the Ypsilanti Reed Furniture Co.
Successor to Dellenbaugh-Alton Manufacturing Co.
SEE ALSO Dellenbaugh-Alton Manufacturing Co.

1914

RANNEY REFRIGERATOR CO.
at least 1901 - 1905

Greenville, Michigan
Manufacturer of refrigerators and kitchen cabinets.

RAUSCH FURNITURE CO.
1965 - 1967

Grand Rapids, Michigan
Manufacturer of furniture.
Successor to Furniture Arts Co.
SEE ALSO Furniture Arts Co.

REDCO MANUFACTURING DIVISION, L. H. L., INC.
1968 - 1992

Grand Rapids, Michigan
Manufacturer of executive office furniture: panel end, parsons, end, cube, waterfall, and cylinder tables as well as tabletops and bases in wood, aluminum, steel, laminates, and veneers for the contract and restaurant furniture industries.
Successor to Wilburn Co.
SEE ALSO Wilburn Co.

REGAL FURNITURE CO.
1921 - 1923

Grand Rapids, Michigan
Manufacturer of upholstered chairs and sofas.

REGOUT, THOMAS N. V.
1990 - present

Headquarters: The Netherlands. U.S. plant: Byron Center, Michigan. Manufacturer of drawer slide hardware for contract furniture manufacturers.

RETAN FURNITURE CO.
1930 - 1951

Grand Rapids, Michigan
Manufacturer of reed furniture for the sun room and porch, made with twisted paper fiber cord.

RETTING FURNITURE CO.
1904 - ca. 1920

1909

Grand Rapids, Michigan
Manufacturer of fine upholstered drawing room, lodge, and ecclesiastical furniture in period styles, including Louis XV and XVI, William and Mary, Queen Anne, Elizabethan, Jacobean, Chippendale, Hepplewhite, and Renaissance. Retting produced the furnishings for many of the lodge halls in Grand Rapids. Successor to Retting & Sweet.
SEE ALSO Retting & Sweet.

RETTING & SWEET
1895 - 1904

Grand Rapids, Michigan
Manufacturer of drawing room, lodge, and ecclesiastical furniture.
Predecessor to Retting Furniture Co.
SEE ALSO Retting Furniture Co.

REX MANUFACTURING CO.
1908 - 1914

1914

Grand Rapids, Michigan
Manufacturer of mahogany novelties, including clocks, footstools, candlesticks, tea tables, book blocks, pedestals, magazine racks, and muffin stands.
Predecessor to Rex-Robinson Furniture Co.
SEE ALSO Rex-Robinson Furniture Co.

REX - ROBINSON FURNITURE CO.
1914 - 1926

Grand Rapids, Michigan
Successor to Rex Manufacturing Co. and C. B. Robinson & Sons.
SEE ALSO Rex Manufacturing Co.; Robinson, C. B & Sons.

RICHMOND MANUFACTURING CO.
1893 - 1894

Grand Rapids, Michigan
Manufacturer of cheap and medium-priced folding beds in seven styles. Advertised in *The Michigan Artisan*.

RIVERSIDE LUMBER CO.
1921 - 1939

1925

Grand Rapids, Michigan
Manufacturer and retailer of window sash, doors, and other built-in woodwork and wood furnishings, including kitchen cupboards, "dinofold" folding breakfast tables, and table-and-bench sets for breakfast nooks.

ROBBINS TABLE CO.
at least 1888

West Owosso, Michigan
Manufacturer of "pillar and common extension tables." Advertised in *The Michigan Artisan* in 1888.

ROBERTS, EPHRIAM A.
1873 - 1876

Grand Rapids, Michigan
Manufacturer of carvings, fancy parlor brackets, wall pockets, towel racks, match safes, and book shelves.

ROBERTS & FURBISH

SEE Furbish, Frank L. Co.

ROBINSON, C. B. & SONS
1910 - 1914

Grand Rapids, Michigan
Predecessor to Rex-Robinson Furniture Co.
SEE ALSO Rex-Robinson Furniture Co.

ROBINSON FURNITURE CO.
1953 - 1968

Grand Rapids, Michigan
Manufacturer of furniture, including the "Converta Sofa."

ROGERS FURNITURE CO.
at least 1888

Fremont, Michigan
Manufacturer of oak, cherry, and walnut chamber suites, oak and walnut sideboards, dining room extension tables, and the "New England Dresser," an Aesthetic Movement-influenced combination chifforobe and chest of drawers. Advertised in 1888 issues of *The Michigan Artisan*.

ROLLER MANUFACTURING CO., THE
at least 1888

Holland, Michigan
Manufacturer of fine furniture, including American Eastlake-style washstands. Advertised in 1888 issues of *The Michigan Artisan*.

ROSE CARVING CO.	SEE Rose Manufacturing Co.

ROSE MANUFACTURING CO.
1917 - 1980

Grand Rapids, Michigan
Manufacturer of "traditional," Early American, and French Provincial upholstering frames.
Predecessor to RoseJohnson, Inc.
SEE ALSO Grand Rapids Craftsman Co.; Michigan Frame Co.; RoseJohnson, Inc.

COMPANY HISTORY
1917: Rose Carving Co. is established to carve arms and legs for upholstered furniture manufacturers.
1946 - 1964: Rose manufactures traditional upholstery frames as Grand Rapids Craftsman Co. division; office chair frames are manufactured by contract division.
1969: Begins manufacture of acoustical screens for office landscapes.
1970s: Screens evolve into connecting panels known as "Progressions."
1980: Rose merges with Johnson Furniture Co. to form RoseJohnson, Inc.

1970

ROSEJOHNSON, INC.
1980 - 1993

Grand Rapids, Michigan
SEE ALSO La-Z-Boy Contract, Inc.; Johnson Furniture Co.; Rose Manufacturing Co.; Rowe International; TimberLine, Inc.

COMPANY HISTORY
1980: Johnson Furniture Co. and Rose Manufacturing Co. merge to form RoseJohnson, Inc., while maintaining separate product lines and manufacturing facilities.
1983: Individual operations fully merge into one.
1986: RoseJohnson is acquired by La-Z-Boy Chair Co. of Monroe, Michigan.
1993: RoseJohnson name is dropped; company becomes part of "La-Z-Boy Contract Furniture Group."

PERSONNEL
James Van Oosten, chairman of the board for predecessor company Johnson Furniture Co., became the chair of RoseJohnson after the merger. Though Van Oosten sold the company in 1986, he stayed on as company president.

PRODUCTS
One of the first large contracts awarded to the new company in 1980 was for wooden office systems for the Playboy Enterprises executive offices in New York. By 1986 the now fully merged RoseJohnson dropped the "Timberline" hotel/motel line of predecessor company Johnson, to concentrate on production of its wooden "RJ Office Systems" for executives, "Progressions" panels for use with free-standing office furniture, "Progressions+" work stations for all office levels, "RJ Chairs," and contracts for other manufacturers including cabinets for Rowe International jukeboxes.

OTHER SOURCES
The Public Museum of Grand Rapids owns archival collections relating to Rose-Johnson and its various successor companies.

MARKS AND LABELS
A red rose, the old trademark of predecessor company Rose Manufacturing, was used as a trademark on Progressions and Progressions+ furniture, between 1980 and 1983. The RJ Office System line was represented by an upper case "R" minus its upright portion, and stylized "J". The Timber Line was represented by an overlapping "TL" in script, with a large red circle. During this same period the company trademark consisted of the name "ROSE . JOHNSON / INCORPORATED" on a decorative plaque. After 1983 the trademark became the name "RoseJohnson" in a serif font. The RoseJohnson name is dropped in favor of "La-Z-Boy Business Furniture".

1983   1983

Timber Line
A Unit of Rose Johnson, Incorporated.

ROSE ● JOHNSON
1985

ROSE•JOHNSON
1983

1983

1986

ROSPATCH, INC.
1915 - 1991

Grand Rapids, Michigan
Manufacturer of wooden ready-to-assemble furniture and cabinets for home electronic equipment.
Predecessor to Ameriwood Industries.
SEE ALSO Ameriwood Industries International, Inc.

ROUND OAK MANUFACTURING
1987 - 1992

Grand Rapids, Michigan
Manufacturer of furniture.

ROWE, HENRY MANUFACTURING CO.
1899 - 1967

Newaygo, Michigan
Manufacturer of turned and shaped wooden components for furniture, manual train-

ing and cabinetmaker benches, and butter molds.

COMPANY HISTORY

1899: Company is established.

1905: Company incorporates.

1967: Company closes.

ROWE INTERNATIONAL - AMI

SEE Automatic Musical Instrument Co.

ROYAL CHAIR CO.
1899 - ca. 1928

1914

Sturgis, Michigan

Manufacturer of reclining Morris chairs, easy chairs, and rockers with push button-release foot rest, in several hundred designs including Mission, Turkish, Golden Oak, and Colonial Revival.

1928

ROYAL FURNITURE CO.
1892 - 1931

Grand Rapids, Michigan

SEE ALSO Irwin, Robert W. Co.; Universal Tripod Co., The.

COMPANY HISTORY

1892: Under the ownership of Alexander Hompe and Ralph P. Tietsort, Universal Tripod Co. becomes the Royal Furniture Co.

1901: A controlling interest in Royal is purchased by Robert W. Irwin.

1919: Irwin buys Hompe's interest in Royal. Royal is combined with the Phoenix Furniture Co. to form the Robert W. Irwin Co. Production continues under Royal and Phoenix as well as Irwin names.

1931: Royal name is discontinued on Irwin furniture.

PERSONNEL

Royal was organized out of Julius Berkey's Universal Tripod Co., although in 1898 both Julius and Charles Berkey are listed in the Grand Rapids City Directory as officers of Royal. Alexander Hompe and Ralph Tietsort were the company's officers when Robert W. Irwin purchased controlling interest in Royal in 1900. In 1919 Irwin consolidated Royal into his new Robert W. Irwin Co.

Alexander Hompe served as the company's head designer. J. Stuart Clingman designed special order furniture for the Tobey Furniture Co. in Chicago before becoming Royal's assistant designer in 1903. Clingman made his mark in the modernization of forms by Hepplewhite and Sheraton. He stayed with Royal well after its reorganization as a division of the Robert W. Irwin Co.

PRODUCTS

Royal specialized in the manufacture of dining room, living room, library, and bedroom furniture "for persons of wealth, who wish a most distinguished home culture and refinement above reproach." Pieces were expensive because of the amount of hand-painted decoration, marquetry, custom fabrics, and imported woods. Most production was in period revival styles, including Colonial, Duncan Phyfe, Sheraton, Chippendale, Hepplewhite, Adam, Spanish and Italian Renaissance, and Louis XIV and XV. Some Art Deco pieces were also introduced in the late 1920s. (For more detailed descriptions of post-1920 products, SEE Irwin, Robert W. Co.)

OTHER SOURCES

Correspondence written by Alexander Hompe between 1889 and 1920 is in the collections of The Public Museum of Grand Rapids. Some of the letters discuss the purchase of Universal Tripod and its conversion to the Royal Furniture Co.

MARKS AND LABELS

An early Royal ad shows the name of the company inside a flourished cartouche which may have served as a trademark. Royal pieces by the mid-1910s carried a metal tag depicting a bust of George Washington, which read, "ROYAL FURNITURE CO. / GRAND RAPIDS, MICH." After the 1919 buy-out, the trademark was revised to read, "ROYAL FURNITURE/ MADE BY/ ROBERT W. IRWIN CO." Sometime in the 1930s, Irwin began to make use of an eye-shaped metal tag that read simply "IRWIN."

1914

1895

1916

1926

ROYAL TABLE BED

SEE Sturgis Table Bed Co.

RYAN RATTAN CHAIR CO.
ca. 1881 - 1914

Grand Rapids, Michigan

Manufacturer of rattan baby carriages, rockers, chairs, settees, and ambulance baskets.

S.F.S. CORPORATION
1970 - present

Comstock Park, Michigan

Manufacturer of quality chairs and custom millwork on contract for other local manufacturers, including Steelcase, Inc.; Stow & Davis Furniture Co.; John Widdi-

comb Co.; Baker Furniture Co.; and Kindel Furniture Co.

ST. JOHNS, INC.   SEE St. Johns Table Co.

ST. JOHNS MANUFACTURING CO.   SEE St. Johns Table Co.

ST. JOHNS TABLE CO.
1868 - 1982

St. Johns and Cadillac, Michigan
SEE ALSO Hekman Furniture Co.

COMPANY HISTORY

1868: Founded in St. Johns, Michigan.

ca. 1880: Company sometimes listed as St. Johns Manufacturing Co.

1905: City of Cadillac, Michigan entices company to move and build a new plant in Cadillac.

1909: Advertisements claim St. Johns is the largest manufacturer of dining tables in the world, with a network of 7,700 stores retailing its products in the U.S. alone.

1978: St. Johns, Inc. is purchased by Hekman Furniture Co.

ca. 1982: Factory closes.

PERSONNEL

Before and directly after the move from St. Johns to Cadillac, George M. Petrie was president of the company. Fred Diggins, D. B. Kelly, and Charles Mitchell, all prominent Cadillac businessmen, headed St. Johns from 1906 until 1922. In 1923 George Petrie reasserted his leadership over the company. Controlling interest in St. Johns Table Co. stayed in the Petrie family from that time until 1978, when it was purchased by Hekman.

PRODUCTS

The 1880 industrial census lists the company's products as window sash, doors, blinds, and furniture. St. Johns ads in *The Michigan Artisan* from the mid-1880s through the early 20th century depict a variety of tables in walnut, mahogany, ash, and oak, including extension, breakfast, kitchen, saloon, library, parlor, office, restaurant, fall-front, and center tables, small stands, kitchen cabinets, and simple washstands. Mid-1880s tables had mostly turned, detachable legs, and were shipped "in the white" or with a natural wood finish. A line of small occasional tables had legs with faux bamboo turning.

From about 1905 to 1915, St. Johns made a large number of quarter-sawn oak pedestal tables in mostly Golden Oak but also Mission and Colonial Revival styles. The oak pieces carried a variety of finishes including Golden, Weathered, and Flanders. Since the company was partly lured to Cadillac to provide a market for its lumber mills, much of what the company produced was constructed of local woods.

In 1925 St. Johns expanded its offerings to include breakfast and dinette suites in American Revival styles. In 1928 and '29, most of the factory was turned over to the production of radio cabinets for other manufacturers. In 1931 the company returned to its production of medium-priced dinette and dining furniture.

During World War II, St. Johns produced office tables for every branch of the military, and provided dinette suites for Federal housing projects that housed wartime workers. St. Johns developed a line of bedroom furniture to complement its Early American dining furniture in 1952, but discontinued it in 1958 to again turn its full attention toward dinettes. "Solid Northern Michigan Hard Rock Maple" became the standard wood for much of its production. The use of plastics on its tables began in 1957, and grew steadily until all its tables used plastic or laminate tops. In the 1960s, a Modern line was developed as an alternative to the company's Early American offerings. In the late 1970s St. Johns produced an Early American-influenced collection for Hekman named "Wayside Oak."

MARKS AND LABELS

In 1909 the company announced a new trademark in the shape of an acorn with a picture of a pedestal table inside, and the words, "ST JOHNS/ CADILLAC/ MICH". The logo changed by at least 1952 to a circle with the name "ST. JOHNS" across the center, "ST. JOHNS TABLE COMPANY" following inside the circle top and "CADILLAC, MICHIGAN" following inside the circle bottom. This trademark was altered slightly when the company name changed, to read "ST. JOHNS, INC." at the top (exact date unknown).

Advertisement for St. Johns Table Co., *Grand Rapids Furniture Record,* June, 1909.

1909

1914

1952

SAKKERS & PEYSTER
ca. 1868 - 1871

Holland, Michigan
Makers of tables, bureaus, washstands, and wardrobes.

Successor to Sakkers and Wakker.
SEE ALSO Sakkers and Wakker.

SAKKERS & WAKKER
1865

Holland, Michigan
Cited as a furniture manufacturer in an 1865 newspaper article.
Predecessor to Sakkers and Peyster.
SEE ALSO Sakkers and Peyster.

SALMON, ARCHIBALD
1837 - 1851

Grand Rapids, Michigan
Cabinetmaker.

SAMPLE FURNITURE CO.
1901 - 1908

Grand Rapids, Michigan
Retailers of sample furniture from the Furniture Exhibition Building.

SANITARY REFRIGERATOR CO.
at least 1898 - 1899

Belding, Michigan
Manufacturer of wooden cabinet refrigerators for homes, hotels, grocers, and butchers.

SARGENT MANUFACTURING CO.
at least 1902 - 1905

Muskegon, Michigan
Manufacturer of Mission and Golden Oak-style desks, shaving stands, wardrobes, and chiffonniers.

SCHOONBECK CO.
1924 - 1956; 1969 - 1980

Grand Rapids, Michigan
Manufacturer of upholstered furniture.

SCHAFER, JOHN J.
1895 - at least 1920

Grand Rapids, Michigan
Maker of furniture. Cited in a list of manufacturers in *The Furniture Manufacturer and Artisan*, February, 1920.

SHANAHAN FURNITURE CO.
1922 - 1927

Grand Rapids, Michigan
Manufacturer of small furniture novelties, smoking sets, sewing cabinets, end tables, telephone cabinets, and coffee tables.

SHAW, H.E. FURNITURE CO.
ca. 1919 - 1933

1920

Grand Rapids, Michigan
Manufacturer of oak, walnut, and mahogany spinet desks, wall desks, secretaries, and dining room suites in Colonial and European Revival styles.

1920

SHAW - WALKER CO.
1899 - 1990

Muskegon and Norton Shores, Michigan
SEE ALSO Knoll, Inc.; Westinghouse Furniture Systems, Inc.

COMPANY HISTORY
1899: Shaw-Walker Co. incorporates.
ca. 1935: Shaw-Walker acquires Master-Craft Loose Leaf of Kalamazoo.
1951: Company is one of world's largest manufacturers of office furniture, with 15 buildings, over 1,200 employees, and 4,000 different products.
1989: Shaw-Walker is acquired by Westinghouse Furniture Systems of Grand Rapids, a subsidiary of Westinghouse Electric Corp. of Pittsburgh.
1990: Westinghouse Electric Corp. acquires Knoll International, and reorganizes both the Westinghouse Furniture Division and the former Shaw-Walker Co. as Knoll Group Companies.
1994: Production moves to nearby Norton Shores, Michigan; old facility in Muskegon closes.

PERSONNEL
Arch Wilkinson (A.W.) Shaw and Louis Carlisle (L.C.) Walker, former employees of the Fred Macey Co. of Grand Rapids, which manufactured office furnishings and sold them by mail order, moved to Muskegon in 1899 to establish the Shaw-Walker Co. In 1902 Shaw moved to Chicago to devote his time to publication of *Systems* Magazine (SEE below); Walker stayed on as head of Shaw-Walker. Walker also became involved in the writing of instructional publications about the office, authoring *The Office and Tomorrow's Business* in 1930 and *Distributed Leisure* in 1931.

L.C. Walker's son, Shaw, came to work for the family business in 1938. In 1952 Shaw Walker was named executive vice-president of the Shaw-Walker Co., and Shaw's brother-in-law, J.D. McKinney, became secretary and purchasing director. In 1958 Shaw Walker was made president. A third generation of the family took over leadership in 1982, when John Shaw Walker Spofford was made the company's C.E.O. In 1989 Spofford and his board resigned in 1989 with the purchase of Shaw-Walker by Westinghouse Furniture Systems. Leadership for the Shaw-Walker facili-

Hand-carved wall plaque depicting the "Jumping Man" logo, mid-twentieth century.

ties then fell to Dave Roberts, Westinghouse's Vice-President of Strategic Operations, who was named Head of Operations at Shaw-Walker. In 1991 he was replaced by Mike Gluhanich, who was named vice-president of operations for Knoll Group - Muskegon.

PRODUCTS

The Shaw-Walker Co.'s first product was a 9" oak filing box which held 3"x 5" file cards and alphabetical tab indexes. It was sold for $1.95 and advertised as a "complete office system." To assist customers in the use of the file card box and other office products, Shaw-Walker printed and distributed a booklet entitled *Systems*. This booklet is generally regarded as the first "house organ" to be published by a manufacturer in the U.S. *Systems* became so popular that by 1903 it was being published separately by the new A.W. Shaw Co., which had been set up just to handle its publication. The name was soon changed to *Magazine of Business*. In 1929 A.W. Shaw House merged with McGraw-Hill publishers. We still know this publication today, as *Business Week*.

By 1903 Shaw-Walker's product line had been expanded to include wooden multi-drawer file cabinets, desks, and office chairs. The company's first steel filing units were sold in 1913. The company compared the steel framework of its filing cabinets to the inner steel structure of the newly built Woolworth Building in New York City, beginning Shaw-Walker's long-standing slogan "Built like a skyscraper." Later revisions of the company's metal filing cabinet in the 1940s made it able to withstand temperatures of up to 1,700 degrees for an hour, making it an important product for fireproofing records. In 1924 the sales department began publication of a new magazine, called *Skyscraper*. In 1929 the "Skyscraper Desk" debuted, again likening its structural support to that of a skyscraper.

In 1946 Shaw-Walker introduced the "Correct Seating Chair," which it later described as the first ergonomically designed office chair. In that same year the company set a new industry standard, by producing all desks with writing surfaces at the same 29" height. By the 1950s the company claimed to produce "everything for the office except machinery." In 1970 Shaw-Walker followed the trend of other manufacturers in producing "TEMPO," its first panel-based office system. This was soon followed by the introduction of a line of computer support furniture. The company also continued to produce wooden furniture, introducing a new line of wooden executive office desks as late as 1985. When Westinghouse, then Knoll, took over production at the Shaw-Walker plants, they were converted primarily for production of their steel panel system lines.

OTHER SOURCES

Information on the company's first products is available in issues of *Systems* magazine, and later in the magazine *Skyscraper*. Some information on Shaw-Walker is available at Muskegon's Hackley Library and the Muskegon County Museum.

MARKS AND LABELS

Shaw-Walker desks and file cabinets were often marked with the company name in gold, uppercase lettering. Sometime during the 1920s, Shaw-Walker developed its famous trademark, the "Jumping Man." It depicted a salesman jumping on the opened bottom drawer of a metal filing cabinet, a tactic often employed by Shaw-Walker salesmen to prove the strength of their product. In the background behind the cabinet was the skeletal steel structure of the Woolworth Building under construction. Underneath was the slogan "Built Like a Skyscraper." Large versions of the Jumping Man logo were hand-carved and placed in Shaw-Walker showrooms around the country, where they were used as late as the 1980s. At the time of the company's sale in the late 1980s, the company used a simple, sans-serif and uppercase version of its name divided by a vertical line as its trademark.

SHAW|WALKER
1989

SHAW|WALKER
1989

SHAW|WALKER
1989

SHEAR - MADDOX FURNITURE CO.
1923 - 1934

Grand Rapids, Michigan
Manufacturer of desks, secretaries, chairs, phonographs, occasional tables, and office suites, including an Italian Renaissance office suite designed by Fred Maddox and produced from American black walnut for Japanese Emperor Hirohito. The company worked cooperatively with Wilson & Beckwith Studios and Grand Rapids Studio Furniture Co., which decorated and finished pieces produced by Shear - Maddox.
SEE ALSO Grand Rapids Studio Furniture Co.; Wilson & Beckwith Studios.

SHELTON & SNYDER FURNITURE CO.
1905 - 1910

Grand Rapids, Michigan
Manufacturer of American Empire and Tudor Revival-style bookcases, desks, music

cabinets, and dining suites in oak and mahogany.
Successor to Central Furniture Co.
SEE ALSO Central Furniture Co.

SHERWOOD MANUFACTURING CO.
founded 1885

Grand Rapids, Michigan
Manufacturer of curtain poles and easels.

SIMPLEX STORE EQUIPMENT
1949 - 1951

Grand Rapids, Michigan
Manufacturer of furniture and equipment for use in retail stores.

SKIDMORE, GEORGE C.
1872 - 1873

Grand Rapids, Michigan
Manufacturer of piano stools.

SKINNER & STEENMAN FURNITURE CO.
1898 - 1905

Grand Rapids, Michigan
Manufacturer of "French" (Golden Oak) and Dutch Mission sideboards, buffets, and cellarets, with inset Delft tiles depicting Dutch boys and girls in peasant costume.

SLAWSON, HIRAM
ca. 1848

Greenville, Michigan
Cabinetmaker.

SLIGH, CHARLES R. CO. / SLIGH FURNITURE CO.
1880 - 1932; 1933 - present

Holland, Zeeland, and Grand Rapids, Michigan
SEE ALSO Grand Rapids Chair Co.; Ply-Curves, Inc.; Sligh Furniture Co.; Trend Clock Co.

COMPANY HISTORY

1880 - 1932: Operates as Sligh Furniture Co.
1933: New Charles R. Sligh Co. founded with assets from Sligh Furniture Co.
1940: Company purchases additional factory in Zeeland, Michigan; name changes to Sligh - Lowry Furniture Co.
1945 - 1962: Sligh - Lowry operates Grand Rapids Chair Co. in Grand Rapids.
1951: Company forms Ply-Curves, Inc.
1953 - ca. 1974: Company operates Sligh - Lowry Contract Furniture Co. subsidiary.
1968: Name changes to Sligh Furniture Co.; Trend Clock Co. becomes a division of Sligh.

PERSONNEL

The Charles R. Sligh Co. was started by Charles R. Sligh Jr. and O.W. Lowry, both former executives of the huge Sligh Furniture Co. which closed in 1933. Charles R. Sligh's experience as a traveling salesman and treasurer with that company complemented Lowry's knowledge of engineering and production efficiency. Their new company was opened in the former Thompson Manufacturing plant in Holland, Michigan with only 45 employees, in a deliberate attempt to operate a smaller, leaner company than their 1,500-employee predecessor. Charles R. Sligh Jr. served as president of the Grand Rapids Furniture Salesman's Club and the Grand Rapids Exposition Association in the 1930s, the National Association of Furniture Manufacturers and the Grand Rapids Furniture Manufacturers Association in the 1940s, and the Grand Rapids Furniture Makers Guild and the National Association of Manufacturers in the 1950s.

Charles R. Sligh III joined the company's sales force in 1948, and was followed by his brother Robert L. Sligh in 1954. When Charles Sligh Jr. moved to New York in 1957 to run the National Association of Manufacturers, O.W. Lowry assumed the role of president. In 1968 Lowry retired from the business and members of the Sligh family purchased his interest in the company.

Other family members continued the tradition of service to the industry. Robert L. Sligh also served in the 1970s as president of the National Association of Furniture Manufacturers and the Grand Rapids Area Furniture Manufacturers Association, and as a board member of the National Association of Manufacturers. Robert L. "Rob" Sligh, Jr. joined the company in 1983, and was made its president in 1990. Like his father and grandfather, Rob was elected president of the Grand Rapids Area Furniture Manufacturers Association in 1995.

PRODUCTS

The company's first orders came from a former Sligh Furniture Co. client, Macy's in New York, for the "Salem" bedroom suite, a line formerly produced by Sligh Furniture Co. It also manufactured a new line of inexpensive 7-drawer kneehole desks, which proved more popular with Depression-era buyers than the high-end bedroom furniture. This marked a long-term shift in production from the old company's reliance on bedroom suites to the new company's desks.

Catalog rendering of the "Cross Country" line by Sligh, ca. 1955.

CHARLES R. SLIGH
Company   Distinction at a Price
HOLLAND MICHIGAN
1937

TRADE   MARK
1941

TREND CLOCKS
by Sligh
1980

SLIGH
Lowry
1980

SLIGH
Furniture
1980

In 1937 a prototype known as the "Aqua Vitae" or "Fishbowl" desk drew considerable attention at Market. It featured fashionable Art Deco styling in an oval shape, with burl veneers, a frieze of mirrored glass, built-in radio, hidden bar, and an aquarium on either end! Unfortunately only the market samples were produced. By 1940 a number of larger kneehole desks as well as coffee and occasional tables, and a commode which concealed a fireproof safe, had been added to the company's offerings; the bedroom suites were discontinued.

During World War II the plant converted to wartime production of parts for gliders, mortar shell boxes, and cargo trailer bodies, as well as nurses' dressers and file cabinets. Due to the restriction of wood for civilian manufacturing during the war, timberland near Holland, Michigan was purchased and used to continue furniture production. At the end of the war Sligh - Lowry purchased the Grand Rapids Chair Co., to expand the line of case goods beyond desks. Some lines, especially the "High-Lo Table" and the "Cross Country Line" continued to be produced under the Grand Rapids Chair Co. name.

The Holland and Zeeland plants produced a series of high-end, traditional desks known as the "Nottingham Group." In the 1960s, desks with hand-decorated and lacquered finishes became popular, alongside patterns in production since the Depression. Traditionally styled desks for homes and offices, made from hardwood solids and veneers, remain a major portion of production today. Beginning in the 1970s, freelance designer David Warren added bookcases and credenzas to the offerings of furniture for the office. In 1989 Sligh introduced a new line of wooden executive office furniture, with 18th-century styling, called "The Corridor Group."

The Sligh - Lowry Contract Furniture Co. subsidiary produced more college dormitory furniture during its period of operation than any other manufacturer. It also produced furniture on contract for hotels, motels, and nursing homes. As contract orders declined, they were more than replaced by the increase in production of clocks by the Trend Clock division, later named Sligh Clock Co. The company has grown to become one of the top three manufacturers of grandfather clocks in the nation.

In 1980, a special Chippendale mahogany Sligh Centennial Desk and Trend 100 Centennial Clock were created, each in limited editions of 1,880, to commemorate the 100th anniversary of the founding of the original Sligh Furniture Co.

OTHER SOURCES

A collection of Sligh family papers is a part of the Michigan Historical Collections of the University of Michigan. Bulletin #29 of the Michigan Historical Collections, entitled *A Furniture Family: The Slighs of Michigan*, was written by Francis Blouin and Thomas E. Powers and published in 1980. Another illustrated history by Blouin, entitled *100 Years: A Great Beginning. Sligh Furniture Co. 1880 - 1980*, was published by the Sligh Furniture Co. in 1979.

MARKS AND LABELS

During the 1930s the trademark was a shield shape with the face of a Dutch woman wearing a traditional cap, and banners over the shield that read, "FURNITURE" and "by SLIGH". In the early 1940s it was changed to a Dutch boy dressed in wooden shoes, resting against a wall. After World War II the company adopted a more contemporary trademark, with the name "SLIGH" in slender letters, enclosed in a box. This same logo was used for the contract line between 1953 and 1974, with the addition of "Contract Furniture" in script under the Sligh name. When Trend Clock Co. was acquired, the mark changed slightly to include the word "Furniture" in script under the word "SLIGH". A logo with companion styling was designed which read "TREND/CLOCKS" in the box, with "by Sligh" in script underneath. In 1980 the company adopted a special circular centennial logo which read, "SINCE 1880 SLIGH 100TH ANNIVERSARY". By the late 1980s the name had been modified again to "Sligh" in rounded letters with no box. The Trend name was also dropped in favor of "Sligh Clocks."

SLIGH CLOCK CO.

SEE Sligh, Charles R. Co. / Sligh Furniture Co.; Trend Clock Co.

SLIGH FURNITURE CO.
1880 - 1932

Grand Rapids, Michigan
SEE ALSO Sligh, Charles R. Co. / Sligh Furniture Co.

COMPANY HISTORY
1880: Charles R. Sligh founds Sligh Furniture Co.
1883 - 1888: Sligh operates Honduras Mahogany Co.

Art Nouveau dressing table in gumwood with malachite finish, designed by John E. Brower for Sligh Furniture Co., ca. 1907.

1919

1919

1922

1922

1926

1895 - 1896: Sligh manufactures bicycles alongside furniture.

1903 - mid-1940s: Sligh operates various timber investment companies.

1932: Sligh Furniture Co. liquidates assets and closes its doors.

PERSONNEL

Charles R. Sligh founded the company in 1880, after working for Berkey & Gay as a finisher and traveling salesman since 1874. In 1883 Charles R. Sligh traveled to Central America, and established the Honduras Mahogany Co., which purchased mahogany timber in Honduras, cut it in New Orleans, and shipped it to Grand Rapids. After the economic depression of 1893, Sligh diversified his manufacturing interests into bicycles as well as furniture. The bicycle operation was merged in 1896 with another manufacturer from Ohio to form the Hamilton-Kenwood Cycle Co. Beginning in 1903 Sligh formed other lumber companies, including the Charles Sligh Timber Co., the Clark-Sligh Timber Co., and the Grand Rapids Timber Co., which invested in timberlands in the U.S. Northwest. These separate companies lasted until the late 1940s. Sligh was a founding member of the Furniture Manufacturers Association of Grand Rapids and was elected to the state senate in 1924. He remained active as president of the company until his death in 1927.

Upon the death of the company's founder, his son-in-law Norman McClave, who had been active in the company since 1907, became president, and Charles R. Sligh Jr. became treasurer. O.W. Lowry became an active voice in cutting production costs after 1929, in an attempt to keep the company solvent after the stock market crash.

Frenchman Rene Guenaux came to Sligh as a designer in 1912, and continued through the 1910s.

PRODUCTS

The company's first products were inexpensive, asymmetrical walnut bureaus with mirrors. In 1882 Sligh introduced matched bedroom suites. Sligh also made chiffoniers, wardrobes, dressers, and other bedroom occasional pieces in maple, curly birch, mahogany, and oak. Sligh bedroom suites were owned by presidents Rutherford B. Hayes and Benjamin Harrison. Sligh began making a line of case goods from Circassian walnut in 1900, and by 1908 the popular line had become a top seller.

Though never considered an "Arts and Crafts" producer, Sligh made at least one notable suite in that style. In 1907 Sligh produced a solid gumwood bedroom suite designed by John E. Brower, with a striking contrasting finish of amber and malachite green. Its functional design was completely unornamented except for circular and oval lily-of-the-valley drawer pulls, and delicate lily cut-outs on the bed. The pieces' gently rounded lines seem more akin to the Moderne movement of the late 1920s than to the other French and Colonial-influenced furniture made by Sligh in 1907.

During World War I, Sligh Furniture Co. made walnut gun stocks for the military.

By the mid-1920s Sligh billed itself as the "largest manufacturer of furniture exclusively for the bedroom in the world." From the 1910s through the mid-1920s it offered more than 80 different bedroom suites and 11 dining room suites, in a wide range of period revival styles including Sheraton, Louis XVI, Jacobean, Italian Renaissance, Austrian Baroque, and Dutch 17th Century. Several of the suites also featured an enameled or painted finish, with hand-painted decoration.

OTHER SOURCES

A collection of Sligh family papers is a part of the Michigan Historical Collections of the University of Michigan. Bulletin #29 of the Michigan Historical Collections, entitled *A Furniture Family: The Slighs of Michigan*, was written by Francis Blouin and Thomas E. Powers and published in 1980. Another illustrated history by Blouin, entitled *100 Years: A Great Beginning. Sligh Furniture Co. 1880 - 1980*, was published by the Sligh Furniture Co. in 1979.

MARKS AND LABELS

From the 1910s through the early 1930s the trademark was the name "SLIGH" in vertical serif block letters, with the "S" and H" in a larger size, over "FURNITURE CO." in small type. It was enclosed in a rectangular outline, and often overprinted with "GRAND RAPIDS MICHIGAN".

SLIGH - LOWRY CONTRACT FURNITURE CO.   SEE Sligh, Charles R. Co. / Sligh Furniture Co.

SLIGH - LOWRY FURNITURE CO.   SEE Sligh, Charles R. Co. / Sligh Furniture Co.

SMITH, JOHN L.
ca. 1834

Grand Rapids, Michigan
Chair turner.

SNIVELY, ABRAM
1849 - ca.1851

Grand Rapids, Michigan
Cabinetmaker; maker of furniture of all kinds, and ready-made coffins.

SNYDER FURNITURE CO.
ca. 1910 - 1919

Grand Rapids, Michigan
Manufacturer of dining room suites, first of plain and inlaid mahogany in Golden Oak, and Mission styles; later in American Walnut, in a variety of 18th century period revival styles.

SOMES, EDGAR R. FURNITURE CO.
1919 - 1920

Grand Rapids, Michigan
Manufacturer of chamber or bedroom furniture, constructed from solid American walnut and "rare veneers," in Louis XVI and other period revival styles.

SPALDING, KLEINHANS & CO.
1873

Grand Rapids, Michigan
Manufacturer of furniture. Listed in the Grand Rapids city directory for 1873.

SPARTA FURNITURE SHOPS, INC.

Sparta, Michigan
A division of Extensole Corp.
SEE Extensole Corp.

Sparta Furniture Shops, Inc. SPARTA, MICHIGAN
1964

SPECIAL FURNITURE CO.
1919 - 1926

Grand Rapids, Michigan
A subdivision of Standardized Furniture Co.
SEE ALSO Standardized Furniture Co.

SPENCER & BARNES CO.
at least 1874 - 1914

1913

Benton Harbor, Michigan
Originally a manufacturer of bedsteads, center tables, and hat racks; later of Mission-style suites and case pieces for the bedroom in mahogany, quarter-sawn oak, bird's-eye maple, and curly birch.

SPENCER - DUFFY CO.
1922 - 1931

1928

Grand Rapids, Michigan
Manufacturer of upholstered furniture, owned by George C. Spencer.
Predecessor to Upholstery Craft, Inc.
SEE ALSO Upholstery Craft, Inc.

STAFFORD - MUNSON CO.
late 1800s - early 1900s

Grand Rapids, Michigan
Manufacturer of quartered oak bookkeeping desks, roll-top desks, and office furniture.

STAFFORD, R. H. MANUFACTURING CO.
1917 - 1918

Ionia, Michigan
Cited in a general listing of furniture manufacturers.

STANDARD BED CO.
at least 1895

Grand Rapids, Michigan
According to a Grand Rapids fire department book, the company's factory burned in 1895.

STANDARD CABINET CO.
1895 - 1909

Grand Rapids, Michigan
Small manufacturer of case goods.

STANDARDIZED FURNITURE CO.
1919 - 1929

Grand Rapids, Michigan
Manufacturer of furniture.
SEE ALSO Special Furniture Co.

STAR FURNITURE CO.
1889 - 1890

Grand Rapids, Michigan
Manufacturer of upholstered furniture and "The Favorite Morris Bed Lounge," a reclining sofa-settee, upholstered in a variety of designs, which opens to create a bed.
Advertised in issues of *The Michigan Artisan* for 1889 and 1890.
Successor to F.E. Morris Co.
SEE ALSO Morris, F.E. Co.

STAR FURNITURE CO.

SEE Michigan Star Furniture Co.; Miller, Herman, Inc.

STAR INDUSTRIES

SEE Miller, Herman, Inc.

STEBBINS FURNITURE CO.
1887 - 1907

Sturgis, Michigan
Manufacturer of wooden living room and dining room furniture.
SEE ALSO Wilhelm Furniture Co.

Company History
1887: Company founded.
1907: Name changes to Stebbins - Wilhelm Furniture Co.
1917: Name changes to Wilhelm Furniture Co.

STEBBINS - WILHELM FURNITURE CO.

SEE Stebbins Furniture Co.; Wilhelm Furniture Co.

STEDMAN FURNITURE CO.
1934 - 1977

Stedman
1950

Grand Rapids, Michigan
Upholsterer of chairs.

STEEL FURNITURE CO.
1907 - 1932

Grand Rapids, Michigan
Manufacturer of school and theater furniture, opera chairs, church, lodge and public seating, office furniture, and metal folding chairs.
SEE ALSO Irwin Seating Co.

Company History
1907: Company founded as Steel Furniture Co.
1932: Name changes to Irwin Seating Co.
In its early history the Steel Furniture Co. sold heavily through contracts in Latin America, and was selling in North, Central and South America, Africa, and China as early as 1911.

STEELCASE , INC.
1954 - present

Grand Rapids, Michigan: headquarters
SEE ALSO Grand Rapids Fancy Furniture Co.; Macey Furniture Co.; Stow & Davis Furniture Co.; Terrell Manufacturing Co.; Turnstone

Company History
1912: Founded as the Metal Office Furniture Co. First products are made on contract for Macey Furniture Co.
ca. 1917: Metal Office severs ties to Macey Furniture Co.
ca. 1920 - 1930: Terrell Manufacturing Co. of Grand Rapids enters a cooperative venture in which it makes cabinets, lockers, and shelving to complement Metal Office furniture lines.
1922: Metal Office begins its independent dealer network, the first in the contract furniture industry.
1936: Metal Office acquires Doehler Manufacturing Co. of New York.
1940: Metal Office acquires Grand Rapids Fancy Furniture Co.
1954: Company name changes to its popular trademark, Steelcase, Inc.
1964: Steelcase acquires Attwood Corp. of Lowell, Michigan.
1965: Steelcase sales exceed all others in the office furniture industry.
1973: Joint venture agreement creates Steelcase Japan Ltd. in Osaka.
1974: Joint venture agreement creates Steelcase Strafor in Strasbourg, France; Steelcase Wood Furniture is formed in Fletcher, North Carolina.
1978: Vecta of Grand Prairie, Texas joins Steelcase Design Partnership.
1980: Steelcase Strafor acquires Polschroeder GmbH G of Dortmund, Germany.
1985: Steelcase acquires Stow & Davis, Inc. of Grand Rapids.
1986: Steelcase acquires Hedberg Data Systems, Inc. of East Windsor, Connecticut.
1987: Metro Furniture of San Francisco, California and Brayton International of High Point, North Carolina join Steelcase Design Partnership.
1988: DesignTex of Woodside, New York and Atelier International of Plainview, New York join Steelcase Design Partnership.
1989: Steelcase acquires Revest of Atlanta, Georgia. Steelcase Strafor acquires: A.F. Sistemas of Madrid, Spain; Gordon Russell of London, England; and Eurosteel of Lisbon, Portugal and Casablanca, Morocco. The Corporate Development Center, also known as the "Steelcase Pyramid," opens in suburban Kent County.
1990: Details formed as part of Steelcase Design Partnership in New York, New York.
1991: Stow Davis joins Steelcase Design Partnership.
1992: Health Design of High Point, North Carolina joins Steelcase Design Partnership.
1993: Joint venture agreements formed with Steelcase Jeraisy Ltd. in Saudi Arabia and Steelcase Modernform Co. in Bangkok, Thailand; Steelcase acquires Anderson Desk, Inc. of City of Commerce, California; Steelcase forms Steelcase Healthcare and Turnstone in Grand Rapids, and Continuum in High Point, North Carolina.

1994: Steelcase forms Steelcase on the Road in Grand Rapids.
1995: Joint venture agreement formed with Godrej and Boyce in Bombay, India.
1996: Joint venture agreement formed with Steelcase OCA in Sao Paulo, Brazil.
1997: Steelcase announces the first public sale of its stocks.

PERSONNEL

For its first two years, the list of officers for the Metal Office Furniture Co. included Alexander Hompe, president, and Fred Tobey, vice-president, of the Macey Furniture Co. of Grand Rapids. Other founding officers were Peter M. Wege (who had already received several patents for metalworking as an executive of the Safe Cabinet Co. of Marietta, Ohio) and Walter Idema, the son of a prominent local banker. After only two years, Hompe left the board of directors and was replaced as president by Peter Wege, who remained active until his death in 1947. David Hunting came to work at Metal Office in 1914, and served on its board from 1920 until 1994. Wege's knowledge of metalworking, Idema's financial abilities, and Hunting's salesmanship provided a team to steer the company for many decades.

In 1961 Wendell Davis was hired as president from outside the company. He was succeeded as president in 1966 by Robert Pew, who came to work for Steelcase in 1952. Pew assumed the position of chairman in 1974, and CEO in 1980. Frank Merlotti, another long-term employee, became president in 1980 and CEO in 1988, while Pew still retains the position of chairman at the time of this writing. Merlotti retired as president and CEO in 1990, and was replaced by furniture industry outsider Jerry Myers, who resigned in 1994. Myers was replaced as president and CEO by Steelcase insider James P. Hackett.

In 1997 Steelcase, Inc. employed 8,200 people in ten manufacturing plants in the Greater Grand Rapids area and more than 19,000 worldwide.

PRODUCTS

The Metal Office Furniture Co.'s first products were free-standing fireproof metal safes and metal filing cases. These were initially produced on contract for the Macey Furniture Co. of Grand Rapids. In 1914 the "Victor" fireproof steel wastebasket was developed. The Victor line was expanded after World War I to include metal desktop accessories.

In 1915, the small, young company was awarded the huge contract to furnish the renovated federal Customs House Tower in Boston. For this order, Metal Office introduced its first fireproof metal "601 desks." During World War I, Metal Office manufactured grained metal "Liberty Bond Boxes." In 1919 the company added steel filing cabinets to its catalog of office furniture. Even though interest in metal furniture was growing for its fireproof qualities, clients still preferred the look of wood. Consequently, Steelcase purchased wood grain roller printing machines from Grand Rapids Panel Co., and used them to give their metal furniture the appearance of oak or mahogany.

During the early 1920s Metal Office redesigned the "601" desks to include a linoleum or "lino-topped" writing surface. In that same period joint manufacturing began between Terrell and Metal Office. Terrell made all of the storage cabinets, shelving, and lockers offered with the "601" line. In 1926 Metal Office introduced its "servidor" for hotel room doors, which allowed mail or laundry to be delivered to a guest room through one door on the outside, then accessed through a second door on the inside without breach of security or privacy.

In the early 1930s Metal Office made beds and other residential furniture for Doehler Manufacturing of New York. In 1937 The Metal Office Furniture Co. was awarded the contract to produce the now-famous custom desks and chairs designed by architect Frank Lloyd Wright for the headquarters of S.C. Johnson & Co. of Racine, Wisconsin. The wooden desk tops were sub-contracted to Stow & Davis, and the tubular steel components were sub-contracted to American Seating, both of Grand Rapids. Metal Office created the sheet metal components, finished them in "Cherokee red," and completed final assembly. In 1939 Metal Office began production of its first line of chairs.

In 1941 Metal Office discontinued production of its metal roll-top desk, a popular model since 1914. Use of metal for civilian production was curtailed, but was more than replaced by orders from the U.S. Navy for "Shipboard Furniture," including metal office furnishings, officer's chairs, and even bunk beds and military chaplain's pulpits. In fact, the Japanese surrender on the *U.S.S. Missouri* took place atop a Steelcase mess table!

Steelcase "C" series chair, ca. 1950.

1928

STEELCASE INC
1956

STEELCASE INC
Grand Rapids, Michigan
In Canada: Canadian Steelcase Co., Ltd., Don Mills, Ontario
1959

STEELCASE
1968

1977

After World War II, Metal Office applied what it had learned from the military, namely the use of standard sizes and interchangeable parts, in its "Multiple 15" desk series. The company also introduced a civilian version of its military "C" chair line, which remained in constant production until 1979. Images of large open office "pools," filled with rows of workers at Multiple 15 desks and C chairs, came to epitomize the post-war corporate world.

In the early 1950s the grey "Multiple 15" line got a new look with mist green, desert sage, autumn haze, and blond tan: colors inspired by the desert, known as "Sunshine Styling." In 1952 the line was expanded with "Convertibles," a system of flexible work surfaces, cabinets and tables. The design of the "Flightline" series introduced in 1956 was inspired by the look of new aerospace technology. The "1300 Line" introduced in 1959 and the "2200 Line" which succeeded it in the early 1960s were completely rectilinear, with polished steel frames, laminate writing surfaces, and convertible extensions. Special furniture for data processing, called "Datacase," went into production in 1961.

Beginning in the early 1960s, several lines moved closer to the notion of the open office environment. "Convertiwalls" featured steel or textured glass panels that slid into slotted uprights, which were wired for phones and electricity. "Mobiles," introduced in 1967, featured flexible storage cabinets and wall panels that could be arranged as room dividers, creating an open office system. This series was replaced in 1972 by "Movable Walls," Steelcase's first office system that hung work surfaces and storage units from hinged panels. It was followed in 1973 by another panel-based system, "Series 9000," which has become the best-selling office furniture system ever. "Context" systems furniture, introduced in 1989, replaced cubicles with curving shapes and work stations that flow one into the next.

In the 1980s and '90s, Steelcase seating was ergonomically designed. The "ConCentrx" chair, which went into production in 1980, was the first chair specifically designed for the worker in an electronic office. The "Sensor" chair, introduced in 1986, was the industry's first to come in three distinct sizes. The 1994 "Rapport" chair featured an adjustable lumbar support pillow and fingertip ergonomic controls.

In 1997 Steelcase offered the most extensive line of products in the contract furniture industry with more than 70,000 different models of furniture, including 6 lines of systems furniture, 34 lines of seating, 14 lines of desks, 6 lines of bookcases, 10 lines of filing cabinets, and 8 lines of task lighting.

OTHER SOURCES

Steelcase, Inc. maintains its own archives of catalogs, photos, and other materials. Steelcase published its periodical for Steelcase users, called *Steelcase Circle*, beginning in 1953. Much of the information in this section is from an illustrated anniversary history entitled *Steelcase The First 75 Years*, researched by Grand Rapids city historian Gordon Olson in 1987.

MARKS AND LABELS

The first safes produced by Metal Office for Macey were marked with an ellipse surrounding the words, "MACEY/ Inter-Inter/ SAFE". The "Victor" trademark appears in fanciful script on the company's early wastebaskets. The tradename "Steelcase" first made its appearance on Metal Office Furniture Co. files in 1920. The name typically appeared on a rectangular tag which read "STEELCASE" in block letters over "Business Equipment" in italics. Items labeled "Terrell" were made by Terrell Manufacturing between circa 1920 and 1930. After 1930 Terrell became a Metal Office trademark for shelving, cabinets, and lockers. In 1925 the Steelcase name began to be placed on desks. Through the 1950s and '60s a variety of stylized "S" designs were used as company trademarks. Steelcase adopted its "spectrum logo," with the name Steelcase in a rainbow of colors, in 1978.

STEIL, A. WOOD TURNING WORKS	SEE Steil Manufacturing Co.
STEIL MANUFACTURING CO. 1919 - 1935	Grand Rapids, Michigan Manufacturer of tables; jobbers (producers by contract) of wood turnings, twists, novelties, legs, and jig sawing for other manufacturers.
STERLING DESK CO. at least 1909 - 1917	Grand Rapids, Michigan Manufacturer of furniture. Cited in a general listing of furniture manufacturers.
STERLING FURNITURE CO. at least 1895	Grand Haven, Michigan Manufacturer of case pieces for the bedroom in birch, bird's-eye maple, and ma-

hogany, and sideboards, china closets, and extension tables for the dining room in Antique, Golden, and Flemish Oak. Advertised in *The Furniture Buyer's Record* for 1895.

STERLING FURNITURE CO.
1926 - 1934

1928

Grand Rapids, Michigan
Manufacturer of occasional tables and small case pieces including table desks, wall desks, bookcases, cabinets and spinet desks, and novelties such as golf tees and chess pieces. In 1928 they introduced a Queen Anne Revival-style "secretary-desk" based on early upright piano designs, and designed by Webster E. Janssen. Its 58-note keyboard slid into place for music, or could be hidden in exchange for a writing surface. The case featured the drawers and bookcases of a secretary, as well as strings, sounding board, and even a player-piano mechanism.

STEVENSON, J. LUZERNE
at least 1873

Grand Rapids, Michigan
Specialized in the manufacture of lounges.

STICKLEY BROTHERS FURNITURE CO.
1891 - 1954

Grand Rapids, Michigan
SEE ALSO Conti, T.A. Co.; Forest Craft Guild; Forslund, Carl Co.

COMPANY HISTORY
1891: Albert and John George found Stickley Brothers Furniture Co. in Grand Rapids.
1897 - 1902: Company opens factory and wareroom in London, England, to supply the European market.
1917 - 1918: Factory is converted to wartime production during WWI.
1954: Company closes; Carl Forslund Co. continues to produce some Stickley Bros. pieces.

PERSONNEL
Albert and John George were two of the five Stickley brothers who made furniture in the United States. All came from a furniture manufacturing background, and had worked together in an earlier company also named Stickley Brothers Furniture Co. which had operated in upstate New York under brothers Gustav, Albert, and Charles. Brothers Gustav and Leopold opened their own company, United Crafts, in 1899. Gustav eventually opened Craftsman Workshops, and became one of the leading proponents of the Arts and Crafts Movement in America. John George left Stickley Brothers and Grand Rapids in 1900, and in 1902 co-founded the L. and J.G. Stickley Furniture Co. in New York with brother Leopold. Albert remained the head of the Stickley Brothers Furniture Co. in Grand Rapids until his death in 1928.

During its early period of production, Stickley Brothers amassed a notable list of craftsmen and designers. The company employed Italian carver Leopold Baillot for three years prior to the introduction of its Mission lines around 1900. Timothy Conti produced marquetry for several of Stickley Brothers' early Arts and Crafts lines, and operated his business (T.A. Conti and Co.) out of the Stickley Brothers' factory. Forrest Mann likely trained some of Stickley Brothers' Turkish and Russian copper artisans, and may have also produced some of their hand-wrought hardware designs. James M. Seino headed Stickley Brothers' decorative painting department from 1914 through 1938. He received his training from the Imperial Academy in Tokyo, and studied art in Paris and New York before becoming the first Japanese resident of Grand Rapids. David Robertson Smith served as Stickley Brothers' staff designer between 1902 and 1915, overseeing most of their Mission lines. Arthur Teal served as staff designer from 1908 to 1911, and again from 1920 to 1924, and 1927 to 1936.

PRODUCTS
Stickley Brothers began as producers of occasional chairs and fancy tables in a wide variety of styles, ranging from Colonial Revival to early Mission designs introduced in 1900. The "Bewdley" line, designed by D. Robertson Smith in 1902, drew influence from the English and Scottish Arts and Crafts Movements. It featured attenuated, stylized floral inlay, which contrasted sharply with the rectilinear forms. By 1903 the "Quaint Mission" line was also in full production. Its lines were blocky with little decoration, except for hand-wrought copper hardware and Spanish tanned leather upholstery. A Stickley Brothers Mission dining room suite won a grand prize at the 1904 World's Fair in St. Louis. After 1904 these influences were merged into the "Quaint Arts and Crafts" line, which was produced for nearly a decade. The "Quaint Manor" line, introduced in 1914, featured slender Austrian

Stickley Brothers Mission arm chair, originally installed in a cafe at the Pantlind Hotel, 1902.

1900

1902

1903

1917

1924

1926

1928

1928

1937

Modern lines, cut-outs, and caned panels.

The company began its stylistic shift away from Arts and Crafts as early as 1909, when straight Mission legs were replaced by heavy turned ones, transforming Quaint Mission into "Quaint Tudor." The company advertised mostly "modernized period styles" by the mid-1910s. These included adaptations of Italian, English, and Early American styles in suites and novelty pieces such as tea carts.

With the arrival of James Seino and other Japanese artisans in 1914, the company also began to offer period revival styles with lacquered or painted finishes and Japanese decoration. The "Quaint American" line of the early 1920s featured naturally finished or polychrome painted Windsor and ladder-back chairs, gate-leg tables, and case pieces that combined elements from a number of American Colonial styles. The "Adam Colonial" line, introduced in 1925, was a somewhat informal adaptation of 18th-century English and American forms, painted in shades of ivory, "peacock," and "colonial" blue. The "Peasant" line, introduced in that same year, was designed to evoke the feeling of folk furniture from Central Europe, and came in painted shades of grey and green.

Stickley Brothers continued to produce adaptations of less formal or provincial Colonial American pieces from the 1920s until it ceased production in the 1950s.

OTHER SOURCES

A number of Stickley Brothers catalogs have been reprinted. Several original catalogs, including a 1903 Quaint Arts and Crafts, are in the collections of The Public Museum of Grand Rapids. Don Marek's *Arts and Crafts Furniture Design: The Grand Rapids Contribution, 1895 - 1915* includes useful information on the company's Mission production. Numerous books and articles have been written about the products of the various companies operated by all the brothers Stickley. Most pay an overabundance of attention to the work of Gustav, though they often provide interesting comparisons of designs by the three major Stickley companies.

MARKS AND LABELS

The Stickley Brothers used a variety of marks, including paper labels, burned-in marks, and brass tags. Marek's catalog cites a gold-colored decal and an oval felt or cardboard tag as their earliest. Burn marks appear occasionally on Arts and Crafts pieces from a range of dates. Most common was a brass tag featuring their signature Art Nouveau "Quaint" logo. Still other pieces were impressed with a mark bearing the company name and "Grand Rapids" in upper case.

Since the company continued to use the "Quaint" brand name for period revival production, its mark changed only slightly. Pieces from the late 1910s and early 1920s are labeled "QUAINT AMERICAN FURNITURE/ STICKLEY BROTHERS CO." and bear the same Art Nouveau trademark. Labels from the late 1920s replace the words "AMERICAN FURNITURE" with "FURNITURE OF CHARACTER".

STOCKWELL & DARRAGH FURNITURE CO.
1883 - 1884

Grand Rapids, Michigan
Manufacturer of furniture in walnut, ash, and maple, and the "Morley Patent Folding Bed." Employed Harvey N. Hall as superintendent and designer.

STONE, GEORGE L., INC.
1924 - 1931

Grand Rapids, Michigan
Manufacturer of upholstered furniture.

STONE - HOULT FURNITURE CO., THE
1919 - 1929

1924

Grand Rapids, Michigan
Manufacturer of medium- and high-grade upholstered chairs, sofas, and davenports in walnut and polychromed wood during the 1910s and '20s. Mostly Italian Renaissance, with other period revival styles. Marketed through other companies associated with William A. Hoult.
SEE ALSO Grand Rapids Furniture Shops, The; Grand Rapids Table Co.

STORE EQUIPMENT CO.
ca. 1950

Grand Rapids, Michigan
Manufacturer of store equipment.

STORY & CLARK PIANO CO.
1895 - 1984

Headquarters and showrooms: Chicago, Illinois. American factory: Grand Haven, Michigan.
SEE ALSO Bergsma Brothers Co.

COMPANY HISTORY
1881: Story & Clark Organ Co. founded in Chicago.
1892 - 1893: Additional factories open in England and Germany.

1895: Story & Clark Piano Co. is founded and incorporated.
1900: Story & Clark Piano Co. takes over U.S. organ production from Story & Clark Organ Co.
1901: Grand Haven factory opens; additions follow in 1905 and 1923.
1984: Company purchased by Norlin Industries, Inc. Company consolidates with Bergsma Brothers of Grand Rapids. Grand Haven plant closes.
ca. 1990: Rights to the name "Story & Clark" sold to a company in Seneca, Pennsylvania.

PERSONNEL

In 1857 Hampton L. Story began to manufacture organs in Burlington, Vermont. A decade later he moved his company to Chicago. In 1881 he merged his company with that of Melville Clark, to form Story & Clark Organ Co. Clark developed the pneumatic player roll for player pianos, and left Story & Clark to start his own company around 1900. Directorship of the company continued in the Story family for three generations.

Story & Clark's post-Depression pianos were designed by Everett Washington. The laminated mahogany sounding board was a key post-World War II invention designed by Charles F. Stein.

PRODUCTS

While still in Vermont, the company produced Story Pianos and Temple Organs, made pianos on contract for Steinway, Weber, and Behning and Klix, and published sheet music and the *Vermont Musical Journal*. Piano forms changed from square pianos to small consoles, spinets, and grands; styles included Sheraton, Louis XV, Chippendale, French Provincial, and Modern. Sales of pianos declined in the 1920s due to the rise of popularity of radios, so Story & Clark briefly contracted to make radio cabinets for RCA until the market crashed in 1929.

In 1935 Story & Clark introduced the "Storytone," the world's first commercially produced electronic piano. World War II halted the manufacture of pianos, which was replaced by production of parts for military gliders and cargo planes. After WWII the company began production of pianos with its unique laminated mahogany sounding board. The merger of Story & Clark with QRS Music Rolls, Inc., which traces its beginnings to the company started by Clark in 1900, made it the only company in the world that still produces perforated roll player pianos.

OTHER SOURCES

The Tri-Cities Historical Museum in Grand Haven, Michigan, has some archival materials on Story & Clark.

MARKS AND LABELS

Through most of its history, the Story & Clark name has been marked in gold on the front of the piano console, above the keyboard. In the 1990s the corporate trademark consisted of an intertwined, uppercase script "S" and "C".

STOW & DAVIS FURNITURE CO.
1885 - present

Grand Rapids and Kentwood, Michigan
SEE ALSO Grand Rapids Desk Co.; Steelcase, Inc.; Stow & Haight Furniture Co.

COMPANY HISTORY

1885: George A. Davis purchases Thomas Haight's interest in Stow & Haight; name changes to Stow & Davis.
1928: Company acquires Grand Rapids Desk Co.
1936: Company recapitalizes and reorganizes.
1953 - ca. 1962: Stow & Davis organizes "Executive Furniture Guild," with exclusive dealerships offering a complete line of decorator services along the lines of the Grand Rapids Furniture Makers Guild.
ca. 1955: Stow & Davis adds former Phoenix furniture factory to its downtown campus.
1985: Steelcase, Inc. acquires Stow & Davis Furniture Co.
1988: Stow & Davis opens million-plus-square-foot plant in Kentwood, Michigan; closes downtown Grand Rapids plants.
1991: Stow & Davis acquires Interior Woodworking Corp. of New Paris, Indiana, and Wigand Corp. of Colorado Springs, Colorado and Avon Lakes, Ohio.
1992: Kentwood plant and wooden office furniture lines are placed under the Steelcase Wood Division name. Upholstered lines, architectural woodwork and custom furniture for offices, hotels, and homes remains under the name Stow/Davis. Headquarters remain in Grand Rapids, but production moves to

newly acquired plants in Indiana, Colorado, and Ohio.

PERSONNEL

The company was originally formed by the partnership of Russell Stow and Thomas Haight. Stow, who also served as mayor of Grand Rapids, retired in 1907. Haight sold his share to George Davis in 1885. Davis remained an officer of the company until 1922. Edgar W. Hunting became an officer of the company in 1896. The firm was reorganized in 1936 by Peter J. Wege, Walter Idema, and David D. Hunting, all of whom also played an important role in the establishment of Steelcase, Inc. Also involved in the 1936 reorganization was Robert Bennett, who served as president into the 1960s, and expanded the company's offerings in the area of total interior decoration planning.

Edgar R. Somes, a prominent Grand Rapids designer, created some designs for Stow & Davis circa 1900 - 1901. Arthur E. Teal, who also served as a designer for Stickley Brothers, designed for Stow & Davis in 1918 and 1919. Giacomo "Jack" Buzzitta began working for Stow & Davis in 1936, and became the first full-time product designer on staff of an office furniture manufacturer. In addition to his role as head designer, which he held until his retirement in 1975, he also produced some of the miniature sales samples which were carried by company salesmen. George Reinoehl designed the 1960s walnut and chrome "Predictor" line. Interior designer Alexis Yermakov was commissioned in the late 1960s to create the "Electa Series." Don T. Chadwick designed Stow & Davis' award winning "Series 1000" line of occasional tables, sofas, and chairs, which was introduced in 1973.

PRODUCTS

The company began as a manufacturer of kitchen and dining extension tables. In 1889 the company produced its first custom and production boardroom tables, a product which remained one of the company's specialties for more than a century. By the 1890s Stow & Davis offered a large range of library, office, and dining tables, including oak pedestal tables. A 1907 article in *The Grand Rapids Furniture Record* described Stow & Davis as "the largest exclusive table house making medium and high grade dining and office tables."

A 1911 article from the *Grand Rapids Herald* states that no hand carvers were employed at the factory, because of the "remarkable simplicity" of its machine-made tables. Circa 1916 advertisements promoted Stow & Davis's ability to produce suites of bank furniture for major clients. They generally included large Adam or Colonial Revival style boardroom tables, wood and leather executive and swivel chairs, and traditional wooden desks in oak or "dull" mahogany.

In 1928 Stow & Davis introduced the first wood and steel framework desk in the wood furniture industry. This method of construction was soon incorporated into all its bank and office furniture suites. Lines with names like Grand Rapids, Kent, Nottingham, Colonial, Baronial, Georgian, Adam, Jacobean, Gothic, and Florentine were made of walnut, mahogany, and oak during the 1920s and '30s, in traditional period revival styles.

Developed in the late 1930s, the Harwood, Croyden, Rapide, Metro, Beacon, Moderne, and Progression lines, and successive versions produced in the 1950s and '60s known as Progression II and III, featured wooden case pieces in walnut or blonde satin finish and leather chairs or sectional seating. All of these lines were characterized by Art Moderne lines, curved tops, rounded corners, and streamlined hardware. The related Nordic suite was made with bleached or gray-silver mahogany veneers. During World War II Stow & Davis manufactured functional wooden desks, chairs, and even bunk beds for naval vessels.

The Custom Executive, Predictor, Sigma, and Transition office groups of the 1950s and '60s consisted of International Modern style free-standing desks, credenzas, conference tables, and occasional pieces of wood with exposed steel frames, chrome hardware, and leather or fabric upholstered seating. The American Colonial, Italian Classic, Kent, York, Georgian, and Sherwood lines continued the offering of more conservative mahogany or walnut executive furniture, with historical English or Italian influences.

The biomorphic "Bubble Chair," produced between 1965 and 1970, had a rounded nylon upholstered form on a chrome or aluminum pedestal base. The "Electa Series" was introduced circa 1968, and featured free-standing pieces with rigid International Modern chromed steel frames, which supported interchangeable panels of walnut, textured vinyl, or smoked glass. Harty desks, designed by M. F.

Board table and chairs by Stow-Davis for the Director Room, Union Central Life Insurance Co., Cincinnati, Ohio, ca. 1935.

1911

1914

1937

1945

STOW/DAVIS
1980

1989

Harty circa 1974, featured massive slabs of rounded walnut floating atop a base of mirror chrome steel. The "Triangle" chair, designed by Robert DeFuccio and produced from 1975 to 1985, won numerous awards for its continuous triangular frame of bent plywood.

The "Free-Dimensional" furniture and wall system, and related "Cube Desk" series, were designed by Warren H. Snodgrass, and introduced in 1974. Finished in a combination of wood veneers, plastic laminates, metals, and fabrics, these were the first open office plan lines offered by Stow & Davis.

OTHER SOURCES

The Public Museum of Grand Rapids has a large archival collection which includes catalogs, furniture plates, awards, upholstery samples, and other materials relating to Stow & Davis, as well as many pieces of Stow & Davis furniture and sales-sample miniatures. The Public Museum also owns The Jack Buzzitta Archival Collection, which includes many plates, design drawings, and interior photos of bank and corporate installations by their most notable designer.

MARKS AND LABELS

In the 1910s the company name was printed in upper-case block letters, with the ends of the first and last "S" extending above and below the name, containing "GRAND RAPIDS" and "MICHIGAN". During the 1930s and early 1940s the name was adapted to italicized upper-case block letters, with the ends of each "S" still extending above and below the name. After World War II the "S" and "D" were printed in script, and the lines above and below the name ceased to be connected to the letters. Pieces manufactured between 1953 and 1962 may carry the trademark of the Executive Furniture Guild of America, with the emblem of an eagle surrounded by the words "Prestige, Character and Integrity". Stow & Davis's logo from the 1950s until 1985 was a streamlined upper-case "S" attached to a "D". After Steelcase's acquisition of Stow/Davis in 1985, all Steelcase wood products were sold under the Stow/Davis or Stow & Davis name. In 1992 the ampersand was dropped from the name.

STOW & HAIGHT FURNITURE CO.
1880 - 1885

Grand Rapids, Michigan
Manufacturer of kitchen and dining extension tables.
Predecessor to Stow & Davis Furniture Co.
SEE ALSO Stow & Davis Furniture Co.

STRAAYER INDUSTRIES
1949 - 1963

Grand Rapids, Michigan
Manufacturer of custom wood products and upholstery frames.

STRAHAN & LONG FURNITURE CO.
1886 - 1891

Grand Rapids, Michigan
Manufacturer of parlor suites and lounges for wholesale only.
Incorporated as Grand Rapids Parlor Chair Co. in 1891.
SEE ALSO Grand Rapids Parlor Chair Co.; Mueller & Slack Co.

STRATFORD SHOPS, INC., THE
1951 - 1958

Grand Rapids, Michigan
Manufacturer of upholstery frames for Michigan Furniture Shops. Eventually merged with Barnard & Simonds Co.
SEE ALSO Barnard & Simonds Co.; Michigan Furniture Shops.

STRUCTURAL CONCEPTS CORP.
1972 - 1986

Spring Lake, Michigan
Manufacturer of office work stations and bakery cases. In 1986 the office furniture division was merged with Interior Concepts Corp. to create Interior Specialists.
SEE ALSO Interior Concepts Corp.; Interior Specialists.

STUART, C. D.
at least 1889 - 1890

Otsego, Michigan
Manufacturer of fine and fancy rocking, dining, and reception chairs with turned components and upholstered or cane seats. Upholstered designs included back cushions tacked directly over turned back spindles, in scallop or crescent moon designs. Advertised in *The Michigan Artisan* in 1889 and 1890.

STUART FURNITURE CO.
1922 - 1929

1924

Grand Rapids, Michigan
Manufacturer of walnut, mahogany, maple, and decorated (painted) bedroom case furniture in Early American, Louis XVI, Duncan Phyfe, and Colonial Revival styles.
Successor to Davies-Putnam Co.
SEE ALSO Davies-Putnam Co.

STUART, JOHN, INC.
at least 1934 - 1956

JOHN STUART INC.
NEW YORK · GRAND RAPIDS
1935

Factory and showroom: Grand Rapids, Michigan. Showroom: New York. Grand Rapids city directories only list the company showroom in Grand Rapids from 1948 through 1956. Even though a John Stuart, Inc. catalog speaks of its factory in Grand Rapids, and pieces sold by the company bore its trademark, John Stuart, Inc. seems to have been a high-end designers' showroom for Early English, Georgian, American, and French Revivals and reproductions, as well as Modern residential furniture, made in a number of Grand Rapids factories.

STURDY CUT NOVELTY CO.
1932

Grand Rapids, Michigan
Manufacturer of wood novelties.

STURGES - AULSBROOK - JONES CORP.
1933 - 1944

Sturgis, Michigan
Manufacturer of furniture; converted to war-time production during WWII.
SEE ALSO Aulsbrook-Jones-Grobhiser Co.
COMPANY HISTORY
1933: Formed as a reorganization of the bankrupt Aulsbrook-Jones-Grobhiser Co.
1944: Last listing in Sturgis directory.

STURGIS TABLE BED CO.
1914

ROYAL TABLE BED
1914

Sturgis, Michigan
Manufacturer of the "Royal Table Bed" for bachelors' apartments, hotels, and Y.M.C.A.s. Consists of a Mission-style oak desk or library table with false center drawers, which fold down to allow a metal cot with cotton mattress to pull out. Advertised in *The Grand Rapids Furniture Record* in 1914.

STYLEMASTER AMERICA, INC.
1977 - present

Grand Rapids, Michigan
Manufacturer of mid-range interior and exterior upholstery frames for custom upholstery shops, and upholstery frames for office, institutional, and hospitality contract manufacturers.
Successor to V&M Manufacturing and Stylemaster H&J in 1994.

STYLEMASTER H & J

SEE Stylemaster America, Inc.

SUPERIOR CABINET CO.
at least 1927 - 1928

Muskegon, Michigan
Manufacturer of medium- and high-grade dining and bedroom furniture.

SUPERIOR CARVED MOULDING CO.
1905 - 1931

Grand Rapids, Michigan
Manufacturer of carved moldings.
Successor to Grand Rapids Carved Moulding & Manufacturing Co.

SUPERIOR FURNITURE CO.
1936 - present

1971

Lowell, Michigan
Manufacturer of solid cherry tables, end tables, consoles, and cocktail tables in 18th-century revival styles. Manufactured all the accessory pieces for the retail store and catalog sales divisions of Carl Forslund Furniture until circa 1965. Circa 1991 Superior also introduced a line of Shaker-style residential furniture.

SUPERIOR MANUFACTURING CO.
at least 1912

Muskegon, Michigan
Manufacturer of church furniture in oak, some with leather upholstery, including pews, altars, altar rails, pulpits and lecterns, pulpit benches, baptismal fonts, confessionals, and hymn boards. Also manufacturer of side chairs, opera chairs, and folding chairs in oak and maple, flat-top and roll-top desks, bookcases, and scientific equipment. Described in a 1912 catalog.

SWEET & BIGGS FURNITURE CO.
1906 - 1909

Grand Rapids, Michigan
Makers of medium-priced upholstered furniture in mahogany, including sofas, divans, davenports, odd chairs, rockers, Turkish rockers, and "Fireside wing chairs" in period revival styles.

SWEET, MARTIN L. BEDSTEAD MANUFACTORY
at least 1883 - 1890

Grand Rapids, Michigan
Manufacturer of bedsteads.
COMPANY HISTORY
1883: Listed at Winegar's Furniture Store Building.
1890: Factory destroyed by fire.

TADD INDUSTRIES, INC.
1973 - present

TADD INDUSTRIES
1239 COMSTOCK STREET
MARNE, MICHIGAN 49435
1978

Marne, Michigan
Manufacturer of wooden children's furniture, including cradles, folding potty chairs, dressing tables, footstools, and doll furniture; daybeds, motel chairs, and grandfather clocks; wooden components for contract furniture and bathroom cabinet

manufacturers, and bowling ball display stands for Brunswick.

TAYLOR CARVING, INC.
1972 - present

Grand Rapids, Michigan
Contract duplicators of carvings and carved parts for the residential furniture industry.

TERRELL EQUIPMENT CO.

SEE Terrell Manufacturing Co.

TERRELL MANUFACTURING CO.
1908 - 1930

Grand Rapids, Michigan
Manufacturer of metal office furniture.
SEE ALSO Steelcase, Inc.
After World War I Terrell entered into a cooperative manufacturing and sales agreement managed by the Metal Office Furniture Co. (Steelcase), in which it manufactured shelving, cupboards, storage cabinets, and lockers to complement Metal Office's "601 Series" desks and "Victor" accessories, and sanitary household food storage cabinets. While Terrell ceased to be a separate company in 1930, Steelcase continued to make shelving and cabinets in the same factory and with the Terrell name through much of the 1930s.

THOMPSON, DONALD C.
1950 - 1975

Grand Rapids, Michigan
Maker of 18th-century American Colonial Revival reproductions of tea caddies, Windsor chairs, and especially veneered looking glasses with carved or cast and gilt medallions, for exclusive retailers and interior designers.
MARKS AND LABELS
Pieces may carry a label or a hammer-punched mark.

Thompson
DESIGNERS AND MANUFACTURERS OF FINE FURNITURE
1960

THOMPSON MANUFACTURING CO.
1910 - 1934

Holland, Michigan
Manufacturer of plumber's woodwork and supplies; novelty and occasional pieces, including tables, magazine racks, plant stands, tabourets, bedside tables, and umbrella racks in Mission style. Some designs are derivative of nearby C.P. Limbert Co. In 1916 Thompson was making "Period Library Suites" in William and Mary, Charles II, Adam, and Mission styles, in walnut, oak, and mahogany. The company's tradename was "Craftstyl."

THOMPSON, STACEY
ca. 1920

Manistee, Michigan
Designer and maker of patented free-standing, collapsible clothing rack.

THWAITES FURNITURE CO.
1919 - 1924

THWAITES FURNITURE CO. PIONEER ALBION MICHIGAN
1924

Grand Rapids and Albion, Michigan
Manufacturer of furniture.
May have moved to Albion, Michigan in 1924.
Successor to Valley City Chair Co. and Grand Rapids Fibre Furniture Co.
SEE ALSO Grand Rapids Fiber Furniture Co.; Valley City Chair Co.

TIMBERLINE, INC.
1959 - ca. 1985

Grand Rapids, Michigan
Contract furniture manufacturer for the hospitality (hotel and motel) industry.
SEE ALSO Harding Parlor Frame Co.; Johnson Furniture Co.; RoseJohnson, Inc.
Timberline purchased Harding Parlor Frame Co. in 1960. Timberline merged with Johnson Furniture Co. in 1963. Timberline name continued as line of hotel-motel furniture manufactured by Johnson and RoseJohnson until circa 1985.

Timber~Line Inc.
1982

TOENIGK, FREDERICK M.
1856 - 1900

Greenville, Michigan
Retailer and cabinetmaker.

TOURIST FOLDING COT CO.
at least 1886 - 1888

Grand Rapids, Michigan
Manufacturer of the "Tourists' Folding Cot," patented in 1886, and consisting of stretched fabric over a metal and four-ply white birch veneer frame, for use by excursion steamers, hotels, military encampments, and campers.

TOWNSEND MANUFACTURING CO.
at least 1952 - 1956

TOWNSEND TMC ZEELAND, MICH. SHOWROOMS Grand Rapids MANUFACTURING COMPANY
1952

Zeeland, Michigan
Manufacturer of "unusually designed quality furniture, reproductions of imported & antique furniture."

TRADEX, INC.

SEE Miller, Herman, Inc.

TRAVERSE CITY REFRIGERATOR CO.
1919: Liquidated due to fire.

Traverse City, Michigan
Manufacturer of refrigerators.

TREND CLOCK CO.
1937 - present

1954

TRENDWAY CORP.
1968 - present

1994

Private and Open Office Environments
1987

TRENK, GEORGE
ca. 1890

TROMP, MARTIN / TROMP MANUFACTURING CO.
1902 - 1924; 1908 - 1916

TURNHAM & BUDDINGTON
ca. 1862

TURNSTONE, a Steelcase Company
1993 - present

turnstone
1993

TYLER REFRIGERATION CORP.
1953 - present

UNILINE, SUBSIDIARY OF HOLIDAY INNS, INC.
ca. 1970

UNION FURNITURE CO.
ca. 1883 - 1886

Zeeland, Michigan
SEE ALSO Sligh, Charles R. Co. / Sligh Furniture Co.
COMPANY HISTORY
1937 - 1968: Small manufacturer of desk and mantel clocks, Early American wall clocks, and wooden novelties.
1968 - present: As a division of Sligh Furniture Co., company manufactures mantel, carriage, grandfather, and regulator clocks designed by David Warren, in historical Dutch and English as well as Modern styles.

Holland, Michigan
SEE ALSO Haworth, Inc.
Manufacturer of open office systems and floor-to-ceiling partitions.
COMPANY HISTORY
1968: Company founded.
1973: Purchased by George, Donald, and James Heeringa.
1976: Trendway purchases Modern Partitions' (now Haworth) floor-to-ceiling partition line. Trendway's original and flagship product is "TrendWall," a gypsum-based, steel framed floor-to-ceiling panel system that is used to create interior walls.
1979: Company adds "Space Management Systems" (SMS), a panel-based open office systems furniture line. Trendway also develops "TrendCentre," a cluster work station that can be configured in different geometric arrangements, along with another office system named "Choices," and the "Prelude Seating Group."

Holland, Michigan
Manufacturer of center tables, furniture trimmings, and small stands.

Holland, Michigan
COMPANY HISTORY
1902 - 1924: Picture framer.
1908 - 1916: Manufacturer of furniture, novelties, picture frames, mirrors, tabourets, pedestals, etc., at the same address as the frame shop.

Grand Rapids, Michigan
Makers of "Cheap chairs sold at auction in Milwaukee."

Grand Rapids, Michigan
Designers and marketers of a line of furniture manufactured by Steelcase for small business and home offices. The company strategy was to sell through some existing dealers, as well as by catalog and "800" number.
SEE ALSO Steelcase, Inc.

Niles, Michigan
Originally manufacturer of metal display stands and racks, produce racks, and tire display stands. In the 1930s the company added ice- and vapor-cooled fish and meat display fixtures. The company later expanded to produce all types of commercial refrigeration fixtures.
SEE ALSO Dry-Kold Refrigerator Co.
COMPANY HISTORY
1927: Company begins as Tyler Sales Fixture Co. in Muskegon Heights, Michigan.
1933: Company moves to Niles, Michigan.
1935: Company acquires Dry-Kold Refrigerator Co.; name changes to Tyler Fixture Corp.
1953: Name changes to Tyler Refrigeration Corp.

Grand Rapids, Michigan
A division of Johnson Furniture Co. that manufactured large contracts of college and university dormitory furniture.
SEE ALSO Johnson Furniture Co.

U
UNILINE
1970

Grand Rapids, Michigan
Manufacturer of furniture, destroyed by fire in 1886.

UNIQUE FURNITURE CO.
1925 - 1927

Grand Rapids, Michigan
Manufacturer of library and davenport tables, and novelty furniture.

UNIVERSAL TRIPOD CO., THE
1887 - 1892

Grand Rapids, Michigan
Founded by Julius and C. H. Berkey, who patented the "universal tripod." The company also manufactured light tables and easels, small writing desks, bric-a-brac cabinets, hall seats, and bedroom furniture in Aesthetic, turned bamboo, Louis XV, and English Arts and Crafts styles.
Predecessor to Royal Furniture Co.
SEE ALSO Royal Furniture Co.

UPHOLSTERY CRAFT, INC.
1932 - 1965

Grand Rapids, Michigan
Manufacturer of upholstered furniture.
Successor to Spencer-Duffy Co.
SEE ALSO Spencer-Duffy Co.

UPHOLSTERY SHOPS, THE
at least 1928

Grand Haven, Michigan
Upholsterers of a small line of seating frames. Advertised in *The Buyer's Guide*, July, 1928.

UTILITY TABLE CO.
1927 - 1932

Grand Rapids, Michigan
Manufacturer of breakfast room furniture.

V & M MANUFACTURING

SEE Stylemaster America, Inc.

VALLEY CITY CHAIR CO.
1902 - 1916

Grand Rapids, Michigan
Manufacturer of oak chairs and rocking chairs in Colonial Revival, Austrian Modern, and Art Nouveau styles.
Predecessor to Grand Rapids Fibre Furniture Co.
SEE ALSO Grand Rapids Fibre Furniture Co.

VALLEY CITY DESK CO.
1889 - 1941

VALLEY CITY DESK COMPANY
MANUFACTURERS
GRAND RAPIDS
MICHIGAN

1911   1937

Grand Rapids, Michigan
Manufacturer of flat-top and roll-top wooden pedestal desks.
Successor to Valley City Manufacturing Co. Predecessor to Valley City Furniture Co.
SEE ALSO Valley City Furniture Co., Valley City Manufacturing Co.

VALLEY CITY FURNITURE CO.
1942 - 1957

VALLEY CITY
FURNITURE CO.
GRAND RAPIDS, MICH.

1950

VALLEY CITY
FURNITURE CO
Founded 1888

1956

Grand Rapids, Michigan
Manufacturer of occasional tables. In 1959 the Valley City plant was purchased by Kindel Furniture Co. Name was used by Valley City Plating Co. between 1977 and circa 1988.
Successor to Valley City Desk Co.
SEE ALSO Kindel Furniture Co.; Valley City Desk Co.; Valley City Plating Co.

Valley City FURNITURE CO.
GRAND RAPIDS • MICH.
1951

VALLEY CITY MANUFACTURING CO.
1881 - 1889

Grand Rapids, Michigan
Manufacturer of moldings, door and window sash products for home construction.
Predecessor to Valley City Desk Co.
SEE ALSO Valley City Desk Co.

VALLEY CITY PLATING CO.
1897 - present

Valley City Plating Co.
3353 Eastern Avenue, S.E.
Grand Rapids, Michigan 49506
1975

Grand Rapids, Michigan
COMPANY HISTORY
1897: Company founded, originally as silver platers of bicycle and stove parts.
1920s: Switches mostly to chrome plating and antique finishing of components for office and household furniture after the invention of chrome.
1976: Begins to assemble complete tables on contract.
1977: Begins to manufacture "Nordex of Grand Rapids" metal household furniture under its own trade name "Valley City Furniture." The Nordex line included mirror black etageres, dining chairs, extension tables, and wall cabinet systems.
late 1980s: Nordex line is dropped.
present: Company continues to make office furniture components, lighting, store fixtures, and high-end metal and glass residential furniture, for companies such as Baker, Henredon, and Drexel.

VALLEY CITY RATTAN WORKS
1884 - ca. 1897

Grand Rapids, Michigan
Manufacturer of rattan rockers and easy chairs.
Predecessor to Falkel Rattan Works.
SEE ALSO Falkel Rattan Works.

VALLEY CITY SPRING BED CO.
at least 1893

Grand Rapids, Michigan
Manufacturer of box springs and mattresses. Advertised in *The Michigan Artisan* in 1893.

VALLEY CITY TABLE CO.
1888 - 1899

Grand Rapids, Michigan
Manufacturer of center tables, pedestals, flat and roll-top office desks, with machine carving and twist turning.
Successor to Clark & Hodges Furniture Co.
SEE ALSO Clark & Hodges Furniture Co.

VAN ARK FURNITURE CO.
1893 - 1894

Holland, Michigan
Manufacturer of Golden Oak bedroom suites and sideboards.
Predecessor to Holland Furniture Co.
SEE ALSO Holland Furniture Co.

VAN BLERKOM, DAVID CO.
ca. 1907

Grand Rapids, Michigan
Manufacturer of gilt, Classical style mirrors, and hall glasses to match hall seats manufactured by the Charles A Greenman Co.
SEE ALSO Greenman, Charles A. Co.

VAN ECKER, P.
1872

Grand Rapids, Michigan
Chair maker.

VANDER LEY BROTHERS
1923 - 1951

Grand Rapids, Michigan
Manufacturer of fine revivals and reproductions of upholstered parlor seating and tables. Vander Ley is perhaps most famous because Warner Brothers Studios used Vander Ley furniture for the set of the motion picture, *Gone With the Wind*. The company became a subsidiary of John Widdicomb Co. in 1951. Members of the Vander Ley family later opened the Homestead Shop.
SEE ALSO Homestead Shop, The; Widdicomb, John Co.

1929

VEIT MANUFACTURING CO.
1905 - 1916

Grand Rapids, Michigan
Manufacturer of wood, marble, bronze, and iron furnishings and fixtures to complete the entire interiors of banks, city halls, court houses, and libraries.

VENNEMA, A.
1864

Holland, Michigan
Cabinetmaker.
Referenced in *Map of Ottawa and Muskegon Counties, 1864*.

VERITY MANUFACTURING CO.
at least 1902 - 1904

Lake Odessa, Michigan
Manufacturer of parlor tables and tabourets.

VYKING REFRIGERATOR CO.

SEE Dry-Kold Refrigerator Co.

WADDELL MANUFACTURING CO.
1879 - 1990

Grand Rapids, Michigan
Manufacturer of wood furniture trim including machine carved and turned moldings, knobs, rosettes, davenport and table feet, victrola legs, and radio grilles for furniture manufacturers and later for the "Do-it-yourself" trade. Because of restrictions on metal manufacturing during World War II, Waddell produced sliding wooden springs modeled after carriage springs, as a substitute for coiled metal springs in upholstered furniture.

OTHER SOURCES
An article by George A. Whinery, Jr. entitled, "and Still Going Strong: Waddell Manufacturing Co." appeared in *The Grand River Valley Review* in Spring/Summer, 1980.

Waddell
Manufacturing Company
GRAND RAPIDS, MICHIGAN
1926-31

WAGEMAKER CO. LTD.
1899 - 1960

Grand Rapids, Michigan
Originally a manufacturer of wooden flat-top and roll-top desks, filing cabinets, filing systems and supplies, "neo-leum" desk tops, filing trays, and specialty cabinet work. Later, the company switched the production from wooden furniture to wooden pleasure boats.

Wagemaker Co
STANDS FOR QUALITY
1937

WAIT & BARNES FURNITURE CO.
1888 and 1893

Sturgis, Michigan
Manufacturer of fine and medium-priced chamber suites, sideboards, and chiffoniers in quartered oak with antique or 16th-century finishes.

WALLACE FURNITURE CO.
1915 - 1927

Grand Rapids, Michigan
Associated with the Berkey & Gay family of companies. Manufacturer of fine wooden residential furniture, including a custom dining suite made in 1923 for movie stars Mary Pickford and Douglas Fairbanks.
SEE ALSO Berkey & Gay Furniture Co.; Grand Rapids Upholstery Co.

WARD, SKINNER & BROOKS

SEE New England Furniture Co.

WATERS, SAMUEL L.
1860 - 1898

Greenville, Michigan
Cabinetmaker.

WEATHERLY, WARREN
ca. 1845

Grand Rapids, Michigan
Chair maker.

WEBER SHOWCASE CO.

SEE Grand Rapids Store Equipment Co.

WEGNER, PETER J. CO.
at least 1928

Grand Rapids, Michigan
Manufacturer of upholstered furniture. Listed in *The Buyer's Guide*, July, 1928.

WELCH FOLDING BED CO.
1886 - 1908

Offices: Grand Rapids, Michigan. Factory: Sparta, Michigan.
Manufacturer of patented folding beds which combined several pieces of furniture such as a writing desk, chifforobe, chest of drawers, and murphy bed all into one unit. Pieces carried lengthy descriptive names like "Welch Cabinet Mantel Bed," "Welch Parlor Cabinet Folding Bed," and "Welch Oxford Junior Folding Bed."
Predecessor to Welch Manufacturing Co.
SEE ALSO Grand Rapids Store Equipment Co.; Welch Manufacturing Co.; Welch - Wilmarth Corp.

WELCH FURNITURE CO.
at least 1917 - 1918

Grand Haven, Michigan
Manufacturer of novelty furniture including tea wagons, knitting and sewing cabinets, folding, gate-leg and end tables, spinet desks, stands, and tabourets.
Cited in a general listing of furniture manufacturers.

WELCH MANUFACTURING CO.
1909 - 1925

Grand Rapids, Michigan
Manufacturer of showcases and equipment for stores.
Successor to Welch Folding Bed Co.
SEE ALSO Grand Rapids Store Equipment Co.; Welch Folding Bed Co.; Welch - Wilmarth Corp.

WELCH - WILMARTH CORP.
1926 - 1927

Grand Rapids, Michigan
Manufacturer of showcases and equipment for stores.
Predecessor to Grand Rapids Store Equipment Co.
SEE ALSO Grand Rapids Store Equipment Co.; Welch Folding Bed Co.; Welch Manufacturing Co.; Wilmarth Showcase Corp.
COMPANY HISTORY
1921: Welch Manufacturing and Wilmarth Showcase run joint design service.
1926: Formed by merger of Welch Manufacturing Co. and Wilmarth Showcase Co.
1927: Name changed to Grand Rapids Store Equipment Co.

WERKMAN MANUFACTURING CO.
1886 - 1890

Holland, Michigan
Originally a manufacturer of wooden farm implements, the company also made low-priced chamber suites.

WERNICKE FURNITURE CO.
1893 - ca. 1905

Grand Rapids, Michigan
Manufacturer of Otto H. L. Wernicke's patented "elastic bookcases," a system of wooden compartments that interlocked vertically and horizontally to create flexible cases for book and paper storage.
Predecessor to The Macey Co.
SEE ALSO Macey Co., The.
COMPANY HISTORY
1893: Company established in Minneapolis, Minnesota.
1897: Moves to Grand Rapids.
1904: O.H.L. Wernicke founds the Globe - Wernicke Co. in Cincinnati, Ohio.

ca. 1905: Wernicke purchases Fred Macey Furniture Co.; name changes to Macey - Wernicke Co.

1907: Name simplified to The Macey Co.

WEST MICHIGAN FURNITURE CO.
1889 - 1984

Colonial Revival dressing table and bench by West Michigan Furniture Co., from *Good Furniture Magazine*, Nov., 1924.

1927

1963

WEST MICHIGAN FURNITURE COMPANY · Holland, Michigan

1965

1966

WEST MICHIGAN FURNITURE COMPANY
Holland, Michigan

1968

WEST MICHIGAN WILLOW WORKS
1917 - 1918

WESTINGHOUSE ARCHITECTURAL SYSTEMS DIVISION

WESTINGHOUSE FURNITURE SYSTEMS, INC.
1983 - 1990

Open Office System installation, from a 1981 Westinghouse catalog. Courtesy, Knoll, Inc.

Holland, Michigan

SEE ALSO Mueller Furniture Co.

COMPANY HISTORY

1889: Company founded.

1904: Company purchases a controlling interest in Engel Land & Lumber Co. of Louisiana, to attain lumber at reduced cost.

1976: Company is purchased by Louis Padnos Iron and Metal Co. of Grand Rapids, continues to operate under its own name.

1984: Assets purchased by and dissolved into Mueller Furniture Co. of Grand Rapids.

PERSONNEL

West Michigan Furniture was founded by D. Kruidenier, Frederick Metz, and George P. Hummer, who later became mayor of Holland, Michigan. After his death in 1920, Hummer's son-in-law, Charles Kirchen, purchased Hummer's interest in the company. Wayne R. Fitzgerald served as its president and general manager from 1955 - 1976, when the company was purchased from the Kirchen family by Padnos. Mitchell W. Padnos became executive vice-president, and Doug Padnos the national sales manager.

PRODUCTS

West Michigan Furniture Co.'s first products were beds and bedroom suites in maple, ash, and oak. By the 1920s it had moved into production of phonograph cabinets, and bedroom and dining suites in 18th-century, period revival styles. West Michigan made Colonial Revival case pieces to complement beds by Kindel Bed Co. in the 1920s. In the late 1920s and early 1930s it produced bedroom suites in a "waterfall" Art Deco style.

During World War II the company made bunk beds and other items for the Army. After the War it made pieces in Modern bedroom groups and storage systems, using solids and exotic veneers, lacquer finishes, and cane and metal accents. From the 1950s to the early 1970s, West Michigan executed numerous contracts for colleges, hospitals and motel chains.

OTHER SOURCES

The business records of West Michigan Furniture Co. now constitute an archival collection, owned by the Holland Historical Trust, and maintained by the Joint Archives of Holland, on the campus of Hope College. They span the company's entire history, and include an extensive run of catalogs beginning in 1908.

MARKS AND LABELS

West Michigan's logo featured a silhouette of a woman in Dutch folk costume carrying a basket, in front of a Dutch windmill. These are partially surrounded by a circle. Beneath the windmill is the name of the company, and the motto, "Style - Stability - Service - Satisfaction." After 1963 the trademark was abstracted to just the turning blades of the windmill.

Holland, Michigan

Cited in a general listing of furniture manufacturers.

SEE Westinghouse Furniture Systems, Inc.

Kentwood, Michigan and Puerto Rico

SEE ALSO Architectural Systems, Inc; Knoll, Inc.; Shaw-Walker Co.

COMPANY HISTORY

1961: Architectural Systems, Inc. (ASI) is acquired by Westinghouse Electric Corp.

1983: Name changes to Westinghouse Furniture Systems, Inc.

1989: Company acquires Shaw-Walker Co. of Muskegon, Michigan and Reff, Inc. of Toronto.

1990: Westinghouse Furniture Systems acquires the rights to manufacture the RACE office furniture system from Sunar - Hausermann; Westinghouse Electric Corp. acquires Knoll International and makes Westinghouse Furniture Systems, Inc. one of The Knoll Group companies.

PERSONNEL

Russell A. Nagel served as president and C.E.O. of Westinghouse Furniture Systems from 1984 until it became a part of The Knoll Group in 1990.

PRODUCTS

At the time of Westinghouse's acquisition of ASI, the company produced floor-to-ceiling partitions. In 1970 Westinghouse introduced its first open office furniture system known as the "ASD (Architectural Systems Division) Group." This was followed by the "WesGroup" in 1984, which updated the product's engineering and aesthetics, and the more design-oriented "Equation" system, both based on the company's "Ultra Panel." In 1990 the company purchased the "RACE" system from Sunar-Hausermann of Cleveland, Ohio.

MARKS AND LABELS

The company trademark incorporated the Westinghouse "W" surrounded by a circle, to the left of the name "Westinghouse Furniture Systems" which was flanked on the right by a horizontal and diagonal grid pattern. This was replaced with the Knoll trademark circa 1990.

Westinghouse Furniture Systems

1990

WHEELER & GREEN

SEE Wheeler, Green & Gay

WHEELER, GREEN & GAY
1873 - 1876

Grand Rapids, Michigan
Manufacturer of milk safes, butter churns, fanning mills, and wash boards.

COMPANY HISTORY
1859: Green & Co. established.
1869 - 1873: Name is changed to Wheeler & Green.
1873 - 1876: Operates under the name Wheeler, Green & Gay.

WHITE CONSOLIDATED INDUSTRIES
1967 - 1991

Greenville, Michigan
Manufacturer of refrigerators and other home appliances.
SEE ALSO Belding-Hall Co.; Gibson Refrigerator Co.; Greenville Product Corp.; Kelvinator, Inc.

COMPANY HISTORY
1967: White Consolidated purchases Hupp Corp., owners of Gibson Refrigerator Co. in Greenville.
1968: Kelvinator, Inc. of Grand Rapids operates as a subsidiary of White Consolidated Industries.
1978: Name changes from Gibson Refrigerator Co. to Greenville Products Corp., while remaining a subsidiary of WCI.
1987: Name changes to White Consolidated Industries Refrigerator Division.
1991: Name changes to Frigidaire Company Refrigerator Products.

WHITE, NEHEMIAH
ca. 1840 - 1859

Grand Rapids, Michigan
Originally from New York, White was one of Grand Rapids' earliest cabinetmakers, and maker of "flag-seat chairs." A number of pieces White made before coming to Grand Rapids are in the collection of Lorenzo State Historic Site in Caznovia, New York.

WHITE STEEL SANITARY FURNITURE CO.
1909 - 1936

Grand Rapids, Michigan
Advertised in 1909 as a department of the Adjustable Table Co. Manufacturer of enameled tubular steel and glass bathroom stands, kitchen tables, and metal cabinets.
SEE ALSO Adjustable Table Co.

WIDDICOMB BROTHERS & RICHARDS
1869 - 1873

Grand Rapids, Michigan
Manufacturer of Rococo Revival and Renaissance Revival-influenced bedroom furniture made from domestic hardwoods.
Successor to George Widdicomb and Sons. Predecessor to Widdicomb Furniture Co.
SEE ALSO Widdicomb Furniture Co.; Widdicomb, George & Sons; Widdicomb, John Co.; Widdicomb Mantel Co.

WIDDICOMB FURNITURE CO.
1873 - 1950

Grand Rapids, Michigan
Successor to Widdicomb Brothers & Richards. Predecessor to John Widdicomb Co.
SEE ALSO Widdicomb, John Co.; Widdicomb Mantel Co.

COMPANY HISTORY
1873: Widdicomb Brothers & Richards incorporates as Widdicomb Furniture Co.
1887 and 1891: Local histories of Grand Rapids describe Widdicomb as the largest manufacturer of bedroom furniture in the world.

1915: Company is purchased by Joseph Griswold, Sr. and Godfrey Von Platen.

1950: Widdicomb merges with Mueller Furniture Corp. to form Widdicomb - Mueller Corp.

1960: Mueller severs ties to Widdicomb.

1970: Widdicomb Furniture Co. name is purchased by John Widdicomb Co.

PERSONNEL

At the time of the company's incorporation, William Widdicomb was president, Theodore Richards was vice-president, and William's brother Harry was secretary. William left the family business in 1883 for a position with the Grand Rapids National Bank. In 1885 he began a wholesale grocery business. But he returned to the company upon the request of its board, after the financial panic of 1893. He managed the company until his retirement in 1915. He was described as a clever mechanic who invented many improvements for machinery in the factory.

Lumber tycoon Godfrey Von Platen, furniture man Maynard Guest, and salesman Joseph Griswold, Sr. purchased the company from Widdicomb in 1915. Griswold served as president until he was succeeded by his son Joseph, Jr. who served as general manager and president from 1941 until 1964.

Free-lance designer William Balbach created designs for Widdicomb beginning in 1917.

English-born designer T.H. Robsjohn-Gibbings served as designer for Widdicomb from 1943 until 1956. Although he began to design lines of Modern furniture from the time he arrived, its production was postponed until 1946, when World War II ended. George Nakashima designed the "Origins Group" for Widdicomb in the late 1950s and early 1960s. Other designers from the early 1960s included Marge Carson, Dave Butterworth, Albert Herbert, and Ray See.

PRODUCTS

The first products of the Widdicomb Furniture Co. were spindle beds that were generally shipped to retailers unfinished or "in the white." An 1878 article in *The American Cabinet Maker, Upholsterer and Carpet Reporter* states that Widdicomb made only "nine styles of work," and specialized in low-priced ash, maple, cherry, and walnut bedsteads.

By the 1880s the line had expanded to include all forms of "medium and fine chamber furniture" including beds, dressers, chiffoniers, wardrobes, washstands, mirrors, and night tables. The company utilized a variety of woods including San Domingo and Tabasco mahogany, Circassian walnut, golden curly birch, bird's-eye maple, and also a white enamel finish. Pieces from the late 1890s were also produced in quarter-sawn oak. The 1906 catalog shows bedroom suites and occasional pieces in all of these woods, in American Empire or Colonial Revival styles, or with vaguely French inspiration.

Between 1918 and 1920 Widdicomb advertised Queen Anne, Adam, and Chippendale-styled phonograph cabinets made by its phonograph division. Bedroom suites from the 1910s and 1920s were produced from mahogany and walnut, or with a polychromed enamel finish, in a variety of period revival styles including Italian Renaissance, Venetian, Georgian, Louis XV and XVI, Chippendale, Hepplewhite, Early American, and "New England Colonial." A number of Adam-influenced designs from the late 1910s featured caned panels overlaid with carved swags and wreaths. The distinctive Spanish suites made of shaded and decoratively painted walnut featured trestle tables, Roman arched panels, and baroque scrolled and carved silhouettes.

The company introduced its first Modern pieces in 1928, and by 1938 had stopped production of all traditional and revival pieces. A 1936 *Grand Rapids Market Ambassador* showed a streamlined Art Deco-style bedroom suite made of white harewood, offered jointly by Widdicomb and the Hastings Table Co.

T.H. Robsjohn-Gibbings's Modern designs in the 1940s and '50s were in a warm blond wood tone, with either tapering, functional Scandinavian Modern shapes, or Modern designs with Neo-classical influences. George Nakashima's "Origins Collection," produced in the late 1950s and early 1960s included bedroom, dining room, upholstered, and occasional pieces of Modern design with Japanese and Shaker stylistic influences. Emphasis was placed on the grain and texture of the woods, which ranged from Circassian walnut table tops to hand-shaved hickory spindles.

Blond mahogany arm chair, designed by T. H. Robsjohn-Gibbings for Widdicomb, ca. 1955.

The Widdicomb Furniture Co.
TRADE MARK REGISTERED IN U.S. PATENT OFFICE
Grand Rapids, Michigan
1928

WIDDICOMB, GEORGE & SONS
1857 - 1863

WIDDICOMB, JOHN CO.
1897 - present

W-80 commode by John Widdicomb Co.,
ca. 1992. Courtesy, John Widdicomb Co.

OTHER SOURCES
The Grand Rapids Public Library owns a large collection of catalogs and original archival materials which spans nearly the entire history of the Widdicomb Furniture Co. and its predecessors.

MARKS AND LABELS
The company's earliest beds sometimes had paper shipping labels on the inside bottom of the headboard, and/or a burn mark on the back of the headboard with "WIDDICOMB / FURNITURE CO. / GRAND RAPIDS / MICHIGAN". The company used a distinctive, cursive type style for the name "The Widdicomb Furniture Co." as its registered trademark between at least 1903 and 1937.

Grand Rapids, Michigan
Cabinetmaker George Widdicomb left Devonshire, England for New Hampshire in 1843. In 1857 George and sons William, Harry, John, and George, Jr. opened their cabinetmaking business in Grand Rapids. William made a selling trip to Milwaukee in 1858, and claimed to be the first traveling furniture salesman from Grand Rapids. The business was closed during the Civil War, when all four brothers joined the Union Army. George, Jr. died during the war, leaving the remaining three brothers, who joined in starting the Widdicomb Brothers & Richards Co. in 1869.
SEE ALSO Widdicomb Brothers.

Grand Rapids, Michigan
SEE ALSO Berkey, William A. Furniture Co.; Bexley-Heath, Ltd; Charlotte Chair Co.; Kent Furniture Co.; Vander Ley Brothers Co.; Widdicomb Mantel Co.

COMPANY HISTORY
1897: Widdicomb Mantel Co. re-incorporates as John Widdicomb Co.
1901 - 1906: John Widdicomb Co. purchases and operates former plants of Charlotte Chair Co. in Charlotte, Michigan, and the Kent Furniture Co. plant in Grand Rapids.
1929: Widdicomb family sells interest in company.
1950: John Widdicomb Company acquires William A. Berkey Furniture Co.
1951: Company acquires Vander Ley Brothers Co.
1956: Company acquires Grand Rapids Bookcase and Chair Co.
1970: John Widdicomb Co. purchases the name and goodwill of Widdicomb Furniture Co.
1973: Hickory Furniture Co. of Hickory, North Carolina buys John Widdicomb Co.
1986: Group of Michigan-based investors purchases John Widdicomb Co.

PERSONNEL
John Widdicomb started his namesake company in 1897 after his short-lived Widdicomb Mantel Co. failed. During his tenure as head of the company, he served as the president of the National Association of Kitchen Cabinet Manufacturers. John Widdicomb's son, Harry, became president of the company upon his father's death in 1910.

J. Fred Lyon purchased controlling interest in John Widdicomb Co. in 1929, with a minority interest held by John L. Stuart. Stuart became the major stockholder and chairman of the board in 1939 when Lyon retired. Stuart and his family owned most of the stock until 1969, when they arranged a management buy-out in 1969.

John D. Hanink first came to work at John Widdicomb in 1935. He became president and general manager in 1964. In 1969 he created the Furniture Corporation of America, a holding company that purchased the John Widdicomb Co. He retired as president and C.E.O. in 1977.

Mike Greengard (former president of the Charlotte Chair Co.) and a group of investors purchased the company from Hickory Furniture Co. in 1986, and appointed Greengard president.

Ralph H. Widdicombe, a nephew of Harry Widdicomb, joined his uncle's company as designer in 1898. He was awarded first prize at the Paris Exposition of 1900 for his American Empire-style mahogany bedroom suite. Even after the family sold the business in 1929, Ralph stayed on as chief of design until his retirement in 1951. English-born designer Stanley Green, who received his training as an apprentice at London's Waring & Gillow, designed English Revival and French Provincial pieces at John Widdicomb from 1933 into the 1950s.

Chad Womack, originator of the company's Russian and British India lines, be-

1920

1926

1942

1956-59

1974

john Widdicomb co.
1974

JOHN WIDDICOMB COMPANY
1990

came a designer for John Widdicomb in 1986. Designer Diane Granda also worked on the development of the Russian line, and was responsible for many of the company's English collection designs from the 1980s and '90s, and the Mar-a-Lago reproductions introduced in 1990. In 1989 interior designer Mario Buatta, known by the nickname "The Prince of Chintz," contracted to design a line of furniture for John Widdicomb.

PRODUCTS

The John Widdicomb Co.'s first products included interior woodwork and fireplace overmantels, like its predecessor company. It soon changed to medium-priced chamber or bedroom suites and kitchen cabinets.

In 1901 Ralph Widdicombe introduced a line inspired by the European Modern movement. In that same year the company contracted with the Singer Sewing Machine Co. to produce cabinets for 200,000 sewing machines. In 1902 a similar contract was negotiated for 25,000 sewing machine cabinets with the National Sewing Machine Co.

During the 1910s and '20s the company continued to produce bedroom suites with matched and contrasting veneers of mahogany, satinwood, harewood, Circassian walnut, and maple burl, and gilt, marquetry, or hand-painted floral and scenic decoration, in Sheraton, Hepplewhite, Duncan Phyfe, Jacobean, Queen Anne, and Louis XVI Revival styles. Some Louis XVI suites from the late 1910s and early 1920s included woven rattan panels and enamelling. In 1928 the company introduced a Modern suite based on Sheraton forms, with matched French walnut veneers and ebony sides. Advertisements from 1929 also list individual pieces for the living room, library, and hall in addition to bedroom suites, for the first time.

Ralph Widdicombe designed the first French Provincial line of furniture in the United States in 1924, based on examples collected in Europe. A large bombe chest featured gilt decoration and a large cartouche with pastoral scenic painting. A small bombe bureau from that line has remained in continuous production for more than seven decades.

John Widdicomb's pre-war production in the early 1940s included groups for the bedroom and dining room, and occasional pieces of walnut, mahogany, fruitwood, satinwood, and bleached maple with gilding, and many all-over decorative paint finishes, in revival styles including French Provincial, English Regency, Chippendale, Sheraton, and Chinese Lacquer. Special lines included "poudre tables," a combination dressing table and lady's writing desk for the bedroom, and "Di-functional tables," which could close into small drop-leaf tables that were placed against a wall, or expand with center and drop leaves to seat up to ten.

1950s lines of bedroom furniture included the Italian Directoire line, and new introductions to the company's perennially popular French Provincial line. 1970s lines for the bedroom, dining room, living room, and executive office followed the company's traditional strengths, including Country French (French Provincial), Louis XV and XVI, Italian Directoire and Venetian, English Regency and Early English, and Oriental styles. A new addition was the "Wellington Group" for the home, which consisted of modern, rectangular case pieces of olive ash veneer with walnut trim, and seating with woven rattan panels. A companion line of executive furniture was also based on the Wellington line, as were several lines produced by the subsidiary William A. Berkey Furniture Co.

The "Treasures From Around The World" collection of antique hardwood reproductions, designed by Lucile Fickett and produced in the mid-1980s, included a Chippendale secretary, Queen Anne bookcase, and a chinoiserie writing table. Chad Womack's first Russian Empire pieces were introduced in 1987 as expansions of the 1986 German Biedermeier line. But the popularity of these masculine styled, richly veneered pieces, with carvings and hardware of lions, two-headed eagles, griffins, and sphinxes, some combined with an end-of-the-Cold-War fascination with Russia to make the Russian line a strong seller in its own right.

The romantic Buatta collection, begun in 1989, featured reproductions and adaptations from interior designer Mario Buatta's own collection of English Regency antiques, and brought designer name recognition to the company. Forms included breakfronts, coffee tables, and demi-lune tables in mahogany, rosewood, ebony, and satinwood veneers. It also featured flowery chintz sofas, chairs, and ottomans, with tufted backs, rolled arms and fringe: the first fully upholstered furniture to be made by the company.

In 1990 Diane Granda began to design the "Mar-a-Lago" collection based on furniture in the 1920s Florida estate built for breakfast food heiress Marjorie Merriweather Post and more recently owned by developer Donald Trump. In 1994 Womack's "British India Collection" was introduced. It featured pieces that combined the traditional forms of English Regency, Chippendale, Adam, and Sheraton with exotic materials such as faux ivory and tortoise shell, and Saracenic and Islamic decorative motifs of the Indian sub-continent.

OTHER SOURCES

The Grand Rapids Public Library owns a large collection of catalogs and original archival materials from the Widdicomb and John Widdicomb Companies, from the founding of John Widdicomb to circa 1951.

MARKS AND LABELS

Circa 1920 the company used a very fluid "JWCO" monogram, framed in a vertical oval, with candle sconces and a tall, fanciful finial. This was modified during the late 1920s and early 1930s to a "JWCo" monogram in a vertical oval, surrounded on the bottom and sides by laurel boughs and on top with a bow. In the 1940s every piece was given a paper label bearing that mark and the words "MADE BY/ JOHN WIDDICOMB CO./ DESIGNED BY/ Ralph H. Widdicombe/ GRAND RAPIDS." In the 1950s the company name was printed in a circular, sans-serif type, with all lower-case letters. In the 1970s the trademark was a "jw" monogram in a square of horizontal lines. Pieces from the "Treasures From Around The World" line were numbered and affixed with a brass plate engraved with the buyer's name, as well as an engraved plate marked "John Widdicomb Co." The 1990s trademark is a somewhat sharp "jw" monogram.

WIDDICOMB MANTEL CO. 1893 - 1897	Grand Rapids, Michigan Manufacturer of interior woodwork and fireplace overmantels. Successor to Gleason Wood Ornament Co. Predecessor to John Widdicomb Co. SEE ALSO Gleason Wood Ornament Co.; Widdicomb Furniture Co.; Widdicomb, John Co.
WIDDICOMB - MUELLER CORP.	SEE Mueller Furniture Corp.; Widdicomb Furniture Co.
WILBURN CO. 1947 - 1968	Grand Rapids, Michigan Manufacturer of bars, back bars, and furniture for restaurants. Predecessor to Redco Manufacturing. SEE ALSO Redco Manufacturing.
WILCOX CHAIR CO.	SEE Northern Chair Co.
WILL, GEORGE CO. 1949 - 1951	Ada, Michigan Engineers and builders of supermarket fixtures.

WILHELM FURNITURE CO.
at least 1913 - 1939

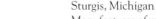

1929

Sturgis, Michigan
Manufacturer of mahogany, oak, walnut, and decorated wood dinette suites, spinet desks, and secretaries; library, sofa, gate leg and tables; and novelty items such as smoking stands, tea wagons, sewing cabinets, magazine stands and radio cabinets in various revival styles including Adam, Jacobean, Queen Anne, and Chinese Chippendale.
Successor to Stebbins Furniture Co.
SEE ALSO Stebbins Furniture Co.; Wilhelm Music Master Co.

WILHELM MUSIC MASTER CO.
1915 - 1919

Sturgis, Michigan
Manufacturer of phonograph record player cabinets. Operated from the same factory as Wilhelm Furniture Co.
SEE ALSO Wilhelm Furniture Co.

WILLIAMS - KIMP FURNITURE CO.
1923 - 1951

WILLIAMS-KIMP FURNITURE CO.
GRAND RAPIDS, MICHIGAN

Federal American Furniture
1951

1949

Grand Rapids, Michigan
Manufacturer of mahogany reproductions of American Federal furniture including dining sets, secretaries, fall-front desks, chairs, and occasional pieces. Purchased in 1951 by Baker Furniture Co.
Successor to C.S. Paine Co.
SEE ALSO Baker Furniture Co.; Paine, C.S. Co.

WILLIAMS MANUFACTURING CO.
1953 - 1973

Grand Rapids, Michigan
Manufacturer of furniture.

WILMARTH & WILMARTH CO.

SEE Wilmarth Showcase Co.

WILMARTH SHOWCASE CO.
1909 - 1926

Grand Rapids, Michigan
Manufacturer of high-grade retail showcases, counters, and wall cases.
Successor to Grand Rapids Fixture Co.
SEE ALSO Grand Rapids Fixture Co.; Welch - Wilmarth Corp.
COMPANY HISTORY
1908: Company founded as Wilmarth and Wilmarth Co.
1909: Name changes to Wilmarth Showcase Co.
1926: Merges with Welch Manufacturing Corp. to form Welch - Wilmarth Corp.

1920   1920

WILSON & BECKWITH STUDIOS
1925 - 1931

Grand Rapids, Michigan
Worked cooperatively with the Shear - Maddox Furniture Co., which manufactured the pieces that Wilson & Beckwith decorated. Grand Rapids City Directory advertisements listed the firm as artists; makers and decorators of furniture, panels, paintings and lacquer work; and interior decorators. The company's stylistic range ran from Japanese lacquer to Renaissance to Art Deco styles. Forms included coffee tables, chairs, benches, screens, boxes, desks, consoles and sewing cabinets.
SEE ALSO Shear - Maddox Furniture Co.

1928

WILSON, THOMAS STUDIOS
1941 - 1946

Grand Rapids, Michigan
Hand decorators of manufactured furniture.

WINCHESTER BROTHERS CO.
1854 - 1857

Grand Rapids, Michigan
Manufacturer of Rococo and Renaissance Revival furniture.
SEE ALSO Haldane, William (Deacon); Nelson & Comstock Co.; Nelson, Matter & Co.; Pullman Brothers Co.
COMPANY HISTORY
1854: Company is formed as a partnership between Enoch W. Winchester and William (Deacon) Haldane.
1855: Haldane sells his share in the company to S.A. Winchester, who came from New Hampshire to join his brother.
1856: Winchester Brothers buy Pullman Brothers Co. Open a new factory described as the largest and best in the city.
1857: Winchesters default on loan in Panic of 1857, and ownership of company transfers to C.C. Comstock.
1863: Comstock forms partnership with Nelson Brothers to create Nelson & Comstock Co.

WINCHESTER & HALDANE

SEE Winchester Brothers Co.

WINDSOR FURNITURE CO.
1923 - 1960

Grand Rapids, Michigan
Manufacturer of upholstered furniture; wholesaler and retailer of furniture and bedding.
Companion company and eventually successor to Windsor Upholstering Co.
SEE ALSO Windsor Upholstering Co.

WINDSOR UPHOLSTERING CO.
1915 - 1938

1923

Grand Rapids, Michigan
Manufacturer of William and Mary and Queen Anne upholstered sofas, arm chairs, and stools, and sofa and occasional tables.
Predecessor to Windsor Furniture Co.
SEE ALSO Windsor Furniture Co.

WIS - KEM CABINET CO.
1912 - 1913

Grand Rapids, Michigan
Manufacturer of furniture. Cited in a listing of manufacturers in *The Furniture Manufacturer and Artisan*, February, 1920.

WITHEY, L. H. CO.
1966 - 1968

Grand Rapids, Michigan
Manufacturer of furniture for homes, clubs, and hotels.

WOLVERINE CHAIR CO.
1887 - 1891

Grand Rapids, Michigan
Manufacturer of "ordered work and chairs."
Successor to Wolverine Chair & Furniture Co.
SEE ALSO Wolverine Chair & Furniture Co.

WOLVERINE CHAIR & FURNITURE CO.
1880 - 1887

Grand Rapids, Michigan
Manufacturer of black walnut, ash, and cherry chairs with cane seats, and patent spring rocking chairs, frames for upholstered rocking chairs, and frames for upholstered parlor suites.
Predecessor to Wolverine Chair Co.
SEE ALSO Wolverine Chair Co.

WOLVERINE FURNITURE CO.
1907 - 1932

1915

Zeeland, Michigan
Manufacturer of medium-grade bedroom furniture.
Successor to Wolverine Specialty Co. Predecessor to Wolverine Specialty Furniture Co.
SEE ALSO Wolverine Specialty Furniture Co.

WOLVERINE SHOWCASE CO.
1904 - 1907

Grand Rapids, Michigan
Cited in a listing of furniture manufacturers.

WOLVERINE SPECIALTY FURNITURE CO.
1932 - 1956

Grand Rapids, Michigan
Manufacturer of nursery chairs and children's rocking chairs.
Successor to Wolverine Furniture Co.
SEE ALSO Wolverine Furniture Co.

WOLVERINE UPHOLSTERY CO.
1925 - 1961

1950

Grand Rapids, Michigan and Fort Worth, Texas
Manufacturer of fine upholstered furniture.
COMPANY HISTORY
1925: Company founded.
1950: A line of occasional tables is added to complement the upholstered lines.
circa 1961 - 1966: Manufacture of Wolverine's own products is discontinued, but the company continues as a showroom and retail outlet for other manufacturers.

Wolverine Upholstery Co.
The Line of Style and Comfort
1950

WOOD BATIK SHOPS
1921 - 1924

Grand Rapids, Michigan
Hand carvers and batch decorators of dining suites, tea tables, gate-leg tables, chairs, mirrors, and lamp bases in Dutch Renaissance, Italian Renaissance, or Venetian Revival styles.

WOOD PRODUCTS CORP. OF GRAND RAPIDS
1923 - 1951

Grand Rapids, Michigan
Manufacturers, turners, and carvers of radio cabinets and novelty tables.
Successor to Hegeman & Drieborg, wood turners.

WOODARD BROTHERS

SEE Woodard, Lee L. Sons, Inc.

WOODARD FURNITURE WORKS

SEE Woodard, Lee L. Sons, Inc.

WOODARD, LEE L. SONS, INC.
1938 - present

Owosso, Michigan
After the conversion of a planing mill, the company's original products were window sash and doors, pine box caskets, and wooden bedroom pieces. An 1896 catalog shows curly birch and oak dressers, bedsteads, dressers, washstands, and chests of drawers, in golden and dark mahogany finishes. In 1935 the company began to manufacture wrought-iron chairs, tables, and chaise lounges for use in sun rooms and outdoors on patios and decks. Well-known lines include the "Orleans Collection" (1940); and the "Chantilly Rose Collection" (1948). The company still manufactures better-quality iron patio furniture.
COMPANY HISTORY
1866: Founded as Woodard Brothers by Lyman E. Woodard.
1896: Operates as Woodard Furniture Works.
1938: New company is formed from assets of Woodard Furniture Works, operates under the name Lee L. Woodard Sons, Inc.

the worth of Woodard
1978

1980

WOODCRAFT CABINET SHOP
1949 - 1953

Grand Rapids, Michigan
Manufacturer of retailing showcases.

WOOSTER, DAVID
ca. 1835 - 1845

Grand Rapids, Michigan
Chair maker.

WORDEN CO., THE
1949 - present

Offices and factories: Holland, Michigan. Factories: Grand Rapids, Michigan.
Manufacturer of wooden teacher's desks, library tables, technical furniture, shelving, storage cabinets, reading chairs, and upholstered lounge seating for schools,

holland, MI   49423-0195
1949

1959

WORDEN FURNITURE CO.
1881 - 1891

public libraries, colleges and universities, offices, and healthcare facilities. Successor to Bolhuis Lumber & Manufacturing Co., a supplier of millwork and construction materials begun in 1906. Worden purchased the Extensole Corp. of Sparta, Michigan in 1978.
SEE ALSO Extensole Corp.

Grand Rapids, Michigan
Manufacturer of medium- and low-priced chamber suites, bedsteads, and tables in maple and ash.

COMPANY HISTORY
1881: Company founded.
1891: Company dissolves when factory is destroyed by fire.

YPSILANTI REED FURNITURE CO.
1901 - 1953

Office and factories: Ionia, Michigan. Additional factories: Portland, Saranac, Lyons, and Lowell, Michigan; and Singapore.
SEE ALSO Overseas Reed and Cane Co.

COMPANY HISTORY
1900: Company is founded as the Phoenix Reed Co. in Detroit, Michigan.
1901: Firm moves to Ypsilanti, Michigan, and changes name to Ypsilanti Reed Furniture Co.
1903: Company moves to Ionia to make furniture using prison labor on campus of the Michigan State House of Correction and Reformatory.
1911 and 1913: First non-prison plants open in Ionia.
1915: Fred Green establishes the Overseas Reed and Cane Co. in Singapore, to purchase and ship rattan to Ypsilanti Reed.
Early 1920s: Besides the Ionia plants, additional factories open in the nearby towns of Portland, Saranac, Lyons, and Lowell, employing a total of 2,000 workers.
1921: Ypsilanti Reed becomes the world's largest producer of reed furniture.
1923: Firm discontinues production by prison labor.
1927: Lowell, Portland, Saranac, and Lyons plants are closed.
1941: Factories convert to wartime production, including military jeep and truck seating, and canvas tents.
1948: Product lines change from furniture to bus seating, automobile and truck bodies, and canvas goods.
1953: Name changes to Ionia Manufacturing Co.

PERSONNEL
Ypsilanti Reed's first sales manager was Fred W. Green, who later became a two-time governor of the State of Michigan. In 1927 Ypsilanti Reed produced a colorful rattan living room line known as "The Governor's Suite" in honor of Green's years with the company. Between 1928 and 1931 Modern designer Donald Deskey was hired to design Art Deco pieces, which were produced from machine-woven fiber. But his most famous designs were for a line of seating made from bent tubular steel. Grand Rapids designer Jess Vennell designed a line of post-WWII furniture, which was produced until 1948 when furniture production ceased.

Reed furniture, painted yellow with orange upholstery, designed by Donald Deskey for Ypsilanti Reed Furniture Co. featured in the *American Annual of Design* for 1931.

PRODUCTS
Ypsilanti Reed Furniture Co. began as a manufacturer of reed and rattan furniture, using materials imported from India, Malaya, and Singapore. Products included hand-woven fancy rattan seating, plant stands, occasional tables, and even bird cages in natural and color stain finishes for the living room, library, sun parlor, and porch. In the 1910s Ypsilanti Reed was second only to the Heywood - Wakefield Co. in consumption of rattan in the United States. After Heywood - Wakefield switched production from handmade reed to machine-woven paper fiber furniture in 1921, Ypsilanti Reed became the largest producer of reed furniture in the world.

During the late 1920s and 30s Ypsilanti Reed produced the Art Deco designs of Deskey, including not only reed furniture but also maple frame chairs with upholstered cushions, and the bent tubular steel chairs upholstered with machine-woven fiber, leather, and Art Deco fabrics.

OTHER SOURCES
There are a number of Ypsilanti Reed catalogs in the collections of The Public Museum of Grand Rapids. The Grand Rapids Public Library has a small collection of company newsletters known as The *Ypsi-Doodler* from 1944 -1946.

1938

YURKINAS & URBAN MANUFACTURING CO.
1951 - 1953

Grand Rapids, Michigan
Manufacturer of unfinished furniture and chests.

ZEELAND FURNITURE MANUFACTURING CO.
1911

Zeeland, Michigan
Advertised in the June, 1911 issue of *The Grand Rapids Furniture Record* as a manufacturer of Empire Revival-style beds, dressers, chiffoniers, washstands, and toilet tables.

ZEELAND WOOD TURNING WORKS
1919 - present

Zeeland, Michigan
Manufacturer of lathe and semi-automatic lathe-turned lamps, spindles, and legs for furniture and home construction.

ZEELAND
WOOD TURNING WORKS
1989

ZIMMER, FRED J.
1906 - 1939

Grand Rapids, Michigan
Manufacturer of davenport sofas, arm chairs, rocking chairs, library suites, parlor furniture, Turkish chairs and couches, Turkish box spring beds, horse hair mattresses, and church and hall seat cushions. Upholstery fabrics used include tapestry, velour, plush, damask, and leather, on frames of mahogany and oak. During the same period of time, Zimmer also worked as an upholsterer and foreman for Retting Furniture Co. and Mueller Furniture Co.
SEE ALSO Mueller Furniture Co.; Retting Furniture Co.

Acknowledgements

This publication is one piece of a much larger puzzle, which has taken many years to complete. Other pieces, including a major permanent exhibition, group and school tours, a woodworking machinery demonstration program, trading cards, and style guides, have been developed under the "Furniture City" name and have been inseparable from this book's development. In fact, it was during the development of "The Furniture City" exhibition that we realized that no recent, comprehensive histories of the Grand Rapids furniture industry existed, and that we would have to write the book just to complete the exhibition. It then became apparent that all the original research should be permanently captured in print.

Even though much of the content of this book was developed in tandem with the exhibition, this is not an exhibition catalog, but a social history of one community and its entanglement with its signature industry. Some of the information in this publication was taken directly from the exhibition, but the content is unique. The many people instrumental in planning and implementing the permanent Furniture City exhibition greatly impacted the development of this work. I wish to thank the exhibition development team, which included Public Museum staff Gary Fraser, Mannie Gentile, and Mary Esther Lee. Michael J. Ettema and Kenneth L. Ames worked as consultants on the original NEH-funded planning phase, and steered the project down many of the paths explored in this work. Consultant John L. Bowditch taught us how to exhibit and interpret woodworking machinery, and Michael Johnston's research on the history of organized labor in the Grand Rapids furniture industry greatly increased my base of information on that topic. Designer and educator James E. Sims and audio-visual producers Rusty Russell and Nancy Haffner taught us all to experience the drama in the thousands of lives affected by the making of furniture in Grand Rapids. Designers Dan Murphy, Janet Pressler, and Caesar Chaves of The PRD Group, Ltd. helped me to see this story's rich colors and textures. Lorraine Schmidt of The PRD Group helped to mold the storyline in the exhibit, and many of her thoughts and words appear in this text.

The research for both the exhibition and this publication was funded in part by the generous support of The Steelcase Foundation, the National Endowment for the Humanities, the United States Department of Energy, and NBD Bank N.A. Specifically, the assistance provided by Kate Pew Wolters and Kathy Partogian of the Steelcase Foundation, and Marsha Semmell and Abbie Cutter of NEH, garnered critical support for these projects. Much of the photography on these pages was funded by the Michigan Out-State Equity Program. The leadership of the Grand Rapids Area Furniture Manufacturers Association, particularly its director Carol Kooistra, and board members Rob Sligh and Win Irwin, deserve my gratitude for providing funding, and for their persistence and patience in seeing this project to its completion. Thanks are also due to the Public Museum Foundation of Grand Rapids and to Gina Bivins and the Publications Committee of the Friends of The Public Museum of Grand Rapids for their financial support.

I wish to thank Public Museum Director Tim Chester, who never questioned my capacity to complete such a mammoth project, and enabled me to succeed. My sincere appreciation goes to Kay Zuris and Jana Wallace, for their competent project and budget management; to Beth Ricker, who helped make this publication a saleable commodity; to Deidra Mayweather, Terri Mawhinney, Deb Washburn, and Nelle Frisch for their marketing assistance; to Joe Kapler, for his collection of maker's marks; and to Joe Kapler, Jeanne Larsen and Rick Jenkins, who managed the location and tracking of images. Thanks to Chris Ham for her assistance with photography at the Voigt House Victorian Museum.

I wish to express special thanks to the many Public Museum staff, interns, and volunteers, who researched and compiled information on the hundreds of companies documented in the directory: Lisa Barker, Gina Bivins, David E. Caplan, Norma Chapman, Laura Cleary, Anna Fraser, Diane Haan, Mark Harvey, Rick Jenkins, Veronica Kandl, Joe Kapler, Nik Kendziorski, Jeanne Larsen, Joel Lefever, Dan McCullough, Marilyn Merdzinski, John Messner, Nancy Powell, Michelle Risany, Kevin Rogers, Anne Salsich, Howard Silbar, Rick and Kathy Stryker, Georgia Thompson, Andy Tzortinis, Wendy Walker, Elaine Webster, and Jean Zimmer. Thanks also to numerous individuals representing current furniture manufacturers and local librarians throughout West Michigan, who answered our requests for histories, trade literature, photos, and sample trademarks for many of the companies represented in the directory.

I owe a debt to contributing authors Ken Ames, Jeff Kleiman, and Joel Lefever for the fresh insights they contributed to the storyline of the book. The amount of research each conducted in his respective area is unequaled in the field. The late Fannia Weingartner, who began as editor on this project, lent us her experience and confidence which were so contagious. Tom Kachadurian made this publication a feast for the eyes and steered its production phase. Karen McCarthy's editorial skills transformed the authors' various writing styles into a cohesive whole. John Corriveau, Craig VanderLende, Steve Milanowski, and Corporate Color are responsible for the beautiful photography work in this book. All images, unless noted with the photo, are from the collections of the Public Museum of Grand Rapids.

Thanks also are due to Grand Rapids antiques dealer Don Marek; Professor of American History and Material Culture Dr. E. Duane Elbert of Eastern Illinois University; Richard H. Harms, former archivist for the Grand Rapids Public Library and now Curator of Calvin College Archives; Blair Tarr, Curator of Decorative Arts for the Kansas Museum of History; and H. Parrott Bacot, decorative arts author and Director of the Anglo-American Museum at Louisiana State University, for their review and consultation over the information presented in this publication, and their guidance in making it the best resource for their respective fields. Weldon D. Frankforter, the Public Museum's Director Emeritus, had a vision for the Museum's documentation of the furniture industry, and worked for many years to collect relevant materials.

Thanks to my family, Vicky, Alain, and Claire, for their patience during the long hours I spent completing this work.

Finally, I am indebted to Frank C. Davidhazy and the other furniture men and women of Grand Rapids, for willingly sharing their own stories, and giving the Grand Rapids furniture industry a personal face.

Christian G. Carron, Curator of Collections
The Public Museum of Grand Rapids

Selected Bibliography

Altenbrandt, Edward, editor. *The Men Behind the Guns in the Making of Greater Grand Rapids*. Grand Rapids: Press of Dean-Hicks Printing Co., 1909.

American Cabinet Maker, 1878 - 1883.

Ames, Kenneth L. "Grand Rapids Furniture at the Time of the Centennial." *WinterthurPortfolio 10* (1975): 23-50.

"Grand Rapids Furniture of the 1870s." Parts 1-3, *Spinning Wheel* (November, December, 1975; January, 1976): 12-16, 33-39, 8-11.

"Meaning in Artifacts: Hall Furnishings in Victorian America." *Journal of Interdisciplinary History* IX:1 (Summer 1978): 19-46.

editor. "Victorian Furniture: Essays from a Victorian Society Autumn Symposium." *Nineteenth Century* 8, nos. 3-4 (1982).

"What is Neo-Grec?" *Nineteenth Century* 2, no. 2 (Spring 1976): 12-21.

The Awakening of Steve Randall: The Story of a Rejuvenated Furniture Store. Grand Rapids: Grand Rapids Association of Furniture Exhibitors, 1913.

Bailey, Perry L. *The Role of The Economic-Geographic Factors in the Origin and Growth of Grand Rapids, Michigan*. Ph.D. Dissertation, Columbus, Ohio: Ohio State University, 1955.

Baker Furniture, Inc. "A Survey of Baker Employees Related to Other Baker Employees." Hollis Baker/Baker Furniture, Inc. Archival Collection, The Public Museum of Grand Rapids, Grand Rapids, 1952.

Bald, F. Clever. *Michigan in Four Centuries*. New York: Harper & Brothers, 1964.

Ball, Ebenezer M. "Letters in the hand of Ebenezer M. Ball." Ebenezer M. Ball/ Powers & Ball Archival Collection, Public Museum of Grand Rapids, Grand Rapids, 1845 - 1853.

Banks, Charles E. and Marshall Everett. *American Home Culture and Correct Customs of Polite Society*. Chicago: Henry Neil, 1902.

Bartinique, A. Patricia. *Kindred Styles: The Arts and Crafts Furniture of Charles P. Limbert*. New York: Gallery 532 Soho, 1995.

Baxter, Albert. *History of the City of Grand Rapids, Michigan*. New York: Munsell & Co., 1891.

Beckwith, John R. " Hand Decorated in Grand Rapids." *Grand River Valley Review*. IX, 1 & 2 (1990): 2-19.

Berenson, Ruth. "Hitchcock Furniture." *Nineteenth Century Furniture: Innovation, Revival and Reform*. New York: Arts & Antiques, a div. of Billboard Publications, Inc., 1982.

Bishop, Robert, and Patricia Coblentz. *The World of Antiques, Art and Architecture in Victorian America*. New York: E.P. Dutton, 1979.

Blouin, Francis X. Jr. *100 Years: A Great Beginning. Sligh Furniture Co. 1880 - 1980*. Holland, Michigan: Sligh Furniture Co., 1979.

Blouin, Francis X. Jr., and Thomas E. Powers. "A Furniture Family: The Slighs of Michigan." *Michigan Historical Collections Bulletin* No. 29, May, 1980.

Bowman, Leslie Greene. *American Arts and Crafts: Virtue in Design*. Los Angeles: Los Angeles County Museum of Art, in association with Bullfinch Press/Little, Brown & Co., 1990.

Brinks, Herbert J. *Write Back Soon: Letters from Immigrants in America*. Grand Rapids, Michigan: CRC Publications, 1986.

Bradshaw, James Stanford. "Grand Rapids, 1870 - 1880: Furniture City Emerges." *Michigan History* 55, no. 4 (Winter, 1971): 321-342.

Bromley, G.W. & Co. *Atlas of the Entire City of New York*. New York: G.W. Bromley & E. Robinson, 1879.

Burchell, Sam. *A History of Furniture: Celebrating Baker Furniture 100 Years of Fine Reproductions*. New York: Harry N. Abrams, Inc., 1991.

Butler, Joseph T. *American Antiques 1800-1900*. New York: Odyssey Press, 1965.

Buzzitta, Giacomo. "Giacomo Buzzitta/Stow & Davis Furniture Co. Archival Collection." ca. 1930 - 1980. Public Museum of Grand Rapids, Grand Rapids.

Caplan, Ralph. *The Design of Herman Miller*. New York: Whitney Library of Design, 1976.

Carron, Christian G., and Veronica L. Kandl. "Mass-Produced Midwestern Furniture." Technical Inserts nos. 47-49. *Illinois Heritage Association Newsletter* Sept. 1990 - Feb. 1991.

Claney, Jane Perkins and Robert Edwards. "Progressive Design in Grand Rapids." *Tiller* II no. 1 (September - October 1983): 33-56.

Clark, Robert Judson, et. al. *Design in America: The Cranbrook Vision, 1925 - 1950*. New York: Harry N. Abrams, Inc., in association with the Detroit Institute of Arts and the Metropolitan Museum of Art, 1983.

Comstock, Charles Carter. *Early Experiences and Personal Recollections of Charles Carter Comstock*. No publisher, 1936.

Dale, Rodney, and Rebecca Weaver. *Machines in the Office*. New York: Oxford University Press, 1993.

Darling, Sharon. *Chicago Furniture: Art, Craft & Industry, 1833 - 1983*. New York: The Chicago Historical Society/W.W. Norton & Co., 1984.

Davidhazy, Frank C. Interviews by Christian G. Carron, Debbie Rotman, and Anne Salsich. Tape recording, Public Museum of Grand Rapids, Grand Rapids, 1992 - 1994.

Decorator and Furnisher, 1882, 1883, 1885.

de Wolfe, Elsie. *The House in Good Taste*. New York: The Century Co., 1913.

Dillenback, J.D. *Grand Rapids in 1874, Sketches of the Trade, Manufactures and Progress of the City*. Grand Rapids: by the author, 1875.

Directory of the City of Grand Rapids. Grand Rapids: J.D. Dillenback & Co., 1870 - 1873.

"A Dixie Industry Goes National." *Business Week*. July 23, 1955.

Dubrow, Eileen and Richard Dubrow. *American Furniture of the 19th Century: 1840 - 1880*. Exton, Pennsylvania: Schiffer Publishing, Ltd., 1983.

Edwards, Clive D. *Victorian Furniture: Technology & Design*. Manchester: Manchester University Press, 1993.

Elliott, Charles Wyllys. "Household Art I - The Dining Room." *Arts Journal* n.s. 1 (1875): 298-300.

Elstner, J. M. *The Industries of Grand Rapids, Her Relations as a Centre of Trade, Business Houses & Manufacturing Establishments*. Grand Rapids: J.M. Elstner & Co., 1887.

Encyclopedia of American Art. New York: E. P. Dutton, 1981.

Ettema, Michael J. "Technological Innovation and Design Economics in Furniture Manufacture." *Winterthur Portfolio* 16, no. 2/3 (Summer/Autumn 1981): 197-223.

Ettema, Michael J., and Catherine Stryker. *Grand Rapids Made: A Brief History of the Grand Rapids Furniture Industry*. Grand Rapids: Grand Rapids Museum Association, 1985.

Fairall, Herbert S. *The World's Industrial and Cotton Centennial Exposition, New Orleans*. Iowa City: 1885.

Fitzgerald, Oscar P. *Four Centuries of American Furniture*. Radnor, Pennsylvania: Wallace Homestead Book Co., 1995.

Flaherty, Viva. *History of the Grand Rapids Furniture Strike: With Facts Hitherto Unpublished*. Grand Rapids: Peninsular Press, 1911.

Foote, Mrs. Clarence Dexter. Interview, tape recording, Grand Rapids Public Library, Grand Rapids, 1971.

French, J. A. and M. T. Ryan. *Grand Rapids City Directory and Business Mirror*. Grand Rapids: Grand Rapids Daily Eagle, 1865.

friendly fellows of furniture town. Grand Rapids: no publisher, 1901.

The Furniture Buyers Order Book and Classified Directory of Furniture Exhibits. Grand Rapids: Grand Rapids Furniture Exposition Association, January, 1928 - October, 1955.

Furniture Dealers' Reference Book. Chicago: American Homes Bureau, 1927 and 1928-29.

The Furniture Manufacturer and Artisan. Grand Rapids Furniture Record Co., Grand Rapids. Vol. 1 - Vol. 44, January, 1911 - December, 1932.

"Furniture Manufacturers Association Records." 1881 - 1987. Grand Rapids Public Library, Grand Rapids.

"Furniture Salesmens' Club Scrapbooks." 1930 - 1935, Public Museum of Grand Rapids, Grand Rapids.

Furniture Sketchbook. Grand Rapids: Grand Rapids Furniture Market Association, Summer, 1957.

Gebhard, David. "The American Colonial Revival in the 1930s." *Winterthur Portfolio* 22, no. 2/3 (Summer/Autumn 1987): 109-148.

"Kem Weber: Moderne Design in California, 1920 - 1940." *Journal of Decorative and Propaganda Arts* 2, (Summer/Fall 1986): 20-29.

Good Furniture: The Magazine of Decoration. Dean Hicks Publishing Co., Grand Rapids, and National Building Publications, New York. Vol. 4 - 37, December, 1914 - September, 1931.

Goss, Dwight. *History of Grand Rapids and Its Industries.* Chicago: C.F. Cooper & Co., 1906.

Gowans, Alan. *Images of American Living: Four Centuries of Architecture and Furniture as Cultural Expression.* Philadelphia & New York: J. B. Lippincott Co., 1964.

Grand Rapids Area Furniture Manufacturers Association Membership Directory. Grand Rapids: Grand Rapids Area Furniture Manufacturers Association, 1989.

"Grand Rapids Bets on Quality." *Business Week*, July 19, 1947: 28.

Grand Rapids Business Journal. 1983 - 1998.

Grand Rapids Daily Eagle and *Grand Rapids Eagle.* 1844 - 1894.

Grand Rapids Furniture Exposition Market Ambassador. Grand Rapids: Grand Rapids Furniture Market Exposition Association, June, 1934 - January, 1937.

"Grand Rapids Furniture Museum Archival Collection." 1935 - 1976. Public Museum of Grand Rapids, Grand Rapids.

The Grand Rapids Furniture Record. Dean Hicks Printing Co. and Periodical Publishing Co., Grand Rapids. Vol. 1 - 64, June, 1900 - January, 1932.

The Grand Rapids Herald. 1892 - 1961.

100th Market Edition, Dec. 27, 1927.

Grand Rapids Market Preview. Grand Rapids: Grand Rapids Furniture Market Association, June 1958 - January 1963.

The Grand Rapids Public Library List of Books on Furniture. Grand Rapids: Grand Rapids Public Library, 1927.

The Grand Rapids Press. 1892 - 1998.

Grand Rapids Weekly Enquirer. July 11, 1845.

Grand Rapids Wood Finishing Co. "Grand Rapids Wood Finishing Co. Archival Collection." Public Museum of Grand Rapids, Grand Rapids, 1895 - 1975.

Greenberg, Cara. *Mid-Century Modern: Furniture of the 1950s.* New York: Harmony Books, 1984.

Greene, Leslie A. "The Late Victorian Hallstand: A Social History." *Nineteenth Century* 6, no.4 (Winter 1980): 51, 56.

Gregory, Michael. "Michigan at the Centennial." *Michigan History* (July/August 1992): 23-32.

Grier, Katherine C. *Culture and Comfort: People, Parlors, and Upholstery: 1850 - 1930.* Rochester, New York: The Strong Museum, 1988.

Haney, David. "Elijah Haney and the Haney School Furniture Co." B.A. Thesis, Central Michigan University, ca. 1975.

Harms, Richard H., and Robert W. Viol. *Grand Rapids Goes to War: The 1940s Homefront.* Grand Rapids: Grand Rapids Historical Society, 1993.

Harold, Steve. "The Furniture Industry." *The Manistee News Advocate Broadside* October 5, 1985.

Heggie, Pauline Johnson. Interview by Christian G. Carron. Interview notes at The Public Museum of Grand Rapids, Grand Rapids, 1992.

Hindle, Brooke, and Steven Lubar. *Engines of Change: The American Industrial Revolution, 1790 - 1860.* Washington, D.C.: Smithsonian Institution Press, 1986.

Howe, Katherine S., Alice C. Frelinghuysen, & Catherine H. Voorsanger. *Herter Brothers: Furniture and Interiors for a Guilded Age.* New York: Harry N. Abrams, Inc., 1994.

Hunting, David D., Sr. Undated interview, tape recorded. Steelcase, Inc. Archives, Grand Rapids.

In Pursuit of Beauty: Americans and the Aesthetic Movement. New York: The Metropolitan Museum of Art, 1976.

Johnston, Michael. *Partners and Adversaries: A Series of Papers on the History of Labor in the Grand Rapids Furniture Industry.* Furniture Research Collection, Public Museum of Grand Rapids, Grand Rapids, 1989.

Kleiman, Jeffrey D. *The Great Strike: Religion, Labor and Reform in Grand Rapids, Michigan, 1890-1916.* Ph.D. Dissertation, East Lansing, Michigan: Michigan State University, 1985.

"Knapp's Dovetailing Machine." Undated pamphlet, Northhampton, Massachusetts.

Knoebel, Lance. *Office Furniture: Twentieth-Century Design.* New York: E.P. Dutton, 1987.

Kurzhals, Richard D. *Initial Advantage and Technological Change in Industrial Location: The Furniture Industry in Grand Rapids, Michigan.* Ph.D. Dissertation, East Lansing, Michigan: Michigan State University, 1973.

Land, Jno. E. *Historical and Descriptive Review of the Industries of Grand Rapids 1882.* Grand Rapids: by the author, 1881.

LeRow, William A. "Our Grand Rapids Letter." *The American Cabinet Maker, Upholsterer and Carpet Reporter* Dec. 7, 1878.

Limbert, Charles P. and Company. *Limbert Arts and Crafts Furniture: The Complete 1903 Catalog, With a New Introduction by Christian G. Carron.* Republished in New York: Dover Publications, 1992.

Lydens, Z.Z., editor. *The Story of Grand Rapids.* Grand Rapids: Kregel Publications, 1966.

Lyon, Robert P. *Standard Reference Book of the Furniture Trade of the United States, Canada, &c.* New York: by the author, 1880.

McClinton, Katherine Morrison. *Collecting American Victorian Antiques*. New York: Charles Scribner's Sons, 1966.

Art Deco: A Guide for Collectors. New York: Clarkson N. Potter, Inc., 1972.

McCracken, S.B., editor. *Michigan and the Centennial*. Detroit: Detroit Free Press, 1876.

Marek, Don. *Arts and Crafts Furniture Design: The Grand Rapids Contribution, 1895 - 1915*. Grand Rapids: Grand Rapids Art Museum, 1987.

Marling, Karal Ann. *George Washington Slept Here*. Cambridge: Harvard University Press, 1988.

Michigan Artisan. White Printing Co., Grand Rapids. 1884 - 1897.

Morningstar, Connie. "The Fortunes of Berkey & Gay." *The Antiques Journal* February, 1972: 10-12.

Narezo, Janet. "Landmark Furniture Buildings." *Grand River Valley Review* III, 1 (1981): 28-31.

Olson, Gordon. *A Grand Rapids Sampler*. Grand Rapids: The Grand Rapids Historical Commission, 1992.

Polakoff, Keith Ian, et al. *Generations of Americans: A History of the United States*. New York: St. Martins Press, 1976.

Polk's Grand Rapids City Directory and *Polk's Grand Rapids Suburban Directory*. Detroit and Taylor, Michigan: R. L. Polk & Co., 1873 - 1997.

Public Museum of Grand Rapids. "The Furniture City." A permanent exhibition at the Public Museum of Grand Rapids' Van Andel Museum Center. Grand Rapids, 1994.

"Grand Rapids Furniture Manufacturers Vertical Files." Containing original and secondary source materials compiled by various researchers between ca. 1970 and 1998, Public Museum of Grand Rapids, Grand Rapids.

"Advertising and Trade Catalog Archival Collection." Containing approx. 4000 furniture trade catalogs and brochures dating between 1890 and 1998, Public Museum of Grand Rapids, Grand Rapids.

Propst, Robert. *The office. A facility based on change*. Zeeland, Michigan: Herman Miller, 1968.

Quaint American Portfolio of Unusual Furniture. Grand Rapids: Carl Forslund Furniture Co., Summer, 1950.

Ransom, Frank E. *The City Built on Wood: A History of the Furniture Industry in Grand Rapids, Michigan, 1850 - 1950*. Ann Arbor, Michigan: Edwards Brothers, Inc., 1955.

Renaissance Revival Victorian Furniture. Grand Rapids: Grand Rapids Art Museum, 1976.

"The Romance of Furniture." Performance program, Grand Rapids Furniture Exposition Association, Grand Rapids, 1936.

Sherwood, Wallace. "Wallace Sherwood/ Grand Rapids Panel Co. Archival Collection." Public Museum of Grand Rapids, Grand Rapids, 1904 - 1964.

Shopmark. Berkey & Gay Furniture Co., Grand Rapids, February, 1917 - December, 1924.

Sikes, Jane E. *The Furniture Makers of Cincinnati: 1790 - 1849*. Cincinnati: Privately published, 1976.

Silbar, Howard. *Notes on The Furniture Industry of Grand Rapids, 1836 - 1964*, 1965. Furniture Research Collections, Public Museum of Grand Rapids, Grand Rapids.

Sironen, Marta K. *A History of American Furniture*. East Stroudsburg, Pennsylvania: Towne Publishing Co., 1936.

Steelcase: The First 75 Years. Grand Rapids: Steelcase, Inc., 1987.

Stowe, E.A. "Some Men I Have Known in the Past." *Michigan Tradesman* 2160 (11 February, 1925): pp. 9-10.

Strasser, Susan. *Satisfaction Guaranteed: The Making of the American Mass Market*. New York: Pantheon Books, 1989.

The Stylist: A Magazine for the Homemaker. Grand Rapids Furniture Makers Guild, Grand Rapids. Vol. 1-35, 1932 - 1967.

Tice, Patricia M. "The Knapp Dovetailing Machine." *Antiques* 73, no.5 (May 1983): 1070-1072.

Tuttle, Charles Richard. *History of Grand Rapids with Biographical Sketches*. Grand Rapids: Tuttle & Cooney, 1874.

United States Centennial Commission. *International Exhibition, 1876: Official Catalogue*. Philadelphia: John R. Nagle & Co., 1876.

International Exhibition, 1876: Reports and Awards. 6 vol., Washington: Government Printing Office, 1880.

Vredevelt, Kirk. *The Reorientation of the Grand Rapids Furniture Industry in the Twentieth Century*. B.A. Thesis, Calvin College, Grand Rapids, 1987.

Wade, Richard C. *The Urban Frontier: Pioneer Life in Early Pittsburgh, Cincinnati, Lexington, Louisville, and St. Louis*. Chicago: University of Chicago Press, 1959, reprinted 1971.

Webster, Elaine. *Directory of Nineteenth-Century Woodworking Machinery Manufacturers in Grand Rapids*. Furniture Research Collection, Public Museum of Grand Rapids, Grand Rapids, 1990.

White, Arthur S. "Grand Rapids Furniture Centennial." *Michigan History* 12, no.2 (April, 1928): 268-79.

White, Edmund. "America's Classical Modernist: Furniture Designer T.H. Robsjohn Gibbings Found Inspiration for the Future in Antiquity." *House & Garden* Vol 163, no. 6 (June, 1991): 100 - 105, 156.

Widdicomb, William. *The Early History of the Furniture Industry in Grand Rapids*. Grand Rapids, 1909.

Williams, C. S. *Williams' Grand Rapids City Directory, City Guide, and Business Mirror*. Grand Rapids: P. G. Hodenpyl, 1859.

World's Industrial and Cotton Centennial Exposition. *Practical Common Sense Guide Book*. New Orleans: 1884.

Index of Chapters 1-9

For more information, please turn to the Directory of Furniture Makers and Their Marks on page 120, a comprehensive listing of manufacturers, which is alphabetized by company name and includes details on history, personnel, products, and labels.